Models and mirrors

Models and mirrors: towards an anthropology of public events

Don Handelman

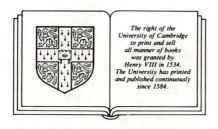

The right of the
University of Cambridge
to print and sell
all manner of books
was granted by
Henry VIII in 1534.
The University has printed
and published continuously
since 1584.

CAMBRIDGE UNIVERSITY PRESS

Cambridge

New York   Port Chester

Melbourne   Sydney

Published by the Press Syndicate of the University of Cambridge
The Pitt Building, Trumpington Street, Cambridge CB2 1RP
40 West 20th Street, New York, NY 10011, USA
10 Stamford Road, Oakleigh, Melbourne 3166, Australia

First published 1990

Printed in Great Britain at the University Press, Cambridge

British Library cataloguing in publication data

Handelman, Don
Models and mirrors: towards an anthropology
of public events
1. Man – Anthropological perspectives
I. Title
306

Library of Congress cataloguing in publication data

Handelman, Don
Models and mirrors: towards an anthropology of public events/
Don Handelman
    p.   cm.
Bibliography.
Includes index.
ISBN 0–521–35069–7
1. Festivals. 2. Holidays. 3. Play. 4. Symbolism. I. Title.
GT3930.H34 1989
394.2–dc19 88–34646 CIP

ISBN 0 521 35069 7

US

For Lea and Ronit, my magic mirrors

Contents

Contents

Figures

Acknowledgements

My thanks are the offspring of kindness and critique, the parents of much intellectual nourishment. My fortune is the bounty of both, for which all of the following persons bear some responsibility. My offering of appreciation is this book.

Bruce Kapferer has shared with me ideas and friendship, sustenance for mind and spirit, during two decades. His creativity and drive are comfort and whetstone.

Victor Turner was a bulwark of comradeship and support in the years before his death. I sorely miss his warm and spirited presence.

On the subject of play, intensive discussions with Jean Briggs, Robert Lavenda, and John Roberts sharpened my wits and focused my perspectives. Tamar Rapoport's questions and comments helped at a crucial stage.

On subjects of symbolism and public events, generous conversations over the years with the following scholars aided in the formulation of ideas, some tentative, others more coherent: T. M. S. Evens, Richard Werbner, Emiko Ohnuki-Tierney, Elihu Katz, Michael Lieber, Riv-Ellen Prell, Harvey Goldberg, David Shulman, Bruce Lincoln, Erik Cohen, Daniel Dayan, Virginia Dominguez, and Robert Paine.

Bruce Kapferer, Robert Lavenda, and Richard Werbner read the introductory chapters of part I. Their comments led to timely revisions.

Parts of this book were written and others revised during a fellowship at the Netherlands Institute For Advanced Study in the Humanities and Social Sciences. NIAS, under the direction of Dirk van de Kaa, is a special place: its atmosphere of contemplation and care is especially conducive to scholarship; and its excellent library services, headed by Dinny Young, deserve special mention. At NIAS, talks on the subject of ritual with Kristofer Schipper, Jonathan Parry, Jan Heesterman, and Henk Driessen were particularly helpful.

To Susan Allen-Mills, my thanks for the encouragement that gave initial impetus to this project, and for the trustworthiness I had wished for in an editor.

Acknowledgements

This book is dedicated to Lea, my wife, and to Ronit, our daughter. Lea's empathy and companionship brighten and gentle my world. The honesty and thoughtfulness of her own scholarship always test mine. Ronit's interest in comparative religion, her keen perception and vivid enthusiasm, are a gift of pleasure ever-renewed.

Wassenaar, The Netherlands, May 1988.

Chapter 4 is reprinted from Don Handelman, *Work and Play Among the Aged: Interaction, Replication and Emergence in a Jerusalem Setting*, Van Gorcum, 1977, with the permission of Van Gorcum & Company.

Chapter 5 is reprinted from *Urban Life*, Vol. 4, No. 4, pp. 433–448, copyright 1976 by Sage Publications. Reprinted by permission of Sage publications, Inc.

Chapter 7 is reprinted by permission from the *1983 Proceedings of the American Ethnological Society*. Copyright (c) 1983 American Ethnological Society. All rights reserved.

Chapter 8 is published by permission of Transaction Publishers from *The Frailty of Authority* (vol. 5 of Political Anthropology), edited by Myron J. Aronoff. Copyright (c) 1986 by Transactions Publishers.

Chapter 10 is reprinted with permission from *Anthropos*, vol. 76, 1981, pp. 321–370.

All of these contributions have been revised for the present publication.

1 Introduction

1 Premises and prepossessions

On the wall are three pictures that evoke my dilemmas in thinking about public events, occasions that people undertake in concert to make more, less, or other of themselves, than they usually do. One is an engraving of the prototype of a seated colossus ('Schema Gigantei Colossi') intended to mark a royal entry into the city of Antwerp in the sixteenth century. The giant is clothed in Roman-style body-armour, helmet, and sandals. One strong hand rests on an eagle-headed sword-hilt. The other curls around a scroll of proclamation. Visible are the bunched, massive muscles of thighs and legs. Enchained, before the colossus, are three small allegorical figures. Around the ornate, rectangular base stand four citizens, gazing upward, who by their posture and gesticulation seem to show awe and wonder at the massive bulk of this dignified, powerful presence.

The second is a color photograph of a Sinhalese Buddhist exorcist who participates in the healing of a patient possessed by a demonic being.[1] The head of the exorcist is covered with a mop of wild, unruly hair. A grotesque, exaggerated half-mask accentuates nose and eyes. Waist and lower body are enwrapped in skirt-like female apparel. His mouth is wide-open in an 'aah' of satisfaction, for he has just farted loudly.

The third is a black-and-white photograph set in the kitchen of a house in a tiny fishing-village in Newfoundland.[2] Seated in a rocking-chair, facing the camera, is a stout woman, the mistress of the home, wearing blouse and trousers, her broad face creased in a wide grin. Clustered about her are three of her small youngsters. Behind the mother, leaning over her, is a strange figure. His face is completely hidden by a horrific halloween mask, from which protrudes a long, lolling tongue. Upon his head is perched a delicate lady's hat. He wears a long dress, and his hands are covered entirely by heavy gloves. His arms are around the seated woman, hugging her, and each gloved hand cups her breast. One of her hands clutches his arm, a wedding band in plain view. The man is one of numerous mummers who visit and hi-jink in the homes of the village during the Twelve Days of Christmas.

The colossus, his seat and feet firmly planted, is a vertical statement of stability, of the power of might and of the authority of edict. He is explicitly demonstrative of these qualities in his carriage, mien, and demeanor. In his composition there are no queries nor contradictions. His design is homogeneous, dominating in its synthesis. Like the giant, the royal entry of which he was a part was an explicit declaration of noble imperatives (cf. Bergeron 1971; Bryant 1986; McCracken 1984), one that showed, or in Foucault's phrasing, inscribed, the impress of power. To put this simply, here power existed because it was seen to be done. Thus Giesey (1985: 53) remarks that during this period, in France, similar occasions 'became propaganda for the glory and power of the ruling monarch'. Little was hidden from participant or spectator (cf. Orgel 1975). The royal entry, in the life of the state, had something of the qualities of an exclamation mark in the punctuation of a text.

Various terms may be used to discuss the royal entry. The royal entry sometimes was part of a 'royal progress'. In its design it had elements of a 'procession' or of a 'parade' in its formal, linear movement. It had qualities of a 'pageant' in its elaborate sets (like that of our colossus). There also were components of 'drama', and so of its 'performance'. It could be likened to a 'ceremony', and perhaps even to a 'ritual' by analysts who see, in the latter, primarily a formalization or a ritualization of behavior.[3]

The appearance of the exorcist is part of a special occasion whose explicit purpose is that of change – the changing of a possessed, sick person into one who is freed of the demonic and so becomes healthy (the occasion has been analyzed in subtle and intricate detail by Bruce Kapferer [1983]). Change is the metier of the event, that which it is designed to do in the cultural codes of the Sinhalese. The exorcism accomplishes this, in part, by building a total cosmological reality that is the demonic antithesis of that which Sinhalese believe is the normal order of things. This cosmos then is subverted, made illusory, and destroyed. This allows the proper ordering of the true world again to emerge. The patient undergoes the same changes, and is cured of affliction. The exorcist in the photograph is a demonic yet comic figure: he is in the process of destroying himself as the kind of being who claims to control the patient. Indeed, much of the work of tearing apart the demonic world, in this event, is accomplished through comedy, through a spirit of play. The qualities of 'play', as I will be discussing in chapter 3, are those of indeterminacy and uncertainty.

The exorcism builds, destroys, and resurrects cosmological worlds. The event works through contradiction, conflict, and synthesis – through antitheses of disorder and order, uncertainty and certainty. To change the condition of the patient, the exorcists tamper and toy with the very premises of an ordered world – precarious and dangerous procedures, as exorcists themselves know only too well. In certain of its phases, the occasion is infused with doubts, and even with terror, as the power of dissolution stands forth, and potentially matters can go very wrong. To prevent this, high degrees of control and of exactitude in action are vital. Just as important is the knowledge that every action is consequential in its effects on forthcoming actions. All acts are interrelated and form a web of intentionality. In the language of social science, the event is structured by a very high degree of functional interdependence among its components. These connections, and the uncertainties and negations that they work through, must be regulated in a homeostatic sense, if the whole program of controlled and directed change is not to disintegrate, with possibly disastrous consequences for those concerned.

The exorcism likely would be called a 'ritual', in both the senses in which this term commonly is used. On the one hand the event is formalized, and is repetitive, in that its enactment is carried out in quite similar ways on each occasion of its occurrence. In other words, it has elements of 'ceremony', as did the royal entry. On the other hand, the event makes recourse to paranatural, mystical powers in order to change the patient. As well, it undoubtedly is a 'drama' whose highly integrated multi-media performance – through dance, trance, music, and comedy – is crucial to the accomplishment of its aim.

The Newfoundland mummer in the photograph participates in a riotous occasion whose aim he and his compatriots simply would describe as 'fun' or as a 'good time', with little further explanation. Among the conservative and circumspect persons of these small villages, mumming is a time of great license, as the photograph shows: of the overturning or inversion of customary moral and social behavior. Although there is patterning in the enactment of mumming, the form of the occasion is looser and more open to ad hoc innovation during its very occurrence than are either of the other events referred to. If we will not settle for 'fun' as the ultimate explanation for the shapes of mumming, then we must engage in intensive interpretation to make sense of the occasion. In formal terms, mumming neither is declarative, like the royal entry, nor does it do change, like the exorcism. It is an allusory occasion, replete with ambivalence and ambiguity that are not necessarily resolved in its enactment. Mumming is infused with the 'carnivalesque'. Perhaps it might be called a 'festival'. But it also contains elements of 'game', 'ceremony', 'performance', and of the simpler sense of 'ritual' as ritualized behavior.

These three pictures, and the events that they index, come from singular cultural worlds and are the creations of very diverse social setups. Many may well contend that their sole commonality is their presence on my wall – that it is my aesthetic choices that brought them into an arbitrary conjunction, one that leaches them of their uniqueness as phenomena of cultures widely separated by space, time, and modes of making meaning and affect. Therefore their significance is regained only by replacing them in their cultural contexts, whose vantages will enable their interpretation primarily 'from the native's point of view' (Geertz 1976). Nor do I deny the value of this: after all, it is a cornerstone of much modern ethnography and cultural analysis.

Yet my dilemma is that we also do comparisons – in this instance, comparisons among public events, within the same society, but also among different ones. Even though, as Pierre Smith (1982: 104) comments, the work of comparison in this domain has lain fairly dormant since the energetic efforts of Sir James Frazer. Any manner of comparison – whether among native conceptions and done by natives, or between conceptions of native and analyst, or among conceptions held by different analysts – requires a profound shift in perspective and perception. This is a radical perspective and a critical perception: it demands grasping something that either was not evident or that, common-sensically, was taken for granted, and comprehending it through another mode of apprehension (in the dual sense of this word). It is in the nature of comparison to be reifying, biasing, partial, and sometimes misguided and wrong-headed as well. This increases the danger that participants will be construed, in Alfred Schutz's phrasing, as 'puppets' that are informed with intentionality by and perform under the aegis of theorist-directors who think for the latter (see also Bell 1987: 106, 111). Yet comparison also may be informative and perhaps illuminating.

Comparison may be treated in different ways. Broadly put, the functionalist position on comparison is to establish analytical categories for their own sake – that is, for the sake of theory – and then to search the worlds of ethnography and history for instances to make the points that these categories formulate. Functional equivalence is attributed to instances within the same category, to be compared with those of other categories. Crudely put, this position eschews cultural worlds, and may be likened to their plunder. (An example of this approach is that of Fortes [1968] on 'installation ceremonies', mentioned in note 7 of chapter 2).

Intracultural comparison is basic to structuralism in anthropology. Like that of functionalism, this general position is criticized for its ahistoricity. As serious is its subjugation of cultural worlds to a hegemony of methodology, one that determinedly molds the constitution of cultural significance to the prerequisites of how analysis is to be done. To no small degree, technique constitutes both medium and telos.

In both approaches there is comparison for the sake of analytical categories, not analytical categories for the sake of comparison, within and among cultural worlds. Both ignore to varying degrees that their own tools are never wholly autonomous, neither of the cultural worlds within which they are created nor of those that these tools are meant to analyze.

My position is that there may be generalizable features that underlie, and that help to constitute public events – but that these can be demonstrated only comparatively. Moreover, these features or forms are neither the significance nor the meaning of public events. Instead, form contributes to the formation of public events, setting broad parameters of likelihood – the likelihoods of certain operations being accomplished through certain forms of public events. Thus, my position is closer to a technology of events, of the identification of logics of their design, themselves embedded in cultural matrices that imbue these designs with significance and that put them to work in cultural ways. Therefore, these designs are never static, nor complete in themselves. They are configurations of potential dynamism that both exercise and limit possibilities of empowerment within social orders. Their status as grounded phenomena, their fullness and their substance, always are constituted and empowered culturally and historically. Put differently, what I am after are logics of meta-design that potentially enable social orders to act upon or to relate to themselves in radically different ways through the substantive media of public events. As should become evident in subsequent chapters, I am not arguing that some social orders have ways of relating to themselves that others lack, but that different logics of design in the constitution of public events index social orders that themselves are organized in radically different ways.

But the problem starts the very moment we (and others) identify a 'species' of event and name it 'ritual' or an analogous rubric. How we allow ourselves to recognize and to constitute these rubrics, and thereby to install and empower them, is a fundamental issue in anthropology. (Indeed, it is where the problem of the constitution and differentiation of praxis begins.) By taking up simple regularities in the logics of form of public events, only a small part of these manifold issues can be addressed. Therefore this advocacy of the conjoining of different public events comes not in order to erect any general theory of occasions, one that lays claim to widespread validity. Instead, the question that guides part I of this book is whether more of a comparative apprehension of public occasions may be informative of matters that, although partial and simplified, are hardly self-evident.

As indicated, once this note of the comparative is sounded, the matter of terminology becomes problematic. In the preceding mentions of the events indexed by the three pictures, I placed in quotation marks some of the descriptive and analytic labels that could be used to discuss these occasions.

These terms are manifold, confusing, and often are used at cross purposes. I do not wish to belabor problems of classification, except to insist that a more incisive sense of coherence is required, even at the risk of aggravating the reification of the phenomena under consideration. Matters of terminology are turned to briefly, further on. For the moment, I will introduce the set of terms that informs my intentions for the study of public events. These terms will be discussed in detail in chapter 2.

In the events that the three pictures index, I see facets of their workings that depend not only on particulars of cultural meaning, but also on logics that organize the ways in which these occasions are put together. All three events are ways of signifying order in the worlds of their participants – lived-in worlds that necessarily, and often in mundane ways, balance precariously on the uncertain footings of contingencies of existence. The royal entry does this by making order to be seen through its own majestic, internal orderliness. It may be likened to a mirror held up to reflect versions of the organization of society that are intended by the makers of the occasion. It is, in the terminology to be developed further on, close to an event that 'presents' aspects of the lived-in world.[4]

The Sinhalese exorcism creates holistic, cosmological worlds – other realities that have built into them their own rules of operation. These are set into motion with the intention to affect or to change directly the lived-in world in regulated and consequential ways. The exorcism approximates an event that 'models' aspects of the lived-in world, in order to operate on the latter. The event makes order by transforming one condition of being into another that contradicts or that is opposed to the former.

Newfoundland mumming neither acts with intentionality and consequentiality on the lived-in world, nor does it mirror the latter in relatively clear-cut ways. Instead, through disguise and license, inversion and play, it courts disorder and uncertainty by allusively bringing to the fore the elusive, yet always lurking underside of social relationships and community. Mumming is akin to a 're-presentation' of aspects of the lived-in world of the villagers. The event signs order by first overturning and then restoring it – not by recourse to transformative processes, but through devices that allusively evoke the terror of disorder in villages with only a precarious sense of their own cohesiveness. Mumming is discussed in detail in chapter 7.

Modelling, presenting, and re-presenting, are the three modes of apprehending the lived-in world through public events that will be discussed in chapter 2. The case studies of this volume then take up, elaborate, and modify aspects of this preliminary discussion. But first let me put the question which to this point has been left unattended: why should one study public events?

Why study public events?

The import attributed to public events (usually in the guise of 'ritual', or a parallel rubric) varies with the theoretical persuasions of analysts. Some, in a more Durkheimian vein, find in such occasions the reflections of collective understandings or of principles of social structure. Others (cf. Gluckman 1962; Ortner 1978) stress that such occasions address, and perhaps redress, problems that are embedded in the social relationships or in the way of life of a people. Still others (for example, Victor Turner, in his later work) emphasize more the necessity for cognitive and emotional experience that can be known to a people only through the doing, the enactment, of dramatic performance. Yet others focus on the interpretive 'reading' of meaning that events provide or make accessible to their participants. Through these 'narratives', people interpret their order of things to themselves. As Geertz (1973: 448), in a celebrated aphorism, wrote of the Balinese cockfight: 'it is a Balinese reading of Balinese experience, a story they tell themselves about themselves'.

Explicitly or not, adherents of one or another view seem to accept the assumption that events are important phenomena because they constitute dense concentrations of symbols and their associations, that are of relevance to a particular people. It is in various public occasions that cultural codes – usually diffused, attenuated, and submerged in the mundane order of things – lie closest to the behavioral surface. Here they are most graspable in various sensory and cognitive modalities, not only by natives but also by ethnographers. To put this otherwise: cultural information makes sense best when imparted through occasions that are set up to do this kind of coded, communicative work. The analyst mines these rich veins of cultural intricacy for insights into the very premises of a people – of their cosmologies, world views, and values. For the ethnographer, public events are privileged points of penetration into other social and cultural universes.

These views rarely address the following: the likelihood that, whether cultural codes are bared to a greater extent within public events or are not, each named occasion of this sort among a particular people communicates only a version of their social order. Versions overlap and conflict with one another, in the knowledge, experience, and affect they convey. If events contain keys to codes, then these unlock many doors, as much to labyrinths as to great halls and cosy kitchens. This multitude of possibilities points up the need for ethnographic strategies that will compare events intraculturally, and so too their versions of order. (This kind of work still is all too rare, and is beyond the purview of this volume, but there are some beginnings [cf. A. Cohen 1981: 155–215; Manning 1977; Da Matta 1977; Ostor 1980; Ortner 1978].)

Another major rationale for the analytical attractiveness of public events is related to certain basic features of their organization. Lévi-Strauss (1981: 672), for example, notes that 'ritual' uses a procedure that he calls, 'parcelling-out': 'within classes of objects and types of gestures, ritual makes infinite distinctions and ascribes discriminatory values to the slightest shades of difference'. So, too, do numerous other varieties of public events that enunciate, specify, and hold out for inspection their component elements, albeit not necessarily with accompanying explanations. In contrast to the frequently confusing, multi-directional, and uncertain flows of mundane living, the divisible elements of public occasions seem eminently available to the engaged observer. Often bounded in fairly demarcated ways in space and through time, they are marked by a relatively clear-cut systematicity of organization. This may help to account for the readiness of ethnographers to endow them with such heavy burdens of meaning, in relation to other domains of life. However, within the domain of public events, not all occasions are constitutive of social order, like the events of modelling I will discuss. Others, like events of presentation are primarily 'expressive', reflecting social order in a more Durkheimian vein. This distinction is crucial to the discussion of performance further on in this chapter, and to the typology of events in chapter 2.

Some basic features of public events

Scholars in anthropology and in cognate disciplines are notoriously cautious about defining domains of activity that approximate my usage of public event. The strong preference is to allow a sense of occasion to emerge from particular contexts of culture, and to remain near to these in specifying that which a public event is about. Although one appreciates this empiricist reticence, the more abstract statements of definition that come forth from the truly massive accumulation of studies on, for example, 'ritual', are strangely uninformative – not only for purposes of comparison, but also merely for getting an idea of what is being talked about. Let me indicate this by giving three definitions of 'ritual' offered by accomplished scholars from separate disciplines.

Writing on 'political ritual', the sociologist, Steven Lukes (1975: 301), suggests that this is 'rule-governed activity of a symbolic character which draws the attention of its participants to objects of thought and feeling which they hold to be of special significance'. Lukes stresses a formality of presentation that provides a special, expressive (i.e. symbolic) diet of cognition and sentiment. 'Ritual' here seems to do work of highlighting ideas and phenomena, but little more.

The social historian, Richard Trexler (1980: xiv), considers 'ritual' as 'formal behavior . . . that, in specific contexts of space and time, becomes relatively fixed into those recognizable social and cultural deposits we call behavioral forms. The purpose of ritual is to achieve goals . . . The result of ritual action is, finally, the small- or large-scale transformation of both the actor and the audience . . .' Again formality, but also purposiveness – the accomplishment of goals that are related to change. Whether these goals are integral to the occasion, or are byproducts of enactment, is hardly clear. Neither is it evident whether 'transformation' is a function of the very operations of the occasion, or again a byproduct 'finally' of these. More-over, change seems restricted to participants. If their cosmos is affected, this is so only through them.

The anthropologist, Bruce Kapferer (1984a: 194), suggests that 'ritual' is 'a series of culturally recognized and specified events, the order of which is known in advance of their practice, and which are marked off spatially and temporally from the routine of everyday life (even though such events might be vital to this routine)'. Once more, a version of formality, but with the added insistence that attention be given to the vital dimension of sequencing, and the hint that this may constitute a program or 'text' of the occasion.

The most remarkable feature of these definitions (and of numerous others that could be adduced) is just how unremarkable, noncommittal, and innocuous, they are. They really tell us almost nothing, apart from some vague sort of instruction, perhaps akin to: PAY ATTENTION – SOMETHING SPECIAL GOING ON HERE AND NOW. Do we want to know what? Then fill in the ethnographic blanks. Apart from this, one might add that all three definitions imply that 'ritual' is somehow implicated in the impress of order.

Culling anthropological writings, one can establish a set of rudimentary features (likely overlapping with the above definitions) that aid in the characterization of public events as signifiers of order.[5] But will these features also inform us, substantially, about the logics whereby order is made in or through events? This issue is more problematic, and yet essential in my view, to any comprehension of how events work. It is the reason for the typology of the next chapter.

As the above definitions, and numerous scholars, tell us, there is in public occasions a comparative formalization of space, time, and behavior that distinguishes these from the living of mundane life. This formality has something of a programatic outline; and some scholars speak of the 'scripts' or 'texts' of such occasions, regardless of whether these are inscribed or not. Therefore, events are put together in accordance with some guidelines of organization: these occasions have relatively evident structures that are conveyed through various media. Thus, in Mary Douglas' (1982: 36) phrasing, 'Public rituals, by establishing visible external forms, bring out of all the possible might-have-beens a firm social reality.'

These structures have relatively high degrees of replicability. That is, whenever a particular occasion is enacted, it is put together from more-or-less similar elements; it is performed by more-or-less the same cast of characters; and it passes through more-or-less the same sequences of action.

That an event is organized as a sequence of practices also implies that it has direction: it has a fairly well-defined outset that points it in the direction of a particular ending or outcome. Therefore, a public event also may contain instructions of how to progress from the former to the latter.

Sequential organization is often associated with goal-directed activity and so is informed with intention. As such, an occasion may be constituted as a causal scheme, without entering here into a discussion of different conceptions of causality. In other words, the occasion may exist in order to do something, regardless of how explicit this can be made by participants or by other informed persons.

That a public event 'does' something is of basic importance. For the moment, suffice to say that this necessarily connects the event to the wider world beyond it. Connectivity connotes the relationship between the event and the lived-in world – that is, it indexes the 'function' of this relationship. This usage can be assimilated too easily, by critics, to an oft-discredited functionalism in the social sciences. As a theoretical position, functionalism depends first and foremost on the premise that the elements and activities of social order are organized as an integrated, homeostatic social-system. It is this premise, of the universal existence of social orders as social systems, that is dubious. But if a public event is goal-directed, if it 'does' something, then likely what it does – whether as product or byproduct – is consequential to social life in some way. This 'functional' relationship lies at the epistemological core of any conception of public events, and I will return to it.

The features of the public event indicate that it points beyond itself: in other words, it is symbolic of something outside itself. Public events are locations of the dense presence and the high production of symbols. Victor Turner (1967:19) went so far as to insist that 'The symbol is the smallest unit of ritual' – that is to say, its 'building-block'.

I am using the term, symbol, in its simple sense. Umberto Eco (1985: 385) writes of the etymology of the Greek word: 'Originally a symbol was a token, the present half of a broken table or coin or medal, that performed its social and semiotic function by recalling the absent half to which it could have been potentially reconnected . . . the verb "symballein" came to mean . . . to try an interpretation, to make a conjecture . . . to infer from something imprecise, because incomplete, something else that it suggested, evoked, revealed but did not conventionally say.' Kahler (1960: 70) notes that the term connotes 'to bring together', or 'to come together'. And Ulich (1955: 205) comments that, 'Since the *symbolon* was conceived of as the representation of the important, yet not existing in concrete actuality, it could also denote the invisible appearing in the visible, the abstract in the real, and the transcendent in the world of immanence.' In our usual understanding, a symbol is something that stands for, that stands in place of, or that points to, something else beyond its presence. Therefore the fuller import, or rather the 'fullness' of symbol is not to be sought in some inherent or essential quality, but elsewhere or elsewhen. This reference to symbol is not to its usage as 'merely symbolic': 'of having only a token effect, being performed only in order to affirm an attitude ... or serving as no more than a ceremonial embellishment which highlights the occasion' (Skorupski 1976: 172). Though these connotations of the symbolic also have their role – for example, to a degree in the royal entry, and more generally in public events of the modern nation-state. The latter will be referred to further on.

A symbol stands for, evokes, or brings into being something else, something absent. Therefore it denotes that kind of relationship where certain components exist elsewhere, but are brought into some sort of connectivity with others that are present. These relational qualities, between presence and absence, are those which constitute a public event as a symbolic structure. A structure or program composed of connections among symbols is one whose integral and integrative capacities are to point beyond itself, to the lived-in world, however the latter is constituted. Or, one may say, the capacity of such a structure is to stand temporarily in place of, to stand for, or to realize that lived-in world. From this it follows that the event itself may be composed as a little world, one that points beyond itself to the lived-in world by incorporating aspects of the latter within itself. Nothing further need be said here about formal properties of symbol. All further references to the organization of public events will be to their formation as symbolic structures, as this was used above.

Formality, replicability, intentionality, symbolic formation, and a connectivity that extends beyond itself – do these features tell us anything beyond that which we already know and use, common-sensically, in relating to public events? Do these features inform us, substantially, about what it is that such special occasions seem designed to do, and how they accomplish this? I doubt it. Even if some anthropologists agree that the above features are relevant to a delineation of public events, once one probes more vigorously into the particular characterizations that are made of such occasions any consensus speedily disintegrates. One is left with a welter of concepts and names for public events that are shaped and honed to the particular ethnographic needs of the analyst. Some of these labels are listed below, simply to illustrate their profusion:

> assembly, ceremony, definitional ceremony, ceremonial, mass cere-monial, crisis ceremonialism, celebration, carnival, contest, feast, festival, pageant, parade, procession, pilgrimage, rite, rite of passage, rite of intensification, calendrical rite, ritual, nascent ritual, ritual of rebellion, ideological ritual, ritual of conflict, ritual of reversal, ritual of inversion, ritual of reiteration, ritual of consolidation, sacred ritual, profane ritual, secular ritual, spectacle, etc.

In part, this disarray is due to a canon of ethnography: that the further one penetrates the ways of life of a people, the more the likelihood of achieving a worthy, if approximate, translation of these into the language of anthropology. But a side-effect of this is a pragmatism in conceptualization that verges on the ad hoc and the piecemeal: abstraction is thoroughly made the submissive servant of particular ethnographic cases, thereby losing much of its substance as generalization.

This disarray is due also to the pernicious presence of fallacies of misplaced concreteness. Thus, some of the terms used to delineate events are translations of indigenous ones that are borrowed by social science. Their status is, at one and the same time, that of indigenous descriptors of events and of social scientific concepts that analyze these phenomena. Given that a name like 'carnival' or 'festival' has indigenous validity somewhere as a description of an event, it cannot be used also to analyze itself as that event. If this is done, then levels of abstraction are confuted and produce paradox. Instead, in order to talk about indigenous events, there should be recourse to concepts that, for purposes of analysis, are understood to envelop the phenomena under discussion. The best of modern ethnographic analyses try to comprehend indigenous phenomena through their own terms; but they then go on to discuss these phenomena in ways that contribute to our own intellectual culture of social analysis. Unless one opts entirely for a position of descriptive cultural-relativism, the development of a language of analysis through abstraction is unavoidable. One expression of the confusion of logic that continues to pervade anthropology is the still prevalent rhetoric that the exception disproves the rule: that a concept loses its validity if it cannot be applied to the particulars of a given ethnographic case. This reflects the pragmatism in conceptualization mentioned above, but misunderstands and misplaces the purpose of abstraction.

I have claimed that the study of public events (under numerous rubrics) in anthropology is in a state of confusion, and that the kinds of rudimentary features of events outlined above are not sufficient for a more comprehensive grasp of what it is that public events do.[6] What manners of premise are needed in order to proceed with an explication of the latter?

Much debate in anthropology about the constitution of social order still revolves around arguments of whether societies are functionally organized, homeostatic entities that are re-equilibrated in holistic ways, or whether they are reproduced continually in ways that also reorganize and change the substance of their structures (cf. Bourdieu 1977). Nonetheless, there is no a priori reason to assume that social order must be grounded in stable and solidary macro-structures, whether in the idiom of homeostasis or in that of reproduction. Still, it is vital to the ongoing existence of any more-or-less dense network of persons that there exist media through which members communicate to themselves in concert about the characters of their collectivities, as if these do constitute entities that are temporally coherent. Public events are conveyances of this kind. There is no doubt that public events exist as grounded phenomena in their own right, and that they can be accorded this status both by participants and by observers. Can one make the same claim for constructs beloved of social science, like 'society', 'culture', 'social structure', 'institution', and 'group' (apart from small face-to-face groups)? Hardly. These, wholly, are abstractions whose phenomenal referents may only be intimated. On the other hand, public events are occasions that meet phenomenal criteria of sense and sight – of boundedness, of degrees of internal coherence, and of a relative unity of organization. So Milton Singer (1972: 71) contended that 'cultural performances' (the units of observation he chose to work through in South India, and loosely cognate with 'public events' in my usage thus far) were discrete, real phenomena to South Indians, and were amenable to direct observation and degrees of comprehension on the part of an outsider. As I commented, not by happenstance do ethnographers of a symbolical persuasion home in on such occasions to unearth evidence that comes to be reified as enduring codes of culture.

Public events are locations of communication that convey participants into versions of social order in relatively coherent ways. As the flow of living so often is not, public events are put together to communicate comparatively well-honed messages. If the flow of mundane living may be quite uncertain in terms of direction and outcome, the converse is true of public events. In the extreme case, they are operators of, and on, social order. Not only may they affect social order, they may also effect it.

The vital point here, one to be made forcefully, is that public events are phenomenally valid forms that mediate persons into collective abstractions, by inducing action, knowledge and experience through these selfsame forms. They are culturally designed forms that select out, concentrate, and interrelate themes of existence – lived and imagined – that are more diffused, dissipated, and obscured in the everyday.

When public events are situated in this way, their special status stands forth. Their standing is that of indigeneous phenomena that exist in the lived-in worlds of their participants, and that are graspable as such by external observers. Their mandate is to engage in the ordering of ideas, people, and things. As phenomena, they not only are cognitively graspable, but also emotionally livable. Therefore, they are devices of praxis that merge horizons of the ideal and the real, to bring into close conjunction ideology and practice, attitude and action. As Hans Buechler (1980: 8–9) argues, they organize both the signifiers of meaning and the referents of meaning. Like the 'aesthetic object', they have strong tendencies towards totalization (Tarn 1976: 29). These thrusts towards totalization as wholeness are discussed extensively by Richard Werbner (1989). Therefore public events tend to be relatively closed phenomenal worlds (or 'limited provinces of meaning' [Schutz and Luckmann 1973]), in and of themselves, that encompass participants and that operate on and through them. Should this perspective seem overly constrictive, it will be qualified to a degree in the following two chapters.[7]

One may well argue that any occasion of face-to-face interaction comes into existence through the selection and reorganization of phenomenal elements, together with a degree of closure, however fragile, that sets the occasion apart from other activities. This was the more profound implication of Erving Goffman's work on the interpersonal 'encounter' in everyday life, but one that he did not pursue (Goffman 1961; Handelman 1973, 1977a). Are there significant differences between the encounters of the everyday and those of special occasions? In their doing, public events seem less open to immediate and ongoing negotiation and reinterpretation of their forms, or are so through different durations, than is everyday interaction. Mundane encounters tend not to constitute relatively closed phenomenal worlds. Instead they are more responsive to pressures from within and without. In this regard, public events perhaps are made more protective of themselves. As foci within which ideation and action are mediated into one another, their logical status in a given social-order likely is higher than that of mundane activity.

If public events are constructs that make order, then the logics of how they are put together is crucial to how they work, and so to that which their designs enable them to accomplish. To enter within such forms is to be captured by, and caught up within, the logic of their design – and so to be operated on by the event, regardless of why it came into being, or for whatever motives it is enacted. Such designs are, in Smith's words (1982:

106), 'snares for thought', snares of mind and sense, snares of Being. William Beeman (1982: 118) calls them 'an ideological hammerlock', one whose logic grips participants in its premises.

Therefore, to get at a comprehension of events in these terms, the following assumptions are necessary. First, that the relative capacities of 'doing' – of making something happen – that an event has is related to its logic of composition. Second, that the logic of composition of an event is intimately related to its organization. Third, that in order to get at the above, one must take seriously that which an event communicates about itself, as well as what an interpreter makes of this.

The positioning of performance

Public events are constituted through their intentionality (their design, or 'structure' in an older parlance) and through their practice (their enactment or performance). Public events are profoundly existential, since no event *qua* event can exist substantively as a phenomenon apart from its practice. Design and enactment are integral to one another.[8] Kapferer (1986: 192) argues that practice ('performance', in his terms), 'constitutes a unity of text and enactment, neither being reducible to the other'. He continues, following Mikel Dufrenne: 'More properly, it is what certain philosophers of aesthetic experience refer to as the Work, irreducible to its performances and yet graspable only through them or, rather, in them'. Nonetheless, in this book, as the whole of this chapter indicates, I give epistemological primacy to design over enactment.

To a degree this primacy is due to the primarily synchronic perspective that the studies of this book take towards particular public events. An examination of how public events are created and are developed through historical time might well move this discussion further towards enactment. All public events began sometime and somewhere, regardless of whether their existence is attributed to 'tradition' or to invention (cf. the essays in Hobsbawm and Ranger [1983], and also Schechner [1981]). In instances of invention, the public event intentionally may be created whole, so to speak; and therefore, its design usually has temporal priority over its enactment. However, even here this design may be tested and tried in various modes, a process akin to that which Schechner (1985) calls 'rehearsal', during which alternatives of form are kept alive, before one is settled on. Then enactment is molded and disciplined by design, although the latter may continue to be modified by the former in ongoing interplay, such that 'design', 'form', or 'structure', are never fixed once and forever (even though persons may refer to these as settled and set).

However, other special occasions emerge and coalesce from the ongoing flow of the ordinary practices or 'doing' of the everyday. The designs of such special occasions are emergent, taking form through the very processes of practice, perhaps even before persons become consciously aware of the overall patterning of their own doings. Here enactment probably has temporal priority over design, if only until the latter takes shape and exerts the emergent logic of its composition, its snares, over the former. During all of these instances, design eventually comes to take precedence over enactment. This precedence is accentuated (and at times exaggerated) when one's analytical optic is synchronic.

Such emergent occasions that are the most elusive in their temporal coalescence (and the least remarked upon and documented), I call, simply, proto-events. 'Proto' refers to their protean character. I hasten to add that such occasions are not public events, in the ways that this rubric has been used in this chapter, although they contain the potentials to develop in this direction.[9] A brief discussion of proto-events concludes this chapter.

Tautologically, yet necessarily, a public event presupposes its own practice. My dictionary defines 'event' as, 'Anything that happens, as distinguished from a thing that exists; an occurrence, esp. one of great importance' (Concise English Dictionary, 1982). A 'happening' can become so only through its own enactment – otherwise there is no 'doing', and so no phenomenon of this sort.

This usage of enactment or performance is self-evident and self-explanatory; and it should be sufficient to remind that the doing of an occasion (and of course, how this is done) is essential to any full comprehension of a public event. Nonetheless, in recent years the enthusiastic adoption by anthropologists of ideas of performance, borrowed especially from dramatistic genres, threatens to reduce logics of design or form to epiphenomena of public events. Enactments are said to question continuously, and so to redo, such forms on an ongoing basis, thereby leaching the latter of the very impress of their designs. If one presupposes that, through their performance, public events necessarily are in a chronic condition of flux and variability, then such occasions lose their principled intentionality and directive force, except for the motives and desires of their performers. No longer are these occasions snares of mind and the senses, nor 'common denominator(s) for consciousnesses who feel themselves counterparts' (Dufrenne 1973: 69).

I deliberately have exaggerated this position to accentuate its implications. I agree with advocates of practice that the experiential dimension of public events is necessary to a comprehension of their operation (cf. Turner 1985), although this project is beyond my aims here. No design or form can itself convey the synesthenic unity upon which many public events depend for their fullness of meaning, and so for their viability (Sullivan 1986: 6). Moreover, advocates of performance studies do acknowledge the requisite of comprehending enactment within, in my terms, the designs or forms of its occurrence. So Grimes (1982: 543) renders performance as per-formance, as a going through form; and MacAloon (1984a: 9) points out that, 'there is no performance without pre-formance' – that is, without form through which performance is done.

The difference between the positions of scholars of performance and my own is, in part, one of emphasis: they stress doing, while I accentuate the logic of forms through which doing is done. For example, my objection to Milton Singer's notion of 'cultural performance' is not to the occasions this term indexes, but to the way the term construes our perception of these phenomena. Singer's wording directs our attention first and foremost to doing. Mine focuses perception more on the forms through which doing is done. My position throughout these chapters is that all types of public events are open to fluctuation and change through their enactment. But that this is so in differing degrees, and these variations in flexibility and openness are related intimately to the logics of design of public events. So these two positions are also in fundamental disagreement.

Whether they recognize this or not, proponents of performance – of the profundity of its emotions and experience – adopt a general view of public events that is primarily 'expressive' in its emphasis on the mutuality, reflectiveness, and solidarity of togetherness. I stress that the design of an event is also its passions, and therefore that the former can help to engender ugliness as well as beauty, hatred no less than desire. Furthermore, that events which primarily are expressive in their logic of design are integral to the movement into modern society, within which our own analytical standpoints on events are formed. To treat primarily expressive occasions as generic of public events is therefore to conflate our own common-sensical comprehension of public occasions with that which is possible elsewhere and elsewhen. Unless proponents of the experiential, expressive functions of events are ready to deal with a variety of logics of design, they simply will continue to miss the substance and significance of many occasions, like those of modelling, whose constitutive, instrumental empowerments are so profound. This should become clear in the course of chapter 2. The relationship between events of presentation, whose designs may be glossed as 'expressive', and modern societies is addressed briefly in the last section of chapter 3.

Nonetheless, the proto-event is indeed one in which the doing of performance clearly has preeminence over its design, in contrast to the types of public events discussed in chapter 2.

Proto-events

Proto-events are identifiable as special occasions, yet ones that have yet to be accorded a status of distinctive phenomena by their practitioners. Thus the rhythm and substance of the observable features of these occasions diverge from routine, expected interaction in patterned and coherent ways that are reproduced through time. But these emergent and divergent configurations are not referred to as holistically distinctive by those who live them.

The chapters of part II take up two cases of this kind in detail. Both were invented in workplaces.[10] The most telling feature of these occasions is an absence of name: both were created and remained as unnamed. The names by which they are known here – respectively, 'donkey game' and 'banana time' – are those of the ethnographers. The practitioners of these occasions neither named them nor spoke of them as phenomena, not even as they emerged. These occasions lacked the most elementary of concerted recognitions – the semantic singularity imparted by name or label that would accord to them an identity as phenomena in the worlds of their practitioners. Yet the persons who did not name these occasions were the very ones who did them – who repeatedly practiced certain actions in repetitive, systematic, regularized sequences. Theirs was 'performance' as the seedbed of form: not the practice of cultural expectations, nor of 'program', 'script', or 'text' that accompany and direct a named occasion, but of doing in concert that which had yet to be cognized consciously and holistically in common, at least through the spoken or written word. In these instances we find the practice of synchronized subtleties that appealed to, that resonated with, and that articulated the sensuous selves of the participants without any discourse or deliberation on rules, roles, or division of labor.

Proto-events are 'happenings' in a primordial sense. For they happen to happen (in the dual meaning of this phrasing), as invented and initially idiosyncratic doings, when the realm of experience seems almost wholly in their practice, and when action in concert supersedes reflection in common. Judging from the studies of part II, such occasions tend to be situational. They emerge in interplay with small-scale local conditions, and make sense only to those who do them. Their significance is localized, restricted to small groups who share these conditions. Negotiations among participants with regard to the form and articulation of practice are done, in the main, without words.

The point I stress here is that in the genesis of proto-events it is doing that is dominant, while it is a logic of form that is created from this practice. How in fact this does occur remains mysterious. Yet it is clear that once such a logic does coalesce, it reorganizes practice in terms of its emergent design. That is, the structure of performance tends to give way to the performance of structure. It is this changing ratio that distinguishes proto-events from public events. Moreover, it is the recognition by participants of an emerging design in their practices that enables them to become self-conscious about their creation. In turn, this likely increases their capacities to alter the design of their practices in intentional and deliberate ways.[11]

There is no small irony here for advocates of performance theory, who eagerly attribute capacities for change more to practice than to structure. I can phrase this best by accentuating the dialectical relationship between the design of an event and its practice. The more coherent practice becomes through its doing, the more practice acquires form. The more such form becomes obvious, the greater the likelihood that its practitioners consciously will recognize in concert that it constitutes a distinct phenomenon, and so will become self-conscious about their relationships to it, and through it. In turn, this self-consciousness will enable participants to alter the form of occasion in directed ways, and so to change its enactment. Therefore, the more structured is the form of occasion, the more potentially malleable it becomes through practice. Nonetheless, these sorts of open-ended developments contain their own limiting conditions. The logics of design of public events will restrain or will expand in varying degrees the impact of form on practice, practice on form.

2 Models and mirrors

The typology that follows could come at the end, the middle, or the beginning of this book. Locating its discussion near the beginning requires some words of explanation. Dorothy Lee (1959: 105–20) points to our tendencies to apprehend realities linearly. More particularly, our texts, our books and articles, are put together both linearly and hierarchically, so that these have a 'beginning' that leads to a 'middle' that in turn points to an 'end'. The typology could fill any of these locations. But each location then would intimate a different logical status to the typology, in relation to the discussions of particular public events that make up the bulk of this book. Each location invokes premises of how its positioning conditions expectations of that which is yet to come, or reflects on that which has come to pass and is already read. Thus, the organization of this book (like all books) constitutes a form that offers guides to the enactment of its text – in other words, to the doing of your reading.

Placed at the beginning, the typology becomes an introduction, one that seems the result of more deductive thinking, and that orientates perception towards all that has yet to come. This location arouses a sense of expectation, that the inscriptions which follow will bear out the typology. Placed at the end, the typology becomes a conclusion, one that seems the result of more inductive thinking, that is the outgrowth of all the discussions that preceded it. These prior inscriptions therefore arouse a sense of anticipation that all will be clarified in conclusion. Placed in mid-book, the typology becomes a way station, a summary and reformulation of that which has been read, reorganizing orientations towards that which is yet to come.

None of these strategies is an accurate reflection of my relationship to both the typology and the later chapters on particular public events. That of mid-book is perhaps the closest, since the typology did not spring forth, full-bodied. Yet mid-book is structurally the most awkward in this sort of text, for it misplaces both anticipation and closure. Nonetheless, the typology did not exist at all when some of these chapters were first written;

it existed as bits of ideas and pieces of ethnography when others were conceived; and was much as it is now, when chapter 9 was written. I put together the typology during years of teaching about 'ritual', 'ceremony', 'festival', and so forth. And so it developed from a growing dissatisfaction with the incapacities of existing rubrics to bring together apparently disparate occasions in order to accentuate their commonalities, while at the same time these rubrics tended to gloss over cutting differences among other occasions. Therefore the typology embodies these tensions, together with an emerging vision of the roles of public events in social life.

This sense of tension between the typological and the particular is the best index of their relationship. And this tension remains: I have not tailored the typology to the public events discussed in subsequent chapters, nor are the latter interpreted in ways wholly compatible with the former. Both continue to have their degrees of autonomy, of fit, of clash. This is so, as well, with regard to the relationships among the case studies themselves of public events. Each case study has its own idiosyncratic history in my work, and its own conceptual thrust. I try to point to these in the brief 'intersections' that precede each of these chapters. Although this text is now set, tremors and at times convulsions reverberate beneath its fixed, linear crust.

The positioning of the coming discussion of types of public events, close to the beginning of this book, is then a compromise between that which the typology is for me and that which I would like it to be for you. For me it is an intermediate approximation of rubrics that help me to think about occasions that seem radically different, but that may have important similarities; and about others that seem quite the same, yet may be otherwise. These typological aids are meta-designs of public events, not the events themselves. They have conceptual autonomy only so long as their existence has value. They themselves are not the aim of this exercise. That aim is somewhere between you and me, and depends on whether these types resonate at all with your data, your experiences and thoughts. If they do so, then your critical and creative response will be the aim of this exercise.

Events that model the lived-in world

The term, 'model', is common in English-language usage, and some words will clarify how it is intended here. In its dictionary rendition, for example, a model may refer to 'a standard, an example used as a canon', and to 'a representation or pattern in miniature ... of something to be made on a larger scale' (Concise English Dictionary, 1982). These definitions include two aspects – thinking and doing – that often are attributed to the term. A model is good for thinking with (a standard, a canon) or for doing with (a miniature of something to be made). This usage parallels the broad distinctions between 'knowing that' and 'knowing how' of Gilbert Ryle (1975: 27–32), and that between 'models of' and 'models for', of Geertz (1973: 93ff.). In these instances, models abstract reality in coherent ways, by selecting out, simplifying, and condensing various of its aspects and relationships. Models also provide directions for the reformulation of these abstractions into action. The most frequent usage in anthropology of the term, model, is that of 'folk model' – the mental or cognitive commonsense constructs through which people grasp and account for their worlds (cf. Holy and Stuchlik 1981). My usage is more restrictive, and bears a limited correspondence to what Max Black (1962: 223) calls an 'analogue model', one that 'shares with its original not a set of features or an identical proportionality of magnitudes but, more abstractly, the same structure or pattern of relationships'. I would qualify the necessity of 'sameness' in structure and pattern, and add that how these are operable or manipulable is crucial. My usage is easier to enter into through a brief digression on models in science where, as basic tools of work, their composition has received greater attention.

Understandings of models in science often collapse the sorts of dualities mentioned above. Barbour (1974: 6), a physicist, defines a scientific model as, 'a symbolic representation of selected aspects of the behavior of a complex system for particular purposes. It is an imaginative tool for ordering experience, rather than a description of the world.' First, therefore, a scientific model is, at one and the same time, a derivation of reality as well as one that should be informative of that reality. Models in science are good to think with and good to do with – often each requires the other for its fulfillment. The scientific model is, in the main, a device of praxis: within it, dualism is specious.

Second, models in science (as in social science, cf. Hagen 1961: 505; Guetzkow 1962; Barth 1966; Wilden 1977) are intended to be purposive in their 'epistemological immediacy': their synopsis of complex relationships is graspable and meaningful as a whole (Barbour 1974: 33). Models are purposive too, in the human intention of their design. The logician, Apostal (cited in Aris and Penn 1980: 3), outlines the modelling relationship as R(S, P, M, T), in which subject S takes, with purpose P in mind, the entity M as a model for the prototype T.

Third, the value of models in science also depends on their anticipatory or predictive capacities. Thus, 'a model always refers to a future event. This event need not necessarily take place but the model creates the possibility that it can do' (Jenkins 1981: 94). Models make space within themselves for probable futures, and specify conditions of the potential attainment of these, through operations upon or with the model. As Mary Hesse (1966: 9–10) points out, models in science contain negative as well as positive analogies. That is, these models are adaptable, in that negative results should lead to the reformulation of the model.

Fourth, that scientific models purposively can do operations that predict changes in their own states of existence, under specified conditions, often requires that the logic of their organization be systemic. That is, the model is set up, and exists, as a miniature system, 'a set of entities mutually interrelated and interdependent, themselves functioning together as an entity at some higher level of organization' (Caws 1974: 1). That a model has predictive capacities, is also to say that it includes within itself the probabilities that can be realized by altering its internal organization in regulated ways. Fifth, such models are informed by what anthropologists, in the main, would identify as functionalist premises – for alterations in certain elements of the model will bring about related changes in other of its elements (cf. Shanin 1972: 8). The result usually is not a different model, but one that systemically has changed something within itself, through its operation. It is systemic relationships that enable Aris and Penn (1980: 4) to say of the mathematical model, that it 'has a life of its own' with an 'intrinsic vitality'. Borrowing from cybernetics one can add that, to effect change purposively within itself, a system must at least be capable of representing a concept of alteration and the alternatives that this can project (Longyear 1979: 514). Thus models likely have 'autotelic' qualities: they are intrinsically rewarding, and contain their own goals and sources of motivation (Anderson and Moore 1960: 207).

Sixth, therefore, the systemic qualities of certain scientific models enable them to make change happen within themselves, regardless of whether this change is wholly theoretical or whether it is used to do something to natural phenomena. Gudeman and Penn (1982: 90) correctly point out that, 'There exists no necessary or a priori connection between a model and that which it models'. Nonetheless, should such a connection be stipulated, and if the models referred to are social or cultural, then their effects on lived-in realities may be profound indeed.

And seventh, models in much of modern science are often 'observer-dependent' (Geyer and van der Zouwen 1978: 1). No longer may we assume with ease that nature (and culture) exist 'out there', to be mapped and discovered without evaluating our own roles and operations at one and the same time. The particle physicist, Werner Heisenberg (1960: 230–231) put it this way: 'When we speak of a picture of nature provided by contemporary exact science, we do not actually mean any longer a picture of nature, but rather a picture of our relation to nature ... Science no longer is in the position of observer of nature, but rather recognizes itself as part of the interplay between man and nature. The scientific method of separating, explaining, and arranging becomes conscious of its limits, set by the fact that the employment of this procedure changes and transforms its object; the procedure can no longer keep its distance from the object.' As we now understand 'forces of nature' (and culture) to be accessible to us through ourselves, so these have become our 'subject'. These views have some prominence in postmodern science, and are discussed at length by Toulmin (1983), Bohm (1985), and others. In current parlance, the relationship between modeller and modelled, through the medium of model, is one of critical self-awareness.

Social scientific models, like scientific ones, are set apart from lived-in realities, apart from those of their makers. They make claims about the world (Barbour 1974: 16), and are used by their makers to think about social life (Rapoport 1978). But what of other models that exist as part of social life, in order to effect some change in the latter? Such models are 'interventionist' – not only do they make claims about the lived-in world, but also for it, and in its name. There is little doubt that many domains of the modern nation-state are organized through premises that consciously are recognized as systemic, and that are planned to be so, in the ways that this term is used here. For example, numerous bureaucracies are put together in accordance with such assumptions; their routines of organization ideally operate in such ways; and the roles attributed to them by their makers are to regulate, to intervene in, and to change social order in mundane ways (see Handelman 1981; van Gunsteren 1976). On the other hand, public events of the modern state largely are devoid of systemic qualities. In the main, these events tend to approximate displays or presentations, like the royal entry. There may be a conundrum here that deserves attention, and I will return to these topics in the last section of chapter 3.

What of peoples whom we gloss as tribal or traditional? Again there is no doubt of their capacities to create forms of organization that are informed by systemic premises; although the identification of the latter frequently requires both indigeneous hints and the interpretations of the ethnographer, since native terms of conceptualization belong to other discourses. Lévi-Strauss (1966: 11) comments with insight that their 'magical thought' differs from science, 'not so much by any ignorance or contempt of determinism but by a more imperious and uncompromising demand for it which can at the most be regarded as unreasonable and precipitate from the scientific point of view ... magical rites and beliefs appear as so many expressions of an act of faith in a science yet to be born'. And Horton (1972: 355), in his discussion of African 'ritual', makes the case that the tremendous concern of traditional religions with explanation and prediction makes 'Ritual Man . . .

a sub-species of Theory-building man'. He adds that the conceptual models of African religions differ from those of science, 'most notably in the absence of any guiding body of explicit acceptance/rejection criteria that would ensure the efficiency with which they pursue their aims'. In Hesse's (1966) terms, 'known positive analogies' are highly developed, but 'known negative analogies' less so.

Of course one may argue over issues of causality, efficiency, and efficacy in modelling, without either denying the existence of such constructs or contradicting that they are informed by systemic premises.[1] Still, one may ask whether tribal and traditional peoples necessarily model their collectivities as systemically organized entities, as does seem to be the case in the modern state. But the concerns here are not with structures of thought.[2] Instead, my question is whether one can identify public events whose logics of composition approximate systemic features that, in turn, set these events apart from others that do not.

What sorts of attributes characterize the event-that-models? First, as noted, the model necessarily is a reduction and a simplification of phenomena of the lived-in world, but it subsumes in its composition certain aspects of the latter. Therefore, it retains its connectivity to the phenomena that it models. In a crude, functionalist sense, the model is put together as a little system of interrelated and interdependent parts. An alteration in any of these requires concomitant adaptation in the others. The rules that set the model to working, and that keep it in operation, may parallel everyday counterparts, or they may be quite artificial ones that maintain only a postulated relationship to the lived-in world, as in numerous games and contests.

The event-that-models, then, is something of a microcosm of the lived-in world, a simplified but specialized, closed system that operates in parallel to the more complex and fuzzy phenomena that it models (Wallace 1966: 238). Yet, while this microcosm is working, it sustains a comparatively high degree of autonomy from the lived-in world, for two reasons. One is due to the closed, systemic qualities of its constitution: so long as it has a mandate to function, it does so in accordance with the in-built relationships among its rules. The other has to do with relationships between determinate part (the model) and indeterminate whole (the lived-in world). From the view of an external observer the model is only a version, or a part, of the lived-in world. But, from within itself, the model fills the world of its participants – it becomes that world by transcending its own partiality as a version of the world. Therefore the model, the part, behaves as if it were the whole, the lived-in world. In other words, the microcosm of the model exists in a relationship of synecdoche to the macrocosm of the world. Put otherwise, it may be that only a 'version' of a macrocosm that is assumed to exist, can presume a totality of discourse about the existence of that macrocosmic whole.

It is vital to stress again that a model neither imitates nor reflects any totality of ordered life. This would defeat its principled purpose, by the introduction into the model of the continuously emerging dynamics that make social life finally uncontrollable. Ultimately the model would become the world, and therefore incapable of acting upon the latter.[3] However, since the model retains its connectivity to the world from which its elements derive, whichever operations are done to the model, the microcosm, also are done to the latter. The problem of the makers of cultural models is one of how to arrest temporarily the flow of living, replete with its unwonted and unwanted occurrences, and to momentarily replace this with a micro-world that either is well-known or is thought to be known fully. Through correct procedures, this microcosm is more controllable, and so the outcomes it can generate are more limiting. As Wallace (1966: 238) writes of 'ritual': 'the contingent probabilities in chains of ritual events are near unity'.

A second attribute of an event-that-models is that it is purposive. It is 'embedded in a means-to-end context' (Barth 1975: 209). In technical language, it is 'teleological' – 'organized action with respect to a specific goal where the goal is itself an integral and explicit part of the activity' (Friedman 1979: 254; see also Sztompka 1974: 74–8). Although scholars (cf. Bargatzky 1984) insist that, to be teleological, social action must have its purpose or goal explicitly enunciated, this criterion may be difficult to meet in an event-as-model. Events are constituted and situated historically, and their purposiveness may have emerged implicitly as their designs altered incrementally through time. (This, I think, is the case with the Palio of Siena, discussed in chapter 6.)

Third, an event-that-models is a maker of change that is neither haphazard nor aimless – it has particular and specified directions. As I commented, these events help not only to affect the lived-in world, but also to effect it. As noted, the purposiveness of an event-that-models is anticipatory: it indexes or pre-views a hypothetical future condition that will be brought into being, and it provides procedures that will actualize this act of imagination. von Wright (1971: 83) writes that, 'Teleological explanations point to the future. "This happened in order that that should occur".' Since this future condition does not exist as yet, an event-that-models must have predictive capabilities. Put otherwise, such an event contains futures within itself. In turn, this requires that the event have a stipulated control over processes of causality, in order to respond, conversely, to the teleological question of 'why something happened necessarily' (von Wright 1971: 84–5).

For my purposes, it is sufficient to say that Western ideas of causality, that also inform much modelling, scientific or otherwise, depend on continuity through time and contiguity in space. Walens (1981: 21) accurately notes that: 'Causality is seen as the interaction of two objects or forces whose relationship involves their direct contact'. He (Walens 1983: 22) offers a useful example of two billiard tables, standing side by side: 'we [westerners] conclude a causal relationship when one ball on a pool table hits a second and "causes" it to move. We do not expect a ball on one table to be able to cause a ball on another table to move, nor do we explain the motion of one ball today in terms of the specific motion of another ball yesterday'. In modern Western thought, relationships of cause-and-effect are not analogical nor metaphorical. By contrast, ideas of causality among non-western peoples may depend upon correspondences of analogy, homology, or iconicity (cf. Daniels 1984). Leach (1968: 525) renders the viewpoint of neo-Tylorians (among whom Robin Horton, cited earlier, is prominent), and with which he disagrees, as follows: 'Since the participants in a religious ritual claim that their actions are designed to alter the state of the world . . . why should we not accept this statement at face value? . . . Ritual acts are to be interpreted in the context of belief: they mean what the actors say they mean'. And Evens (1982: 388) argues for the 'distinct analytical advantage' of a 'theoretical capacity to take primitive man at his word'. Walens (1981: 22), for example, notes the following about Kwakiutl Indian premises of cause-and-effect: 'Two items stand in a causal relationship if they can be shown to have inherent similarities in their structure; if some action is performed that utilizes that underlying structural similarity, then an event will be caused'. So one should recognize that causation may be experienced as a gestalt, in which it is the complex of factors occurring together that is perceived to do something (Lakoff and Johnson 1980: 70–1), rather than their weighted parcellation into distinct 'causes' and 'effects'. It falls then to the analyst to do this work.

Fourth, to operate as a little system, an event-that-models should regulate itself to a degree. In other words, as the processes of these events approach or attain their goals, the former should be slowed down, switched to other goals, or stopped – whereupon the event ends, and phases out its own temporary existence. Moreover, self-regulation enables an event-that-models to monitor its own progression and progress, as this is being made. The devices that accomplish such operations are called, in the language of cybernetics, 'feedback'. Feedback may be defined as 'a process in which the factors that produce a result are themselves affected by that result' (Geyer and van der Zouwen 1986: 216). Negative feedback signals that process should be slowed or stopped; positive feedback signals the converse. The relationship between feedback and the experience of causation as a gestalt likely is an intimate one. Chapter 10 discusses the clown in 'ritual', in part as a monitoring device of this kind that enables the event in which this character appears to switch from one phase to another. Self-regulation is crucial, for example, to events of divination, as the work of Richard Werbner (1989) clearly intimates – since the protagonists must actively reflect upon and interpret signs and portents while the occasion is in process, in order that it can continue to progress.

Anthropologists seldom recognize the salience of self-regulation within the operation of such public events. One exception was the late Michael Egan who studied Sinhalese exorcisms of a variety quite similar to those analyzed by Kapferer. Egan (quoted in Tambiah 1979: 150) wrote that: 'what is lacking in ritual techniques is any sort of direct and immediate empirical feedback from the occult about the effects the ritual techniques are having on [the progress of ritual operations], and in consequence the [Sinhalese exorcist] lacks the necessary information for knowing when to stop one set of operations and start another'. Nevertheless, I think that Kapferer's analysis of the organization of sequencing in these events demonstrates that exorcists do receive that which they perceive as empirical evidence of this sort; and therefore that such devices of feedback are present in the designs of these exorcisms. Nonetheless, though self-correcting, events of modelling seem less self-transforming. Since they tend to lack 'known negative analogies', their self-adaptation and evolution in relation to negative results is less prominent.

Fifth, an event-that-models has built into itself incompatible, contradictory or conflicting states of existence, and in the course of its working it must overcome, synthesize, or otherwise solve these. Thus, the Sinhalese exorcism begins with a person who is ill, who is controlled by the demonic, and in the course of its operations makes of the patient a person who is well (see also Sharon 1978).[4] The Isoma of the Ndembu peoples, analyzed by Victor Turner (1969), turns an incomplete person (an infertile woman) into a complete one (a fertile woman). Occasions of renewal (whether of cosmic order, social order, and so forth) commonly turn one kind of process and momentum – for example, that of entropy – into its converse of regeneration (cf. Beidelman 1966; but especially Schipper and Wang 1986, on Taoist ritual). Or, as in many of the occasions that Van Gennep (1960) called 'rites de passage', an immature youngster is turned into a mature adult. Writing of women's initiations in comparative perspective, Lincoln (1981: 103) calls these 'metamorphoses', and adds that these occasions change the 'fundamental being' of the initiands, by addressing 'ontological concerns'. These examples, and many others that could be adduced, are of events that are called upon to do transformative work within themselves – they do not simply validate changes that have occurred elsewhere, or by other means.[5] At the very least, should people say or show that an occasion is transformative, then we too should look very carefully for a logic of transformation and for a kind of organization (one that I am calling transformative) that enables such operations to be done in controlled, predictive ways.

Sick/healthy, infertile/fertile, entropy/regeneration, immature/mature – the terms of each of these sets are contradictory or mutually negating. These are qualities that cannot or should not co-exist within the same person, the same social space, or through the same duration. The designs of events-that-model are premised to transform one term of each set into the other. Terence Turner (1977) argues convincingly that transformative work in occasions like these depends on the inclusion of higher-order premises, often paranatural, that themselves are not embedded in the usual features of the phenomena to be transformed. Put otherwise, these systemic models are not 'natural' systems. They are human constructions, cultural epistemologies, that bring into powerful and determining conjunction disparate levels, codes, and forces that ordinarily remain separated, or that are thought to have more complicated ontological relationships.

'Transformation' is an overworked word. In its commonplace usage, the words 'change' or 'alteration' would do as well. The term, 'transformation', should refer to processes whereby one kind of phenomenon is utterly made over into another. This is a qualitative change in whatever is thought to distinguish one phenomenon from another.[6] Events that are transformative, in the above sense, often are understood to be dangerous. For this there are good epistemological reasons. Transformation requires the introduction of uncertainty into the presumed stability of the phenomenon that is to undergo this radical transmutation.[7] This intervention into the very structuring of cosmos and person may threaten to unleash forces that potentially are subversive and destructive of human and natural orders. Yet, when such forces are set loose within models that are organized in accordance with systemic premises, then transformative work can proceed apace in controlled and predictive ways. 'Uncertainty' is crucial to the logic of events-that-model, and I return to this in the following chapter.

In order to exemplify these features of an event-that-models – especially that of systemically organized relationships that I take as necessary to controlled, transformative work – let me turn to a reanalysis of a more extended ethnographic case.[8] In 1956, Audrey Richards (1982) published a by now classic monograph on *chisungu*, an occasion held among the Bemba peoples of present-day Zambia. Richards had observed *chisungu* in 1931. She described it as a 'girl's initiation ceremony'. In previous times, *chisungu* may have lasted up to six months. The enactment Richards observed was truncated to less than a month's duration; but she believed that the elementary structure of the event had remained intact. Here my sole concern is to expose some aspects of the design of this elaborate and complicated event: therefore ethnographic detail is kept to the bare minimum, unlike the chapters of this volume that deal in detail with particular public events.

According to Richards, the intention of *chisungu* was to turn an immature girl into a mature woman, one who would be ready for marriage, and capable of undertaking the dangerous tasks of purifying her husband and herself following the pollution of intercourse and menstruation. Contacts with ancestral spirits were vital to the well-being of the household, and these could be attained only under conditions of purity. *Chisungu* was held not at puberty, but just prior to marriage. Upon its success depended the viability of future households, and so too that of the Bemba peoples.

At the outset, and for the duration of the event, the girl-candidates were secluded and placed under the expert supervision of older women. These elders stated that the purpose of *chisungu* was to 'grow' the girls, to 'teach' them, to make them into women (1982: 121). A girl who had not had her *chisungu* performed remained simply 'rubbish', an 'unfired pot'. Richards (1982: 125) adds: 'the women in charge of this ceremony were convinced that they were causing supernatural changes to take place in the girls . . . as well as marking those changes. They were changing an alarming condition to a safe one, and securing the transition from a calm but unproductive girlhood to a potentially dangerous but fertile womanhood. They were making the girls grow as well as teaching them'. La Fontaine (1982: xxxvi) commented in her introduction to the reissued volume, that the purpose of the event was 'the transformation of human nature into responsible social beings'.

It is clear that *chisungu* is purposive and goal-directed, and that these attributes are built into the event itself. Therefore the operation of the event is teleological. It should also be evident that the event encompasses contradictory and conflicting states of existence: one kind of person, an immature one, enters; another kind of person, a mature one, exits. The change that is made to happen in the interim is an essential one, in the very being of each girl. The event, in other words, makes transformation happen. To do this, the occasion must overcome, solve, or synthesize the contradictions that it itself postulates as incompatible: the candidate cannot leave as some amorphic conglomeration of pre-pubescence and pubescence. *Chisungu* models what it is to be an immature girl, and a mature woman, and the relationships through which the former is transformed into the latter.

On the first day of *chisungu*, the girls, covered with blankets, were made to crawl backwards on all fours into the initiation hut, where much of the event would take place. They were understood to be 'forsaking their old way of life . . . concealed from others . . . passing through a tunnel, a dark place . . . into the heart of mysteries, the knowledge of how to build up their future homes' (1982: 64). The girls intentionally were made to look foolish, and were mocked and ridiculed by the older women. During the evening of the first day, and later on, this relentless and unmerciful teasing would continue. Thus Richards (1982: 79) describes the evening of the seventh day:

Everyone watched anxiously to see whether they would cry. One girl burst into tears at once and was greeted with roars of appreciative laughter. The other did not weep at all, and was immediately smacked by her relatives who shouted, 'You child you! Cry a bit! Cry a little bit!' . . . The rest of the evening was spent in similar efforts to make the *banacisungu* [the girl-candidates] cry. I watched seven different singing games in which the girls were pulled about and tormented . . .

The purpose of all sessions of teasing during *chisungu* was to bring the girls to tears. This teasing may be understood as a technique that helped the girls to 'unlearn' their state of immaturity and their status as pre-pubescents. This state was 'broken down', in part through teasing, to prepare and to aid the girls to learn to become other than they were. The weeping of the girls was taken as evidence that this process was working, that the girls no longer were true-to-type, no longer consistently immature. As teasing intensified, so did the weeping of the girls. In Gregory Bateson's phrasing, this process could be summarized as one of 'learning to learn'. Teasing/crying was prominent on the first, the seventh, and the eleventh days, after which it ceased entirely.

Throughout this period the older women imparted new knowledge to the girls that was necessary to their growth. As well, numerous symbolic acts, that were paranaturally transformative in themselves, were performed to change the girls. The relationship between teasing and crying (that is, unlearning) is teleological. Teasing brought the girls to tears, while this weeping was itself a monitor of the success of the teasing. The evidence of crying might lead the older women to intensify their teasing, or to decrease this. In the former instance the relationship became one of positive feedback, and in the latter, one of negative feedback. The important point is that this was a variable, adjustable relationship. Thus this relationship was self-regulating to a degree, in bringing the girls to the correct condition. Weeping, therefore, had the character of a 'test' of the effects of teasing, although it was not accorded this exegesis either by Bemba women or by Richards.

Also on the first and seventh days, there took place what Richards calls 'magic omens' or 'ordeals'. On both of these days the girls first were teased, then passed through an ordeal, and then tormented again during the evening. On the first day the girls were made to jump over a pile of boughs, some two feet in height, from a particular variety of tree with meanings of fertility and fruitfulness. The girls jumped 'to the accompaniment of screams of encouragement and threats from all around. ['Don't tremble!' 'Don't be frightened, you silly girls'. 'Jump now! Jump high'.] The girls were evidently nervous to a degree, and one failed to manage the moderate jump expected and had to try again and again. When both the girls were over, there was an outburst of congratulation' (1982: 66). In the ordeal of the seventh day, the girls had to catch water insects in their mouths (1982: 75).

Richards (1982: 138) considers that 'the critical moments [of *chisungu*] in Bemba eyes were those I have described as magic omens or ordeals'. Asked what would happen if a girl failed an ordeal, an older woman responded: 'Nothing ... anyhow she must jump it. We do not let them fail' (1982: 123). Another stated that through the ordeals, 'They [the older women] try to find out if the girls have grown up' (1982: 76). Richards (1982: 162) comments that these ordeals were 'tangible proof' that the girls were maturing. La Fontaine (1982: xxxvi) adds that the successful results of ordeals 'establish that the girls have indeed been changed by their experience ... the girls are material that is shaped'. These ordeals, then, were also 'tests' that provided evaluations of the progression of transformation within the girls.

The relationship between 'testing' (the ordeals) and learning also is a teleological one – a device of variable self-regulation that is built into the event. Not only did the tests monitor the progression of transformation in the girls, but, like crying, they provided negative feedback that either slowed down the event, or that enabled it to proceed. For the girls had to pass each test, regardless of the number of attempts that were required to do so. Crying and testing seemed to do similar kinds of work in *chisungu*; though during the first seven days that of crying monitored more the progression of 'unlearning', while that of the ordeals monitored more the progression of learning. But the relationship of learning/testing was of greater scale and compass than that of teasing/crying. Weeping seemed to provide a more immediate index of the effects of teasing; while the tests supplied more of an overall summary of the accumulated unlearning, learning, and growth that had happened to the girls during lengthier periods.

These two sets of relationships also were connected to one another, for learning and growth did appear to depend, in the eyes of Bemba women, on the 'unlearning' or the 'learning to learn' of the girls. The girls, as material to be shaped, had to be made malleable if learning and growth were to proceed

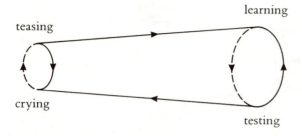

Figure 1 Self-regulation in *Chisungu*

apace. This more comprehensive relationship may be abstracted, as in figure 1. From the ethnography, one cannot claim that these aspects of the first days of *chisungu* were as neatly organized a set of self-regulating causal relationships as figure 1 depicts. Nonetheless, this figure does abstract from the ethnography a thrust of logic of design that can be called systemic. The figure may be read in the following way. On the first day, teasing leads to crying. This indexes or 'tests' the effects of this tormenting of the girls and the success of their beginning to 'unlearn' their immature state. The first ordeal follows: this encompasses and tests the success of the whole vertical relationship (in the figure) between teasing and crying. The success of the ordeal leads to an ensuing period of learning and growth. On the seventh day, this entire pattern is repeated, beginning again with the teasing of the girls.

An additional point of importance follows from figure 1. The upper plane of this figure, labelled 'teasing' at one extremity and 'learning' at the other, does not depict a dichotomization of these two factors. They are not discontinuous binaries. 'Unlearning' and 'learning' are part of a greater, more comprehensive conception of learning. Their presence on the same plane of the figure indicates that they are continuous with one another – they are different aspects or functions of a continuum of meta-learning that has as its ultimate aim the growth of the girls. During the early days of *chisungu*, both the 'unlearning' and 'learning' functions of the continuum are operative, for distinctive purposes. In the later days the emphasis of the continuum shifts, 'teasing' ceases, and only 'learning' remains. The same depiction holds for the lower, lateral plane of this figure. Again, 'crying' and 'testing' are not dichotomous binaries, but are continuous with one another. Both are functions of a continuum of testing, or of meta-testing, that, in one mode or another, monitors and regulates the progression of *chisungu* from beginning to end. This entire structure of relationships, then, is informed by causality, by self-regulation and correction, and by progression towards the accomplishment of goals that are integral to the design of the event.

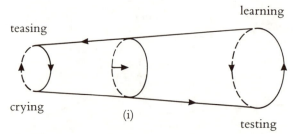

Figure 2 Further feedback in *Chisungu*
(i) temporary unfired clay-images

Following the severe teasing of the evening of the seventh day, another relationship of learning came to the fore. From the ninth through the thirteenth day the older women shaped large, complicated images of unfired clay, each with its own set of meanings. Towards the end of the day on which they were made, these images were shown briefly to the girls, to teach them, and then were destroyed (1982: 88). One may suggest that these clay images were demolished because the girls were still in the process of being 'grown' – their transformation was still to be completed. The images prefigured a state of fuller knowledge and corresponding growth. Their molding signed the development of the girls; their destruction, that this was yet unfinished. Fresh clay is itself incomplete, still malleable like the girls, and perhaps paralleled and reflected their unfinished condition.

During this period the emphasis of *chisungu* seemed to shift more towards 'learning' and away from 'unlearning'. The girls advanced in their maturation: they became sufficiently grown to offer food, then to eat more freely, and then learned how to purify their future husbands after intercourse. During this period there were no ordeals, but the last session of teasing/crying took place during the evening of the eleventh day, and thus overlapped with the construction and destruction of clay images. Therefore the relationship between learning and testing appears to have been maintained, with teasing/crying also providing evidence of the progress of the girls. With the progression of *chisungu*, one could add additional feedback loops to the structure of the model, as in figure 2, that continued to sustain the relationship between learning and testing. The teasing/crying of the eleventh day was the final session of 'unlearning' in *chisungu*, and the last negative feedback of this sort. On the thirteenth day (there was no activity on the twelfth) the making and breaking of clay images also ended. On the fourteenth day the girls were washed, cleansed, and painted with white-wash. Richards (1982: 90) comments that this, 'seems to mark a definite stage in the ritual. It is a rite of purification from the menstrual blood and a form of beauty magic.'

The teaching and growing of the girls continued. Additional images of unfired clay were shaped by the older women, but these no longer were demolished. On the seventeenth day the girls underwent a third major ordeal, intended also to make them grow (1982: 98). They had to leap over two crossed hoops, one from a tree that signified maleness, and the other, femaleness. This test greatly exceeded in difficulty that of the first ordeal of jumping, for this structure was at least twice the height of the earlier one. One of the girls failed twice to clear this obstacle:

It was apparently a terrifying thing to have happened. Her mother looked really angry and distressed and beat her on the legs with a branch. She herself looked petrified with fear and had obviously lost her nerve. Everyone shouted advice . . . The girl was by this time sobbing miserably, but with a final whack on her shins from her mother, she made a supreme effort and cleared the jump. The relief of the crowd was tremendous . . . *(1982: 97–8)*.

That evening the girls were presented with forty-three fired, pottery images, each with its own meanings of propriety, duty, and morality. Following on this, the bridegrooms (in this instance for various reasons, enacted by others), entered the hut carrying bows and arrows. The girls sat against a wall, beneath circular, painted marks that signified them. The bridegrooms fired their arrows at these targets: 'Their husbands had come to claim them in marriage' (1982: 107). On the morning of the eighteenth day, the girls underwent their final major ordeal: the slow killing of chickens by banging their heads on the ground, as the girls sat and rose, sat and rose, in time to drum rhythms. One of the older women commented: 'if she can't kill the chicken we shall know that she isn't grown up yet. We shall call her a *citongo* [an uninitiated person]' (1982: 107). The girls then prepared the chickens for cooking. Later that morning, the women and girls partook of a communal meal, during which the latter were made free to eat once again with other members of the community. On the twenty-third day, the girls – freshly bathed, oiled, in new clothes, with their bridegrooms by their side – sat on mats before their huts, and were presented to all the villagers. *Chisungu* had ended and the now mature women were ready for the wedding rites.

The systemic aspects of *chisungu* that I have outlined may now be depicted as follows, in figure 3.

Although a simple schematic, this figure highlights those self-regulating relationships that were discussed in this section. Through 'unlearning', or 'learning to learn', the girls were made culturally malleable. Progress was monitored by teasing/crying and by ordeals. Parallel to these, the girls were taught and grown. Emphasis shifted entirely to learning and growth, and the progressions of these also were checked periodically. The figure can be read

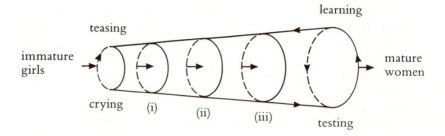

Figure 3 Systemic design in *Chisungu*
(i) temporary unfired clay-images
(ii) permanent unfired clay-images
(iii) permanent fired clay-images

synchronically, as a structure of dynamic relationships, or diachronically as a sequence of additive progressions – as permanent clay-images replaced temporary ones, and in turn were replaced by fully-baked, fired-pottery images.

Chisungu is a complicated occasion, rich in symbolic action, and permeated by the complex cultural exegeses of the Bemba – of the meanings that its acts had for them – as well as by the explanations and insights of Richards. I have not discussed *chisungu* as a creation of Bemba culture. Nor have I addressed the bulk of sub-events that occurred within the design of the occasion. My intention was to demonstrate that certain crucial aspects of *chisungu* are put together in ways that are not simply a matter of organization, nor for that matter of sequential (diachronic) organization, nor even of systematic, sequential organization. The logic of the event is that of a causal, predictive scheme; and its premises of causality are pointed to the making of directed change. It begins with one kind of phenomenon, and makes of this another that stands in contradiction to, and in place of, the former. The prediction of transformation, its direction and actualization, are done within the event itself. The outcome is not the product of the more variable, uncontrolled, and therefore uncertain interface between the event and conditions of the wider social-order (as is the case in the other types of events to be discussed). Moreover, this scheme is self-regulating, to a degree: it monitors its own progression to ascertain whether the operations of its enactment are having their desired effects and consequences. It is put together as a model that neither reflects phenomenal and existential realities (a model of), nor that merely offers directives to those realities (a model for). Instead, this model brings into systemic interaction those forces that grow the girls, paranaturally and didactically.[9] This kind of controlled, transformative work is peculiar to what I call an event-that-models.

No other case study in this book is as comprehensive in its emphasis on modelling as is *chisungu*. Nonetheless, chapter 6 does continue themes of systemic modelling. It is set in the Italian city of Siena, where the Palio Festival is held. Part 'parade' and part horse-race, with religious undercurrents, and eddies of politicking, the Palio has attracted the attention of a number of anthropologists whose studies form the basis of my reinterpretation of the event. The argument to be offered is that, in this public event, the city of Siena models itself systemically in ways that work to accomplish the regeneration of the entire urban entity. Through its model of itself, the city takes itself apart in intense competition on a lower level of urban structure. While this is occurring, a higher and encompassing level of urban structure ensures that the conflicts between the fractious and fragmented parts of the lower level do not spiral out of control. The modelled city is then put back together again, in a renewed and revived condition. The logic of this transformation differs from that of *chisungu*. The purpose of the latter is the creation of a new being. That of the Palio is, as I interpret this, the return to a similar state of being, but rejuvenated. Yet in my understanding, such controlled, transformative work through a public event is possible only when the occasion is organized as a model that operates in accordance with systemic premises.

'Banana time', discussed in chapter 5, is in my terms a proto-event, yet one that acquired an emergent logic of modelling. A seminal piece of industrial ethnography done by the late Donald Roy in the 1950s, it describes the commensality, the arguments and antics, of three middle-aged workmen employed in an American factory. In my interpretation of his description, their doings constituted a remaking and hence a new experiencing of reality – one that altered a repetitious, numbing, and isolating routine of work into one of conflict, playfulness, and solidarity. These men reinvented the ordering of their working day as a design of sub-events that transformed their long hours of work into another reality, one predicated upon extraordinary occurrences. Still protean in its unnamed doings, this design was emerging as one with systemic properties. These properties enabled the same framework of sub-events to be reproduced through the same sequencing of activities, day after day and, moreover, to withstand threats to its existence. Within this workplace, this emergent modelling did not have a special, ontological status, one that set it apart from mundane reality. Instead it was the reality of the everyday that was re-modelled comprehensively, to operate in accordance with systemics of order that had little to do with the culture of the factory, as this was understood there. To say any more at this point, would be to give the game away.

As well, chapter 10 on clowns in 'ritual' has particular relevance for events of modelling. A problem of organization not addressed in the discussion of *chisungu* is how one phase or stage of an event is turned into the next, so that the progression of the occasion can continue. This problem was hinted at in the quotation from Michael Egan, earlier in this chapter. With regard to *chisungu*, one possibility is that the episodes of teasing/crying, and those of the ordeals, also contained information on how to do these transitions, and so to move the event into a subsequent phase of activity. However, whether these episodes were also mechanisms of sequencing, in addition to those of monitoring and self-regulation, is not clear from the ethnography. Certain of the occasions discussed, in which clowns appear, approximate events of modelling. These clowns seem to do precisely this work of sequencing: they break down the phases or contexts within which they perform, and so open the way for the occasion to be reconstituted as its subsequent phase. These clowns have this capacity because of their peculiar compositions. The chapter discusses the logic of composition of 'ritual' clowns, in part to argue that these figures switch an event from one phase to the next, in sequence.

Chapter 10 also shifts the angle of vision from the event as a point of departure and unit of discussion to certain specialized roles that I call, generically, 'symbolic types'. In that chapter, with a view to work in the future, I argue only for the value of this kind of conceptualization, in public events and beyond. However, it is clear that a full analysis of a public event would include evaluations of the composition of roles that constitute the event, on the ground, so to speak. Thus the internal, compositional logics of roles, and their articulation and coordination in performance, likely will vary with the logic of design of the particular public event that contains them.

Whenever they occurred, occasions that approximated events of modelling were inventions of the first magnitude – for they showed the capacity to break with ongoing realities of social life, in order to act on these through controlled and predictive modes of organization.[10] Of course, one can attribute such power to humankind's invention of more or less comprehensive explanations of how and why the world was constituted as it was – to that which we may call cosmology, religion, and so forth. But it is in events of modelling that ontology and action are brought into causal syntheses to act in, and to act on, the lived-in world. Short of transforming the premises of social and cosmological orders, there is no more radical action that a people can take than to set up intentional simulations of their worlds: systemic models whose instructions are to act upon and to change the ordering of these worlds in comprehensive and consequential ways.

The sharpest, principled contrast to the logic of the model is that of the mirror, the reflecting surface that displays how things are, but that in itself, and through itself, acts directly on nothing. These are the events-that-present the lived-in world, to which I turn to next.

Events that present the lived-in world

There are public events whose comparative directness of themselves in display is striking. One may call them declaratives, sometimes imperatives, but rarely interrogatives. Writing of Renaissance Venice, Muir (1979: 35) comments that, 'Doge Gritti was active in reforming the public ceremonies so that they might reflect the full dignity of the state'. 'All such pageants', he continues, 'began or ended with a procession on foot around Piazza San Marco and a visit to the basilica ... the ceremonial and liturgical stage devoted to the presentation of the ideals of the Venetian republic' (1979: 37). '[P]ageantry had thus evolved into ... a public mirror', he maintains, 'meant to reflect images of political power' (1979: 50). On a great civic procession of eighteenth century Montpellier, another scholar (Darnton 1985: 120) notes: 'It was a statement unfurled in the streets, through which the city represented itself to itself', and, 'It existed in the way many statements and works of art exist – as sheer expression, a social order representing itself to itself' (1985: 124). In such occasions, as Raymond Firth (1967: 12) argues: 'the emphasis is more upon symbolic acknowledgement and demonstration of a social situation', than it is on that which he calls 'procedures' for altering that situation.[11]

Statements, mirror-images, reflections – these are hallmarks of events-that-present. The pivots of such occasions often are the very visibility of symbols throughout. Their relative plenitude of orderliness is the product of the over-signification (Babcock 1978a) of exactness, replication, and uniformity in detail. This quality of might on sight, of the presence of power, may overwhelm in its mass and magnitude. Nowhere was this more in evidence, for example, than in Nazi Party, Nuremberg Rallies, in which hundreds of thousands of marchers participated in the totalitarian unity of fascist design. The directives for a Rally, concerning the order in which the formations of the various party groups enter the parade, show the extent of synchronization in choreography that went into its planning (Burden 1967: 119):

The required formations had to be formed on the approach route to the main square, where Hitler reviewed the parade. By the time the ranks moved into his sight, they were to be twelve men deep, the distance between the marchers 114 cm (30 inches). (Diagrams of the distances to be kept between individuals, between rows of men, and between the hundreds of standard bearers are attached to the document). The left hand of the marcher was to be placed on the belt buckle; the thumb was to be inside, behind the buckle, and the other fingers slightly bent, with the finger-ends at the right edge of the buckle.

The document gives the exact timing of the cues for the hundreds of bands to begin to play – when they reached a certain distance from Hitler. The exact order in which the huge parade was to disband, after each formation had passed Hitler, was also carefully prearranged.

At first sight, other public occasions of presentation appear to be informed by a more complex logic of organization, especially when allegory (in European traditions) played a part. For example, Mona Ozouf (1975) has shown that the matrix of space in public 'festivals' that celebrated the French Revolution was infused with messages that separated the new order from the old, and that exalted the former and decried the latter. Thus, space used for such occasions was to be universal (not localized and overly known), arbitrary (unconnected to the past), empty (open to innovation), without visible limits (in the open air of liberty), without fragmentations or divisions (that connoted hierarchy), illuminated (so that all was clearly seen, for illusion and despotism lurked in shadows and depths), and so forth. Within such space the allegorical allusions of these occasions did carry more complex messages – of conflict and of its victorious resolution. Thus Hunt (1983: 99) describes a festival 'which aimed at nothing less than a review of the Revolution's development. It was a morality play with a set of striking, allegorical messages.' At stations, along the processional route, allegories were presented through tableaus (like the Antwerp giant) or dramas: 'At the statue of liberty, delegates ... put the torch to the hateful symbols of monarchy, and thus reenacted the ritual sacrifice of the monarch to the goddess of the Republic' (1983: 101).

These occasions were vivid and vibrant expositions, in which what was done was seen fully to happen. They undoubtedly were designed to arouse emotion and to evoke sentiment, and it is likely they indexed conditions and aspirations of wider social orders. But can one claim – given conceptions of causality of that age, as well as of this one – that in and through their operations these public events directly impacted on and changed the lived-in worlds of their peoples? No more so than a war game during a Nuremberg rally in 1935 (Burden 1967: 111) had any direct effect, through its own workings, on the rearmament of Nazi Germany.[12]

In the civil armatures of the modern, bureaucratic state, events-that-model are scarce. But events of presentation are the dominant forms of occasion that publicly enunciate and index lineaments of statehood, nationhood, and civic collectivity. For example, the rudiments of the great celebrations of statehood in the Soviet Union are known superficially to many Western television viewers. The formalization and rigor of these occasions, like that of the march-past of the Great October Socialist

Revolution in Moscow's Red Square, are strange to the citizenry of Western, democratic states (except, perhaps, in the contexts of national funerals), yet we readily apprehend, if superficially, their totalistic character.

Red Square is a location of Soviet centricity, a juncture of Russian historicity, of the enduring revolution, and of the pinnacle of political and bureaucratic power. This locale is bounded by markers that remind demonstratively of these features: the Kremlin wall, the mausoleum of the embalmed Lenin, the obelisk in memory of the heroes of the October Revolution, and the tomb of the Unknown Soldier of World War II, all are iconic displays of Soviet ancestry that resonate with public occasions held there. Just as these icons mark the Square, and index its relationships to social order, so too does the leadership of the state in receiving the march-past. The political and military elites stand on the tomb of Lenin, above the marchers, centrist and static. During this time, in this place, they too are icons and indices of ideal Soviet order. The overall arrangement is stratified clearly, with the elites at the mid-point of the parade – pillars of the state resting on the foundation of the ancestor of the revolution – and at the apex of the living hierarchy.

In counterpart to this vertical and stable centricity, the other major characters, the marchers, move through the Square and past the elites in lengthy formations that themselves are elongated, but horizontal, statements of hierarchy: officers to the fore, rank-and-file behind. In uniformity of dress and in rhythm, the marchers replicate and adumbrate one another, both men and machines, and space, place, and motion. The political centre is high and embedded: rooted in place along with other of the icons. The nation of disciplined marchers passes through the centre, for its place there is transitory. But the marchers do so with coordinated precision, to the beat of their leadership. Man and machine, on such occasions, are virtually interchangeable signs. If there is any sense of crescendo, or of the climactic, then often this is accomplished by increasing mass and magnitude. In point of fact, if the logic of organization of these events can be said to have an internal dynamic, then this is one of simple addition (or subtraction) of signs that magnify (or reduce) the accumulation and embellishment of the occasion.

Binns (1980: 171) comments that by the end of the Stalin era, Soviet ceremonies were characterized by regimentation, standardization, and displays of power. This certainly holds for the occasion referred to above. Throughout, there are no questions – no contradictory or discordant notes, no puzzles or paradoxes, no challenges. Instead, a profusion of exclamatory signposts: all components point to the overwhelming consistency of the overall organization; and each component, in itself, helps to replicate the whole pattern. All components reflect, and are reflected in, one another. There are no knots in the linear weave of this event. There are no loose ends with which to unravel this weave. The elites, who here embody the state, hold up a highly polished mirror of great clarity to the nation, and the nation sees an incisive vision of itself stand forth. This version of course is constructed, a fiction, but one that permits no intruders or competitors during its doing. Here there is no space for multiple visions nor for the contradictions of transformation (cf. Lane 1979: 264; McDowell 1974: 271, 276). To no small degree, like other occasions of this kind, 'its formal properties mimic its message' (Moore and Myerhoff 1977: 7). Public events like this say, 'Look, this is how things should be, this is the proper, ideal pattern of social life' (Skorupski 1976: 164).

These remarks echo those of Soviet scholars themselves. They emphasize the display functions of these occasions, which provide 'graphic examples' – ideological and normative – of proper conduct (Lane 1979: 262), while contributing to the social control and the regulation of Soviet society. In contrast to events of modelling, if events-that-present make something to happen in the lived-in world, then the search for this must concentrate at their interface, rather than within the event itself. In other words, these events have teleonomic rather than teleologic properties. Should they have any causal effects, these would be more a byproduct of the uncertain interaction between the enactment of an event and the wider social order in which it is embedded, rather than a direct consequence of the internal logic of the event itself.[13]

This distinction, then, is between public events that are predicated as causal schemes, in terms of their internal logic of controlled transformation, and those that are predicated as proclamations, whose uncertain effects (intended or not) are products of the highly variable interface between event and social order. Susan Davis' study of 'parades' by strikers in nineteenth century Philadelphia is instructive here. Davis (1985: 106) calls these parades 'ways of acting on the world', for they were shaped not only 'by their own logic or internal rules ... [but were] a technique of communication – full of possibilities but shaped at least as much by history, society and culture as by the particular men who wished to wield it' (1985: 114). In my terms, the form of the strike parade, and so its internal logic of operation, derived from conditions of the wider social order. Yet its ways of acting on the world, its relationship between premise and outcome, clearly were teleonomic. As her examples show, the effects of strike parades on the wider social order were highly contingent and unpredictable, and were determined primarily at their interface. 'Full of possibilities' indeed, but somewhat akin to a blunt instrument applied to the body politic, with uncertain consequences. The unpredictability of the interface between public event and wider social order is evident through numerous occasions that approximate presentations of protest (cf. Thompson 1971; Jasper 1980; Goldberg 1977; Lofland and Fink 1982). Or, one may say that sometimes the intentionality of such events deliberately is to make this interface problematic and uncertain, so that their presentational force will impact directly on the wider social order. But given their internal logic, the direction and effectiveness of this expressive impact always is volatile and unpredictable.

Lloyd Warner's analysis of an American public occasion helps to explicate aspects of a logic of presentation. In the 1930s, Yankee City (Newburyport, Massachusetts) celebrated the tercentenary of its founding with five days of parades, games, religious ceremonies, sermons, and speeches. The climax of the festivities was a 'grand historical procession' through which the townspeople 'stated symbolically what the collectivity believed and wanted itself to be . . . At that moment in their long history the people of Yankee City as a collectivity asked and answered these questions: Who are we? How do we feel about ourselves? Why are we what we are? Through the symbols publicly displayed at this time . . . the city told its story' (Warner 1961: 90). The historical procession was close to a year in gestation. Among the strengths of Warner's discussion is to show that choices on themes to be included (and excluded), on the specific guidelines for their enactment, and on other preparations, lay with the elites of the community. Their emendations and revisions of history to produce the historicity of Yankee City required profound decisions about that which Warner (1961: 99) called the 'living chapters of the Yankee City Book of History' that were made manifest in the event. The substance of these decisions – their polemics and politics – were discussed, argued over, and altered, over and again.

In these decisions there undoubtedly was the 're-presentation' of history, and at times even its radical alteration. But this was integral to the phases of planning and preparation, and remained outside the enactment of the event itself. The historical procession evinced no problematics, no contention or conflict, in the course of its action. Displayed as 'fact' and truism, the thematic contents of the procession demonstrated a determinate sense of certainty and consistency. There were no internal contradictions or oppositions to be resolved or synthesized in its performance. In other words, these thematics were self-validating in their very display, especially as no alternative or clashing visions of the historicity of the collectivity, nor of its class and ethnic composition, were permitted entry. In its presentation of itself the event was deeply informative and perhaps emotive, but neither transformative nor re-presentative in relation to its own constitution.

There is again a thorny problem of terminology here. Semioticians and symbolic anthropologists of all persuasions likely would insist that any and every public occasion is necessarily a 're-presentation' of some reality – at the very least, as metaphor or trope that, common-sensically, remain the basis for ordinary language usage of the terms, 'symbol' and 'symbolic of'. But they should recognize that this is so if one focuses only on the immediate relationship between social order and public event. This focus necessarily entails, in all cases, the utter privileging of social order over its own creations – public events – thereby denying any phenomenal auto- nomy to the design and practice of the latter. Then public events of any type are reduced to mere 'expressions' of social order. Here symbolic anthropology and Durkheimian functionalism become intimate bed- fellows. Although certain public events are indeed 'expressive' in the sense used above, this is something to be determined, not assumed. Therefore, my concern here is first and foremost with the logic of design of events themselves. And one of these logics I call 'presentation'.

The historical procession, as it was put together, included neither transformation nor re-presentation in the logic of its design. The event was teleonomic, not teleologic (unlike a Sinhalese exorcism, or *chisungu*). If the event did something of transformation or re-presentation, then again this was a product of the interactive interface of event and social order; and not because the event contained, within itself, any program of controlled transformation or of re-presentation. In itself, the historical procession was not a self-regulating, causal scheme that, in predictive ways, determined that something would be made to happen to the wider social order outside the event.

The procession was composed of forty-two tableaus or historical scenes that were carried on truck-beds past the throngs of spectators in a prearranged chronological sequence, one that told the linear tale of this social space from its inception to the present. Warner (1961: 91) com- mented that the overall sense of movement was one of a 'preordained "inevitability" supposedly bound to the imposed irreversibility of chrono- logy'. As duration was thought to move 'like an arrow' of evolutionary progression, so did the procession. In its enactment, the procession was all of a piece. Although composed of numerous segments, it was put together as a single context of action and comprehension, without any radical disconti- nuities – as a statement of how things got to be the way they were, and so a pronouncement of how things were. Together, all of the scenes adumbrated the same bundles of thematic messages. The procession of history processed through the spaces of the city, made historic in their passing. Time and space were mapped onto one another with a high degree of fit, each reflecting and reinforcing the claims of the other.

Nonetheless, this narrative-in-motion did tell a story, and so it was more than a summational pronouncement on the character of Yankee City history. To be understood, the story had to be seen to progress. One example of this – Warner's analysis of the presentation of gender in the procession – will suffice here. The first scene in the procession was of 'the forest primeval': a virginal girl standing amidst a land empty of people, but replete with rivers, lakes, and forests. Here the abundance of nature was presented as wild, pure, potentially fertile, and female. In later scenes, the landscape came to be settled, ordered, and dominated by powerful males. These developments resulted in the founding of Yankee City. The technological, moral, and sacred orders were all given a masculine cast. Females were prominent as males settled the fertile land, but as women in the custody of men, 'mothers' from whom the great nation came forth. The occasions that 'made history' stemmed from the actions of powerful and prestigious males, to whom females were submissive and subordinate. When women of superior social-standing appeared, this was due to the status of their guardians, their husbands or fathers. 'Time' also shifted through these scenes: from the far-distant timelessness of nature and the feminine, to time in progress – that is, to culture dominated by the masculine.[14]

Now, one cannot insist that the major organizational dynamic of this presentation was simply that of addition and subtraction of mass and magnitude, for each scene was designed to be different, to tell a different part of the story. Still, each scene was framed and packaged in the same format; and each was a segment of continuous time that moved through the same space as every other. Therefore, there were major elements of replication, and so of addition, in how the procession was organized. Moreover, one cannot claim that the telling of these narratives was subject to self-regulation within the procession. Regulation and control were external to the event itself (essentially, they were functions of planning and preparation). Should there have been difficulties in its enactment, the whole occasion would have ground to a halt, to be reorganized and re-ignited by some impetus from without. As well, there was little or nothing in the way of internal checks that could monitor the progress and impact of the event, as its enactment was taking place.

One also can see, given the modular organization of the procession, that scenes hypothetically could have been added or subtracted without necessarily altering the story lines of the event. With an act of imagination, one can conceive of the entire progression of the procession being run in reverse – from the present to the distant past – and of sense being made of this. A different narrative, but a viable tale nonetheless. Much the same could be said for the other public events discussed in this section. By contrast, one is hard put to conceive of an event of modelling – a Sinhalese exorcism or *chisungu* – being run backwards and still making sense to participants, since this would obviate the relevance of the systemic attainment of its goals. (See note 6, this chapter).

The event of modelling makes transformation happen that directly affects wider social orders. The event of presentation holds up a mirror to social order, selectively reflecting versions of the latter that largely are known, if in more dispersed and fragmented fashion. Within the event, these reflections are delineated with greater clarity and precision. In their play of images, uncertainty has little or no role. Events of presentation deal in the substantiation of affirmation (cf. Chaney 1983: 122). They are, in the main, societal icons in which connections among the whole and its parts are visibly displayed and open to inspection. And, like icons, their metaphors tend to lead elsewhere, but not otherwise. Cultural particulars aside, modelling and iconicity are polar opposites: both in their logics of internal organization and in their relationships to lived-in realities. The logic of transforming someone or something under controlled conditions is other than that of display, no matter how evocative or indexical are the associations of the latter.[15] The event of presentation may be of profound significance, but it is comparatively simple in the logic of its constitution and operation. Put otherwise, the only purpose of such events is to assert the determinacy of the significance they close and enclose; and so they are given over wholly to the making of expressive meaning through interpretation.

Chapter 9, on two national occasions of the Israeli state, continues themes of presentation in public events. The opening ceremonies of Remembrance Day and Independence Day each present a different version of the moral ordering of citizenry in relation to statehood. Although I have argued here that the organizational logic of presentation is comparatively simple, I stress again that this is not to say that such composition lacks significance in relation to wider social orders. Quite to the contrary, as chapter 9 endeavors to convey.

However, that chapter also raises a problem of methods – of units of analysis – to which I return briefly at the close of this chapter. Thus, each of the opening ceremonies analyzed in chapter 9 is autonomous unto itself, as is the Day it introduces, and can be discussed as such. Nonetheless, by intention these two Days are linked chronologically and thematically to one another. Discussed jointly, these two ceremonies can be understood to make meaning together, to tell a dramatic narrative of this nation-state. Then, although each ceremony presents its own version of moral and social order, each also re-presents the other, as parts of a more comprehensive narrative structure.

Events that re-present the lived-in world

For my purposes, a wide variety of events may be summarized under the rubric of re-presentation. If events-that-model make change happen within themselves, that directly effects social realities, and if events-that-present are axiomatic icons of versions of such realities, then events that re-present do work of comparison and contrast in relation to social realities. This kind of event re-presents lived-in worlds by offering propositions and counter-propositions, within itself, about the nature of these realities. Whether through the juxtaposition and conflict of contraries, through the neutralization of accepted distinctions, or through their inversion, the more hidden or controversial implications of the propositional character of the world are exposed. These implications may pose alternatives to the ordering of social realities. They may offer a grab bag of options. They may thrust towards relationships of thesis and antithesis. But, at the bare minimum, they work through contrast and comparison within the event itself. In turn, such work may raise possibilities, questions, perhaps doubts, about the legitimacy or the validity of social forms, as these are constituted in the lived-in world. Events that re-present are like multiple or magic mirrors that play with forms of order – that refract multiple visions of the possible, from among whose uncertainties there re-emerge probabilities. These are public events within which, in Fernandez's (1986: 162) apt phrasing, the 'argument of images' predominates – sometimes resolved, sometimes kaleidoscopic.

The following instances amplify and develop these remarks. The first – the Nuremberg *Schembart* Carnival – juxtaposed contraries that themselves were inversions of social reality. The resolution of inversion revalidated the world as it was. The second – the *Kalela* Dance – enabled a more coherent version of social reality to come into focus, one that was then at the cutting-edge of social reality, as it were, and that in the future would become integral to the emergent, African social order. In both examples the ideation and action of 'play' take more forceful parts than in those events discussed previously. The presence of 'play' in the design of public events is discussed in chapter 3.

The annual Carnival of late-medieval Nuremberg took place frequently between the years 1449 and 1539. Its legendary origins recalled civil order and virtue. In 1348, when mutinous artisans rebelled against the patrician council of the city, the butchers' craft remained loyal. As a reward, the butchers were granted an annual dance that, over the years, evolved into the *Schembart* Carnival. Writing in 1548, a commentator stated that the occasion was a 'mirror of a bygone revolt, to remind the common people never to participate in such rebellious madness' (Sumberg 1966: 30). Thus a real overturning of social order was displaced by a metaphor, cast within a medium of play, fun, gaiety, and laughter. In turn, this provided an aperture for commentaries on that order.

The '*läufer*' (runner/dancers), a main attraction of the event, were one of the few groups permitted to mask. The act itself of masking in public had qualities of inversion. In particular, qualities of subversion, of the potential overthrowing of the political order, or at least of its incumbents. For sedition and revolt were thought to flourish under the mask. (This is brought out vividly, in the France of that period, by Le Roy Ladurie [1980]. As Scribner [1978: 319] comments, though carnival itself rarely led to rebellion, the latter often assumed carnivalesque shapes). Initially, half the *läufer* were to come from patrician families and half from associations of artisans. The *läufer* paid the butchers for the privilege of participating. Not surprisingly, in practice the patricians came to predominate among the dancers (Sumberg 1966: 60–62). Given the financial resources of the patricians, after 1468 all the *läufer* were sons of these elite families (Kinser 1986: 4). Nonetheless, this change was not promulgated by edict. Therefore, in principle (although never again in practice), the composition of the *läufer* was intended to be marked by an uncharacteristic egalitarianism. That is, by the dissolution of boundaries of wealth, power, and occupation. Masked and concealed, the *läufer* often sang songs that commented on the everyday: obscene, gossipy, and scandalous (Sumberg 1966: 89). The themes of their critiques were urban and civic; and the *läufer* danced both in brothels and in the homes of the wealthy, along their route.

The *läufer* were accompanied by groups of 'grotesques' who amused, amazed, and terrified the onlookers with their costumes and antics. Some of their outfits clearly were satiric. Sumberg (1966: 108) describes a costume, made entirely of letters of indulgence, that attacked this practice of selling absolution. He comments: 'The character of [this guiser] ... is a very dramatic one, representing the great conflict that became the basis for the Reformation.' This, and other burlesques and parodies, allegorized the distorted boundaries between the morality of the ideal order and the immorality of the mundane – and attacked the venality of those whose task it was to serve the sacred.

The highlight of the *Schembart* Carnival was the *Hölle* (literally, hell), a pageant or float drawn on runners or wheels, and introduced in 1475 by patrician families (Kinser 1986: 5). The *Hölle* was a condensation and summation of the playful overturning of the world, messages that were intermittent in the songs of the *läufer* and in the costumes of the grotesques. In the *Hölle*, complex metaphors of the infernal, of themes that plagued humankind, were brought into the centre of the city and made the focus of attraction. The *Hölle* embodied in miniature the world of the city – a magnified and exaggerated agglomeration of images of the undergrowth of life, of life as it should not be lived.

The *Hölle* often took the form of a castle (a motif of feudal power), or that of a ship of fools. Frequently it held or conveyed a plenitude of symbols of evil: dragons, basilisks, demons, child-devouring ogres, and old women. A favorite allegorical theme was that of folly: fools were cleansed in wells, baked in ovens, polished on wheels, and ground down in mills (Sumberg 1966: 186).

In the climax to the event, the *läufer* laid siege to the *Hölle*, and a burlesque struggle ensued between two sets of inversions: the masked, concealed (and in principle, egalitarian) *läufer* and the evil beings of an overturned cosmos. The *läufer* climbed siege-ladders, set off fireworks hidden within the float, did battle with the demons and fools, and eventually burned the whole edifice (Sumberg 1966: 139) – in a sense, re-turning the world on its normal axis. It is especially significant that the *läufer* – the temporary, dangerous concealment of identity, whose visibility was valued in the everyday – stormed the *Hölle* that revealed the more tacit or 'masked' moral undergrowth of the everyday. In the world right-side up there was no place, as it were, for the evil that mushroomed in hidden spaces – whether that of sedition, egalitarianism, theological corruption, or the demonic. As the concealed *läufer* destroyed the revealed *Hölle*, and righted the world, they eliminated their own semiotic significance. Both *läufer* and *Hölle* had meaning within the event, yet in relation to the implausible, that in this instance was also the undesirable.

In this event, forms of social order were put to question, in ways that were in keeping with a medieval European world-view (see Bakhtin 1968; Gourevitch 1975: 75). Order not only was restored and revalidated through the destruction of the *Hölle*, but forms of order were hidden in that very imagery and allegory of a world out of kilter. Thus in one carnival the motif of the *Hölle* was that of a windmill, within which a fool-miller fed fools into his mill in order to grind them into better men. According to Sumberg (1966: 160–1), the grinding of the mill also was an erotic metaphor. But its grinding also signified 'the mill of holy wafers', that in turn signified 'the renewal of life through Christ'. One metaphor led to another, that enhanced the former. This re-emergence of propositional truths, often of the revalidation of the ordering of existence, is central to phenomena of inversion, that are discussed in brief, momentarily.

According to criteria used to discuss the other types of public events, the following may be said of the *Schembart* Carnival. It was predicated on internal contradictions that inverted aspects of the ordering of lived-in reality through concealment and revelation. Alive in the world of the event, neither of these contrasting versions of social reality were intended as viable in the lived-in world outside the Carnival. Within the event their respective re-presentations and relationships were explored, as they were pitted against one another. The triumph of the *läufer* righted the world, yet in this reality the *läufer* too had no space. Unmasking, they resumed their places in the setup of the city. From Sumberg's description, this mutual negation through conflict and clash effectively ended the formal program of the occasion. Carnival may have evoked a sense of 'poetic closure' (Swiderski 1986: 20), as it dismantled its own edifice.

In its logic of organization, this event was distant from the iconics of presentation discussed beforehand. Did it have something in common with the transformations of modelling? There was a small measure of self-regulation in the *Schembart* Carnival, but one that had less to do with transformation than it did with the device of inversion. An introductory word then, on inversion, to be continued in chapter 7, on Newfoundland mumming.

Inversion does query the validity of existing order – and through critique it may offer alternative visions. Yet it is a widely-accepted dogma in anthropology that inversion, far from up-ending order and opening avenues to its redoing, instead revalidates and reinforces it (see, for example, Gluckman 1954, and some of the papers in Babcock 1978b). Although anthropologists do offer some structural (as distinct from functional) explanations of the mechanics of inversion (see Leach 1961), they rarely examine the ways in which these devices work. If inversion tends strongly to reinforce normative realities, then built into this device there should be mechanisms that will direct it to the work of reaffirmation rather than to that of revolution.

My own view is that inversion keeps to the mold of the phenomenon, the foundation for inversion, that actually is inverted. Therefore, inversion maintains the relevance of its foundation, and is a discourse about its validity. For instance, the inversion of a stratified order is still a discourse about that very order of stratification that is inverted. The inversion of gender remains a discourse on gender, and so forth. Inversion maintains mode of discourse (Handelman 1979). The aspects of order that are inverted remain the mold for the inversion. If from the outset there is any consensus that the original order, from which its inversion must derive, is the more valuable or valid, then that of the inversion is falsified and invalidated. Therefore, the inverted order is not self-sustaining. It is an inauthentic version that reverts to its normative counterpart, from which it derived. The same manner of relationship will hold, for example, if one replaces an emphasis on consensus with one on differentials of power.

This formulation suggests that, built into the totality of potential change that an inversion indexes, there likely are limits to the degrees to which this inversion can proceed and still hold to its discourse on the phenomenon that is inverted. The phenomenon that is inverted posits limits to which the inversion can go. Beyond this, the inversion no longer is true to its foundation-for-form: it is no longer an inversion, but becomes another phenomenon in its own right. If there is the potential for transformation through inversion, then this is likely to happen only when inversion exceeds itself and breaks its connectivity to the phenomenon it inverts – thereby creating a new phenomenon. Inversion has topological qualities, something akin to an inflated pillow case turned inside-out: the material of the pillow case still encloses the same space, or volume of air, but the surfaces are inverted. Other conditions remaining equal, the device of inversion regulates itself to a degree. Yet this offers a very limited range of homeostasis – one whose very premise of reversion (i.e. self-regulation) seems to preclude the attainment of a new state of being or reorganization, which is the *raison d'être* of transformation. Instead, inversion tends to mitigate against the emergence of new phenomena or ways of reordering existence; and as noted, sustains the status quo.

In the *Schembart* Carnival there is little evidence of internal self-regulation, beyond that noted for inversion, or beyond the ending of the occasion through the mutual obliteration of contraries. There certainly are no hints here of a systemic scheme that monitored its own causal progression, and little evidence that the effects of the event were other than teleonomic. The occasion obviously commented upon and criticized the lived-in world through irony, satire, and allegory. But, so long as the event remained true to itself, one would have to insist that any change this Carnival occasioned in the lived-in world had to be a product of the interface, and not predicated on the internal logic of the event. This Carnival may have decentred the world to a degree, but it did not make change to happen within itself in predicated and predictive ways.

Compared to events of presentation, uncertainty existed within the Carnival, an event of re-presentation. This was especially salient when paired with another feature of some events of re-presentation. Certain occasions that are called 'festival' or 'carnival' are more similar in their logic of form to events of presentation. Others are closer to events of re-presentation. The latter have what I can only call more 'loose' or 'flexible' forms of organization than events either of modelling or of presentation. Some flexible public occasions (cf. Lavenda 1983) offer participants a multitude of ways to connect to the event, whether through simultaneously occurring sub-events, or through open and pragmatic criteria of participation (such that mere presence enables participation – or abstinence – in activities of one's choice).

At their interfaces the boundaries of these events are more permeable (in both directions, inward and outward) than the other types of occasions discussed. An event is a potentially explosive medium when it offers alternative visions to lived-in realities, within a form that largely lacks premises of systemic self-regulation or a well-structured program. This is especially so if conditions of uncertainty outside the public event resonate with those within.

One may argue that contention and conflict are intimated, implicated, or actualized in the performance of all public events. But in the approach advocated here, this point raises questions of probabilities of location: Before, during, or after? Within or without? The flexible format and permeable boundaries of events of re-presentation suggest their greater likelihood as arenas of confrontation than events of modelling. Thus, of the public events of early modern Europe (or of this tradition) that at times sparked conflagrations in their wider social-orders, it is not coincidental that many tended to be of a re-presentational form that was 'loosely-organized'. It was these 'carnivals' or 'festivals' whose internal dynamics could be more unstable, unpredictable, and emergent in their interaction with their social environments, and that therefore could pose serious threats to the latter (cf. Le Roy Ladurie 1980; Davis 1982: 124–151; Bezucha 1975; Lavenda 1978, 1980). And it was this variety of public occasion (including the *Schembart* Carnival and urban, Newfoundland mumming) that was put down and outlawed by the power structures of wider social orders (cf. Burke 1978: 178–204).

This is the qualification of the self-regulation in inversion that I referred to earlier: here inversion is stretched beyond the limiting self-containment of its foundations-for-form. Whether due to initial intentions or not, its connectivity to its foundations is snapped. It ceases to be an invalid (in the dual sense of this), or ultimately false, version of those foundations. Instead, the inversion emerges as an authentic, transformative alternative, one that attacks in all seriousness the foundations on which it was erected.[16]

This section closes with a brief mention of a further instance of an event that is close to re-presentation, one that will bridge the discussion to the idea of 'play' in public events, in the next chapter. This instance is the *Kalela* Dance (the 'dance of pride'), discussed by Mitchell (1959), as it was performed in the towns of the Central-African Copperbelt during the 1950s. The Dance manipulated aspects of social stratification, themselves salient features of African urban experience, and made the unity and rivalry of tribalism the focus of attention. *Kalela* erected an as-if world of experience in the urban situation, one of make-believe, but of serious implications that were given expression through playful modes of interaction.

The Copperbelt was characterized by a rigid class structure, divided along lines of European and African. Within the African sector there were high rates of labor migration and labor turnover. Men from many different tribal groups were thrown together arbitrarily as co-workers, in low-status occupations. Mitchell (1959: 22) notes that, in town, there was little opportunity for the elaboration of traditional relationships and sensibilities, since neighbors and workmates were continually changing. Africans were alienated from sources of power; while their bases for communication amongst themselves changed. In these conditions the 'tribe', as a web of relationships and collective identity, had little saliency. However 'tribalism' – mundane interaction on the basis of categorical, stereotypical tribal contrasts – was a prominent creation of African urban experience, and a harbinger of the ordering of social life in the future.

Kalela was a phenomenon constituted by the African urban world. *Kalela* consisted of dance and song, performed by teams that tended to the homogeneous in terms of tribalism. The organizer of the team, called the 'king', dressed in dark suit and tie. All of the dancers too were garbed carefully in the 'smartest of European wear' (1959: 9). The team was accompanied by a play-doctor, dressed in a white, surgical gown, whose task was to encourage the dancers in performance; and by a play nursing-sister, dressed in white, who made certain the dancers were tidy.

Kalela songs extolled the origins, the unity, and the landscape, of a performing team's tribal grouping, and in a rivalrous manner denigrated the distinctive features of language and custom of other tribal categories, whose members were assumed to be spectators at the dance. Other songs, topical and witty, lampooned and parodied the urban Copperbelt, again in a lingua franca. Thus the Dance excluded from performance the African experience of dominant and oppressive European power, while it stressed the substance of categorical tribalism as the centre of urban African life. The Dance commented upon the power and ambivalence of tribalism, and upon its growing prominence in African urban life; even though, apart from the dancing teams, tribalism did not yet form the basis for categorical corporativeness in the towns. Nevertheless, at the very growing edge of structure, *Kalela* previewed a future in which the determined constitution of African life was to become determining.

Through the Dance the conditions of one sort of class rigidity were altered. The dancers playfully inverted their identities, by donning the attributes of Europeans. Done in play, these features of European power and status were neutralized; and so the dancers effaced the hegemony of these class distinctions in their lives. Put otherwise, through inversion the dancers held constant this factor of class within the world of *Kalela*, and denied import to its presence. (References to Europeans were virtually absent from the lyrics of *Kalela* songs – though this was not remarkable, given the accentuation of tribalism.) At the same time, the whole performance positively valorized the categorical distinctiveness of tribalism in the towns. And it was within this context of tribalism that the insignia of dress and occupation reemerged as indices of the aspirations of status and class among Africans, that they were unable to attain as yet in the wider social order, but that would be theirs in a future constituted through the formations of tribalism. Therefore *Kalela* also previewed the profound shift to the making of meaning through categorical contrasts, and the joining of categories of tribalism and class, that were alienated more and more from traditional webs of social relationships.

Joking behavior (in the sense that Radcliffe-Brown [1952] discusses this) between members of different tribal groupings was also a new but prevalent feature of urban life, one that showed the emergent significance of categorical contrasts. Mitchell (1959: 41) argues that the Dance had qualities of a joking relationship between team-members and their audience: the dancers taunted and spoofed the categorical tribal identities of the onlookers, and the latter responded in kind, without animosity. The performance was enjoyed by all.

The negation of rigid, class hierarchy and the exuberant exhortation of tribalism and social mobility, re-presented aspects of the wider urban world within the Dance. One can argue that the Dance reified the phenomenal and existential import of tribalism and class mobility in ways that still were embryonic in the mundane life of the towns. Thus *Kalela* isolated and re-presented playfully certain distinctions, their contrasts and contradictions, with their implications for the emerging order of African pluralism, mobility, and conflict. But the participants were not held immediately accountable for these messages of conflict, since they were communicated in play.

Kalela was a micro-world of make-believe, given life through playful modes of joking, lampooning and spoofery. A magic mirror of the relevance of tribalism, it premised an alternative order that was yet neither fully coherent nor viable. *Kalela*'s world was a governed one. Its fictional premise of a world filled only by tribalism and its correlates was played out in accordance with fairly rigorous guidelines. It was akin to what we would call a 'game' – an occasion that verged on the teleological in its workings. Through it, Africans were able to experiment with the evocation of categorical distinctions in a group context, that of the dancing team, and this may well have contributed to the production of this reality in the wider social order. Although *Kalela*, like the *Schembart* Carnival, obviated itself playfully in the immediacy of its doing, among those who practiced and watched the Dance there likely were persons who became members of elites and institutions that were to implement the serious substance of the emerging visions of tribalism, mobility, and class formation.

Earlier on, in different terms, I implied that the validity of inversion also was predicated on make-believe. Not by happenstance, inversion in public events frequently has a playful mien, as was the case in the *Schembart* Carnival. In both instances, plays–upon–form came to decentre and to question aspects of their respective worlds. This capacity of the ideation of play to critique seemingly stable and accepted order also appears within *chisungu* – in the cruel, teasing humor of the mature women; and in their laughter and enjoyment at the discomfort and tears of the girls. I suggested that this teasing helped to break down the immature state of the girls – in other words, to decentre and to destabilize their condition. In each of these instances, the ideation of play (whose absence from events-that-present is by now unsurprising) was molded, controlled, and put to use for particular purposes of destabilization, in keeping with the respective forms of these events. This relationship between the ideation of play, its capacities to dissolve centres of social gravity, and its appearance in public events, requires further discussion in the following chapter.

Three chapters discuss themes of re-presentation. Chapter 4 takes up the 'donkey game', a proto-event in my terms. Invented in a Jerusalem workshop, this game constituted an alternative reality, predicated on the premise of make-believe. Through this temporary reality, certain workers were able to communicate messages of dissatisfaction and desire that attached to their position in the workshop. Nonetheless, put together through play, this alternative vision had no material effect on their conditions within the workplace.

Chapter 7 discusses mumming in village Newfoundland, a phenomenon that has intrigued a number of anthropologists. During the Christmas period, villagers don disguises and visit families of the community. Re-presented as 'strangers', these visitors evoke the strangeness and alienation hidden within the Newfoundlander sense of collectivity and self. The behavior of the mummers is wild and grotesque, an inversion of the mundane. They re-present the amorphous disorder that is thought to underlie sociality. Brought to the surface, as it were, this 'evil' puts the question of whether the collectivity is a viable entity. But the mummers are tamed through game. They then unmask, re-emerge as moral beings, and engage once more in the civility of sociality. The viability of social relationships and community is demonstrated, despite what are perceived as their own structural and emotional flaws. Again, the outcome of inversion is the reaffirmation of norm and custom.

Chapter 8 addresses a variety of holiday celebrations in Israeli kindergartens. Through inbuilt contradictions that emerge in their sequencing, these occasions engage little children in the directions of maturation expected of them. In particular, these re-presentations show to children the shift in ultimate allegiance, from family to nation-state, that with time they are intended to make.

Qualifications

As I indicated near the outset of this chapter, anyone who does typologies should know full well their lacunae and weaknesses, as well as the dangers of their reification. In this chapter I have stressed aspects of the organization of public events and, more generally, of the impetus of form. What the useful catchments are, of the three kinds of events delineated, is difficult to estimate. This would require trying their arguments on a much wider and more diverse range of public occasions, in order to see whether the interplay between typologizing and case analysis tells us anything that was not self-evident before. This is beyond the scope of this volume. Here the endeavor is limited to attending to ways of thinking about public events that try not to respect conventional assumptions and distinctions that dominate, and that retard, the study of such occasions. My claim on the worlds of events is that the scheme offered here (and parallel efforts by others) merits further critical thought, if there is to be any progress in apprehending and comprehending these prominent phenomena of social life.

Lacunae in the types are highlighted should we simply reverse perspective and relate to these as meta-designs – that is, to treat the types as instructions with the capacities to design public events. The occasions so generated would emphasize logics of form and a sort of aesthetics of organization. But they would lack elements that we and others believe are integral to public occasions: from the obvious matter of beginnings and endings, to the extremely subtle ones of media of enactment and their experiencing, whether as performer or spectator.

Thus there are five major issues that I have not addressed. One is that of parameters: what series of coordinated actions should constitute the units of analysis? Put otherwise, where does a public event begin and end? For instance, James (1983) discusses *Corpus Christi* in a late-medieval English town in terms of 'procession' and 'dramatic play'. The procession mirrored and indexed the unity and differentiation of the social-body and the body of Christ, and their functional interdependence, through the lineal unfolding of precedence, status, and hierarchy. This version of social and cosmic order was understood as an ideal and eternal depiction. The dramatic plays, performed by guilds, mirrored each year and indexed the changing fortunes, the rise and fall in status, of occupational groups. This version of order was situational and shifting. In itself, each of these occasions was close to an event of presentation. However, if the unit of analysis is the marking of *Corpus Christi*, then these two occasions contrasted and re-presented their respective images against one another. Together, these two became a magic mirror that refracted the projections of each through the other.

A second issue concerns the changes that a given event may undergo with time, and so whether it remains the same sort of occasion. For example, Custer's Last Stand was marked in 1926, on its 50th anniversary, and in 1976 on its 100th (Linenthal 1983). The 50th anniversary commemorated the historicity of the Last Stand, as an event of presentation. The 100th, again largely as an event of presentation, emphasized reconciliation between Euroamericans and American Indians. Over time, the intended meanings of the event had undergone considerable reinterpretation. Moreover, the 100th anniversary was also marked by protests of members of the American Indian Movement, who hung the United States flag upside-down and who held their own 'victory' celebration that conflicted with the official theme of reconciliation.[17] Thus the 100th anniversary re-presented that of the 50th, while the former also contained within itself elements of re-presentation.[18]

Third, event-forms may be relatively unstable – especially for certain events of re-presentation, as I suggested earlier – and so may have a greater potential for shifts in their logic of organization during any given occasion of their performance. Thus Abner Cohen (1982: 124) describes a polyethnic London 'carnival' as a 'contested cultural performance', one that holds within itself a tense balance of 'conflict' and 'alliance'. Clearly an occasion of re-presentation, this event may shift radically towards the extreme of alliance; and so become an affirmation of hegemonic order (cf. Lukes 1975: 301). In Cohen's terms it has become a 'political rally'; in mine it has neared an event of presentation. Or, the relative fluidity and lack of systemic control in this occasion may shift it towards the extreme of conflict with, and opposition to, established social order. Cohen calls this a 'political demonstration'; while I would stress the generation of uncertainty and the possible effects that might emerge from the interaction of event and social order.

Other public events are relatively stable through time, even though their composition is predicated on multiple re-presentations, within the same event. Here genres of performance are 'nested' within one another, although their logic of interrelatedness is more systematic than systemic. MacAloon (1984b: 268) calls this nesting 'ramified', given the algebraic interplay among genres during their enactment.[19]

Related to the idea of 'contested cultural performance' is that of the event as an arena within which conflicting definitions, or overt and tacit agendas, coexist uneasily or clash during enactment (cf. Greenwood 1977). Here the boundaries between social order and event are highly permeable, and the event becomes a reflection not of frozen cultural ideals, but of the turbulence that wracks social order during that time and place. In effect, the event then loses any claim to special ontological status. Instead, it is, or becomes, a direct extension of ongoing or emergent struggles that coopt any and all venues for their conflicts (cf. Lincoln 1985; Goldstein 1984; Le Roy Ladurie 1980).

Fourth, the typology raises the issue of hypothetical relationships among the types. The types were discussed as if they, and so too the real events that they index, are truly distinct from one another. But as indicated by the examples discussed, the probability of a given, real event fitting neatly within one type is necessarily small. Then what is the relationship between the types? Should they be understood as continuous with one another, so that a given public event, say (X), could be located hypothetically as a 'mixture' of types somewhere on this continuum, as in the following example?

$$X^1 \qquad\qquad\qquad X$$
MODELLING — RE-PRESENTATION — PRESENTATION

In this kind of classification the greatest disadvantage of the continuum is its utter linearity. The event (X) can be discussed only as the interplay of two types, whereas qualities of all three may feature in its design. Moreover, if the relationship between types is understood as developmental, as a temporal progression, in this example an event (X^1) can turn into event (X) only by becoming more like one of re-presentation in order then to become one less like re-presentation. This imparts a unity to the predication of human phenomena, and to their change, that skews reality even more than the types themselves.

A more accurate image of my position is that of figure 4. Here the boundaries formed by the ideal interaction between the three types create a hypothetical space that encloses the qualities of all the types, and that enables their interaction so that they can cohere in different combinations and formations. Then a given public event can be said to be more like one type than the others, or to contain qualities of all the types. Although beyond the purview of the book, such 'quality space' also could be used to grasp the logic of different moments or phases within the same event, and the movement between moments. Such space also might be used to discuss shifts among public events in a given cycle of occasions, one whose own logic of operation influences those of the events that compose it. Or, such space could be used to map the historical development of a particular event.

Note that the ideal relationship, the border, that connects events of presentation and re-presentation in figure 4 is left partially open, as a dotted

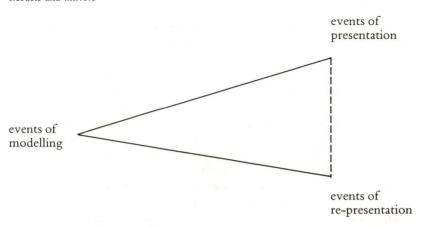

events of
presentation

events of
modelling

events of
re-presentation

Figure 4 Relationships among types of public events

line. This is so for the following reasons. The event of modelling is the most clearcut; and therefore its contrasts and relationships with the other two types are distinctive and strong – those of the solid line. So too, it is shown as more distant from the other two types. However the relationship between events of presentation and re-presentation is less stable and more ambiguous. Furthermore, the resolutions of this relationship may lie even beyond this enclosed space – therefore the dotted line.

Fifth, in my preoccupation with the logics of form in this chapter, I have not addressed various concerns that are integral to many public occasions. The orchestration of experience and affect is among these. How do public events structure, coordinate, and play with the mood-states, the emotions and sentiments, of participants and onlookers?[20] Do they move people? And, why? Regardless of the kind of event concerned, the experience of participants will be affected, and this may well be of wider import. Thus, what to make of Iranian *Ta'ziyeh* drama that Beeman (1982: 95) tells us is intended and designed to evoke weeping among spectators? These issues are related to questions of meaning: what is it that a public occasion signifies to and for those involved? Should one at all speak of 'signification' in relation to feeling? Are 'feeling' and 'meaning' separable ontologically, and if so, in which terms? Thus, what to make of Mosse's (1975: 201) statement that German audiences 'lived' Hitler's speeches? And, most critically in relation to the claims I have made for modelling, should such occasions be understood as ones that mold affect, such that transformations (for which duration?) are accomplished in the feelings of masses of people (see note 15, this chapter)? In other words, are such events self-regulated, predictive schemes for the teleological transformation of affect (cf. Schieffelin 1976)?

All these issues relate directly to the discussion of performance at the outset of this chapter, and to my insistence there that experience is tied closely to the logics of design of events.

In turn, such questions insist that close analytical attention be given to the communicative capacities of various media through which a public event is enacted – media like rhetoric, narrative, music, song, dance (cf. Langer 1953; Straus 1966; Bloch 1974).[21] These subjects are of integral importance to public events, yet I do think that they are best addressed through the particulars of cultural traditions, and are more impenetrable to the sorts of comparisons that I have tried to outline here.

Mention of 'meaning', likely the greatest bugbear of scholars who deal in symbols, leads me to close this chapter less on a note of lacunae left vacant than of a correlation unconnected. We are wont to believe that the more complicated is the organization and elaboration of a public event, the richer, deeper, and more profound are the cultural 'meanings' that the event generates, conveys to, and evokes among participants. The typology I have posed is based on one order of complexity – that of organizational logics of form. In these terms (and clearly there are many others), my guess is that there is no necessary correlation between the organizational complexity of a public event (regardless of whether we call it 'ritual', or something else) and the complexity or resonance of 'meaning' it produces.

Public events vary from the explicitly ontological to the insistently pragmatic, from the unreflective to the exegetical, from the constitutive to the expressive. The positioning of an event in these terms may well implicate profundity, but profundity of meaning does not implicate complexity of organization. The latter tells us more of how something works, but not of the quality or resonance of thought that goes into its phenomenal formation. Even the profound goal of 'transformation' and the more complex logic of modelling do not require any extraordinary attention to the generation and exegesis of 'meaning' (although, of course, they may be embued with this). Modelling requires rules, or modes, of procedure and inference that are put together in certain ways. How (and why) particular cultures ground, contextualize, and substantiate the above is quite another matter. Similarly, events of presentation may be signal repositories of 'meaning' (as is the case, I believe, of the state ceremonies discussed in chapter 9), even though in my terms such occasions 'do nothing' in relation to their own logic of operation.[22]

3 Precariousness in play

Westerners commonly identify the ideation of play with the make-believe, with artifice and frivolity, and with the impossibilities of fantasy – and, enamoured of cognitive dualism, compare this unserious ideation with its opposite of the 'serious', whose apex is the sacrality of 'truth'. Sacred truth and frivolous falsehood are among the extreme binary opposites of our modern conceptual universe. But, with this radical disjuncture, we almost have banished from serious discourse the relationships between centres of social-gravity and their dynamic absence.

I have noted in passing the affinity of the idea of 'play' with that of 'uncertainty', identified with the unpredictable play of forces in flux. In many traditional cultures, such uncertainty, and its concomitant indeterminacies, resonate deeply with conditions that were antecedent to the creation of the cosmos, or that were integral to this. In the beginning . . . there was turbulence/chaos, or the absence/negation of anything and everything. Stories of cosmogenesis tell of the creation of phenomenal order out of, or through, these conditions. Cosmogenesis necessarily is inherently dynamic and processual. By whatever agencies, the uncertainties of indeterminate occurrences are turned into the certainties of determinate and predictable courses of action.

This turbulence or absence is not symbolic of anything else. It is non-derivative. It is inherently itself, more so than any order erected by humankind. It existed prior to the creation of order, and is the unalterable baseline that demarcates human doings from their nullities. Perhaps the extreme of antithesis to human order, it is also as near as cultural thought comes to conceptualizing a total, or near total, absence of order. There are cosmologies that embed the existence and interplay of such forces in the very premises of their metaphysics. These cosmologies (among the major belief-systems, the prime case may be that of Hinduism) are pervaded by qualities of instability, of ongoing fragmentation and re-constitution, in their logics of operation.[1] Within such cosmologies, for example, the boundaries that divide the paranatural and human realms are more matters of continuous and contingent gradation, than they are of absolute demarcation. The characters that populate these cosmologies (i.e. deities, spirits, demons, tricksters, and so forth) tend to be positional and transmutive types, rather than enduring centres of gravity. The significant status accorded to premises of uncertainty have profound effects on how these cosmologies operate. Other cosmologies give little recognition to these primal antitheses, or accord them at best minor metaphysical roles. These latter cosmologies are less self-transformative, and more centristic: their cosmic centres, or cosmic apices, are characterized by enduring stability (Handelman 1987a).

Cosmologies that embed forces of flux at a high level of abstraction in their ontologies seem to keep an ongoing accounting of, and relationship to, the conditions that are thought to precede, or that participate in, cosmogenesis. Within these cosmologies, stability tends not to be the natural order of things, not necessarily self-perpetuating, and not part of a grand evolutionary design that, through the discovery of knowledge, inexorably moves humankind further and more towards a total control over social orders and their environments. Whether or not cosmologies that largely deny a significant role to forces of flux also are self-deluding in this, is beyond my purview. But I might note in passing that certain of the modern exact sciences seem to understand better than the social sciences that any making of order also changes, in the process, that selfsame order. This perspective echoes the dialectical view that any social arrangement carried to its logical conclusion liquidates itself.[2] In other words, stability and uncertainty are not remote from one another: each is the immanent shadow-side of the other, whether peoples recognize this or not.

Few viewpoints in anthropology seriously entertain the likelihood that the existence of social order is eminently more problematic than is its absence. One seeming exception is that of Sally Moore (1975: 232), who put forward the view that 'the underlying quality of social life should be considered to be one of theoretically absolute indeterminacy ... in this model social life is presumed to be indeterminate except insofar as culture and organized or patterned social relationships make it determinate ... even within the social and cultural order there is a pervasive quality of partial indeterminacy'.

For Moore, the absence of order is theoretically as much of a possibility as is its presence. The possible is prevented from becoming probable by the ongoing and unceasing work of reproduction that social orders perform on themselves. Thus, reproduction implicates the presence of change in its doing, even if such change is limited, repetitive, or cyclical.

Another exception, one especially relevant to the study of public events, is that of the late Victor Turner's interpretations of liminality. These probe where, in traditional social orders, we may look for the structured praxis of reproduction. In my understanding, the idea of liminality is a logical expansion of that of pervasive indeterminacy in social order, and requires some discussion here (see also Handelman 1985).

The term, 'liminality' (from the Latin, *limen*; literally, threshold), we owe to Van Gennep (1960: 11, 21). He delineated a type of occasion, one that he called *rites de passage*, that specialized in the doing of change among tribal peoples. The mid-phase of his tripartite analytical scheme, the liminal, was characterized by the programmed deconstruction of routine social-structural perceptions and arrangements – in a sense by their negation. There, the persons to be changed came into contact with transcendental sources of power (1960: 114) that transformed their being, before they were returned, transmuted, to quotidian social order.

According to Kimball (1960: viii–ix), Van Gennep understood social order in terms of its entropic degeneration and periodic regeneration through occasions that often had the format of symbolic death and rebirth. The condition of transition, the liminal, was dangerous precisely because it dealt with the taking-apart of customary order. It made indeterminacy explicit – and necessarily questioned the arbitrariness of customary patternings in social life; thereby raising the potential for variability in their reconstitution. In my view, Van Gennep located a focus in the ordering of traditional life that specialized in the controlled dissolution of cultural and social integration; that recognized the necessity and danger of such a project; and that related the malleability of the liminal condition to extraordinary forces with the capacities to destroy and to create order.

Turner made explicit certain implications in Van Gennep's work. Turner recognized the affinity of liminality to the very absence of structure – in other words, to conditions of uncertainty and indeterminacy. 'We are not dealing with structural contradictions when we discuss liminality', he wrote, 'but with the essentially unstructured (which is at once destructured and prestructured) and often the people themselves see this in terms of bringing neophytes into close connection with ... the unbounded, the infinite, the limitless' (Turner 1964: 8). This absence of structure, of the decentering of order, was a locus of the relatively free recombination of cultural elements: 'Liminality may perhaps be regarded as the Nay to all positive structural assertions, but as in some sense the source of them all, and more than that, as a realm of pure possibility' (Turner 1967: 7). Liminality, he maintained (Turner 1977: 69–71), provided 'acultural means of generating variability' among tribal peoples. Hypothetically, it was to be considered a major source of change (Turner 1977: 76).

A populist concept in anthropology and cognate disciplines, liminality was applied indiscriminately to a wide variety of contexts. Too often it became simply a metaphor for the unclarity of situations that struck us as 'betwixt and between' in some manner.[3] More recently, Turner (1978: 281) drew back from this unbridled diffusion of the liminal condition: 'It is true that I have . . . stressed the potentially subversive character of liminality in tribal initiations . . . but this potentiality never did have any hope of realization outside a ritual sphere hedged in by strong taboos'. Therefore, he added, liminality should be restricted primarily to ritual with a *rites de passage* structure. Beyond this, the application of this concept would be mere metaphor (Turner 1978: 286; see also Turner and Turner 1978: 249).

This recantation was overly restrictive. Turner's recognition of liminality is a complementary, focused counterpart of Moore's depiction of indeterminacy. Concentrated, in accordance with cultural design, it is buffered and labelled Handle With Care, or defused in other ways. Uncontrolled, it is corrosive. Not only the contexts of its occurrence, that may or may not buffer it, must be addressed, but also (at the risk of sounding idealist) its essential condition. This is still a no-place in no-time that perhaps resists classification (Turner and Turner 1978: 249).

In chapter 10 on clowns in ritual, I argue that liminality, the fluff of indeterminacy in its focused condition, is best understood as a medium that is intensively processual: fluid, shifting, vital, and replete with energy; yet without the capacity to stabilize itself. It may be likened to the generation of randomness in social life (Mahoney and Sutton-Smith 1976), with all of the potentiation that accrues to this. But the processuality of indeterminacy is essential to the projects of transformation of events-that-model. Within these occasions, processuality is hedged-in, is strictly controlled, and is put to cultural usage in accordance with the systemic design of the occasion. Nonetheless, and this Turner avoided enunciating, should the liminal condition shatter its cultural buffers and instead concentrate in quotidian contexts, then its impact is searing and destructive. If the condition called liminality is, as Turner referred to it, the *fons et origo* of structure, then structures of destruction also may be formed from this under conditions – of alienation and anomie – that are well-known (cf. Goldberg 1977). In events of re-presentation, the liminal condition is less systemically controlled. When such events are enacted in times of social inconsistency, or of the more extreme anomie, that resonate with the volatility of liminality, the latter may shatter its buffers and spurt forth, like an uncontrolled spread of antitheses without syntheses. This randomizes and disrupts the connectivity among elements of culture, unravelling the weave of customary integration. However, as noted before, in events-that-present there is a distinct absence of indeterminacy and uncertainty, and hence of 'liminality'.

The condition of controlled uncertainty that is found in certain public events, and that Turner identified with liminality, resonates deeply with the qualities of indeterminacy that Moore considers are pervasive throughout social order, and that implicate all established structures in the sowing of their own negation. In turn, both of these conditions have affinities to the unpredictable and uncertain qualities that characterize the chaos or nullity that precedes cosmogenesis – qualities that may be embedded at high levels of generality, as cultural premises in particular cosmologies.

What has all this to do with play, as we know it? That which we commonly gloss as 'play' is infused with qualities of flux and the processual that are devalued thoroughly in a positivist age, and that are believed to be controlled utterly – eventually. Our modern sense of play, as the rando-mized play of forces, is of the minute epiphenomenal: of rationalist and salvationist discourses on the unreal, the invalid, artifice, pretense, false-hood, and 'just play', that are contrasted with the ponderous gravities of serious and substantial realities (Manning 1983: 23–25). These qualities of play, that are also negations of determinate realities, circumscribe part of the phenomenon. Whether they are epiphenomenal is another matter, and not a laughing one.

Our point of view undoubtedly is telling – witness the embrace of bureaucratic and technological power it has spawned in the modern age. But it is no more universal than the mind/body duality of our hellenist heritage, with the blind spots built into that. That which we call 'play' is play and little more, given the constricted role that we surrender grudgingly to uncertainty in the construction and conduct of social realities.[4] This 'play', I should point out, is not the psychologistic notion, tailored to our conception of the individual, of the realization of self-fulfillment through fun, game, and group therapy. The deeper play of forces to which I refer is closer to what would be understood by cosmic physicist and cosmic metaphysician alike. Nor is the view put forward here a romanticized one. Uncertainties of play and terror are not necessarily genteel kissing cousins, but intimate, perhaps incestuous bedmates. The play of forces is never more exhilarating nor frightening than when boundaries are breached and identities blurred, as every aficionado of horror films and Sinhalese exorcisms knows. As Eugen Fink (1968: 25) puts this, 'Play can contain within itself not only the clear apollonian moment of free self-determi-nation, but also the dark dionysian moment of panic self-abandon'. Terror and play are forceful modes of introducing uncertainty, and their affinities are undeniable.

Unlike ourselves, and our purposive beliefs that order can be made, and made to progress inexorably by the suppression of forces of deep flux and uncertainty, other peoples acknowledge and actively utilize these dangerous forces to precariously undo and redo social order. This, in my view, is what lies behind the concept of liminality. That is, what lurks behind ideas of play is cognate with what stares forth from ideas of liminality and cosmogenesis. Play, as Fink (1968: 23) comments, 'is always a confrontation with Being'. If we are to comprehend the seriousness of the deep ideation of play – literally as the inter-play of elements of order that are in-play – then this ideation, and the actions through which it gains expression in the phenomenal world, should be understood as affinities of some more comprehensive notion of uncertainty.

Uncertainty is the recognition that cosmos (or whatever entity is under discussion) exists as much through the deep flux of unpredictability, as it does through determination. Therefore, that this is another mode of thinking and talking about change, rather than rest, in the world. Uncertainty may be valorized as beneficial (true, moral, sacred, etc.), as harmful (evil, immoral, demonic, etc.), or as neutral (amoral, uncaring) – but all of these continue to index the ultimately uncontrollable nature of cosmos, and yet the needs of humankind to acquire some measure of regnant control and predictability that make humanly designed orders probable.

The ideations of play have their own roles in this, ones that seem related to the very processes of change, to changeability itself. In these, the fluff of the make-believe (and cognate ideas) is crucial. However, the unseriousness of play must not be confuted with irrelevance. Its relevance to human existence is this very quality of absence of gravity, of the flux and fluff of ongoing change, of the everpresent sense of the possible. To deny the relevance of the serious unseriousness of play is, to a degree, to exile forces of uncertainty from an accounting of how phenomenal worlds hold together; and, of equal importance, from an accounting of how these worlds operate to change and to reproduce themselves in ways that are thought controllable.

In public events, change often is presaged by the presence of the playful; and, through this intimation, foci of uncertainty are made explicit. Most frequently, the playful springs forth to shatter routinely accepted arrangements (especially in events-that-model), or to figure possible alternatives to these (particularly in events of re-presentation). The playful may control itself to a degree (as in inversion), but not fully; and its volatility depends on the kind of event in which it is given a role. I have suggested that the uncertainty of the playful is most controlled in events of modelling, and less so in events of re-presentation. Uncertainty seems to have little or no role in events of presentation, at least in those that mirror formations of the modern state. An abbreviated survey of certain of the attributes of playful ideation will indicate how it may have the roles in public events that I attribute to it.

Gregory Bateson (1956, 1972) pointed out just how problematic was the border between serious reality and that of play. He attended especially to the constitution of this boundary, to the passage between realities of perception. He concluded that, in terms of a system of logic like that of Whitehead and Russell's Theory of Logical Types, this crossing was inherently paradoxical.⁵ Bateson argued that the passage to play, and the creation of a reality predicated on play, was keyed cognitively to a meta-message that informed persons on how to relate to, and so how to do, this transition. He called this particular meta-message, 'This is play', and implied that it created the paradox of which the boundary itself (or frame, in his usage) between serious reality and play was constituted. Among the examples he used to illustrate this paradox was that of the 'bite' and the 'playful nip'. The playful nip looks like a bite, but it signifies something quite different. It is a bite, and it is not a bite. It is a bite, and it is not a bite, at one and the same time. It is an imaginary bite – a bite that does not exist, yet does, for it is consequential as a bite that wasn't. Keeping this example in mind, the message, 'This is play', was spelled out as follows, by Bateson (1972: 180): 'These actions [the nip], in which we now engage, do not denote what would be denoted by those actions [the bite] which these actions [the nip] denote'.

My concern here is not with the logical status of this paradox, but with a blatant aspect of its form. The meta-message, 'This is play', is a clear declaration of conditions of uncertainty, as these were discussed above. A phenomenon is one thing (a bite) and another (a nip) simultaneously. Therefore, at one and the same time it is both, and so it may be neither. Uncertainty permeates this meta-message of play. And this, of course, is the lesson of true paradox: so long as one holds to its internal logic of operation, one cannot solve or escape its ongoing self-contradictions and self-negations that continually resurrect their antitheses. True to itself, the paradox is in perpetual motion, in a sort of fluidity and flux that know no resolution or stability except that of movement. In Bateson's formulation, the meta-message, 'This is play', creates the doing and the comprehension of that which follows – in other words, play. And, as I have argued, this medium is characterized throughout by attributes that correspond to the meta-message. This is the 'enigmatic realm that is not nothing, and yet is nothing real' (Fink 1968: 23).

The medium of play is conditional: within it, nothing is immutable; its normality is transmutability; processuality is its reality. Play stabilizes neither this nor that, neither truth nor untruth. For Hegel it was like the free, unconstrained descent of the waterfall, the 'water-dust', for which no static form is adequate (cited in Clayre 1974: 24). It is an amoral medium, as Huizinga (1970: 85) pointed out: 'Play lies outside the antithesis of wisdom and folly . . . truth and falsehood, good and evil . . . it has no moral function. The valuations of vice and virtue do not apply here'. Its qualities of plasticity, lability, and levity, together with its rejection of propositional validity, give to the medium of play the potential to meddle with, to disturb, and perhaps to dissolve, centres of social gravity. Subversive, it can rock the foundations of a given phenomenal reality by making their presumptions uncertain and unpredictable. Given the logic of its meta-message, perhaps the greatest import of the play medium within public events is its capacity to communicate, with simultaneity, multiple messages that may be (but are not necessarily) mutually contradictory. In its uncertainty, the medium of play routinely mixes metaphors, and, as a corollary of its subversiveness, it can comment with immediacy on anything and everything. As we know well, there may be a world of meaning in a wink or a joke. The profundity of the play medium lies with its uncertain changeability and in its capacities for commentary. This was brought forth in the analyses of the *Schembart* Carnival and the *Kalela* Dance, and will be evident as well in a number of the chapters to follow.

Nonetheless, it would be in error to take the meta-message, 'This is play', as inherently or necessarily paradoxical. It has the status of paradox in our cultural traditions, in our cosmologies that tend to dichotomize phenomena, and to assign absolute values to these dualities, so that they are neither interchangeable nor interpenetrable. Here cosmic (and social) stability are thought to dominate utterly their counterparts of instability and fragmentation. Still, it is doubtful whether this meta-message has the status of paradox in cosmologies that place a high value on uncertainty, and so on its corollary of more ongoing self-transformation. Our conceptions of play are dominated by a domestication of uncertainty. We enfeeble the forces of uncertainty in play by assigning to them values of the unreal, of fantasy and pretense, and of the make-believe. Given these valuations, the messages that can be transmitted through the play medium to weighty social realities are diminished in their impact, since they are received as frivolous, and as inconsequential to those realities (see Handelman 1977b). Sent in play, or through 'just play', they are not to be held accountable within serious realities for their innuendos and implications. Yet, in another dimension, such messages that emerge from play media nevertheless are sent back to serious realities, albeit as unstressed, or through ambiguous genres of allegory, irony, and so forth. This ambivalent, or perhaps poly-valent, communicative work features prominently in chapters 4 and 10.

The idea of 'game' is integral to chapters 4, 6, and 7. For present purposes it is sufficient to understand game as rule-bound play (Miller 1973; Caillois 1961). 'Game' may be thought of as a derivative of 'play', brought into being by the same meta-message that creates the latter – but the regnancy of rules in the former has important implications. The game is a distinctly moral medium, one that is keyed by instructions that specify how it is to be played, and that distinguish between correct and incorrect behavior, between right and wrong. Itself predicated on a fiction, its world of order may be related to with the utmost seriousness. Moreover, it is a profoundly purposive medium, with well-defined goals that specify the means of their attainment. A game makes change happen within itself, often by positing an initial condition (for example, sets of opponents) that is to be turned into another (winners and losers). Therefore, built into the idea of 'game' are contrasting or contradictory states of existence, which must be resolved through its action. The game form also depends upon predictability, by limiting possible outcomes, and by specifying the causal scheme to attain these. As well, the game form is self-regulating, for it often contains rules to correct for deviant or obstructive occurrences that emerge in the course of its action.

A game, in other words, is also a temporary system that may have a role in an event of modelling (as does the horse race in the Palio of Siena), or in one of re-presentation (as does the game of guessing the mummer's identity in Newfoundland). In the terms of this chapter, game is a further domestication of the ideation of play: it is uncertainty dominated in its doing by systemicized control. Within it, the flux of play is harnessed to orders of cosmos and world, often as a metaphor for regularity, rather than the antithesis of this. If one removes its predicate of make-believe, game shares much in common with phenomena that anthropologists identify as 'ritual' – itself an ironic commentary on the ceaseless inter-play of order and indeterminacy.

The ideation of play, as make-believe, resonates vibrantly with particular (certainly, Western) cultural sensibilities that render it paradoxical. Nonetheless, the affinities of play to conditions of uncertainty suggest that the meta-message, 'This is play', could be rewritten to give it a broader transcultural catchment. The meta-message might be rendered as: 'This is uncertainty'. This message, in my view, is of a higher order of abstraction than that of play, and so would encompass the latter. As I discussed above, to address a phenomenon as uncertain is to put into question the validity of its certain status and determinate existence in the world.[6] Such a meta-message brings into being phenomena that are neither this nor that, are both, but perhaps are neither. It denotes processuality in the creation of phenomena, and within phenomena themselves. Valorized, it may be understood as part of the epistemologies of cosmogenesis, and of transcendental forces and playful moments. Within forms of organization like public events it encompasses the ideation of liminality, and of play and game.

At a high level of abstraction all of these ideas, and more, denote 'having change happen', 'making change happen', or 'being in change'. A premise that underlies all of this must be that of uncertainty – of the world being taken apart unceasingly, both haphazardly and deliberately; and, antithetically, of there being culturally constituted forms and means of putting it back together again, as it was or differently. The introduction of uncertainty is integral to controlled change among traditional peoples; and public events, especially those that model, are crucial to this work of change. But, should traditional peoples lose the means to reconstitute their worlds, so that they remain primarily within conditions of uncertainty, the unsurprising result is disaster and despair, as the next section describes.

Let me suggest that the presence in public events of that which we identify as play signifies uncertainty, processuality, and therefore the presence of change in its happening. Consider the following. Sinhalese exorcism: the validity of the demonic reality that has captured the patient is destroyed through humorous byplays. *Chisungu*: the determinate prepubescent state of the girls is broken down through teasing. The *Schembart* Carnival: the upside-down world of the *Hölle* is wrecked in fun. Christmas mumming: the wild, amoral mummers are tamed in game. The *Kalela* Dance: the play world resurrects ethnic-tribal relations in place of those of class. In all these instances, and in chapters 4, 5, and 6, as well, play is implicated in uncertainty and processuality.

A final point here: a meta-message like that of, 'This is uncertainty', may avoid or make possible the kind of paradox that Bateson used to delineate play (and that I use throughout this volume). Still, either instance is predicated then on particular cultural perceptions of uncertainty and of paradox.[7] If, for example, the beings of Hindu cosmologies undergo continuous transformations, and if the logics of these cosmologies do not recognize this as paradoxical, then why invoke paradoxicality to find an epistemological status for these phenomena? Perhaps it would be more fruitful to think about the role of uncertainty in such cosmologies. Similarly, if Catholic theologies accord a paradoxical status to the figure of the Virgin Mary, then it is to the logic of cosmology that questions should be addressed.

Predicaments in play: the laughter of the Ik

What happens when a traditional world collapses, and agencies of reconstitution no longer work? When controlled determination in the cosmos is reduced to a near minimum, and therefore so too is meaning? When this is not due to the tangible terror of oppression, in which there is something to resist, or to succumb to? What is left in human existence? Perhaps a sense of absurdity, of the horrors of unravelling lives, when things hardly hold together, and then precariously. In other words, the pervasiveness of reverberating uncertainty, in modes that we might recognize as untrammelled and amoral 'play'. These are the dark aspects of play – the indeterminate play of forces ordinarily kept at bay and introduced in small, controlled measures into models that operate on the world, or virtually suppressed in favor of its tamer significance as make-believe. Colin Turnbull's (1973a) depiction of the Ik offers an instance of such an annihilative existence among a traditional people.

The Ik lived in Northern Uganda, in mountainous terrain that borders the Great African Rift. They were hunters and gatherers who dwelled in unstable social groups composed of family units. Like other African hunter–gatherers, their social relationships likely were predicated upon sharing and reciprocity in food and other resources. The government of Uganda expropriated their hunting lands, and turned them into a nature preserve. Placed in a reservation area, the Ik were expected to practice agriculture, at which they were poor. Famine became endemic, and the Ik lived on the edge of starvation, or did starve. Their modes of making order in the cosmos, through 'ritual' means, became ineffective and fell silent.

As Turnbull depicts them, the Ik survived by shaving to the minimum all forms of cooperation and reciprocity. Their temporary villages were constructed to minimize contact between persons within the village stockade. Spouses foraged separately for food, and ate apart, lest they be pressed to share. Until the age of three, children were raised within the household, but then were thrown out to fend for themselves. Youngsters formed two age bands (one of children aged, roughly, three to seven; and the second of those aged eight to twelve) that foraged together for protection. But there was little sharing among their members. Over-age children were driven forcibly from the companionship of the bands, until as young adults they were left wholly on their own. As the young were abandoned to survive or to die, in accordance with their own capacities, so the old were left to starve or to succumb to disease and to other privations. In Turnbull's estimation the Ik shed almost all qualities and sentiments of sociality, belief, and hope, that impeded their survival as individuals. The decimated and desolated Ik, he argued (Turnbull 1973b: 518), survived by becoming supreme egoists: 'a totally passionless, empty people whose nature, as humans, has been reduced to what must surely be the absolute critical minimum . . . What has happened is the utter destruction of sociality that we have been pleased, for so long, to consider the essential element of human nature'. The book abounds with examples of unconcern and cruelty towards the young, the aged, the infirm, diseased, and helpless.

Yet the Ik sought out one another's company to sit together in silence near their dwellings. They cooperated sporadically to provide goods and services to neighboring peoples; and Ik men maintained a small number of instrumental, dyadic 'partnerships' with neighboring pastoralists, and dyadic 'friendships' with other Ik. Nonetheless, the Ik world was pervaded and shattered by uncontrollable uncertainties that questioned the validity of any nexus of sociality and cooperation. And, on occasion, the Ik laughed in concert, with overtones of mockery and ridicule, and undertones of mutual helplessness.

There were acidic critiques that excoriated Turnbull's depiction (cf. Barth 1974: 99–102). Other commentators tried to comprehend the disastrous devolution of the Ik condition, together with their laughter. Thus McCall (1975: 345) suggested: 'I see the Ik as very much a cohesive group, who are trapped in their disastrous situation. They accommodate their collective misery by using laughter. Jokes, humour, and a sense of the comic serve not only as redirection of internal aggression, but also for the purpose of group definition'. McCall may have been on the right track, but his conclusion with regard to 'group definition' was erroneous. Here are two brief instances of Ik laughter.

> Turnbull (1973a: 49) shook hands with one of two older men. As he tried to remove his hand, the old man tightened his grip, and Turnbull almost lifted him from the ground: 'he fell back and collapsed and lay on the ground, all skin and bone, and he was laughing . . . he apologized for his behavior. "I haven't eaten for three days", he said, "so it's difficult to stand up", whereupon he and his companion dissolved into laughter again'.

> Turnbull (1973a: 204) came across one man stealing food from another. The latter cried, but had not the strength to resist. 'As soon as I appeared Lomongin [the former] reversed his actions and pretended he had been feeding Lolim [the latter], saying that the old man was so blind he could not see where to put the food. The old man had enough strength to retort, "At least I didn't put it in yours!", at which they both rocked with laughter and held onto each other as though they were the closest of friends'.

In these instances, Ik laughed together, apparently displaying sentiments of mutual appreciation. The play of the first instance seems predicated on the awareness of starvation, and that of the second on the stealing of sustenance. If there was any recognition of 'group definition' in these, then it was only that of mutual predicament, and of how each Ik contributed to the catastrophes that befell the other. Their common recognition was that of sheer expression. Just that: nothing was altered by this. These instances, and others, seemed not to offer any information on how Ik could create greater cohesion in their relationships.

The phenomenal predicament of the Ik was that of the uncertainties of fragmentation and extreme individuation. Their existential apprehension of this was expressed through humor, through a form of play. Yet play itself was an expression of conditions of uncertainty, and so it denied the stable validity of whatever it communicated to the Ik world. Therefore any sporadic and unregulated attempts to alter the Ik condition through 'play' could only be indeterminate.

The Ik order of things was disintegrating, and the domain of 'making order', the 'ritual' domain, had fallen silent. Alone, each Ik pursued the uncertainty of his future in the predicament of his present. Ik were unable to comment on their situations in terms of morality, faith, or belief, for these modes had dissolved. McCall (1975: 346) aptly noted: 'For the Ik it is their entire predicament that is barred from discussion, except in humour-ous joking references'. Time and again, through these alternative modes, Ik expressed mutual commiseration of their common tribulation that each was fated to suffer separately. In their daily lives the Ik expected to be hurt, to go hungry, to fail, and to find that the promising masked only disappointment. The seeds of indeterminacy were sown in all Ik endeavors, wild growths that flowered suddenly. To struggle to escape was absurd. Over and again, Ik laughter was triggered when together persons perceived the despair, the hopelessness and helplessness, that was their lot, trapped in the play of forces of flux.[8]

This existential apprehension was present in instances that appeared wholly callous and brutal:

Sitting ... men would watch a child with eager anticipation as it crawled toward the fire, then burst into gay and happy laughter as it plunged a skinny hand into the coals ... a mother would glow with pleasure to hear such joy occasioned by her offspring, and pull it tenderly out of the fire. (*Turnbull 1973a: 112*)

Here, in a dense moment of collapsed meaning, was the lifeline of every Ik. As the child moved alone through space and time, buoyed perhaps by measures of faith, fascination, and anticipation, it headed with determi-nation for shock, pain, and disillusion. In concert, the men gave recognition to self-mockery in the child's fated progression. They could appreciate the terror of their mutual dilemma through the uncertainty of play, but through this they were powerless to change it. In other instances, the old mocked the young for that which they inevitably would become, and the young teased the old with what the latter undoubtedly had become. Over all, these playful modes could communicate only the intimacy of despair. Turnbull himself acknowledged, if implicitly, that the messages of Ik playfulness were fleetingly sociable, but of little substance or sustenance:

And I thought of other old people who had joined in the merriment when they had been teased, knocked over or had a precious morsel of food taken from their mouths. They knew it was silly of them to expect to go on living, and having watched others, they knew that the spectacle really was quite funny. So they joined in the laughter. *(1973a: 228)*

Among the Ik, suggests McCall (1975: 347), 'The priest's incantations are replaced by the jester's repartee as the force to bind society together'. Yet this play was more a shadow-plaiting of elusive fragments, than it was social cohesion. Bereft of the means of making cosmic and social order, or at least of increasing the probabilities of their cohering, the Ik were tossed about in a reverberating uncertainty that denied any alternatives or antitheses. Play, I argued, may communicate contradictory messages: here, a sociality of negation and a negation of sociality. Left to spiral through its own logic, this play could not define a moral or social collectivity, nor even revive or strengthen this. Any sentiments on the making of order only through the flux of the playful remained merely impotent illusion.

The Ik are an extreme instance of the play of forces beyond control. Usually out of sight, the submerged potency of these dynamic conditions lurks in the depths of surface appearances of solidarity and stability. It is against the incursions of these forces of dissolution that public events work among traditional peoples. These potentials held at bay – but also their controlled usage, necessary to the making and renewing of order, that peoples must practice incessantly upon themselves. But, however necessary, these practices are precarious. This, as I have noted, tells us something about how (and perhaps, why) certain kinds of public events have the logics of design that they do.

Events and societies

Max Gluckman (1962: 2) once asked: 'why is it that in tribal society there is on the whole greater ritualization of transitions in social status . . . than there is in modern society?' Gluckman's query went in an interesting direction, but his reply was wanting. He contended that this formalization clarified the patterning and problematics of social relationships; and thereby indicated the means available for dealing with the latter. By contrast, the implicit position of part I of this book has hewed closer to that which John Roberts (1964) called the 'self-management' of cultures (see also Leach 1966). Let me clarify here my suppositions on the connections between public events and social orders. Roberts argued that, to be self-sustaining and self-reproductive, a cultural (or social) unit had to have the capacities to conserve and to process information about itself. My view is that public events are culturally constituted foci of information-processing. In these activities lie crucial junctures of events and the social orders that formulate them. The capacities for the processing of information are highest in the systemic properties of events of modelling, and lowest in the reflecting mirror-images of events of presentation. In this scheme, the magic-mirrors of refraction in events of re-presentation occupy an intermediate position.

To this point I have tried to treat the types of events as heuristic devices. That is, to relate to them seriously, but not too seriously. I have implied that they are good to think with, but not to believe in. Here, for a bit, let me alter the optic and relate to the types as if they are indeed phenomena that exist in the world, rather than meta-designs. And so, to speculate upon their correlation with different orders of society.

Any given people likely will have public occasions that approximate all types of events discussed here, since each type is a distinctive construct for the processing of information. Nonetheless, albeit hypothetically, I would suggest that the relative centrality of these types will vary with different kinds of social order. Broadly glossed: events of presentation seem associated especially with modern, bureaucratic states; events of modelling with tribal and traditional peoples; while events of re-presentation tend to an association with traditional, hierarchical societies. In this I am not implying any unilinear development among societies, one that spatially places the 'primitive' on the temporal downslope. (In this regard, see Fabian's [1983: 17–8] critique of the scientific spatialization of time and society.) Instead the hypothetical relationships among societies are akin to the possibilities within the space of figure 4.

The edge of contrast here is between social orders that recognize themselves to be organized systemically and as relatively autonomous of the natural cosmologies within which they are embedded, and those that have less or little awareness of this. This argument is not part of the ongoing debate over how people think: whether there are significant distinctions between 'modern' and 'primitive' thought, between digital and analogic cognition, and so on. My point is a simpler one, discussed elsewhere in some detail (Handelman 1981).

The paradigmatic form of organization of the modern state is that of bureaucracy. The most elementary feature of bureaucracy is that it is a device for the ongoing generation of taxonomies – of ways of classifying aspects of the world, and of relating to these categories. The ideal practice of bureaucracy is that of orthopraxy – in a way, it has much in common with Levi-Strauss' idea of 'parcelling-out' in 'ritual'. Moreover, the premises of bureaucracy accord with those of autonomous, systemic organization: teleological, predictive, self-regulating, and making change happen within itself. Like the event of modelling, the *métier* of bureaucratic organization is the making of controlled change through the creation and manipulation of taxonomy. Unlike the event of modelling, bureaucracy does all of this in the most mundane and routine of ways. The intersection, the coordination, and the mutual reinforcement of numerous bureaucratic organizations brings modern society nearer and nearer to the 'iron cage' of bureaucracy of which Weber warned – in other words, closer to a conception of an autonomy of total system (even though this in turn generates basic contradictions. See van Gunsteren [1976]).

Now, any network of information can be systemicized, whether this be termed government, economy, science, the media, the military, all of these together and many others as well. And this becomes even more so, as surveys of attitudes, tastes, and preferences become more integral to the self-regulation of public life. In modern states this is quite the case. The key is whether those persons, who exist within a network of information, come to construct its logic of operation as systemic. If so, then it becomes systemic for them, and they become its operators, setting it to do work in ways that are expected to be self-regulating and predictive.

The major implications are four-fold. Firstly, the ratio of the force used to the effects achieved alters radically (Foucault 1979): thus, although little force is applied, decisions have causal ramifications of vastly greater magnitude. Secondly, experts and managers often think that social orders can be planned comprehensively – in their magnitude, duration, and effect – through modelling. Therefore there is 'forecasting' of numerous sorts – predictions that in turn generate further decisions whose effects are thought to be controllable. Thirdly, social order can be treated as autonomous, as independent from what we euphemistically call the natural environment (but that really refers to the continuousness of 'naturalized cosmology'). The future course of social order no longer is thought to depend on its place in a cosmic scheme of things, but rather on its plans for itself. 'Nature', in its manifold aspects, becomes perceived as an exploitable resource, for the benefit of state and citizenry. Wolin (1985: 239) neatly summarizes these developments: 'the transformation of ritual into rules not only prepared the way for the unprecedented concentration of power associated with the modern state; it destroyed the myth-ritual conception of power as repair of the world and it replaced it by a conception of power as domination over both nature and man'. Therefore, fourthly, there is hardly any need for 'transformative work', as this term has been used here. The continuous, routine modelling of worlds of living, through various modes and in a multitude of domains, often is intended to change phenomena in ongoing ways. 'Change', the most complex kind of information-processing, becomes a function of the bureaucratic, scientific, and technological ordering of, and impact on living – whether in the name of 'progress', 'advancement', the 'betterment' of humankind, or other ideological tenets.

If causal change is understood to be built into the systems that mundanely regulate so many domains of living, then there is little space for the transformational work of events-that-model. 'Systems' incorporate within themselves all that is needed to know about the predictive management of life – or so their planners and managers seem to believe. And, the simple fact is that on the plane of the state, events of modelling are conspicious by their absence. On the other hand, much of the life of the modern state is put together by organizations that are quite aware of their own systemic premises, and that continually engage in predictive modelling in order to do the work of transforming the values of information they process. The magnitude of this hegemony over transformational work is astounding. Thus, a wry aside, one that also is no laughing matter: what is one to make of a newspaper headline announcing that 'time stood still' in order to enable the vagaries of the earth's rotation to fall into line with the timekeeping of the USA's atomic clock – TIME STOPPED TO LET THE EARTH CATCH UP WITH OFFICIAL CLOCK. 'If we didn't do this', said an official, 'the sun would be rising at noon or something'.[9]

Events-that-present are summarizing pronouncements and indices of the known: they contain little or no sense of uncertainty. Within them, shapes rarely have shadows. These occasions are condensed magnifications of that which social order knows itself to be, and they validate this knowledge. Modern states work on the premise that the necessary information relevant to their functioning either is available and is included in the making of decisions, or, if insufficient (as of course, it probably must be), such information will be attainable with progress. Since these networks of information relate to themselves as systemic, regardless of how complex is their interdependence, they postulate their own autonomy and their supposed capacities to control the development and direction of their own destinies. Therefore these structures are understood, as a matter of course, to be self-correcting: through bureaucratic promulgation, legislative action, juridical decision, scientific experimentation, attitudinal surveys, and the like. The transformational, causal work that is done by events of modelling already is incorporated into the parameters of social orders that are aware of themselves as relatively autonomous systems. There such events are, in the main, epiphenomenal and irrelevant. Instead, events of presentation display social order quite as their creators understand this – as determinate images that mirror collective or elite perceptions of what the mind-sets and the feeling states of participants ought to be.

In the vocabularies of modern states, the usage of the 'symbolic' denotes the 'merely symbolic', the 'just symbolic', the 'expressive': these commonplace phrasings accurately connote the condensed mirroring of the already known, if perhaps more dimly perceived. The symbolics of social order become its expressive extensions. No longer are symbols or metaphors causal connections that rivet relationships between domains of existence, the boundaries of which are understood to be, in large measure, beyond human ken.

Social orders of tribal and traditional peoples likely are known to their members as systematic: that is, as organized in patterned and repetitive ways. Yet one wonders whether they are apprehended as systemic. These orders are known to exist through intimate interdependencies with other phenomena, including those of nature and paranature. But the awareness of the closure of a totality of order, of macrocosm, is located beyond mundane routines of existence, and often is shrouded in uncertainty. Peoples have access to those sources of knowledge and instruction, yet accessibility is limited, and at times hazardous; and finally these sources are beyond human control. Social order exists within a more comprehensive and encompassing cosmos that may be influenced by peoples, but whose control, the certainty of control over an assumed totality of information, is vested elsewhere. Social order is nowhere near coterminous with macrocosm.

It is especially among peoples whom we gloss as tribal that events-that-model have their particular significance. It is there that model, as microcosm, is constituted as a temporary system that acts on the inaccessible macrocosm. Therefore given the sorts of cosmos that often are the foundations for events-that-model, social processes often are understood through natural ones. By contrast, the systemic orders of modern states are perceived routinely to incorporate the macrocosm and to act on it. In these perceptions, the macrocosm is remade continually in the determinative images of social and technological orders. Among tribal peoples, social order is remade through the forces of macrocosmic uncertainty that subsume the former. Here, more inaccessible and uncontrollable aspects of the macrocosm are incorporated into the modelled microcosm, to be controlled by its predictive rules of operation. Events of modelling are explicit transformers of social order among these peoples. These are occasions during which peoples may envision, and transfigure, the holistic properties of their manners of living, and the ways in which these are related to macrocosmic order. And, such visions likely are most crucial when one kind of phenomenon is changed into another.

Events of re-presentation seem to have a more interstitial position in relation to social order. These occasions might be more prevalent among traditional collectivities that have strongly hierarchical structures, but that are not fully objectivated to themselves. The validity of their orders still must be seen to be done, in order to be known as done. In part, this is accomplished through events of presentation, that display order; and in part, for example, through the temporary transpositions or inversions of hierarchy, that bring out the falsifiability of alternative orderings, and so that revert to the authoritatively acceptable.

Let me restate emphatically that there is no neat or simple, functional correlation between a people and the kinds of public events they create for themselves. All social orders likely work through variants of all three types, and others that have not been broached here. Still, I would suggest that there are tendencies that differentiate the appearance of forms of events. To be sure, in the modern state, but especially among its localized collectivities, certain transitions of kin and community (birth, marriage, death) may be done through events of modelling; as, more infrequently, are occasions of local community solidarity. But it is clear that many of the most pressing dilemmas – of the allocation and use of power, of relationships among social strata, or of the historical validity of a society – are not treated transformatively in the events of the modern state. For the 'solutions' to these and other issues are assumed to be built into the routinely systemic operations of social order. This is much less the case among peoples glossed as tribal, where social order must invent special devices to bring about transformations within itself.

All public events, in their creation of limited social worlds, are exercises in holism. It is in events of modelling that the organization of holism is the most sophisticated – for these occasions fully synthesize morphology and processuality. The signal irony of all this is that the logics of designs of public events in so-called 'simpler' collectivities are most complex, while those of 'complex' ones often are quite simple. In the case studies that follow, my focus shifts from logics of design to the finer points of public events – to their elaborations of significance, as snares of thought, in particular places.

2   *Proto-events*

Intersections

Some twenty years ago, believing I was a student of aging, I passed many months in the company of the older people described in chapter 4. So, chronologically, this book really begins here, with their invention of a game. Sentimentally too, for their antics wakened me to the powers of play, an interest that has not waned.

The game continued for about one month. There was no exegesis, just as there was no name. Protean, the game happened to happen. Along the way its form took shape. During its existence I asked no questions, fearing to alter or upset its delicate balance. But too, I had difficulty believing the neatness and regularity of its patterning, even though I made little sense of this at the time.

Afterward, my questions on the game met with shrugs, smiles, and summary glosses of 'fun', 'entertainment', and the like. The puzzles remain. Sometimes I return to the game, adding another cornerstone of meaning, changing an emphasis, seduced perhaps by its symmetry, but I always was, according to my field notes.

My concerns and worries were not theirs, and so I was a sometime player, probably seen as a sympathetic outsider, but likely not a very empathetic one. But writing this, in a retrospective mood with prospective intimations, I recall the wry amusement of one of the women. 'If I was rich', she chuckled, 'I'd have a grave with electricity'. Amen.

4 The donkey game

The invention of the donkey game occurred in a sheltered workshop in Jerusalem that employed the indigent elderly. In my interpretation this form of make-believe created an alternative reality through which certain enduring problems of the players could be broached systematically and experienced in multifaceted ways. Therefore I will ask why this game was practiced in this place by these people. If this question seems simple, it is deceptively so. In terms of the wider society, the game seemed quite idiosyncratic. In relation to the little world of its invention it was significant. This may be a hallmark of proto-events.

At one time I worried about the tight match between the form of the game and the predicaments of the players that I think it played to. Now I am less concerned, given two provisos. One is that ideology, the conscious formulation of principled aim and motivation, seems lacking in proto-events. The comparative absence of intervening, collective reflexivity permits emergent behavior to respond more directly to whatever impulses led to its formulation. Collective reflexion likely mediates, changes, and skews this more immediate relationship. The second, to which I alluded in earlier chapters, is that public events more generally are designs with strong instrumental components (even when these are called 'expressive' by scholars). Whether they operate through transformation, re-presentation, or presentation, their practice rather than their theorizing is essential. They are not hypothetical designs to be thought on in the main, but ones to be done. Therefore something of the direct relationship between social impulse and behavior is kept, the importance of ideas notwithstanding. This, even though there often are conflicting definitions of the viability and worth of special occasions, and opposing views over what these are about and whom, if anyone, they serve. As I indicated in earlier chapters, it is important to distinguish whether contradiction and conflict are integral to the design of an event, as well as the mechanisms (or the lack thereof) for handling such uncertainties. In a rudimentary way, this was important even for the donkey game, since the cooperation required by the game rested, in my understanding, on quite different views of what was happening in play. This is discussed in the last section of this chapter.

Before describing play in this shop, and then the emergence from this of the game, some contextualization is necessary. The workshop was one of a number run by a Jewish voluntary organization I call SAGE. The mission of SAGE was that of the redemption of the indigent elderly, of their self-esteem, through productive work for which they were paid. The administrators of SAGE were middle-aged women of the middle-class who believed in serious good works. Their attitude was that of patrons who knew what was best for their charges. Their behavior towards the latter was caring, authoritarian, abrupt, and indeed, patronizing.

The workshop made ceramic jewelry. The shop employed sixteen people and a female supervisor, all of whom worked five mornings a week. Workers were paid according to the number of days they came to the shop. The sixteen had emigrated to Palestine, and later to Israel, from a variety of North African, Middle Eastern, and Mediterranean locales.[1]

The shop consisted of two rooms, back and front. The shop was entered through the small front room, that opened onto a courtyard, around which were clustered other of the SAGE workshops. Access to the back room was through the front room. Seven of the workers were women. Six were widows, living alone and responsible for their own upkeep. All the women worked in the cavernous back room, itself part of an old building of thick stone walls, narrow windows, and perpetual gloom. The women ranged in age from sixty-six to eighty-four. Of the nine men, six worked in the cramped front room, a newer structure, airy and often sunlit. The men ranged in age from sixty-one to over ninety. Six were married, and four of them were breadwinners of households still with children of school age.

The clustering of women and men in different rooms was important, for to a high degree it also marked differences in personal history and in attitudes to work in the shop. These differences had a direct bearing on the invention of the game.

All the workers had been shunted to SAGE by the local welfare department. The men had become dependent on welfare for subsistence mainly for reasons of ill-health. Over the years the welfare department made determined efforts to erase them from its rolls. Given their age, limited skills, and declining personal resources, the men were employable only in organizations like SAGE. There they earned less than the social assistance benefits they had received. Nonetheless, this income was necessary for their well-being, and often that of their households. They did not perceive work in the shop to be valuable or rewarding, but their capacities to resist this placement had eroded as their dependency had increased.[2] Given their cultural origins, their loss of autonomy and lessened capacity to govern their own fate were deeply painful.

These patterns of dependency continued in SAGE. One man said of the situation of the workers there, 'We're like broken shoes, they walk in us.' The administrators valued serious attitudes towards work, and often recognized these through a demeanor that conveyed involvement in tasks of production. Most work was done seated in place. Workers thought to be committed to work sat at their places, eyes and posture pointing towards the work space before them, their interaction with others sedate, with little movement out of place.

Work in the main was the making of clay beads. With a couple of exceptions, the men thought the work infantile. Although their levels of production were good, their demeanor said otherwise. Those of the front room spent much time in sociable but raucous conversation and horseplay, wandering about the shop, seeming to neglect their tasks. These men were thought poor workers by their superiors, and they often were reprimanded and criticized in public.

The women also reached the workshop through the welfare department. But none had ever held a steady job in the past. Now, living alone in the main, their earnings were sufficient for personal upkeep. Moreover, the tasks of the shop were not unlike the kinds of handwork to which the women were accustomed. Yet more than this, employment provided the women with independent incomes, to be disposed of as each wished, and the occasion to compete for prestige on an equal footing with men. The women found these opportunities exciting. They identified with work and frequently were praised by their superiors. The shop constituted a reality that reversed traditional gender-linked hierarchies on a routine basis, with the women at the top and most of the men at the bottom.

Just as administrators would burst into the front room from the courtyard, to upbraid the men there, so too the latter were continually and critically sniped at from behind by the women of the back room who denigrated their work habits and personal behavior. Short of surrendering their improper behavior and adopting the demeanor of serious workers, the men could not counter these cross-pressures. Discontented with being in the shop, the sole enjoyment of these men was their sociable behavior with one another. Through play these men could express their disaffection with the shop while subverting momentarily its dominant reality of work. Later, through the game, they would regularly substitute a reality within which they regained their rightful place in the moral order. Or so it seemed, from one angle of understanding.[3]

Play in the workshop

Recurrent modes of play in the shop were spontaneous and intermittent, with variable content and uncertain outcomes. Play characterized by minimal physical movement was more the province of the women, and of those few men who also identified with work. Play that moved about the shop, and that was more physical in substance, was the domain of the disaffected men, most of whom were located in the front room. As I will indicate, it was the play of these men that contributed to the invention of the game. The following is an inventory of modes of play in the shop.

> Quips, jokes, and humorous stories: These were largely the domain of the women, and were interjected in conversation to emphasize or to illustrate a point. Since these conversations were dyadic in the main, held between persons who were seated at work, they were not seen as disruptive of productive routines.
>
> Singing: On occasion one or two of the women broke into song at their workplaces. Again, this was not seen as disruptive.
>
> Traditional tales: Story-telling was the domain of one backroom man, whose tales were directed at everyone within earshot. Although others were attentive, interjecting excited comments, proper demeanor was maintained.

All of these playful forms reinforced the views of superiors that the shop could be used properly for sociable intercourse that was subordinated to the work process.

> Joking activity: This was prominent in contacts among the disaffected men. Joking was predicated upon an extended message of 'this is play', included at least two active participants, and was composed of both utterance and physical movement. Themes of mutual insult, violence, and sexuality were prominent in these interchanges. One example will suffice here.

A frontroomer, Shlomo, entered the backroom and approached Zackaria who was seated at his place of work. Shlomo loudly called out, 'Crazy Zackaria', and then, 'Zackaria the donkey, you're crazy!' Zackaria grinned and continued to work. Shlomo advanced on Zackaria who lunged at him with a pair of pliers. Shlomo dodged nimbly and chuckled. The following interchange ensued:

Zackaria: 'Watch out, Shlomo, this [the pliers] is a revolver. I'll shoot you into little pieces for the cats to eat'.
Shlomo: 'Crazy Zackaria, I'll cut you into pieces and throw you down the toilet'.
Zackaria: 'I'll sell you to the Arabs for steak'.
Shlomo: 'I'll sell your brain to Barazani the Kurd to chew'.

Zackaria: 'I'll sell you piece by piece for soup in the market'.
Shlomo: 'I'll cut off your ears to put on a donkey'.
Zackaria: 'I'll cut off your penis for a donkey's tail'.
Shlomo: 'I'll cut off your balls to hang in the women's toilet'.

The women averted their heads. Zackaria embraced Shlomo, and they pummelled
one another, giggling and chuckling.

In the context of the shop, this interchange expressed the mutual
acceptance of absurd identities. Although its overtones were aggressive and
hostile, the exchange was embedded in a relationship of friendship, and it
likely commented on the place of these men in the shop. The fantastic
content of their utterances reflected self-estimations of the absurdity of their
work situation and their dependency. In the back room, identified with
work, these men acted out themes of metaphorical violence and mutilation.
If mature, responsible men were to be dismembered and equated with
fodder, then what indeed was their manhood worth in this place? To
pursue this line of interpretation, when Shlomo cried, 'I'll cut off your balls
to hang in the women's toilet', he commented implicitly that Zackaria was
the 'castrated' victim of the women, although the testicles hanging there
reaffirmed the capacity of the mature male to sexually dominate females. As
is claimed more generally for commentaries communicated through play,
these were contradictory yet complementary, contrasting in a sense the
ideal and the real. As the men hugged and pummelled each other, their
mutual equality and enjoyment were evident in activity that excluded the
participation of women and, moreover, that embarrassed them.

> Role play: On occasion workers enacted roles that were more
> relevant to the wider society. The initiators often were disaffected
> men. Their play mocked roles of power and expertise, upon which
> they were dependent in their lives outside the shop. Here are a few
> examples.

In terms of the process of production, Mashia.ha frontroom worker, had to deliver
his output to the most powerful of the backroom women, who at times derided the
quality of his work. Sometimes he phrased his contact with her through role play, as
in the following instance: 'Here comes the social worker to help Zohara', he began,
handing her a penny and adding, 'Now Zohara, if you're a good girl and behave
yourself properly, I'll give you another penny at the end of the month. Now be a
good girl'. Others in the back room might take up the chorus, 'Look at the social
worker who comes to help. Give me a penny too. With only a penny I can be young
again'.

In this encounter, Mashia.hmocked the criteria of allocation and the
small benefits of the welfare department. He showed that clients had to

present themselves as personally and morally worthy of aid in order to qualify for benefits. Therefore Zohara had to be a 'good girl', attributes far removed from her age, marital status, and position in the shop. By playing the social worker while casting her as a young, female client, Mashia. h momentarily altered the balance of power between them. Proffering the penny in the guise of a social worker paralleled giving her his output as a shop worker. As the first warned that she would benefit only so long as she remained a worthy recipient, so it intimated that he would supply her only so long as she behaved with propriety. Thus admonitions that he hesitated to communicate to her openly could be embedded in role play.

Men who initiated these byplays commonly did so towards women who then were cast as subordinates and supplicants within the frame of play. On another occasion, Shalom, a backroom worker, adopted the role of doctor towards a backroom woman. 'Now I'm the doctor', he chuckled, 'beware of the gasses. All day, boom boom, a whole night boom boom'. He waggled his forefinger at her, 'You mustn't eat so much. Now the gasses catch you, boom boom.' He snorted, 'When you fart in the street, soon soon, look left, look right, to see if anyone's coming, lift your leg a little, and boom boom.' He laughed and handed her three olives, 'Take these pills. One in the morning, one at noon, and one at night. I'm a good doctor. Here, I'll write you a prescription.' He scribbled on a scrap of paper, 'No more gasses, no more boom boom.' He handed her three more olives, 'And here are the pills for tomorrow. I'm the doctor. If you don't feel better I'll give you an appointment here tomorrow.' In the guise of a make-believe doctor he commented on bodily odors that he attributed to her. In this there was humiliation, but not serious confrontation (from which the women tended to emerge triumphant).

At other times the men played the role of 'host', entertaining their 'friends' (other workshop men) or 'guests from America'. SAGE depended on private donations, and numerous tourists and other potential benefactors passed through the shop. Therefore playing 'host' to such guests contained elements of self-ascribed status. On these occasions the kiln speedily became an oven, plates piled with beads became portions of chicken, kebab and rice, tools became eating utensils, and settings would be laid for the feast, as imaginary cognac and arak were drunk from empty water glasses. Outside the shop, at home, these occasions were times of mutuality and conviviality among kin and friends. Within the shop these playlets stressed the solidarity of male camaraderie and the exclusion of women.

> Pranks: These were part of the play repertoire of the men, particularly those of the front room. Simple in conception, pranks were predicated upon elements of anticipation, tension, and surprise, followed

by an outburst of emotion when the victim discovered the hidden twist in a routine context. A favorite merely entailed slipping an object, like a smooth stone, into a jacket pocket, and awaiting its discovery and the reaction of the victim. Other pranks were more elaborate. Mashiaḥ regularly shopped in the market before work. One morning he brought back a white hen. When he went out to the toilet, another frontroom worker put the hen within a cabinet in Mashiaḥ's worktable. On his return he of course missed his hen. One front roomer said that he himself had been too engrossed in work to notice anything. Another questioned the existence of the hen. The perpetrator added that the hen had escaped outside. When Mashiaḥ went out to search, the hen was placed under a table in the back room. Mashiaḥ returned, suspicious and empty handed. He searched both rooms, but no one betrayed the fowl's location. The eventual discovery of the hen was accompanied by the laughter of both men and women. This intensified when Mashiaḥ seized a length of wood and lightly beat the perpetrator, who pretended to cringe in an exaggerated manner and laughed along with the rest.

In another instance a front roomer stuffed a stray cat into a drawer of Mashiaḥ's worktable, while the latter was out. On his return he went into the back room. There the women told him to stop wasting working time, and steered him back to his table. He sat, lit a cigarette and leisurely took a few puffs. Then he opened the drawer and the yowling cat leaped into his lap, tightly gripping his clothing with its claws. Shocked and shouting, amidst cheers and clapping hands, Mashiaḥ almost fell over, but joined in the laughter.

The play of the women was sedate and did not disrupt the rhythms and routines of work. That of the frontroom men often was raucous, disorderly, and critical of the social order of the shop. Women's play did not contribute to the substance of the emergent game. Men's play did: joking activity contributed the terminology of the absurd; role play added well-defined play roles; and pranks, the extraordinary concealed within the mundane. But the modes of play discussed so far were spontaneous and intermittent, with uncertain outcomes. The invention of the game constituted a routinization of play and uncertainty, and so too of commentaries on the local order of things that were embedded there in the make-believe.

Two further aspects of workshop play are relevant here. At times the women used the metaphor of 'theatre' in referring to these goings on. Such references were not made by the men. As one woman commented, 'This place is like a theatre, every day another play'. And the women observed that one should pay admission in order to watch the antics of the men.

These references were congruent with their frequent roles as spectators who watched from the sidelines as the frontroom men riotously subverted the reality of work through play.

References to 'children' and 'childhood' were common, invoked usually by administrators to denigrate men at play. When a superior interrupted men's play, the following sorts of comments were evident: 'All of you are here to work – you aren't children'; 'Children, sit down and stay quiet'; or, 'Stop behaving like little children'. Given the dependency of the men and the authoritarian attitudes of superiors, admonitions that only children performed such antics were themselves an absurdity for the frontroom men. When they themselves remarked that, 'This place is like a kid's school', or that, 'When we graduate we'll go to kindergarten', the men seemed to comment that their position of dependence and subordination was akin to that of children; that 'childish' behavior was an appropriate response; and that only as little children could they acquiesce to and cope with their conditions of livelihood. As well, perhaps the imagery of childhood projected a more innocent state, when play hardly was separable from the serious world, and when players enclosed themselves within a reality of make-believe that resisted the intrusion of external demands.

In the context of the above the men invented the donkey game. I call it this because the motif of 'donkey' was prominent in the talk of the men; the motif had been associated jokingly with the parentage of the men; and the cry of 'donkey' became part of the game. But, as I noted, the game was never named, either by players or spectators. Nor, to my knowledge, was there ever any discussion about its purpose, ground rules, substance, or tactics.

The donkey game – a tell-tail sign

During a session of joking in the front room, one of the men introduced the motif of the 'donkey tree' to mock Zackaria's paternity. 'You know', he began, 'in Tunis they have a tree, a donkey tree! Every night at midnight, all is quiet. Only the animals are about. All good people are sleeping with their wives. The moonlight shines on the donkey tree. Boom! From out of the tree comes a donkey, a baby donkey comes out. That's how Zackaria was born, out of the donkey tree!' To their amusement, variations of this story were applied to others of the men. Not long after, Shlomo elaborated on Zackaria's paternity, explaining that a donkey had sprung full-grown from the donkey tree and impregnated Zackaria's mother. He was the offspring of this union. Again the motif was applied to others of the men.

Within a few days, Shlomo constructed a device of a length of wire with a rag fastened to one end, the other bent into a crude hook. He started hanging this device onto the collars, pockets, and belts of his friends – those men who did not identify with the dominant reality of work in the shop. He did this with stealth and deftness, and his victims appeared unaware of what he had done to them. When each discovered the device, Shlomo would cry, 'donkey, donkey'. The device came to be called a 'tail', and its victims joined in hanging this tail on one another. Here the idiom of the absurd was consistent with that used by these men in their joking activity. The only utterance required in transferring the device was the cry of 'donkey', as the victim discovered his tail. This call was not limited to the players, for the onlookers, the other workers in the shop, often joined in. However, this utterance and the tempo of transference were conditioned by situational factors. If the supervisor or an administrator were present the utterance was eliminated, while the number of transfers was scaled down or held in abeyance.

In their doing these actions became more consistent in form. These conventions may be called the 'ground rules' of the emergent game. As with all else related to this activity, these were never enunciated as rules. But they specified the cues that signaled the onset of a round of play and the manner in which this was to be done. In the main these rules were followed faithfully. Otherwise the doing of the game broke down. Thus, only one tail could be in play. Two basic roles had emerged in the game, that of the transferer and that of the recipient, or more to the point, the 'victim'. More than one tail would have blurred the distinction between these roles, and so would have made the order of turn-taking uncertain. Like other modes of play among these men, the game over time took the form of balanced, reciprocal interaction. Possession of the tail was evidence that its possessor had been the previous victim, and so the next transferer. With one tail in use its possessor knew what his role was to become. Each successive victim thereby earned the right to become the next transferer.

There was no specified period of time, nor any particular context, within which the tail had to be transferred. This indeterminacy heightened the anticipation of the players. They knew who would hang the tail, but not when or how this would be done. This flexibility also meant that the game could be adapted easily to the momentary exigencies of the shop, the risks entailed scaled up or down, and so forth.

There was no specified order of transfer. The last victim chose the next. This too heightened anticipation and tension, for the previous victim but one also could become the next. No player was excused from the game because he had just played a turn.

Transfers were made within the shop. In other words, the game was played within the social order upon which it commented. To play elsewhere was to invite disruptions by outsiders who saw only spontaneous horseplay. This the players learned through experience. Within the shop the game was played in either room or both, thereby enabling the momentary subversion of the backroom identification with work. But the women were completely excluded from active participation. Their place in the game was always that of the spectator. Similarly excluded (with occasional exceptions) were those few men who also identified fully with the importance of work and with the prestige that this conferred.

Playing the game took the following form. The previous victim, the 'donkey', took out the tail at a time of his choosing. His intended victim could be anywhere in the shop, in either room, seated at work, standing, interacting. With casualness or stealth the transferer approached his victim, as he would in perpetrating a prank, and hooked the tail onto his target. Part of the fun lay in the 'donkey' being unaware of his acquired identity. The absurdity of the victim's condition, essential to his donkiness, was most heightened by his self-ignorance. That dumb donkey continued to attend to his concerns even though in a state of identity transformation of which everyone else but he was aware. But those others did not know whether the victim really was unaware of his acquired identity or pretended this. Nor could they know when his transformed identity would be revealed publicly. In a few instances the donkey carried his tail about for periods of up to an hour before acknowledging or discovering his new identity.

During these interstitial periods the overt identity and behavior of the victim conveyed the usual, yet were intertwined with a sign of the absurd, one that called forth aspects of the 'true' identity of the players in the workplace. The contradictions within this 'double vision', together with the inability of players and spectators alike to resolve these discrepancies until they received the proper cue from the victim, likely also heightened anticipation and tension. The revelation of the absurd identity concealed within the seeming normality of things signaled that others should recognize this 'true' identity by calling out, 'donkey, donkey'. Sometimes the label of donkey stuck to a victim beyond a particular round of play, since his donkiness became a topic in conversation until he initiated the next session of the game. These elaborations on the identity of donkey added to the enjoyment of all concerned. The following is an example of a lengthy round of play, held while the supervisor was out.

Hanging tails on the angels

Shlomo, the last victim, entered the back room and silently approached Zackaria whose back was turned. He deftly hung the tail on Zackaria's coat and moved off to wash his hands at the sink. Zackaria rose and strolled about the room, seemingly unaware of the dangling tail. Two of the nearby women muffled their chuckles. Yiḥye, another of the frontroom players entered. Zackaria scratched his upper back and discovered the tail. Players and spectators laughed and called out, 'donkey, donkey'.

Note that although some of the women attended to the transfer they did not talk about it, and so cooperated in the play. Zackaria, whether purposively or not, paraded his identity; while the others behaved as usual. This heightened the discrepancy between his identity in the shop and that of the game. Anticipation mounted as the eyes of others followed him about, awaiting his discovery of the tail. As that happened, most of the others responded as they were expected to.

Yiḥye was examining the kiln as Zackaria came from behind and hung the tail from his coat collar. In turn, Yiḥye hung the tail on one of the backroom men, who speedily hooked it back onto Yiḥye. Each transfer followed the rules of the game. Each was marked by stealth and deftness, while the others waited until the victim revealed himself before labeling him publicly.

Yiḥye was taken unawares in the last transfer. He knew the tail hung between his shoulder blades but he had difficulty grasping it. His efforts were spurred on by the women who urged him to reach higher. After he succeeded, and under the cover of washing his hands at the sink, he crept up behind David and hooked the tail from his shirt collar. David, a backroom worker, was not a player. To the contrary, he thoroughly identified with the reality of work and competed vigorously with the women for the praise of superiors. David must have felt the tail, for he stood immediately and denounced 'this game for children during work time'. His words were blown away by the gales of laughter of the others.

Given that the players systematically excluded from active play those who identified with work, it is unlikely that Yiḥye tried to seduce David into becoming a regular participant. Perhaps he tried to expose David as one subject to the same frailties as the players, and so as less committed to work than he insisted. If David acquiesced, he would deny momentarily but publicly his intense involvement with tasks on which he based his identity in the shop, and for which he was rewarded. But David speedily denied the validity of the game, likening it to children's activity, and thereby echoing the sentiments of the workers' superiors. He clung to his image as a paragon of work. Nonetheless, all around him the public definition of the work-place had shifted temporarily from one of work to one of play, and his diatribe was stunted by the fun of the others.

David brandished the tail and hung it on Mashiaḥ who had just entered the back room. As Mashiaḥ removed the tail to cries of 'donkey', Shlomo tickled him. Mashiaḥ and Shlomo struck one another on chest and arms with much flourish but little force, while others chuckled, grinned, and pointed. This round of the game had ended. Mashiaḥ called out, 'Shlomo and Zackaria will be gentiles even in their graves'. Zohara grinned and added, 'Right, they'll hang tails on the angels'. Another woman quipped, 'Then no one will know who is an angel and who is Satan'. At these remarks, players and spectators broke into renewed laughter. The front-room men returned to their places, with Mashiaḥ in possession of the tail.

Although David played a turn, he did so demonstratively and openly, in disregard of the rules, showing that he refused to enter into the spirit of play. At this point the round started to break down. Shlomo's tickling Mashiaḥ further contravened convention and aborted the round, effectively locking the latter into the identity of 'donkey'.

In their quips the women acknowledged that the game had subverted their reality for a brief period. By hanging the tail the players gained the attention and tacit cooperation of the 'angels', of those who identified with work. Satan commonly is depicted with a tail. The angels thereby acquired an attribute of Satan. This obscured the moral distinction between right and wrong. The back room was pervaded by an ambiguous atmosphere, within which the workers there were tempted by enjoyment to shed their serious reality for that of play – and so to blur the distinctiveness of their proclaimed morality of work by which they habitually separated them-selves from the players. Momentarily, Satan and the angels were indis-tinguishable, and the make-believe unified the workplace. (Of course, many rounds of the game never penetrated the back room, and so did not affect the reality of the latter.)

The sign of the tail

The messages of an alternative reality embedded within the donkey game were not qualitatively distinct from those in other modes of men's play. But within the more complex game these messages were simplified, honed, and reproduced. Where joking, role play, and pranks were spontaneous, haphazard, and somewhat idiosyncratic, with negotiable courses and uncertain outcomes, the game was directed consistently towards a particular outcome. Mary Douglas (1968: 365) writes that, 'The joke merely affords opportunity for realizing that an accepted pattern has no necessity. Its excitement lies in the suggestion that any particular ordering of experience may be arbitrary and subjective. It is frivolous in that it produces no real alternative, only an exhilarating sense of freedom from form in general'. This is often what we would call 'fun'. Without doubt the game was fun for the players and most spectators. However, even though they did not explain the game beyond its sense of 'fun' and 'entertainment', it was not just any 'freedom from form', any frivolity, that made the game fun. This is attested to by the invention of 'rules' by which the game was played. These were arbitrary yet methodical conventions that increased the degree of certainty that not just any fun was made in the practice of the game. Instead these conventions orientated the players to certain kinds of fun, to certain varieties of performance and experience that played with particular ambiguities safely hidden from view in the usual order of things, but that were acutely felt by the players. It is with this note of pointed fun that any interpretation of the game should begin. In other words, why this variety of fun in this particular place?

The game altered boundaries of relevance. The women who held centre stage in the serious reality of work were excluded from active participation and relegated to the periphery of the play world. Those men perceived as peripheral to work moved to the centre of attention. More than any other practice, the game distinguished the disaffected from other men and all women.

At the same time there was an overall reduction in other modes of men's play. It was as if the messages of those play practices had found a steadier state of expression in the game. This rendered those other play practices more superfluous. Although this is at best a correlation between forms of practice from which I am inferring meaning, it does suggest strongly that play was significant for these men. They did not do play for the sake of folly (although folly was integral to the identities they took on through play). They communicated with one another through play, especially through the game, about their predicaments. And they believed that they could not do so baldly and openly without jeopardizing their employment and livelihood.

The game was invented and refined by men who were friends, whose interaction with one another was characterized by mutuality, reciprocity, and equality. Within the frame of the game the men held to these attributes, and so they sustained its practice through time. Indeed, the reciprocal redistribution of roles through the taking of turns, and the sharing of the identity of 'donkey' both point to the cooperative tenor of the game. Apparently the game only made sense within the workplace, for it was not practiced elsewhere. Its cachet was restricted to these men, to their relationships, to their predicaments.[4]

Within the game, players cooperated to accomplish anticipation and release. Transferrers often chose times and contexts that were fun for the players. By doing transfers they linked not only themselves and their victims but all the players who practiced this unity that otherwise was absent from their workshop lives. Moreover, the very manner in which transfers were made seemed to symbolize the hazards of male sociability in the front room. The exaggerated stealth and caution of stalking the victim, the suddenness of surprise in discovering the tail, paralleled the precarious course that these men steered between superiors and backroom women in order to practice their friendship. But instead of being surprised and admonished by superiors in the routine course of shop experience, through play they were reminded of whom and what they were by sympathetic, kindred spirits.

Although the practice of consensus might be accomplished more loosely through other modes of sociable interaction, it was integral to the game. The victim cooperated by behaving as if all was ordinary while the tail was hung, and for as long as he wore it. Others cooperated to sustain anticipation and tension until the tail was discovered. Once a transfer was done, control of the round passed to the victim. Although labeled donkey, others became dependent on him for release. This points again to the symmetry of the game. So long as the transferrer controlled the round, anticipation and tension were lower. His control during this phase was matched by the lesser dependence of others. While the tail actually was hung, joint coordination and finesse often were required of the transferrer, the victim, and others in order to exchange game roles and identities. Here dependency was more symmetrical. Once the target became the victim, all were dependent on him for their fun, and this balanced his labeled condition.

The interdependence of the players also was highlighted by contexts of play. Doing a transfer with superiors present was riskier. They knew nothing of the game, and saw it only as the sort of raucous horseplay they deplored. The choice of playing in these contexts lay with the transferrer. The fun would be greater, but so was the threat of humiliation. If he played, this obligated his victim to cooperate. In these conditions, joking could be stopped, a prank aborted. But the game obligated players to share the entailed risks. Here play likely strengthened interpersonal bonds in the sense that Huizinga (1970: 31) intended: 'the feeling of being "apart together" in an exceptional situation, of sharing something important, of mutually withdrawing from the rest of the world and rejecting the usual norms, retains its magic beyond the duration of the individual game'.

Since the game was played as well in the back room, the cooperation (or at least the disinterest) of the women was needed so as not to destroy a round before the victim revealed himself. In fact, the women did behave as a proper audience and seemed to enjoy the game. This may have raised the value of the game for the play group. The women were excluded, yet they paid attention and followed convention. Thus the game was legitimated by those persons central to the reality of work, but here relegated to the periphery and rendered more passive.

Yet for all this the game probably buttressed that serious reality in which those who identified with work were valued. In other words, the experience of the women watching the game may have been quite different from that of the men who played. The revelations of male identity in the game were quite congruent with how the women perceived the character of these men through the dominant reality of work. For the women these men were indeed donkeys most of the time. By supporting the game the women saw performed before them the weaknesses of its players. But more than this, they saw these players admitting to their flaws (as they did not do otherwise), thereby validating the inferior status they were accorded by superiors and by the women themselves. Here the very dominance of the players in the make-believe of the game reproduced their inferiority in its absence.

For its players the game evoked that which Goffman (1961: 108) called 'role distance': how persons constitute and express the distance between their perception of their selves and how their formal roles would have them. Goffman (1961: 113–4) added that, 'Situated roles that place an individual in an occupational setting he feels is beneath him are bound to give rise to much role distance'. Through the game the players distanced their selves from the subordination and depreciation that their roles entailed, and so reasserted their rightful place in the moral order of their lives.

The sign of the tail requires further discussion here. Its connection to animal anatomy is obvious. Less forthright yet suggestive are its connotations of an obverse potency. The epithet of 'donkey' was common in workshop talk. Its usage usually connoted dumbness and stubborness – qualities of the proverbial beast of burden transposed to humans. In part, the origins of the game may have derived from jokes about the unnatural births of the men as offspring of donkeys – perhaps to their 'rebirth' as dumb, ill-used beasts of burden. The remaking of the human is evident also in the joking byplay between Shlomo and Zackaria, described earlier. Yet in these men there was an absence of that potency associated with the animalistic. In that earlier byplay, Zackaria likens Shlomo's penis to a donkey's tail. But this is an emasculated Shlomo, his penis taken to make that tail – a penis worn on the hindquarters, pointing backward. In other words, an obverse penis, limp, ineffective, impotent. Is it surprising that Shlomo's device, which he usually hung on the back, came to be called a tail?

Looked at this way, the sign of the tail condenses the entire tale of social and psychic emasculation that these men, from their perspective, experienced in the shop (and prior to this). Potentially (and retrospectively, in their self-imagery) these men were powerful and potent in their male animalism. In actuality they were futile and impotent. The sign of the tail looked both ways – to what these men should have been in their own estimation, and to what they were. So too, the game itself, an elaboration of the condensed sign and a metaphor for the life of these men in the workplace. Thus the tail was a powerful trope, a device of passage that turned one reality into another, yet that lost neither the triumph of futility nor the futility of triumph, and so enabled the simultaneous experiencing of both.

Therefore there is a juxtaposition of messages in the game, through which the routine and the extraordinary contrast, yet acquire attributes of one another that thereby inform experience with an integration that contains its own negation. For ordinary life and play are both serious and absurd, and the condition of one informs the other. The players saw themselves as helpless and hapless persons controlled by hierarchy and authority. These experiences they found absurd. They did not want to be in the shop, needed to remain there, and had no way to conjoin these sentiments except through play. As their life-situations were absurd, so their play was serious commentary; but as their play was by definition unserious, that they played as they did was a commentary on the seriousness of their life-situations.[5]

Intersections

My doctoral work in social anthropology was done in the late 1960s at the University of Manchester, under the direction of Max Gluckman. The reanalysis of the ethnographies of others was a hallmark of study at Manchester, of learning to think as an anthropologist. Gluckman's view was that there was something of value in most work, and so the purpose of critical analysis was constructive, not destructive – a position that I took to heart (in principle, at least) early on. Although Manchester insisted on specialization in an ethnographic area, the Mancunian style also encouraged the critical reading of ethnographies outside one's own particular area of research. This style demanded a close, often excruciating attention to ethnographic detail, and an appreciation of the significance, if not the meaning, of the most mundane of social intricacies. As I learned later on, this was a style of study well-suited to the interpretation of public occasions.

Reanalysis is a peculiar genre in a discipline that gives pride of place to the firsthand collection of information through fieldwork. At least twice-removed from that interface we so often call the 'field' (with its connotations of a distant, wild, natural habitat to be tamed through disciplined study), reanalysis is necessarily dependent upon the frailties and faculties of the field ethnographer. To be engaging a reanalysis requires especially an act of imagination that in my view is somewhat akin to the idea of parallel worlds in science-fiction. In other words, the world of reanalysis accepts that of the 'original' in most respects, yet puts this together as a different version to bring out something latent or implicit in the original – just as the latter likely is at best (and frequently for the best) a version of 'what actually happened' in the field. Thus reanalysis refuses to privilege the authority of the ethnographer. Ethnographers are the authors of their own works, not of the peoples they inscribe. Yet it is not clear to whom reanalysis owes its faithfulness, its craft, in the first instance – to the ethnography that gave it birth, or to the natives that enabled both to exist at all.

Banana Time was one of the first reanalyses I attempted. The shortest case study of this volume, it was the most difficult to formulate. Donald

Roy's (1959–60) brief ethnography of the antics of three workers, often cited but little discussed, seemed to have much resonance with my observations of the donkey game. I was convinced there was more method to the doings of his protagonists than he made of these. But for a lengthy period I could not get a handle on this. One day, quite abruptly and unexpectedly, there was pattern within passion – a moment of the comic-strip bulb lighting up inside my head. For that experience alone I am fond of 'banana time'.

Over a decade later, while rewriting portions for this book, I realize that this little piece owed much to my Manchester experience, and that it was crucial to the formulation of certain ideas I've used ever since. Among these is that of the reproductive interplay between 'integration' and 'conflict', which appears in somewhat different guises also in chapters 6 and 7. More generally, banana time taught me that the 'ritualization' of behavior could have a much more powerful impetus than that of mere formalization and customary repetition – just as the donkey game showed that play should not be relegated casually to the garbage-can category of 'expressive behavior'. I also am indebted to the late Donald Roy for the grace and helpfulness with which he responded to my rereading of his materials.

5 Banana time

Roy's ethnography recounts the commensality, fighting, and play among three middle-aged naturalized Americans in a small workplace. His primary aim was to discuss how industrial workers managed the tedium of their work roles, and their alienation from the means of production, through 'expressive' activities that enabled them to gain some sense of control over their fates in such places.

The activities Roy discussed emerged tacitly from interaction among the protagonists, who neither discussed nor negotiated their practices. Nonetheless, these activities were repeated daily, in the same serial order. Now one could argue that such an arrangement was predicated on the invention of custom, that was implemented daily in somewhat mechanistic fashion. But I will suggest that the organization of this sequence of activities contained its own power of reproduction. This dynamic, one that I will call dialectical, enabled the sequence of activities in the workplace to be reproduced on a daily basis. This logic is more complex than that of the donkey game. The donkey game played the interstices of social order, opening apertures to a momentary alternative reality that subverted work, but a reality constituted through Western assumptions of the make-believe, and so of the inauthentic. The uncertainty introduced by the make-believe was controlled by its game form, whose predication on pretense thereby negated its own substance.

The activities discussed in this chapter were put together otherwise. These spanned the entire working day, the daily period that the protagonists spent together. As I will indicate, the protagonists reinvented the working day as an integrative framework of sociability, within which they worked, argued, and fought. Still, the very complexity and interdependence of the activities that constituted this framework made it less flexible and more fragile in response to crises than that of the donkey game.

First I will recapitulate the salient features of Roy's description, and then consider how these may be treated as a synthetic framework for action that reproduced itself through time.

'Times' and 'themes' in the workplace

George, Ike, and Sammy, the three protagonists, worked in a room closed off from the rest of the plant. One door, usually shut, led to a storage room. They had few contacts with other workers or with management. Their lengthy working days were spent operating punch presses that cut out various patterns in leather and plastic, using steel dies of various shapes that were changed by hand. The following is Roy's (1959–60: 160) description of work in the room:

This was standing all day in one spot beside three old codgers in a dingy room looking out through barred windows at the bare walls of a brick warehouse, leg movements largely restricted to the shifting of body weight from one foot to the other, hand and arm movements confined, for the most part, to a simple repetitive sequence . . . and the intellectual activity reduced to computing the hours to quitting time.

But Roy noticed that the three engaged in a series of activities that were repeated daily and enjoyed greatly. These 'times', as Roy called them, are the focus of reanalysis here. The following 'times' were discernible in the interaction of the three.

1   Coffee time: George and Ike came to work before Sammy. The two shared a pot of coffee brewed on George's hot plate.
2   Peach time: When Sammy arrived he announced 'peach time'. He then produced two peaches that he divided into equal portions among the three workers. Ike complained about the quality of the fruit; and this led to banter and joking between the two.
3   Banana time: Sammy always brought a banana in his lunch pail. After peach time, Ike stole the banana, crying 'banana time', and gulped down the fruit. Sammy protested, denouncing Ike; while George remonstrated with Ike, yet scolded Sammy for the fuss he made.
4   Window time: Sammy continued to criticize Ike's character in an echolalic fashion, until Ike retaliated by opening wide the window facing Sammy, letting cold air engulf the latter. During the prologue to the opening of the window, Ike would threaten and feint. In return Sammy protested, argued, and claimed he would catch cold. Finally he closed the window. George encouraged Ike, declaring that fresh air was healthy, and chided Sammy for not appreciating Ike's consideration.
5   Lunch time: Prior to the lunch break Ike tampered with George's alarm clock (that kept the work schedule) by setting it ahead by a

few minutes so that they could eat earlier. George always discovered this and berated Ike.

6   Pick-up time: Every afternoon another worker came to collect the punched out patterns. He scoffed at the output produced by the three, while they deprecated his easy job. Usually the three related their antics of the day to the visitor. George and Ike often belittled Sammy, while Ike joked at George's expense.

7   Fish time: During the afternoon George and Ike took a break to eat pickled fish that Ike provided.

8   Coke time: In the late afternoon the three took turns making the trip to the fourth floor vending machine to buy drinks for one another. The hours ending the working day were staggered: Sammy left first, followed by Ike, and then George.

Throughout the working day, interspersed between 'times', the three engaged in what Roy called 'themes': acts of kidding, joking, prank, and horseplay. Unlike 'times', 'themes' had no particular order, although their form often was repeated. So, whenever Sammy went to get a drink of water, or to the toilet, his machine was switched off. Invariably, on returning, he fell into the trap of behaving as if his machine were in operation. Or, striking a worker over the head with a paper sack would set off exchanges of slaps, laughter, and echolalic utterances, like those of Sammy: 'Ike is a bad man, a very bad man! George is a good daddy, a very fine man!' At other points Ike would repeat snatches of doggerel, like: 'Mama on the bed, papa on the floor, baby in the crib says giver some more!' And together the three returned to choruses like: 'Are you man or mouse? I ask you, are you man or mouse?'

Roy concluded that the organization of 'times' constituted an 'interactional frame' (1959–60: 163); that the activities of this frame 'represented a distinctive subculture', and that, 'Tensions born of long hours of relatively meaningless work were released in the mock aggression of horseplay.'

It is indeed to Roy's credit that he recognized that these activities were patterned through time, and this no doubt bears on problems of tedium and alienation from work with which he was concerned. But the power of his material is enhanced if one looks more closely for the dynamic that enabled, indeed encouraged, the reproduction of these activities on a daily basis. However the sequence of 'times' was invented (and we are not told how), it was followed quite faithfully. This suggests that this sequence was at least systematic in its logic of organization, for it was constituted through both the certainty of consensus and the uncertainty of conflict.

The integration of 'times' and 'themes'

Some anthropological studies of 'ritual' point out that when conflict is expressed within occasions that stand for the highest affirmation of moral order (for example, the legitimation bestowed by the sacred), the very practice of dissent is itself a restatement of the value of the order that permits its expression (see Gluckman 1954). In such instances the practice of disharmony often is not an attempt to alter the basic morphology of the social order. Instead, the sacred is the strongest societal vessel within which to demonstrate cleavage and contain conflict. The highest affirmation of order thus encourages and yet controls the most elementary expressions of its dissolution – thereby reaffirming once more the moral worth of this ordering. In this way, structure generates its antitheses that in turn reproduce and reintegrate the set-up. This constitutes a dialectic that energizes the continuity of moral order.

This idea of dialectic, returned to further on, is that of what I call 'encapsulation'. It differs radically from classic ideas of dialectic – of thesis, antithesis, synthesis – that are both processual and productive, and therefore constitutive of new social forms. The dialectics of encapsulation are those of process that is reproductive of social order. Encapsulation is itself predicated on the assumption that certain kinds of activity (including a good deal of that which is termed 'ritual') exists within the confines of cultural rubrics or frames that constitute, existentially, a different 'logical type' of experience (see Bateson 1972: 189). As a different logical type, the frame that encloses these activities specifies that they are not to be experienced and evaluated according to criteria that guide interpretations of other sorts of activity. However the major lesson of the analogy of the 'ritual' frame for secular, framed occasions is the possibility of the encapsulation of opposition within the confines of integration, such that conflict is shown in a manner that 'tests' successfully the strength and viability of that integration. This has a direct bearing on the organization of 'times' described by Roy.

These 'times' were of two forms, that may be called respectively, consensual and oppositional. Their serial ordering located times of conflict within an overarching frame of integrative, consensual relations between the workers. The opening of the working day began with 'coffee time', a commensal and consensual occasion that marked the onset of interaction between George and Ike. They partook in the sharing of drink, brewed on George's hot plate. This occasion of solidarity roughly paralleled the beginning of a day of work that was predicated on solitary activity. Although the solitariness of the work routine rendered irrelevant any sense of mutuality, coffee time initiated the integrative frame of action and experience that reiterated daily the cohesiveness of social bonds. Thus the condition of existing as a 'person alone' among other solitary beings was counter-balanced by one of existential unity within which personal identities were appreciated.

On Sammy's entry, he initiated 'peach time', providing two peaches that were shared among the three. So Sammy entered the integrative frame through the sharing of sustenance. One may speculate that the invariable division of two peaches among three persons required especial attention to the minutiae of sharing in order to attain an equitable distribution; and that this again emphasized bonds of mutuality. Ike's decrying the quality of the fruit led to banter among the protagonists, but this already occurred within the integrative frame, and so did not alter the initial definition of cohesiveness that guided the subsequent actions of these workers.

The working day ended for the three with two other occasions of mutuality and solidarity. During 'fish time' George and Ike together shared food that the latter provided. Later, during 'coke time', the three shared turns buying drinks for one another. According to Roy's description the relationship between George and Ike was stronger than their relationships with Sammy. So Ike reciprocated for the use of George's hot plate during 'coffee time' by providing their sustenance for 'fish time'. But it is most important to note that once Sammy entered the workplace all three engaged in 'peach time', and that they ended the serial ordering of times with the reciprocity of 'coke time'. Thus coffee time, peach time, fish time, and coke time constituted the frame of integrative occasions that bracketed the onset and end of the working day. All other activities during the working day, including those of production, were contained within the comradeship of this integrative frame.

Within this frame of integrative times the protagonists practiced their times of opposition: banana time, window time, lunch time, and pick-up time. These times communicated disharmony and conflict in social relationships (to wit: theft, quarrel, disparagement). Put differently, these times communicated dissatisfactions with the tedium of work and its arousal of sentiments of alienation, but with one important proviso. Times of opposition existed not only within a frame of integrative times (a reality that here also subsumed that of the individuation and solitariness of work) but also within a subframe of play that was intimately keyed to the integrative frame.

Keeping in mind Bateson's formulation of the make-believe in the message, 'this is play', discussed in chapter 3, within this workplace the signs of play were those that signalled the onset of times of opposition. In this usage, play also communicates that its doing is not to be interpreted according to serious criteria. Thus its substance of antagonism in the workplace was discounted by the protagonists, without setting aside the enjoyment experienced through participation. Play in this workplace constituted a further extension of the frame of integrative times that controlled, in serial fashion, the times of opposition that occurred between integrative times. The frame of integrative times included an 'inner lining' of integration, as it were, constituted through play that leached occasions of opposition of their ferocity, yet without blocking the pointedness of their messages (see Handelman 1977b).

I suggest that the following formulation of occasions in this workplace is more comprehensive and dynamic than that given by Roy, for it indicates that these people reinvented their working day as a systematic (and perhaps systemic) form of organization that enabled the routine reproduction both of sociability and of controlled conflict. An experiential frame of integrative times established the master context of reciprocity, mutuality, and solidarity for interaction in the workplace. This integrative frame provided information as to how opposition and conflict were to be practiced. The messages of this subframe took the form of play, and so supported the integrative frame by discounting the seriousness of times of opposition while enabling the expression of conflict. That the integrative frame could be sustained in the face of conflict signified its overarching value for the protagonists, and strengthened their mutual solidarity.

I would argue further that the great value placed on solidarity encouraged the expression of conflict in counterpoint to, but contained within the overarching integrity and strength of the integrative frame. Yet, since the practice of times was an emergent formation in the workplace, the protagonists also fashioned a safety valve for the expression of conflict by doing it in terms of play, which constituted an ongoing articulation between integrative times and their serial guidance of times of opposition. Thus the unity of the workplace was predicated upon an encapsulated dialectic, of opposition within integration. This dynamic reproduced the daily round of activities.

My interpretation of the ordering of times is supported by the pattern of reintegration that these activities took, after the disintegration of relationships that Roy called 'black friday' (1959–60: 165–6). While Sammy was on vacation, relations between George and Ike collapsed after Ike, in introducing a new joking theme, grated a sensitive aspect of George's workplace identity. The organization of times and themes broke down completely for thirteen days. During this period all utterances and actions were interpreted strictly in terms of the individuating and alienating context of work. When reconciliation was achieved it took the following sequence. (1) George and Ike again ate fish together one afternoon. (2) Later that same day Ike and Sammy began to play together, and Ike burst into song. (3) This was followed by a return to times of conflict, as other elements of integration and opposition were reintroduced during the next few days. In other words, through the sharing of sustenance the protagonists first resurrected a portion of the integrative frame of times. Then, within this context they began to recreate the subframe of play. And then they returned to times of conflict.

This resurrection reproduced the hierarchy of relevance of the elements of the integrative frame, as this had existed prior to 'black friday'. It shows clearly how important it was that the protagonists contain opposition within integration. Although they returned only in part to the exact kinds of times that had existed before the collapse, these did include at least one new 'time' of opposition that communicated Ike's atonement for his black friday gaffe. This 'rush to the window' seemed to replace 'window time', and Roy (1959–60: 166) describes it as follows: 'Ike broke wind, and put his head in his hand on the block as Sammy grabbed a rod and made a mock rush to open the window. He beat Ike on the head, and George threw some water on him, playfully'. Thus the resurrected, integrative frame proved sufficiently resilient to incorporate messages that responded to changing conditions, in this instance the moral opprobrium that attached to one who had damaged the shared mutuality of the frame.

One further problem should be explicated. Earlier I implied that the practice of work was constituted through a logical type of behavior different from that which permitted times and themes. Therefore work should have precluded the practice of the latter, whose implementation would subvert work activity. Given the coexistence of work and times in this workplace, how did the protagonists accomplish the passage from one context to the other, when ideally these alternatives excluded each other?

Some scholars of transition suggest searching for modes of organization that denote detachment from one sort of context to deposit protagonists on the threshold of another (see Turner 1969: 94–6). So Kapferer's (1983) analysis of shifts between phases in Sinhalese exorcisms discusses how humor can awaken audience, and then patient, to alternative sets of meaning, the acceptance of which by participants enables the event to proceed to its successful conclusion. I suggest that the 'themes' Roy described did something similar within the workplace.

'Themes' were brief segments of action that occurred between 'times'. Although their form and substance were relatively consistent, their practice was spontaneous – they did not occur in any particular serial order, as did 'times'. So a serious discussion on the high cost of living suddenly could be turned into horseplay or prank; or a worker might begin to utter a string of 'oral autisms'. The practice of themes were thus temporary, somewhat idiosyncratic excursions into the experience of play; and each protagonist experimented in his own way, and to some extent at his own pace, with these leavetakings of the context of work.

The periods between times were filled, therefore, with short but ongoing alterations of reality that did not correspond exactly to the form and substance of times, but that did constitute transitions to a similar logical type. This would mean that each phased shift from work to times was not an abrupt transition; for such passage was preceded by actions that simulated this transition, and so prepared protagonists for these experiential shifts. Themes interspersed among serious actions held the protagonists perpetually on the edge of shifts in context – since none could predict when one of their number, unannounced, would make this transition.

In this workplace, themes performed the vital function of existentially preparing the protagonists to perceive work as one kind of arbitrary context that could be penetrated with an act of will (see Douglas 1968: 370). And so themes, as flexible, social experiences of passage, prepared the way to the more coherent alternatives of times of integration and opposition.

That the reorganization of the working day into one of 'times' constituted a radical change in quality of experience is evident too in its consequences for lived time. Roy gives no information on workplace experience before 'times' were invented, apart from stressing its tedious and alienating sameness. Still it is fair to assume that, before the creation of times, workplace periodicity was dominated by moments and durations (minutes, hours, etc.) that were reckoned in terms of work and production. This rhythm of time was largely monotemporal. Workers punched out and counted units of piecework that were equivalent in value to one another, as were the units of time through which this was done. Temporality and production had an analogous rhythm of being, one of even and similar intervals rather than peaks. Monotone and monotime – the absence of differences in value, in both the acts of work and their temporal ordering, may well have signified the absence of value itself in this kind of existence.

The invention of the sequence of 'times' radically and comprehensively changed the temporal ordering of the working day. The experiential frame of times was also a temporal matrix, one of highs and lows, certainties and uncertainties, and inclusive of just about everything that happened in the workplace on a daily basis. Moreover, different values were associated with integrative times and with those of opposition. These workers had created a hierarchy of values keyed to the new temporal rhythm of the workplace, one that nullified the solitariness and alienation of work without subverting the act of production (that would have endangered their jobs).

The viability of this framework of 'times' depended on its capacity to reproduce itself through time. In my interpretation this reproductive capacity depended on a dynamic of dialectics. As I noted, classical dialectics are open-ended and generative of form. Simply put, the idea of thesis contains the seeds of its own obviation, of anti-thesis. The development of antithesis produces a synthesis that is itself different from both thesis and antithesis. The major theoretical advantage of this sort of conceptualization is that the impetus for change is located in the very centricity and stability of social form, changing this from within, as it were.

The interpretation of this chapter points to an obverse process through which social order is reproduced – the dynamic I called the dialectic of encapsulation. This momentum of conservation is especially suitable to numerous occasions that are called 'ritual', and to the 'ritualization' of behavior. The particular advantage of this dynamic is that it depends necessarily on the idea of opposition to established, normative order. But it is the very uncertainty carried by such conflict that is reproductive of this order. This formulation is indebted to Max Gluckman's (1954) concept of 'rituals of rebellion'. In terms of chapter 2, the dynamic of encapsulation is relevant to events of modelling and re-presentation. In line with the thinking of that chapter, the effectiveness of this dynamic for the reproduction of an event would depend on how well uncertainty is controlled.

The dialectic of encapsulation depends on a delineation of hierarchy, such that the idea of 'thesis' can be identified with higher-order values, and that of 'antithesis' with lower-order ones that are in opposition to the former. Therefore the actions identified with higher-order values may be said to encapsulate or to encompass the uncertainty expressed through those of lower order – in the case of banana time, the encapsulation of times of opposition within the frame of integrative times. Thus lower-order values reaffirm those of higher order, and synthesis is analogous here to the revalidation of the status quo. Each practice of this kind of event is in a way a 'test' of the viability of its higher-order premises. In turn, the reaffirmation of these premises once more encourages the practice of opposition to their validity. Dissension and validation are both integral to this dynamic of encapsulation and to its ongoing reproduction.

In terms of the workplace of this chapter, integrative times were of a higher order than those of opposition. The practice of times of conflict did not destroy this integrative frame, but was contained by it. This control of conflict revalidated the viability of this frame, and so of the values that constituted it. In turn, the tested frame encouraged opposition to itself, thereby enabling the expression of dissension and conflict – but this generated once more the hierarchical superiority of integration over opposition. In this way, through its own implicit logic, the entire set-up reproduced itself day after day.

3   Public events

Intersections

Works, like this chapter and chapter 10, sometimes get written through the confluence of coincidence. In 1977–8 my wife and I spent an enjoyable sabbatical year at the University of Pittsburgh, and visited good friends, Davydd and Pilar Greenwood at Cornell University. I love looking through books and bookstores. In Israel, academic books are scarce and expensive. Davydd took me to the university bookstore, and there reduced to half-price was *La Terra in Piazza*, a study of the Palio of Siena, a monograph I had not known on a public event I hadn't heard of. Old friends and a new book. I was elated, and took to the Palio even before reading the monograph. The following year I was invited to a conference sponsored by the Center for Medieval and Renaissance Studies at UCLA, and thought the Palio an apt subject. A reanalysis of the Palio duly emerged.

In working on the Palio materials the relevance of modelling to public events occurred to me. Much later it became the cornerstone of the typology of chapter 2. In this present version of the reanalysis I treat the Palio more explicitly as an event of modelling the world. It may or may not be something like this. More importantly, it likely is an occasion that revolves around relationships between a whole and its parts, such that, simultaneously, a social entity can be taken apart yet held together. The relevance of this for events of modelling and re-presentation is clear. I am indebted to Terry Evens, a warm friend since our Manchester days, who some years ago pointed out to me the relevance for the Palio of the part/ whole relationship. At that time I hadn't the wits to see its significance.

6   The Palio of Siena

In chapter 2, I suggested that major public occasions of the modern world tended strongly to be organized through a logic of presentation and sometimes of re-presentation. Altogether, a systemic logic of modelling with its capacities for transformation is rarely a hallmark of these occasions. However there is one well-known case in the contemporary ethnography of the West that may usefully be rethought in terms of its model of urban rejuvenation. This is the Palio festival of the *comune* of Siena in Central Italy. My phrasing above is hesitant, since there are fierce differences of opinion over the ethnography of Dundes and Falassi on which I rely, and I refer to some of these in endnotes.

In existence continuously since the seventeenth century, this festival, as it is called, has been treated by popular commentators as an unusual horse race, preceded by an elaborate historical parade. Some scholars have argued that it continues cultural patterns of medieval Siena, and is a metaphor for a particular Sienese view of the world (Dundes and Falassi 1975). Others have argued that it reconstructs the past glory of Siena, and reinforces the existence of the ward, the *contrada*, as a viable entity in the Sienese world (Logan 1978). Sydel Silverman (1979, 1981) is adamant that, far from being a medieval survival, the forging of links between palio and *contrada* by the Florentine conquerors of Siena elevated allegiance to the *contrada* at the expense of the *comune* and stunted the development of more broadly-based interest groups, whether those of patriotism or of social class. Through the politics of divide and rule the Palio mystifies economic and political realities. However all commentators agree on the centrality of the Palio festival in Sienese life.

I will argue that regardless of their historical origins the occasions of the Palio are constituted as a model that transforms the *comune* by taking it apart and putting it back together – thereby yearly regenerating the *comune* as a holistic urban entity.[1] The logic I discern in the festival is one that can neither be traced directly to medieval remnants, nor to a peculiarly Sienese world view. In accordance with this position the festival is not simply an event of *contrade*, but one in which the place of the *comune* should be given much more attention. Other discussions treat the role of the *comune* in the festival as an epiphenomenon, and stress that of the *contrade* above all else. I will return to this uncritical acceptance of *contrada* rhetoric and ideology in the last section of this chapter.

Through its festival the *comune* can 'totalise the consciousness it has of itself' (Pierssens 1972: 10). Through its modelling of the everyday the festival can act on the *comune* in controlled and predictive ways. Twice yearly a particular configuration of the *comune* is passed through the Palio model to have its viability tested, and so to be regenerated in the process. This cannot be done through the everyday social order of Siena.

The self-testing by social entities of their own viability and validity is often overlooked but should not be disregarded. Qualities of coherence may be well-known, yet neither self-evident nor static, and thus require the repetitive experience of being so. That which I call 'testing' is then a function of social reproduction, but one whose outcome is controlled and therefore predictive. Testing depends on the introduction into social order of predicated uncertainty that puts the validity and viability of that order to the question, but that has the regularized means to resolve its own contradictions and oppositions.

The next section discusses the two most prominent secular components of the festival model – the respective levels of 'city' and '*contrada*'. Next I turn to the model's most prominent religious figure, the Madonna in whose honor the races are run, and her spiritual and 'earthy' aspects. The third section addresses how the *comune* is broken down through the model, through the distancing of Virgin and city from the lower, earthy level of *contrada*, and how nonetheless these levels remain articulated through the figure of the racing horse. The fourth section pursues these themes through the sequencing of occasions within the festival, as the framing of disorder within order. The fifth discusses the reconstruction of the urban entity through the parade and race, as aspects of the Madonna, and city and *contrade*, are put back together in proper relationships of scale and quality. The sixth addresses issues raised by this analysis.

Comune, city, *contrada*

The social structure of the everyday *comune* is composed of a multitude of different subsystems and social units, and of relationships of different scale, complexity, and quality. Patterns of stratification, economic infrastructures, religious institutions, occupational structures, political parties, trade unionism, ties of patronage and brokerage, parishes, and *contrade*, cleave, compete, cooperate and overlap with each other in myriad ways. Many of these connections clearly do not cease at the boundaries of the *comune*, but pass through to link Siena inextricably to the economic and political life of region and nation-state. In this picture of social structure there are no inherent or inbuilt limitations on political and economic competition, on social inequality and mobility, or on degrees of machination and maneuvering – except as 'statistical' products of numerous additive and countervailing forces whose outcomes are shifting and comparatively indeterminate.

Looked at on the ground, so to speak, Siena is divided into seventeen *contrade*. In the metaphoric centre of the *comune* is the piazza of the Campo, around which or nearby are grouped some of the major institutions of the *comune*: the city hall, the soaring bell-tower, the archbishopric, major churches, hospitals, and so forth.[2] In terms of the visual impact of spatial organization, the conjunction of tower and Campo is striking and suggestive. The Campo is shaped like a shell, a concave bowl sloping downhill, its focal point adjacent to the tower. In the middle of the Campo is a fountain dedicated to the Madonna, the Virgin Mother, who is the patroness of the *comune* (Dundes and Falassi 1975: 231).[3]

Among the prominent components of everyday Sienese life is the ward, or *contrada*. Nonetheless it is but one among many that together constitute the substance of mundane living. However the *contrada* is a corporate group with membership mainly through birth, with preferred endogamy, owning property in common, and operating as a mutual-aid society and social club (Dundes and Falassi 1975: 2). Each *contrada* has its own government, elected officials, symbols, patron saint, church and priest (see Falassi and Catoni 1983: 27–8). Of especial importance, each *contrada* has its own demarcated territory.

The administrative offices of the *contrada* are occupied by adult men. Hypothetically these may be filled by women but, like those of the *comune* administration, this happens rarely. These offices are contrasted with those, like that of the capitano, whose task it is to win the Palio race. In comparison to all of these secular officials who are answerable to their *contrada*, church and priest, although integrally identified with their *contrada*, owe allegiance to the archbishopric of the *comune* (Dundes and Falassi 1975: 33–5).

Grading by age and sex is important in the *contrada*. The age grade of the Little Ones' Group includes all children up to the age of twelve; and they celebrate holidays together. The adolescents compose the Young Peoples' Group, with its own officials and activities. At the adult level there is a Women's Group, but no parallel organization of adult males. Thus as adolescents mature, females are relegated to their own less prominent group, as were the peripheral children and youths, while adult males 'are the contrada, in the sense of being the locus of its power and authority'

(Logan 1978: 49). Like the *commune*, the *contrada* is identified primarily as a male domain.

Although its members are divided by class, politics, sex and age, the *contrada* is a major focus of sentiments of solidarity; while there is opposition among *contrade* in daily life, when this kind of contrast is made relevant (Dundes and Falassi 1975: 21, 26). Each *contrada* considers itself an 'independent republic or state' (Logan 1978: 49), or 'a city within the city' (Dundes and Falassi 1975: 46).[4] Some *contrade* are formally 'twinned' with other cities and towns (Falassi and Catoni 1983: 28).

There are three important points in this description. First, each *contrada* is theoretically equivalent in scale and quality to every other *contrada* (although in practice they differ in size of territory and population, and in economic strength). Second, each *contrada* is the *comune* in miniature – for it duplicates or parallels major secular and religious institutions of the *comune* on a small scale. Third, together the *contrade* ideally encompass the territory of the entire *comune*, apart from its central piazzas and institutions. These points will become relevant in discussing the palio model.

In daily life the *comune* is a complex entity within which the *contrada* exists as one kind of social unit and as one basis for affiliation. But in the Palio model the *contrade* rise from within the complex order of the *comune*, like a territorial and social grid that radically simplifies, reorganizes, and circumscribes the overall urban entity – erasing, cross-cutting, or obfuscating other distinctions, cleavages, boundaries, and forms of cooperation so important to the order of daily life.[5] This shift is from the *comune* as a product of factors of different scale, quality, and complexity (one of organic solidarity, in Durkheim's terms), to a closed model of the urban entity that, in its secular domain, is composed of the following features. A core of municipal institutions that regulate the secular domain of the festival, and that I will call the 'city' (to distinguish it from the everyday, complex *comune*). Equivalent segments that replicate one another and that I continue to call *contrade*. And a high degree of replicability of institutions between the higher level of city and the lower one of *contrada*. Quite unlike everyday Siena, this version of social structure is organized along lines similar to those of segmentary opposition, of fission and fusion, in a relationship of parts to a whole (that is akin to what Durkheim called mechanical solidarity). On the one hand this enables the spatial and social composition of the modelled *comune* to be taken apart along predetermined axes. On the other it suggests that within this model each *contrada*, each segment or part, can come to behave as if it were the urban entity – as if its boundaries can expand momentarily to correspond to those of the city. Within this model, opposition and conflict and their outcome are predetermined and controlled, in contrast to the indeterminacy of the everyday.

The advantage of eliciting the Palio as a model is that the operations of its dynamism may be specified or hypothesized. The Sienese Palio is unlike so many other public events summarized under the rubric of 'festival', that in their logic of design are more akin to occasions of re-presentation, or even of presentation. The Palio also is unlike many other Italian festivals that are based on competition between named groups or categories, territorial or otherwise.[6] For the Palio accomplishes the reproduction of social order through the predicated and controlled transformation of conditions of uncertainty.

The Madonna

The second major domain of the Palio model is that of the sacred. At numerous junctures in its history the *comune* has been dedicated to the Madonna – the spiritual Virgin Mother – to whom its population turned for intercession and protection. For Sienese she is the patroness of the *comune*. Her relationship to the Campo is evinced in spatial terms. For example, there is a popular belief that the Campo is shaped in the form of a cloak that the Madonna is depicted as wearing in various paintings (Dundes and Falassi 1975: 203). The Palio race, held in the Campo, comes under her protection.

According to Dundes and Falassi, in Sienese folk perception and parlance the Madonna is not quite a homogeneous figure. At times she has somewhat ambiguous connotations. She is the Virgin, but also the Virgin Mother. The essence of purity, she also has latent connotations of bearing her child out of wedlock. Within her figure are subsumed attributes of dominant, virgin purity and of its inverse quality, a minor theme of profanity.[7] One may call these dual aspects spirituality and 'earthiness', and note that this dualism likely is more embedded in the perceptions of men than those of women (cf. Reuther 1977: 72). This dualism renders the Madonna a figure embued with the strength of eternity and the power of regeneration; and these aspects become clearer within the Palio model. With reference to the *comune*, the Madonna embodies an ambiguous female principle that is related to a solidary urban entity that, in turn, is thought of primarily as male.[8] While city and *contrada* replicate each other in mechanical fashion within the model, the virginal (or spiritual) and earthy aspects are transformative of one another. The relationship of Madonna to city is thus the articulation of a sacred principle, containing properties of continuity and generation, to a secular and mechanical version of social structure.[9] Through this articulation the analogue of the *comune* can be informed of itself reflexively, of its nature and composition, within the festival model of Siena.

The strength of the Virgin is in her purity, verity, and transformative potential. As intercessor she is at the service of men. The power of the earthy aspect is in the control of males. Separated, these aspects are respectively immaculate and chaotic. Combined, they are complementary and generative. Within the religious domain of the model the latent connotations of the Madonna separate out and are given expression through the behavior of *contrada*, while her spiritual aspect is articulated to the higher level of the city. At the same time, the city is separated from its *contrade*, while this relationship of distance between higher and lower levels of modelled social structure is mediated by the Madonna, who subsumes all of her own aspects. Given this mediation, the city and *contrada* levels of the secular domain are opened to the transformative capacities of renewal contained in the Madonna.

Dundes and Falassi argue that there is substantive etymological and connotative evidence in Sienese thought for the dualism of the Madonna. Each summer two Palio races are run. Each race cycle is independent of the other, and each celebrates a different representation of the Madonna: that of 16 August honors the Madonna of the Assumption, while that of 2 July the Madonna of Provenzano on the occasion of the Feast of the Visitation. The Feast of the Assumption venerates the Madonna as a universal Christian figure, the very embodiment of purity and holism. The Madonna of Provenzano is venerated as a local figure of intercession whose image (in the sixteenth century) was located in an area notorious for prostitution, and that was reputed to cure venereal disease (1975: 7–8). Note that each year in the modern Palio festivals, two representations of the Madonna are honored: one is the pan-Christian Virgin Mother of God, the *Theotokis*, while the second, particular to Siena, carries connotations of sacred powers amidst earthy excesses.[10]

The term 'palio' refers to the festival, to the horse race, and to the banner – painted with the image of the Madonna and the emblems of the competing *contrade* – that is presented to the victor.[11] Dundes and Falassi (1975: 198–202) argue that the palio banner is a female symbol. The term 'palio' may derive from the Latin *pallium*, which means 'cloak'. In ancient Rome this referred to the garment worn by prostitutes. The Madonna frequently was depicted wearing a cloak. '*Palio*' refers to a headcloth, and the Madonna at times was depicted wearing one. '*Pallio*' also refers to a cloth canopy, a baldequin, held over important personages. Such a silk cloth was thought to come from Babylon, called '*Baldacco*' in folk idiom, which also meant 'bordello'. Women who wore the '*pallio*' were called '*baldracche*', the plural form of '*baldracca*', an idiomatic term for harlot. In a complementary vein, the palio (as cloak, headcloth, or canopy) suggests a protective covering – and Siena sometimes is depicted as sheltering under the Madonna's cloak. In the iconography of the palio banner the painted image of the Madonna is given pride of place.

The dualistic connotations of the Madonna may be found also on the *contrada* level. So in Sienese slang the palio banner is called *'cencio'*, which means both 'rag' and 'faded woman'. These connotations are complementary to those of *'palio'* as *'pallium'*, the cloak of a prostitute, itself with connotations of the mantle of the Virgin. I will argue further on that each horse is the embodiment of its *contrada*. The saddle blanket worn by the horse during the parade is called *'gualdrappa'*, of which another meaning is a 'ragged slattern' (1975: 209). The saddle blanket as a protective covering would seem to complement the *palio/pallium* as cloak, headcloth, or canopy.[12]

I turn now to discuss the separation of levels of city and *contrada* – the taking-apart of the urban analogue of the *comune* through its festival model – and the unusual articulation of these distanced levels through the dualism of the Madonna.[13]

The *contrada* and the horse

Through the Palio model the grid of *contrade* rises to extreme prominence from its everyday, more submerged position, to take over the social and territorial space of the urban entity, to slice this entity from the wider regional and national contexts in which it is routinely embedded, to make the boundaries between Sienese and all others more exclusive, and temporarily to make over the social structure of the *comune*. Within the secular domain of the Palio model the grid of *contrade* can be said to constitute a lower level of social structure, while the city – the municipal organs of the *comune* – constitutes a higher one. Within this model the two tiers of the secular domain are kept separate, but through a relationship of parts to whole that accentuates their potential transposability.

However, on the lower tier the relationship between domains of the secular and the sacred is not that of potential transposability, but of the effacement of the boundaries that distinguish them. Moreover, the scale of each *contrada* is magnified in the direction of the attributes of the city, and each becomes an exaggeration of its everyday counterpart. In addition, each *contrada* puts forth an analogic extension, a metaphoric counterpart of its own dilation, in the form of the horse that becomes the embodiment of the segment it represents. The horse, an ambiguous figure according to Dundes and Falassi, has strong affinities to the Madonna. But, as I will indicate, its attributes are an inversion of the spiritual aspect of the Madonna. In this predicated, controlled, and predictive taking-apart of sacred and secular order, the Madonna retains her relationship of patron to the city, and dynamically articulates the city to the *contrada* through the horse. Then, through the race, the dualism of Madonna and horse is used to put back together the correct moral and social order of the entire urban entity.

In the days preceding the race each *contrada* becomes a dilated version of itself, one that stresses its opposition to other segments. The *contrada* closes its doors, incorporates more fully its less prominent members, and reinforces its solidarity. In part this is accomplished by degrees of role inversion. As mentioned earlier, the everyday *contrada* is dominated by adult males, while children, youth, and women have their own societies. But within festival time certain of the customary attributes of the latter categories are inverted, becoming more like those of the adult male. The *contrada* is 'masculinized'. Children and women become more aggressive towards rival *contrade*. Groups of teens and young men walk around the *comune* exchanging insults, and on occasion fisticuffs. Scuffles are prominent after the trial races that precede the Palio race. These fights rarely occur on that part of the track directly in front of the city hall (in space strongly identified with the level of the city), but erupt instead in locations associated more with *contrade* territories. This distanced neutrality of the level of the city in the face of dilated opposition on the level of the *contrade* is a theme to which I will return. The point here is that all such aggressive behavior usually is avoided, apart from the festival (Logan 1978: 54; Dundes and Falassi 1975: 43–4, 67).

Internal *contrada* solidarity peaks at a dinner for all its members the evening before the race. Before this dinner, wives belonging to *contrade* different from those of their husbands will return to their natal corporate groups until after the race. During the race itself, women are known to scare the horses, to knock jockeys from their mounts with handbags, and to return insults to their *contrada* with punch and kick. Logan (1978: 54) comments: 'They are as adamant as the men when it comes to asserting the nobility and force of their *contrada* and the inferiority and lowliness of their enemy *contrada*'.

Through these diverse behaviors the *contrada* closes rank, modifies status differences among its membership, and stresses its conflict with other parallel segments. Indeed it is commonly believed that only through a maximum of internal unity and strength will a *contrada* win (Logan 1978: 57). Through its self-maximization within the palio model each *contrada* dilates, becoming an aggrandizing force in relation to other segments, and in a highly predictable way the *contrade* together fragment the urban entity on its lower level of social structure. Each segment becomes more akin to a 'miniature city'.

Within this lower tier of the model, each *contrada* more fully incorporates its religious institutions, temporarily attenuating their fealty to the archbishopric. On this lower level, religious power is earthier, devoted emphatically to aiding the corporate group. As the secular *contrada* is distanced from the city, so the *contrada* church and priest are separated from their superiors. This opens the way to inversions of religious order on the lower tier, to the confounding of sacred and secular domains, without affecting their distinctiveness on the higher tier.

The patron saint of the *contrada* is expected to be devoted wholly to the fortunes of his segment in the race, and not to higher religious authority. Before the race a patron saint receives offerings of candles from *contrada* members. If he does not help his *contrada* in the contest he often is punished, typically by having his candles extinguished (Dundes and Falassi 1975: 89–90, 44). Logan (1978: 54) comments that, 'The saints are regarded as obligated to live up to their supporting roles as contrada patrons' (see also Heywood 1904: 241).

The confounding of sacred and secular domains within the *contrada* is most evident in the figure of the horse. Until a horse is assigned to a *contrada* it is simply an animal. Once assigned, the horse is said to be 'owned' by the *contrada* (Dundes and Falassi 1975: 147). Then it becomes a malleable vessel, to be embued with the image of the dilated *contrada*. The horse (and so its *contrada*) has affinity to the wilder, earthy aspect of the Madonna.

In almost all instances the horses are either mares or geldings. Both are thought of by Sienese as 'feminine' animals (Dundes and Falassi 1975: 199–200). This characterization of the mare is straightforward; while that of the gelding brings to mind a beast made more female. The horse is then a female representation of the masculine *contrada*, one that has an affinity to the earthy aspect of the Madonna, itself an inversion of the Virgin. Thus the masculine *contrada* produces a female analogue of itself that is articulated to the earthy aspect of the Madonna, while the city remains articulated to its patroness, the Virgin. In the race, female runs for female, while each represents a masculine group.

The affinity of horse to Madonna is also brought out in those qualities thought desirable in the mare or gelding. Sienese agree that the best horses for the race are not thoroughbreds, but 'halfbloods' (*mezzo sangue*). This term connotes that the animal (or person) is a mixture of good and bad qualities. The preference for such horses is suggestive of their ambiguity: the horse 'is a combination of both good and evil, and one cannot know for certain which will prevail until the very end of the joust' (Dundes and Falassi 1975: 145). The ambiguity of the horse can be likened to that of other relationships within the model (within the figure of the Madonna, and between levels within secular and religious domains).[14]

The horse is transformed into an unnatural vessel for the dilated *contrada*. Kept separate and protected, the animal becomes the sign of the destiny of its *contrada*. Within the lower tier of the model, boundaries of the sacred and secular are dissolved, and these domains flow together in earthy union to reinforce the dilation of the *contrada* and its inverted analogue, the horse.[15] This is evident the day before the race when the horse must be blessed within the *contrada* church by its priest. Normally such animals are not permitted to enter a church. The priest often departs from the text by blessing the horse before the jockey, indicating that the horse is the more important of the two. In fact a horse can win the race without its rider, supporting the interpretation that the animal becomes the analogue of its *contrada*. Should the horse defecate within the church, this is perceived as an omen of good fortune in the coming contest; and the capitano may step carefully into this auspicious ordure (Dundes and Falassi 1975: 97).[16]

I underline here that this dissolution of boundaries has its own logic within the festival model. Separated from the higher level of the city, the *contrada* swells to encompass fully its sacred precinct and to produce the horse as the analogue of its own distorted image. The figure of the horse condenses and embodies the dissolution of boundaries within the *contrada* and the hardening of borders between *contrade*. Thus the horse is made indecently and earthily powerful, as is its *contrada*. The dilated *contrada* has cast forth a figure that is compatible with its own aggrandizing image, with that of the distorted relationship between lower and higher levels, and between domains of the sacred and secular on the lower level.

In contrast to the immaculate unity of the city, the expansive *contrada* becomes a powerful disordering force. The *contrada* horse, a female animal or animalistic female, conjoins male and female attributes. Both Madonna and horse are female and powerful. But the dominant aspect of the Madonna is spiritual, while that of the horse is earthy. Thus the horse articulates the masculine *contrada* with the earthy aspect of the Madonna. In turn, the earthy aspect is subsumed by the dominant, spiritual aspect of the Madonna, that remains articulated to the masculine city, within the model.

The Palio model is a radically simplified and transformative version of Siena, one that enables its lower level to be taken apart in predictive and controlled ways through the exaggerated fragmentation of segments and the conflation of the sacred and secular. Simultaneously, the higher level of the model retains its pristine integrity, to contain the wildness and chaotic power that is being generated on the lower level. Since together the *contrade* ideally take in all the social and territorial space of Siena, one can say that within the Palio model the urban entity has been taken apart; and that although hierarchical relationships between levels have been distended, they remain operative throughout the festival.

Before the race the structure of Siena within the palio model may be depicted as follows:

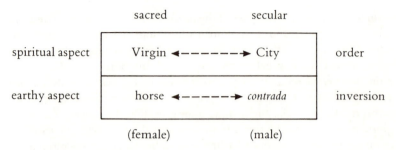

Figure 5 Levels in the Palio model: hierarchy and fragmentation

Mention must be made here of the jockey, as a male participant in the race. In the great majority of cases the jockeys are strangers, outsiders to Siena hired by the *contrade*. Each jockey is a node of suspicion for *contrada* members, as one who tries to make deals for his own benefit at the expense of the strategic designs of the segment. After the race the jockeys leave the *comune*. More than any other figure, the jockey bears the brunt of his *contrada*'s displeasure at failure. In the race itself there are only two male figures of consequence. The jockey, portrayed as a character of guile and disloyalty who is motivated by money rather than natal ties, represents the *contrada*. The other is the starter of the race, again usually a stranger to Siena, who acts on behalf of the city. But he behaves with impeccable neutrality and impartiality, as does the city level within the model.

In terms of the tacit logic I have explicated, the race itself may be regarded as a 'female' event: the horses are female or feminized; the race is in honor of and under the protection of the Madonna; while the horse can win without its rider. The males active in the race are strangers to Siena. As a male outsider in a female-dominated occasion, the jockey appears as an inversion of male-female relationships in everyday public life. For in the major political, economic, and religious arenas of the male-dominated *comune* (and *contrada*) women are the 'outsiders' to a certain extent. By the same token, the powerful feminine horse is an inversion of the place of the female in the everyday. Thus there is a strong sense of complementariness in this pairing of amoral jockey and indecently powerful horse: both have an inbetween character, and both represent aspects of the unusual condition of the *contrada*.

The sequence of occasions in the festival model: frames of integration and opposition

In the face of the fragmentation of its parts and their swollen opposition to one another, the city level remains thoroughly impartial and behaves with impeccable, apolitical neutrality (Silverman 1981: 177, 1985: 99). In contrast to mundane behavior, one may say that the city level has become 'spiritualized'. Within the festival model, secular and religious occasions on the higher tier enunciate order and balance.[17] In terms of sequencing and duration, the higher level frames the heightened imbalance of the lower within occasions of stability and integration. The basic relationship between these levels remains asymmetrical, one of subsumation. Thus the capacity of Virgin and city to sustain this model of the *comune*, in the face of the conflict and uncertainty of its disordered lower level, also becomes a controlled test of the viability of the entire urban entity. The festival model encourages this framed testing, by the *comune* of itself, through alternation and adumbration in which occasions of major significance to the *contrade* are preceded by subsuming events sponsored by civic and religious institutions of the higher level. By framing its internal fractures in this way, the city ultimately ensures the putting together of its parts in their normal scale and interdependence.

The first of these occasions is the choosing of the competing *contrade*. In each independent Palio cycle only ten *contrade* race each year (see Heywood 1904: 222–3). In a given cycle the seven that did not compete the previous year participate by right. Three additional *contrade* are added from among the ten that did compete the previous year. The selection of these three takes place in the city hall, in the presence of the mayor and the capitani of all seventeen *contrade*. The mayor chooses three *contrade* by lot. The capitani of these three then choose, by lot, three from among those ten that competed the previous year. Again by lot the mayor selects in sequence the names of the seven *contrade* who will run the following year in this Palio cycle. The order in which the names of these seven are chosen determines the order in which they will march in the current festival's parade (Dundes and Falassi 1975: 49–51). Done by lot under mayoral auspices in central civic space alongside the Campo, the choosing of the *contrade* epitomizes the dispassionate impartiality shown within the model by the city, towards its own rivalrous segments.

Through discussions amongst themselves, the capitani pick the ten competing horses. Since these have yet to be assigned to particular *contrade*, choices are based on impartial criteria of horseflesh. The strongest and weakest contenders are eliminated. The Sienese ideal is an evenly matched field, in which all the ten have an equal chance at victory (Dundes and Falassi 1975: 48; see also Heywood 1904: 218, 236). From the perspective of the city level, the horses like the *contrade* should have competitive equivalence.

A few days before the race, again by lot under mayoral auspices, the ten horses are assigned irrevocably to the competing *contrade*. This marks the first time a *contrada* and a particular horse are identified together. Once more the city level highlights its own neutrality and impartiality in these assignments. Then six trial races organized by the municipality are held in the Campo. Their obvious functions are to learn about the horses and to accustom them to the track. The order of position for the start of each race is worked out according to precise and complicated statutory formulae, as were the selection of the competing segments and the assignment of horses (Dundes and Falassi 1975: 66–7). All these procedures of the city level emphasize equality, chance, and fairness.

From the time the racing *contrade* were chosen, the Palio banner and those of the segments were hung from the city hall. In the afternoon of the day before the race the Palio banner is carried in procession by city officials to a city church associated with the Madonna of that race. There the banner is blessed by the archbishop (Falassi and Catoni 1983: 60). In the August procession each *contrada* offers wax candles to the Madonna, while the city offers one enormous candle, some ten feet high. After its blessing the Palio banner is hung in a special location within the church. In effect, this intensified icon of the festival is separated from the jurisdiction of secular authority and is dedicated to the Madonna. That evening each *contrada* holds its own festive meal.

The day of the race an early mass for the safety of the jockeys is said by the archbishop in a city church. In the early afternoon the horse is blessed in the contrada church. Then the *comparsa* (a group of adolescent males in historical costume) of each *contrada* performs its elaborate flag–gymnastics, first for the membership of its own segment and then before secular and religious institutions of the city level.

This sequence of occasions is framed in alternation by the upper and lower tiers of the model. Initially, the distanced arbitration of the city level frames the exaggerated opposition of the dilated *contrade* – in the choice of contenders, in the order of march in the parade, in the assignment of horse to *contrada*, and in the starting positions in the trial races. Next, these trials bring to the fore the conflict of *contrade*. The focus then shifts to the domain of the sacred on the upper tier of the model: city and *contrade* together venerate the Madonna, while the archbishop blesses the Palio banner. The highest-ranking representation of the sacred now frames both tiers of the secular domain. Next, solidarity within the *contrada* climaxes at its festive meal. The following morning the horse is blessed in the *contrada* church – the peak of identification of *contrada* and horse, and the dissolution of boundaries between spirituality and earthiness on the lower tier. In counterpoint to this particularism, the *comparse* begin their round of entertainment before their own *contrada* members, and then move on to link their segments to institutions of the upper tier.

In this sequencing the *contrada* level never fully escapes the subsuming control of higher-order secular and sacred domains. Nonetheless this lower tier, that in principle is inclusive of the city's territory and population, has been fractured, and its smallest fragments – the *contrade* – opposed to one another. By the same token, the higher tier of the model has been distanced from the lower one, without altering their hierarchical relationship.

The parade and the race

The parade and race respectively reorder and transform the fractured urban entity through its festival model. The parade restates the correct relationships among components of the *comune*. The race activates this through the amplification of emotion and the setting loose of dynamic form, fusing together the alienated aspects of purity and earthiness, city and *contrada*. The race, the climax of the festival, is the most frenzied yet controlled of its occasions; and its unleashing of wild competition among the equivalent *contrade* is framed by Madonna and parade, by sacred strength and historical verities. The parade is wholly a male occasion, the race preeminently a female one. Both are re-formations of order, respectively in the idiom of city and Madonna. These operations of rearticulation and transformation may be shown in figure 6.

The tolling of the tower bell signals the beginning of the historical parade. The course of march is around the Campo, and the lengthy procession is orderly, stately, and well-coordinated. In essence the procession is a recapitulation of the illustrious history of Siena. The first groups to appear represent prominent sites and social categories of the days of the Republic. There follow the *comparse* of the ten racing *contrade*: each includes acrobatic flag-wavers, its *duce* who is chosen for his virile good looks, the horse wearing its *gualdrapa*, and at the tail end of each *comparsa*, the jockey riding a stallion.

Then there is a shift in reference, from the historical to the eternal. A group of boys appears, representing Siena itself. Here the city is characterized as 'male' and as 'youthful' – in a sense as eternal. There follow the *comparse* of the seven non-competing *contrade*, who are considered 'temporarily dead'.

After these there enters the 'triumphal chariot'. This wagon flies the Palio banner and holds, among others, four elderly men who represent the ruling council of Siena at the height of its glory in the days of the Republic. Accompanying the chariot are seven horsemen representing the *contrade* not competing in the current race. They are eternal in the sense of being retrievable, for they will 'return to life' in the race of the following year (Dundes and Falassi 1975: 109). The historical groups and those that stand

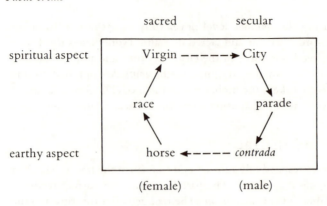

Figure 6 The Palio model: transformations through parade and race

for eternal verities then give way to a group that is 'dead' indeed. This consists of six masked riders and horses who represent six suppressed *contrade* – wards that no longer exist.[18]

There is some evidence that the whole procession progressively moves back in time. The first group contains references to the end of the Republic, while the chariot group makes reference to its high point, its beginnings in the thirteenth century. As the procession retraces Sienese time it nears those eternal values upon which the *comune* was founded. Lasting secular values are conjoined with those of the sacred: together in the chariot are the wise men of the Republic and the Palio banner on which the Madonna's is the dominant depiction. Thus the race will begin framed by that point in the parade at which eternal secular and sacred verities intersect. The eternal is also the nexus at which the secular hegemony of the city derives from that of the sacred – where the Madonna reigns in place of the Council of Elders.

Accordingly, the transition between parade and race is not abrupt: moving back towards its origins, the city gives itself over to the hegemony of the Madonna. The Palio banner, iconic of the Madonna and the only 'female' presence in the entire procession, appears at the end of the parade and its interface with the race – at the point of transposition of the Madonna at the service of the city and the city in the service of the Madonna. The shift from parade to race is a transition from secular solidarity eternal, guided by a 'male' principle, to its rejuvenation through the intercession of a sacred and dynamic female principle.

The race itself consists of three turns of the Campo, and lasts some ninety seconds. It is a wild and chaotic run. The jockeys beat one another and the opposing horses. The enormous crowd roars at a feverish pitch. Some appear almost in trance while others faint from the excitement, the heat, or the press of the crowd. The profane power of the dilated *contrade* is released within space central to the city, beneath the metaphoric cloak of the Madonna. The race clearly has crucial functions within the festival model. First, it is a metaphor of motion and dynamism, of processuality. Second, as a game form it stabilizes and directs the resolution of uncertainty and conflict, since it is predicated upon the acceptance of an identical goal and the means of its attainment. This goal (the winning of the race) specifies in a highly predictive manner that the festival model is to end its operations, and so close itself down. Third, the race amplifies sentiment and enthusiasm, so that even though onlookers root for different *contrade* their outpouring of emotion is fused into a mass demonstration of support for the belief in city and Madonna. This fusion of emotion complements the logic of putting the city back together through its model.

Of particular interest to this analysis is that, from the viewpoint of the city, of the upper tier of the model, there is only one official finisher. There are no awards for any other places.[19] Once the first horse crosses the finish line the race is over. Why is it that the contest is limited to a first-place finish? I think that this lies at the heart of the metaphoric renewal of the *comune*, through its festival model. There is only one official finisher because there is only one city – for the race may be understood as a contest of metaphoric succession to the city on the part of its 'miniature cities'. The winning *contrada* is an artificially-dilated version of itself that becomes like the city, but that returns to its normal magnitude, for in its usual condition it lacks the spiritual and institutional features to become really akin to the *comune*.

Dundes and Falassi (1975: 51) comment that after the race 'the city symbolically belongs for the moment to one *contrada* alone'. Logan (1978: 57) adds that 'For the days immediately following the Palio the winning *contrada* "owns" the city.' Moreover, there are strong sentiments of rebirth associated with the victorious contrada. It is referred to as 'a little one is born'; while the Palio banner is called 'the infant sucking' (Dundes and Falassi 1975: 211), and the 'new-born son' (Falassi and Catoni 1983: 60). The new-born son is the victorious *contrada*, the analogue in miniature of the city, reborn within the womb-like space of the Campo, with its affinities to the Madonna. The morning following the race the victorious *contrada* parades through the entire city.[20]

From the viewpoint of the *contrada* its own 'rebirth' is all important. But the festival model encourages synecdoche – a relationship in which part stands for whole, such that the special qualities that accrue to the part also become integral to the whole that encompasses the former. In the transformations of the Palio model it is the momentary isomorphism of levels, of the whole of the city and its *contrada* part, that is crucial both to the renewal of the *comune* through this model and to the feeling of civic unity that characterizes the close of the festival.

Through victory one *contrada* is identified symbolically as the city – it 'owns' the city and is momentarily its 'reborn' successor. City and *contrada* are brought together. Through its horse the triumphant *contrada* is articulated to the earthy aspect of the Madonna. Through the race the earthy (horse) and spiritual (banner) aspects of the Madonna are reintegrated in generative union, producing the reborn *contrada*. The winning horse gains the banner, that then is referred to as the 'new-born son'. But the horses run under the dominant spiritual aspect of the Madonna, and so the race reintegrates and subordinates her earthy side – the Madonna is restabilized in correct relationship to herself. And, although the rejuvenated *contrada* does substitute for the city, its dilated magnitude is artificial and it reverts to being one segment among many, all of which are subsumed by the city. The great fractures generated by the festival model before the race are erased in its running; and the city is put back together in the correct form of unity among its sacred and secular components. Since the festival model of Siena derives intimately from the social structure of the everyday *comune*, one may say that the latter too has been renewed.

The logic of design I have elicited suggests that the dynamic of metaphoric renewal is energized by the figure of the Madonna. Her implicit, asymmetrical dualism makes it possible for the sacred to articulate simultaneously the two levels of city and *contrada*, each of which links with one of her aspects. In the process the version of the *comune* modelled through the festival objectifies its components and itself – and so it can come to know itself, and to test holistically its own validity, as it cannot through its everyday activity. Then, through the contest, in a location that conjoins sacredness and urban centrality with historicity and energy, the fragmented and confounded parts race back towards union with the wholes from which they derived – and correct part/whole relationships are restored.

The Palio festival is a rigged game, a twice-yearly dialogue in which the urban entity engages itself through contest in such a way that the only ultimate victor is the *comune* itself – for time and again it successfully tests its own viability as a holistic entity.

Alternative views

Of scholars who commented on drafts of this chapter, a number were especially critical of the role attributed to the Madonna in the model of the Palio.[21] There is an absence of any explicit evidence of dualism in the popular imagery of the Madonna, even though one might expect this sort of incipient complementarity, given differing Catholic perceptions and interpretations through the ages, and the difficulty of resolving these through dogma. This questions the following aspects of the model. Is gender of relevance in the interplay of sacred and secular domains? And if so, may city and *contrada* be identified as male metaphors, and the horse as female? More generally this questions the role of religious dynamism in the festival, upon which transformations in the model depend.

As it should be practiced, reanalysis is a highly playful genre of scholarly work, one that fiddles with, emends or dismantles its own constructions in trying to make different sense of the sensibilities of others. These critical comments are substantive. I cannot speak to their validity, but I can suppose this. Then how would I go about taking apart my own reading of Palio ethnography, and putting it together in a way that partially responds to these comments? Let me pursue this for a bit, leaving it to you to decide whether you prefer one version to another, or neither.

I am strongly persuaded that the Palio festival is structured hierarchically, since two levels are distinguished clearly – the higher-order one of the city and the lower one of the *contrade*. Furthermore that these levels are related through synecdoche, of part to whole. On the basis of these premises the following kind of analysis takes shape. Just as the city can be divided into its *contrade*, so it subsumes all of these, while each *contrada* is the city in miniature. During the festival the behavior of each *contrada* is something of an overdetermined inversion of the everyday. Each *contrada* dilates its capacity to be like the city. On its lower level, constituted through *contrade*, the city is fragmented. In the opposite direction the pristine integrity and unity of the city is overdetermined on the higher level. This relationship between levels is maintained throughout the festival occasions I have discussed as frames of integration and opposition. At the climax of the festival the historical parade restates the correct articulations between city and *contrada*. The race actualizes these articulations by producing one victor that is called reborn. The reborn *contrada* momentarily becomes like the city, levels merge, inversions are erased, and one of its parts is identified with the whole of the urban entity. Thus the latter too is rejuvenated, its viability tested successfully once more.

In this version the role of the Madonna, and generally that of religion, are merely those of ideological underwriters, insuring the legitimacy of the festival in its entirety in terms of a level of axioms higher still than that of the city, and therefore protective of the latter just as it is protective of its *contrade*. This version, one that could be related in detail, has a much more straightforward and less dynamic logic than the one I discussed at length. The concerns of this less complex version are still those of the social reproduction of the urban entity. Yet whether the logic of the festival now constitutes a model that does transformative work is quite another matter.

This version seems more mechanical, more akin to re-presentation and simple transposition, and perhaps to the dialectics of encapsulation discussed in the previous chapter, than to a logic of causal transformation.

In either instance I am convinced that other analyses of the Palio all miss one crucial point. They all accept at face value the ideology and rhetoric of the *contrade* – that these entities and their relationships are subject and object of the entire occasion. By accepting this version of discourse, these analyses look no further, to what the Palio may accomplish in more comprehensive terms and to how this works. But the more profound discourse of this public event must be on the *comune* as a whole, and not just about its parts. If the population, social composition, and territorial claims of the *contrade* together cover virtually the whole of the *comune*, then how can that holism not be at issue when together all of these *contrade* do their competition? If holism is fragmented, is not its integrity at issue? Put otherwise, these parts necessarily implicate their whole, since by all accounts the *contrade* never cease being parts and therefore the hierarchical holism of the city is never in question on a higher level. The issue of holism is implicated both by what fragmentation does do here, as by what it does not.

In this case to maintain that the explicit ideology and exegeses of the *contrade* are sufficient grounds to explain the impetus of the festival is misleading. Their very existence as parts continually and inexorably leads to and implicates the city that contains them. As divided as they are against one another during the festival, their horizons merge because they are so like one another. And their horizon is the whole.

Whatever the reasoning used to analyze the Palio, the relationship of part to whole cannot be circumvented. This raises other issues. Why has this public event survived for so long? Regardless of the kind of explanation offered to date – a peculiarly Sienese world view; or structures of hegemony that stunt countervailing tendencies – pride of place goes to the *contrade* (both positions in fact are straightforward arguments for the strength of tradition translated directly into social action, regardless of how radically they seem opposed). Can the survival of the *contrade* fully explain the kind of organization the festival has? Clearly the festival would not survive without the *contrade* and their particular constitution. But this is as tautological as saying that the *contrade* would not survive as *contrade* without the *comune*. *Comune*, *contrade*, and Palio have existed together for a long time in complex interdependence. I would expect there to be a particular epistemology that articulates all of these through some mechanism that rhythmically does their social reproduction without sacrificing any at the altars of the others.

During its lengthy history the Palio has not had a unitary existence. Its constituents, contents, and procedures continually have undergone promulgation, revision, and replacement. The conquerors of Siena adapted the Palio for the *contrade*, whom they fostered as allies at the expense of the *commune*. Somehow the Palio became keyed to regularly reviving the *commune* in terms of those very qualities of viable autonomy that were denied it by its incorporation into larger bodies politic. But revival can take many forms, and so it is unlikely that during all these years the Palio was one and the same festival. The Palio may have begun as a competition that verged on the self-presentation of *contrade* statelets. Given the dynamic power attributed to the sacred in earlier periods, the Palio may have acquired characteristics of modelling and a systemic logic of organization. Today it may be an event of modelling, or closer to one of re-presentation that is ended systemically through the competition. This sort of history of the Palio would actively question the capacities of public events to act on the social orders from which they derive, and so too their role in their own survival.[22] But this kind of history has yet to be adduced.

Intersections

On the surface my own fieldwork in Newfoundland was far removed from the isolated fishing villages of Christmas mumming. I learned about the complicated workings of an urban, public welfare bureaucracy, a world of rules, segmented lives, and personal humiliations. There I was drawn to the intricacies of official decisions. Later I became fascinated by the most mysterious of these – how officials decided whether parents suspected of maltreating their children had done so or not. A world without innocents, of victims and victimizers. These cases often had attributes of classic tales of detection. But at times their dispositions were muddy, messy, and unjust, leaving me in no doubt of the positivism of classical sleuths and of the struggles of modern social workers to be so. I won't dwell on this, for this work is reported elsewhere (Handelman 1978, 1983). Still, for me Newfoundland is a space of mysterious involution that never unravels itself, and this tinges and tints whatever I write on this place. It is of course what attracted me to mumming.

The world of Newfoundland welfare I knew was one of ongoing suspicion about the hidden motives of others, and of the demeanor and face-work that allayed and yet used these suspicions. On the surface my own fieldwork was far removed from the substance of this chapter ... but these themes recur.

Many of the people I spoke with, passed time with, and observed, were former villagers or their offspring. Few in Newfoundland are that far from there ... But on the surface my work was distant from the topics of this chapter.

Responding to the symposium in which this chapter first appeared, Edmund Leach (1984: 363) wrote: 'No Newfoundlander participant could possibly understand what Handelman is talking about.' I wonder ... In November 1983 I presented this chapter in seminar at Memorial University of Newfoundland to a sympathetic and highly aware audience of anthropologists, sociologists, and folklorists. Sharply critical of many of my contentions, they knew very well what I was talking about. And more than a few of them are not far removed, in life and work, from the locales of this chapter.

In his remarks Leach championed the cause of folly as just that – the jumble of fun that people play with and feel for its own sake. With reference to this chapter he added: 'The process of analysis has served to destroy the Festival of Folly which, from the local point of view, was quite certainly the occasion for the whole enterprise' (1984: 363). And should folly have such an exacting patterning, as I discern in mumming? If it is folly for fun's sake, then why its peculiar regularities? Is it then not specious folly to disregard these? But this is what many portions of this book are about.

7 Christmas mumming in Newfoundland

Concealment and revelation often alternate in the inversion of social personhood. Seemingly opposed, yet complementary, their relationship circumscribes a recurrent device for the alteration of social order. Of the two, the concealment or rearrangement of one's familiar and public persona has been accorded pride of place in numerous studies. Modes of symbolic inversion have been called rituals of reversal (Turner 1969), dramas of conflict (Norbeck 1967: 209), and rituals of rebellion (Gluckman 1954). Edmund Leach (1961: 135) likens role reversal to the playing of everyday life 'back to front', in its systematic alteration of signs. Inversions often are associated with hierarchical orders, with the periodicity of transition (Davis 1982; Phythian-Adams 1972: 67–8) and are characterized by mockery, mimicry, and the ridiculing of one category or conception of person by another.

Inherent in the logic of inversion is the cultural recognition that these conditions are unusual and temporary. These are conditions that mark the incorrectness of their own changes, and so the validity of a further reversion to normal personae. Thus the concealment of personhood leads also to its revelation. As scholars repeatedly have argued, an inversion of personhood and the revelation of its reversion to familiarity strongly underscores the moral correctness of everyday social order.

If much attention is paid to the aspect of concealment in inversion, then little is focused on its complement – that of revelation, when the mask is removed, when the masquerade is over, when the inversion proves a false representation of person, and when inverted personhood reverts to its everyday analogue. To decipher inversion, in dramatizations of personhood and collectivity, one should recognize that its mechanics operate through two aspects of a single device: concealment and revelation. For the moment let me state that with inversion to conceal is to reveal, while to ask what is concealed is also to pose the question of what is revealed. As such, inversion is an instance of re-presentation, one that begins to limit severely and so to control its outcomes within the public events of its practice. I return briefly to this point in the concluding section of this chapter.

This chapter addresses the logic of concealment and revelation that operated in 'mumming', as this custom was practiced during the Twelve Days of Christmas (26 December to Epiphany) in the small, rural fishing villages (called outports) of Newfoundland. There Christmas mumming flourished during the period of the family fishery, roughly from the mid-nineteenth century until World War II, although it is still practiced in not a few of these communities.[1]

In order to mum, persons disguised in costume. As mummers they visited households in the community. If householders guessed their identities, the mummers then removed their facial coverings and accepted food and drink before departing for the next house.[2] I argue that this deceptively simple device of concealment and revelation effaced a disjunction in perceptions of the exterior person and the interior self, a duality that was echoed in perceptions of the social relationship within the community and in the absence of such bonds beyond its external boundary. Mumming not only harmonized person and self but also the community in relation to itself. I argue for a conception of personhood in outport Newfoundland that was predicated on a disjunction between perceptions of the self, perceived by others as hidden, and perceptions of the social person. In accordance with this conception, selfhood was masked in much of daily life, while personhood was revealed and open to inspection.[3]

My interpretation of mumming depends on the ethnographies of others. In the next section I use these materials to bring out the distinctions mentioned above. I then describe the outport mumming complex itself. The third section takes up certain safeguards, of sign and structure, that protected the collectivity against the disordering force of mumming. These safeguards included the taming of mumming through shifts in social space, through shifts in control in the discourse between disorder and moral order, and through the guessing game. The fourth section addresses the mechanics of inversion and reversion in mumming to show how this device could erase disjunctions in the domains of personhood and community. In the conclusion I discuss certain general issues that emerge from this analysis.

Interior and exterior attributes of person and community

Scattered along the rugged 9,600 kilometres of Newfoundland shoreline, outports were isolated and small in population. The basic unit of social organization was the household, and ties of kinship among households constituted the major lineaments of community. Beyond the household there were hardly any communal institutions.

The household was akin to a solidary and enduring bastion in the village: a dense locus of sentiments of solidarity and of comparative openness and cooperation. Only within the household was information shared freely (Chiaramonte 1970; Faris 1966). The emotional bond between husband and wife is described as the most resilient tie within the household, and as stronger than those between members of different households. Relationships between households were characterized by 'separateness', with each as a highly privatized and contained locale of self-protection (Chiaramonte 1970: 13). Social relationships between members of different households were dyadic, reciprocal, instrumental, and fragile, and were open continually to renegotiation.

Houses, built closely to one another, reproduced in their use of space the duality of extreme privacy and a transparency before others. This dualism echoed that of relationships between members of different households. Houses offered a surface appearance of openness to familiars, although the great bulk of household space was hidden from their view. The main entrance was through the kitchen, and familiars freely entered this region without knocking. Once within they were restricted to the kitchen, where householders socialized with one another, and so kept their personae on view. In the kitchen, familiars were constrained by the strict etiquette of the host-guest relationship that, like most contacts between persons, was infused with formality, reserve, respect, and outward cordiality (Faris 1969: 142; Szwed 1969: 108; Firestone 1967; Chiaramonte 1970).

Most households earned their livelihood through the family fishery. Fishing in the main was based on relations of kinship, pervaded by the attributes noted above. The ideal unit of production consisted of a group of brothers who held property for fishing in common, who fished together, and who divided the returns into equal shares. As the sons of brothers grew older, they fished with their fathers. Later on these sons would fish together as a group of brothers (Firestone 1967, 1969). This suggests a phase in the domestic and productive cycles – when a father fished with his sons – that made the nuclear family autonomous of other households, and so more of a solidary bastion. Although this did not occur in practice, for a variety of demographic and social reasons, such contraction of a village into relatively self-sufficient households was perceived as hypothetically possible, at least on certain parts of the island.

The average crew of the family fishery was composed of two to four men who were closely related. The skipper owned the boat, but he rarely told his crew where, when, or how to fish. Complementing the work of the crew was that of the 'shore crowd': the womenfolk and children of the crew who together did the complex, technical work of processing the fish and preparing the catch for sale. The maintenance of crew and shore crowd led to much tension. Even brothers who worked together intensively would drift apart after the fishing season until Christmas time, after which they would ready the equipment for the coming season.

These exigencies created conditions of that which Firestone (1978) calls 'role transparency': familiars knew well the social personae of one another and they lived fully in one another's gaze. Within the home this held for the kitchen, the interface of transparency and privacy protected rigidly by host-guest etiquette. Ethnographies imply that the transparency and moral restraint of social personae were complemented by perceptions of the deep, interior privatization of the self. There, hidden from view and rarely exposed, an individual was at home to himself, unrestrained by the moral structures of the social person. There, others perceived that one experienced the motivations and desires that were not to be shown to familiars. However, one's 'face' reflected the cordiality of good neighbor and workmate that one also saw reflected in the visages of others.[4]

These accounts imply that familiars were perceived in terms of a dualism composed of the following. An overt, moral aspect of personhood, bound by ties of kinship and social contract and corresponding to the social person; and an inner and hidden self, freed of moral restraint and constituted in part of feelings and sentiments that if given rein would damage social ties. This is a crude separation that hardly serves to address the complexities of personhood and the convolutions of selfhood. Yet it does highlight a distinction that had currency in the daily life of these villages.

Faris (1968, 1969: 142, 1972: 161) writes that adult behavior was characterized by formality, caution, inhibition, and rigid role expectations. Children were taught to avoid close personal ties with peers and to suppress the expression of emotion, since any exposure of self could lead to exploitation by others. Szwed (1966) echoes these observations.

In daily life there was little visiting among households, especially by men (Chiaramonte 1969). To a degree this was due to the exigencies of fishing. Still, outside the household men tended to congregate in small groups only in neutral locations (shops, the churchyard, the government wharf; see Faris 1966). There conversation took the shape of monologues rather than discussion (Chiaramonte 1970: 15). Thus they could avoid making commitments to one another, even that of offering hospitality.

Descriptions emphasize the centrality of an ethos of egalitarianism and reciprocity among villagers. Szwed (1969: 107) argues that this was maintained in part by 'the highly ritualized nature of interpersonal relations'. Any striving for mobility or status was met by techniques of leveling, like gossip, ridicule, and the withdrawal of reciprocity (see also Firestone 1967, 1978: 102).

The caution, the reserve and wariness, that pervaded contacts outside the household were conjoined by the deep suspicions persons held of what they perceived as the amoral (but not malicious) hidden motives of others. Suspicion and hostility were kept well concealed, and there were strong proscriptions against verbal confrontation and physical violence (Faris 1966, 1969: 139; Szwed 1969: 108). Thus the formality and moral distancing of etiquette protected social persons from one another, and buffered them against the unknown and socially dangerous desires of which their inner selves were suspected (Chiaramonte 1970: 12). As social persons, villagers were familiars of one another while their inner selves, secluded and privatized, were mysterious and forbidding and, so to speak, 'strangers' to one another. Szwed (1969: 108) comments that social relationships were known only as 'surface facts', while the motives that underwrote such ties were perceived as an unknown, 'threatening mystery'.

These observations support the interpretation of a duality of social person and private self. The social person was perceived as a 'social fact', well-known in various personae, while social relationships themselves were characterized by role transparency. By contrast, there was the deep suspicion that if the social person were quite transparent, the self would be opaque to the gaze of others. And it was to the mysterious self that villagers ascribed the causality of motivation, a point that fits well with their valuing individualism and self-reliance. In turn this suggests that villagers perceived the inner person, the self, as the location of 'authentic' feelings and sentiments that animated personae yet that were kept from others.

The word 'authentic' is used here with reservation. I will not suggest that this perception of self and other was constituted merely and wholly in terms of attributes that potentially threatened the idea of social contract and the persons this connected. But I do argue that outport people conceived of the inaccessible self as composed in part of hidden qualities that were authentic in their very inaccessibility. This authenticity of the inaccessible was continuously validated in these communities where information valuable to the living of one's life was strategically withheld by other familiars outside the household. Inaccessible resources and the motives that underwrote their manipulation often determined one's quality of life, and outport people were well aware of their predicament.

This use of information on the level of community is well documented in the ethnographies I have cited. Of equal importance to community life was the monopolization of crucial information by the merchants who bought the villagers' catch and who issued credit to the latter. Put simply, fishermen received credit in food and other commodities that enabled them to eat and fish, without knowing the actual price they would be charged for these resources. Similarly, fishermen sold their catch knowing neither its price nor the amount of credit they would be issued for the coming year. In order to balance their gains and losses from year to year, merchants averaged their costs against returns, doing this for entire villages and thereby penalizing the more industrious fishermen while the less diligent benefited. Thus the trade of the family fishery was dominated by outside, merchant capital, rigged by statute and practice to exploit outport families. Sider (1980, 1984) argues that these pernicious practices set outport families against one another, encouraging suspicion and distrust, and fragmenting these villages into households that to a degree still had to depend upon one another. In my terms these were quite the sorts of conditions that could engender perceptions of a disjunctive dualism between interior self and exterior person within the village.

If the self were a wellspring of authentic motivations that endangered others, then the social person and the social contract between persons did not accurately reflect this authenticity – and so they contained prominent elements of artifice and inauthenticity. Just as the social person masked the self, so the social relationship, that linchpin of community, masked the selves of persons thereby conjoined. If, through social contract, persons were familiars, then their concealed selves were strangers.

Together the households of an outport constituted a moral community of familiars (Faris 1968; Sider 1976: 111). Within the household this was predicated on bonds of kinship, trust, and interdependence. Among households, morality depended on a code of etiquette and social contract, mainly between individuals. Familiars within the community 'masked' their grievances, their suspicions and hostilities, through privacy and social distance, through formality and reserve, through egalitarianism, and through the avoidance of overt emotionalism.

Although social distinctions within the moral community were ill-defined and weak, its external boundary was strong and resilient. Strangers were regarded openly in precisely the ways in which familiars were perceived covertly. The typical stranger was received with courtesy, hospitality, and formality. But he was perceived as amoral, unpredictable, untrustworthy, and potentially malevolent. The devil, the night, and things dark by nature, including the dangerous interior condition of anger (called 'getting black'), were associated with evil, and evil with strangerhood (Faris 1969: 134, 138; see also Firestone 1969).

Two contrasts and two affinities, in the domains of collectivity and personhood, stand forth from the preceding discussion. These are restated here, for they are used intensively in my analysis of concealment and revelation in mumming. In the daily life of the outport these contrasts and affinities were best regarded as tendencies. Nonetheless, in mumming these themes were concentrated and honed to a glittering edge.

The first contrast distinguishes between the inside of the community, its social relationships, and the strangerhood that lies beyond it. This contrast is of a disjunctive dualism, since it opposes the morality of community to the amorality of strangerhood. The second contrast distinguishes between the social person, the exterior of personhood, and the interior self. This contrast is also that of a disjunctive dualism, for it opposes the moral social person to amoral aspects of self. The first affinity is between the interior of the social person, the self, and the exterior of community, the realm of strangerhood. The second affinity is between the exterior of the social person and the interior of community.

Aspects of the self, of the submerged desires and antagonisms that were suspected to lurk there, were negatively valued but were regarded as 'authentic' in the sense used previously. The covert self contained negative attributes that charged motivation towards familiars and that were perceived as 'true', but that were concealed from view by the exterior social person who in no small measure was the reflecting surface of a moral code of conduct. The self was affective, charged with emotion; the social person was orientated instrumentally and showed little feeling. The exterior of the social person was positively valued but was perceived as inauthentic, since it was the product of the constraints of community and of interpersonal relationships, and not of a person's inner sentiments, as these were perceived by others.[5]

In this interpretation, mumming was a drama of deception and truth, of concealment and revelation that the collectivity played through itself. It was a dramatic construction on the value and, as it were, the authenticity of person and community – one that manipulated the dualism of interior and exterior, of the covert and the overt, to invert their everyday contrasts and affinities. In so doing, mumming showed what the person and the community of relationships were 'really' like. But then it reverted this apparent 'truth' to demonstrate its artifice and deception. The mechanics of inversion and reversion effaced the dualism of person and self, of familiar and stranger, and brought these into congruency with one another. There emerged an analogous structure of person and community that was harmonic in its moral valency. Further on I will suggest that this was accomplished through the manipulation of three sets of opposition: the covert and the overt, the positive and the negative, and the authentic and the inauthentic.

My treatment of mumming is programatic, in order to bring these features to the surface of discourse. However you should note that there were variations among villages and individuals, and that practices of mumming certainly could be more haphazard and less synchronized than in my argument. To date these variations have yet to be addressed systematically and in depth.

The mumming complex in outport Newfoundland

The Christmas season was the only annual period when villagers did not work (Faris 1972: 140). The men slept late; Sunday clothing was worn daily; evenings were given over to drinking, dancing, and singing; and special foods were eaten. This interlude was a time of social intensification through which the isolation and self-containment of households diminished.

There was a sharp increase in social visiting between households, whether by entire families or by groups of male social drinkers who stopped in succession at the houses of each of their number, who in turn became the host and reciprocated the hospitality previously received. Unlike much of the more sporadic visiting of daily life, that of Christmas had no special instrumental purpose. Villagers participated in communal occasions (parties, dances, Christmas Eve gift-giving) held in locations central to the community (Faris 1972: 160; Chiaramonte 1969: 83). These shifts towards social solidarity were clearcut. In additive fashion they involved increasingly inclusive levels of integration: the household in relation to itself, links between households, the giving over of public space to socializing, and collective participation in communitywide events.

Transversing this momentum of increasing solidarity was the counter-flow of mummers, commonly called '*janneys*' or in places the 'Dark Ones' (Faris 1968). The basic features of mumming were simple (see Halpert 1969). Groups of adults – mainly men but including women and, more recently, youngsters – donned costumes. These were assembled from oddments of clothing often belonging to others. Special attention was given to the concealment of well-known features of the social person. Faces were covered with transparent cloths, commonly called 'veils', and sometimes by masks. In some villages these coverings were called 'false faces' (Faris 1969: 131). Hands, well-known in the village, were covered. Padding changed body shape and image. Voice was altered through ingressive speech.[6] Although men often dressed as women, and women as men, the emphasis was not on the inversion of gender as such, nor on the impersonation of particular characters. Instead preeminence was given to dis-guise, to concealing one's known persona and to becoming anonymous and mysterious. In other words, strange, since one concealed knowledge about oneself and so about one's relationships.

Anonymous and anomalous, groups of mummers intruded into the community after dark and made their way along the narrow pathways among houses. (But never on Sundays. See Robertson 1982: 177.) In general they were seen as malevolent, threatening, and frightening creatures who in earlier times may have had connotations of amorphous ghosts and other malign beings ordinarily kept at bay beyond the borders of community (Widdowson 1977: 229, 233). Mummers were especially fearsome and feared when encountered along the byways between houses: in the interstices, among dense nodes of solidary intimacy. Here their behavior was patently aggressive and threatening towards others. It was not playful. In extreme instances, persons were reported to run, to climb trees, or to jump into the harbor to escape them (Widdowson 1977: 233–4; Firestone 1969: 68). Groups of mummers sometimes fought one another with staves, physically attacking those they encountered (Halpert 1969: 44). Faris (1969: 132) comments that in earlier times mummers were especially rough with persons seen as deviant. Williams (1969) quotes an informant: 'Outdoors you're more afraid of them than in the house – you never know what they're gonna do. You try to keep away from 'em as much as you can.' Intruding into the community the mummers brought disorder into its open public spaces and controlled these by their presence. One did not reason with mummers out-of-doors: one submitted, resisted, or bolted. Outside, after dark, the context of contact was quite that of the mummer: wild, emotional, aggressive, and menacing.

On reaching a house they intended to visit, the mummers knocked on the kitchen door and requested admittance, as would strangers to the village. Within, their behavior continued to be the inverse of that expected of familiars, and people would say that 'anything can happen' (Faris 1969: 132). Unrestrained, the mummers acted oddly, shouting, making sudden and violent movements, and engaging in horseplay, trickery, and mock intercourse with the women of the household. Mummers nudged, jostled, and poked fun at householders (Szwed 1969: 110–11). They intruded into the private regions of the home and frightened the children, perhaps threatening to abduct them (Widdowson 1977: 234). Much of this behavior was scary like that out-of-doors, but it also was seen as playful, as 'fun'.

In turn the householders initiated a guessing game with the mummers to unravel the 'true' personae of these guisers. They too were not restrained by customary formality. They felt the bodies of the mummers, tickled and poked them, and on occasion ripped off their facial coverings (Faris 1969: 132). They asked mummers to sing and dance in order to discern some familiarity in voice, gesture, and movement. The transitions from outright fear outside, to an admixture of playful and scary interchange within the home, and then to the guessing game are returned to further on.

If the persona of a mummer were guessed correctly he removed his facial covering. The householder then became host and the mummer, guest. Customary etiquette prevailed and all chaotic behavior ceased. The host greeted his guest, placed him in a seat, controlled their conversation, and offered food and drink (Szwed 1969). If the mummer's persona were not guessed correctly, he departed concealed and anonymous, without partaking of commensality.

This invasion by grotesque and malign beings was most discomfiting for the family. Yet the house visit was summarized as 'fun'. But there was no fun for either householder or mummer if the persona of the latter was not guessed correctly and he left without revealing himself. So too there was no fun if the concealed persona were guessed too quickly. Crucial to an accomplished performance of mumming was first, successful concealment and then, successful revelation.

Why mumming in its outport form? Explanations focus on the social conditions that fostered mumming and on its functions. Little attention is given to the logic that encouraged its controlled accomplishment. Explications take mumming as a period of sanctioned license that offered cognitive freedom from the everyday. Thus Faris and Firestone link the mummer to the idea of strangerhood that freed mummers from mundane strictures of role and relation. As surrogate strangers, mummers could express suppressed hostilities. Szwed echoes these sentiments. Chiaramonte considers that mumming and associated social drinking shattered the isolation and alienation of households, and so allowed dyadic ties to be formed or renewed. In varying degrees all these scholars agree that through mumming the outport celebrated and reaffirmed its sense of communal identity.

Recently Firestone departed from the functionalist tenor of these arguments, taking a position closer to that of this chapter. He contends that in confronting the anonymous mummers the householder also faced the anonymous community on whom his perception of self depended. By unmasking them, and 'the fantasmagoria of what one might be in others' eyes', the householder revealed the familiar personae and the honorable intentions that lay beneath the mask (Firestone 1978: 109). This legitimized his perception of himself through their eyes.

My own understanding of mumming borrows liberally from all of the above: the affinity of mummer to stranger; the expression of suppressed suspicion through licensed behavior; the revelation of self and other through unmasking; and the ways in which these factors commented on social relationships and community. Yet I seek an interpretation at a more abstract level, one that is not dependent on a direct relationship of form and function and that does not rely on the vagaries of persons in interaction for the logic of its structure.

Of more importance, the interpretation offered here operates at one and the same time on the domains both of personhood and of collectivity. These domains are linked together through affinities of analogy and through a common device of inversion and reversion that harmonizes the incipient duality in each domain, bringing each into congruence with itself, with implications for the other. This can be of value for the study of public events, particularly those of re-presentation: for here the dramatization of altering personhood through performance within an event may be a medium for the symbolic reproduction of social order.

Time, space, and control in mumming

That mumming first came to be associated with the Christmas period in the outport may have been idiosyncratic and practical. That this association continued contributed profoundly to the circumscription of mumming by devices of protection that tempered the degree to which it could spread chaos within the collectivity. Examined closely, the contextualization of mumming emphasized its control, although its anomic presence was given extensive expression. These safeguards are evident in the social intensification that surrounded mumming, in its timing, in the places of its practice, and in its taming through game. These safeguards are discussed in turn in this section.

Two kinds of intensification were at work during the Christmas season. One was the great increase in social visiting among households, in social drinking among groups of men, and of community-wide social occasions. These took in the major configurations of the collectivity: dyads, groups of familiars, households, and the whole community. Given the paucity of information on religious beliefs and practices in outports, I cannot discuss the embedment of mumming in the Christmas season. Still, the intensification of collective solidarity likely gained import from a central theological tenet of Christmas: the birth of moral community among Christians. The time of Christmas, with its encompassing cosmogenic mood, provided a resilient context for the predations of mumming.[7]

The second process of intensification flowed in the obverse direction, towards that of the breakdown of relationships and of the idea of community. Its vehicle was that of mumming. Successful mumming was predicated on the turning of familiars into strangers. I argued that alienation and unpredictability were suspected to lurk within the selves of others and beyond the community. These two loci of strangeness, beyond the social person but inward and beyond the community but outward, were the basic signs of the paradigm of mumming that linked personhood and collectivity. The appearance of the mummer – shapeless, formless, and anonymous –

keyed the strangeness and potential for badness hidden within the self of everyman to the external boundary of the collectivity of persons, beyond which everyman was openly suspect.

In mumming, the insider became an outsider who was inside – that is, a stranger. The disguise of this outsider brought out the shadow side of person and community: the breakdown through disorder of morality as the grounds for sociality, for the mummer fitted no accepted category of familiar. The implication is that the person-as-mummer was turned inside-out, while the mummer-as-stranger who intruded within the moral community was turned outside-in.

These two processes of intensification pulled the community in opposing directions: mumming was centrifugal, vacuous and anomic, and so reified the worst fears of the villagers; socializing was centripetal, warm and friendly, and so confirmed their hopes. Here there are two contrary conceptions of collectivity: one of moral and social solidarity and the other of alienation and chaos. And the second, ordinarily hidden in the everyday, glared forth. If the first could be likened to a sort of renewal of the moral community, then the second was more akin to its demise. But this was temporary: the very cessation of morality contained within itself the embryo of moral rebirth – for the amoral mummer, unmasked and revealed, was again a basis for meaningful communication among persons. This suggests strongly that mumming mediated these two processes of centrifugality and centripetality. Mumming began with the premises of centrifugality, but by falsifying its own claims to authenticity it transformed these into the premises of centripetality.

Everyday contacts were mediated on the one hand by the formality and morality of etiquette among familiars, and on the other by trust and intimacy among householders. Through mumming these links became mediated by anonymous and monstrous strangers. In more semiotic terms, relationships among signs as media of communication were blocked and displaced. Unable to relate to others who had become strangers, one also may have peered within oneself, to one's strangeness of self, to that which one suspected to be secreted within others, and to that which one thereby discovered to be present in oneself as others saw one. One's strangeness of self was amplified in relation to others who were strangers.

This blockage of communication suggests that mummers as strangers infiltrated the interstices of contact between familiars, thereby displacing and replacing everyday signs of connectivity. This semiotic displacement was a key to the disorder that mummers brought in their wake. Disorder was not accomplished merely by the presence of these feared characters, but by the displacement of the known sign from the connective substance of relationships. In turn this made the mummer the fulcrum of interpersonal contact. Any sense of relationship and community then passed through the matrix of the mummer figure who turned the network of the known – from its closure as the external boundary of the collectivity to its highest density in the intimacy of the home – into a frayed fabric of indeterminacies.

An inspection of mumming in different locales indicates that the capacity of the mummer to mediate the chaotic into the known, and so to disorder the latter, was a graduated one in which the known began to be mediated back into the amorphic, as control shifted from mummer to familiar. Outside in the dark, mummers were most authentic to others. In an ideal way these spatial interstices between homes were closest to the moral boundary of the community. In daily life the use of these locations was dependent on the formality of etiquette and was the least leavened by the intimacy and open sharing of the home. Of course the night heightened the vulnerability of these spaces and impartially blurred the seen and the unknown in its blackness. It was in these locations that persons bolted from mummers. Here the latter were most violent towards others, and others towards them. Here mummers were without restraint or obligations of mutuality towards others, and others towards them. Here one could be uncertain whether a familiar, indeed anyone human, lay beneath the costume. In other words, whether appearance was guise or authenticity.

As mummers knocked for admittance the internal consistency of their character began to alter. Although they still behaved as did strangers, they acknowledged the moral integrity of the home. Control started to shift towards the reconstitution of morality at the very interface of public and private space, of exterior and interior. Yet with their entrance the mummers penetrated this core of solidarity and intimacy. Moreover this locale was highly protective of the most vulnerable sector of the community – its children, the products of its past, the predicators of its future. A lengthier perspective points to the contact between mummer and child as one of the more profound of the entire mumming complex. The capacity of children and parents to withstand and to tame the onslaught of the mummers was an index of the likelihood of the community to reproduce itself through youngsters who would become properly socialized adults.

Within the home, control oscillated between householders and mummers. The latter inserted themselves between householders by behaving like intimates of the former. They behaved as could householders who shared intimacy. Yet the mummers mocked this closeness, and so questioned its integrity. They teased and threatened householders; they entered the inner reaches of the dwelling; and they chased the children. For their part, householders ridiculed and took liberties with the mummers.

Although rules of etiquette were in abeyance, the result was not intimacy as this was experienced within the home, but its converse: a condition of distance that bore an icy resemblance to intimacy. As mummers mimicked intimacy within the family, so the character of trust among householders was mocked and mediated by strangeness. The home, the moral core of community, teetered on the edge of its own metaphoric disruption. In the anonymous and forbidding mummer the householders likely saw not a mere mirror image of themselves but perhaps their extinction as a family. This may be the deepest if implicit truth that mumming touched upon – and therefore the importance of proving the artifice and pretense of the mummer. This revelation would mediate the knowledge of morality back into the chaotic unknown, and so extirpate the latter. Strangeness would be concealed again within the self and beyond the collectivity.

The guessing game was crucial to this. The behavior of mummers within the home is described as frightening but playful. There is no contradiction between these. In chapter 3 I argued that the power of the idea of play is in its capacities for dissolution. It is an amoral medium, and this is its particular terror. It can 'play' with any foundation-for-form, rendering alien the known. But the medium of 'game' is ruled. The freedom of play is keyed to the rules that specify and constrain the conditions of its existence. As a ruled medium, game is a moral domain. This was so of the guessing game. There the mummer no longer played out his own authenticity and destructive design, for these were made contingent by the rules of the game. His acceptance of the game placed the mummer in a moral domain within which he no longer commanded his own fate. Therefore, degrees of control continued to pass to the householders, since they held a mandate to falsify the presumed authenticity of the mummers. With the transition to game, morality was ascendant, although its triumph hardly was assured until the mummer was shown up as sheer disguise.

If the identity of the mummer were guessed accurately, control passed wholly to the householders. Here special attention should be paid to the act of naming oneself: this revelation of biographical person was a moral act that committed the ex-mummer to the obligations of sociality. Thus mummers whose personae were not guessed, and who departed as authentic strangers, left themselves and householders anxious and dissatisfied. The revelation of personhood was a triumph of morality and civility, in a contest won by the household over those concealed forces within person and community that could erode and destroy it. Once the mummer was revealed as familiar, the determinate form of the host-guest relationship replaced the agonistic oscillation of the guessing game, the outcome of which was not predetermined, at least in accordance with the ideal form of mumming.[8]

The banishment of the strangeness and amorality of the mummer through inversion and reversion is now considered. I argue that the device of mumming linked perceptions of personhood to those of community, such that concealment and revelation operated at one and the same time in both domains.

Inside-out, outside-in: inversion and congruency in mumming

To recapitulate the argument so far: the evidence suggests that perception of outport personhood was dualistic. The exterior of personhood, the social person, was accorded positive value. Yet this exterior, molded by social strictures, was perceived to a degree as inauthentic, as camouflage. Lurking within the interior of the person were aspects of a more authentic self that were not to be trusted, and these were accorded negative value. Not that the self as a whole was perceived as negative, but aspects of it that were crucial for interpersonal contacts were comprehended in this way. These negative aspects of self were rarely on display, for the social person conducted his everyday life in accordance with the cordiality of formality. Still one suspected their presence. People were correctly and courteously sociable to one another, yet deeply suspicious and distrustful of one another's 'true' but secret intentions and sentiments. I argue that the outport perception of personhood differentiated, if implicitly, between one's overt social person and one's covert self; that each was accorded a relatively positive or negative value; and that each was perceived as relatively authentic or inauthentic.

In daily life the overt social person was accorded positive value but was perceived as inauthentic, as a moral artifice of social relationships. By contrast the covert self was perceived as authentic but was accorded negative value, since it was not constrained by morality.[9] In other words, the outport perception of personhood contained striking incongruencies between the exterior person and the interior self.

An analogous set of relations can be posited for the outport perception of community and strangerhood, with one signal difference. Strangerhood lay outside the community, covert and hidden from view, beyond moral compact. And although strangerhood was accorded a negative value, it was perceived as authentic and 'true', if amoral and dangerous. This points to an affinity of signs that connoted aspects of the covert self of a person within the community to those that connoted the covert but external condition of strangerhood beyond the community; and an affinity of signs that connoted the overt social person to those of membership within the community. Aspects of both the overt social person and the social relationships of community were accorded a positive value but were perceived as inauthentic. The exterior appearance of the person masked the suspect, negatively-

valued authenticity hidden within the self; while the etiquette of relationships between persons masked the suspect, negatively-valued authenticity
that underlay sociality but that was banished to hidden regions exterior to
the community.

The mummer raised this submerged quality of personhood into view and
made others anxious that it indeed could be authentic – that there was no
radically different quality of being beneath the mummer's surface, nor any
different implication for social relationships. That which had been concealed was revealed, and that which had been revealed was concealed. This
turnabout erased the disjunction between the authentic, but negatively-
valued covert character of self and of the community of familiars, and their
inauthentic but positively-valued overt character. In each of the separate
domains of personhood and community, exterior and interior attributes
became congruent and harmonious with one another.

The donning of mummerhood was an exercise in concealment, the
hiding of the overt and familiar person. Yet it was also a revelation, for it
surfaced and reified a representation of the negatively valued but authentic
aspects of self that persons were suspected to have. Inside-out, negative
aspects of selfhood were revealed; and aspects of the social person, positive
but inauthentic, were concealed. The signs of personhood were inverted in
a manner in keeping with the deepest fears of villagers about others.
Authentic strangerhood that lurked in everyman was amongst them.

With the presence of mummers, outside-in, strangerhood struck at and
burrowed into the interior of the collectivity. Mummers as strangers
inverted the relationship between interior and exterior, replacing familiars
and reversing the signs of social relations. The concealed character of the
social relationship, suspect but authentic, was revealed. To interact with the
mummer was to experience the authentic fragility of the mundane social
relationship, a vulnerability ordinarily hidden in the everyday. Mumming
inverted person in relation to self and in relation to others; and so it also
inverted the social relationship. The inversion of a number of relationships
exponentially subverted the very idea of community as a nexus of
connectivity among households.

If mumming revealed a suspected truth about personhood and about the
social relationship, then it did so as dis-guise. The deep structure of disguise,
as concealment, once more implied that surface appearance was not
authentic. Penetrated, it would become mask and therefore inauthentic.
Thus the rendition of personhood that would emerge from within would
be perceived as authentic. Since the personhood of mummer was of
negative value, its replacement likely would be perceived in a positive vein.
This phase depended on the validation of mumming as mask, as an artifice
that concealed another version of personhood within itself. But the proof of

deception was conditional, not predetermined: in programmatic terms this penetration of artifice could be unsuccessful, and then the mummer would exit as an authentic representation of personhood.

The moral nexus of the guessing game tested the validity of the mumming version of personhood. If this were falsified, it was peeled away to reveal both a familiar AND an authentic personhood, now proven to have been concealed within the mummer. With the validity of mummerhood nullified, the mummer removed his 'veil' and the now authentic person-as-self emerged from within. This reversion cancelled those negative qualities of self that were concealed within the everyday version of personhood. In this moment of revelation there was no contradiction between social personhood and covert selfhood.

The revelation of the falsity of mummerhood likely was one of the few occasions in the outport when there was no disjunction between the positively valued perception of the person and its authenticity. Instead these qualities of personhood were harmonized with one another, while the negatively valued perception of the covert self momentarily became inauthentic and so rendered itself irrelevant. I suggest that in such moments the harmonics of personhood and selfhood were experienced fully and holistically as surface facts. Their congruency was open wholly to public inspection and validation.[10]

One understands once more why mummers and householders were uneasy and distressed if the deception of the former was not falsified. Then the mummer's version of personhood remained authentic and negative, a confirmation of the worst suspicions of villagers about familiars. The mummer departed as he had come, an anonymous stranger outside the morality of etiquette and beyond the incorporation of commensality. As villagers said, then there was no fun, for mummerhood froze in its phase of authenticity and so continued to signify the fracturing of sociality.

I argue that the intrusion of mummers into the community, the outside-in flow of strangeness, reified fears that amoral disorder was the authentic basis of relationships. But the revelation of the familiar hidden within the mummer falsified the latter and authenticated the former. In programmatic terms the mummer-as-stranger, who belonged outside the community, once more was banished beyond its borders. Within the community, relationships were governed again by etiquette, a morality no longer merely formal but also positive and authentic. Therefore in the domain of community the falsity suspected to lurk within everyday relationships was banished, inside-out, beyond the collectivity of familiars. Here too, the previous disjunctions between the overt and the covert, between the positive and the negative, and between the authentic and the inauthentic, were brought into harmony with one another.

In these small settlements a sizable number of individuals participated in mumming and took turns being host and mummer. Programmatically, one can state that the idea of personhood, if not all persons, underwent the harmonic process that to my mind composes the deeper structure of mumming. In turn, relationships were constituted in the main of persons who underwent the host-mummer interchange. Therefore relationships also went through this process. The collection of relationships that connected households to one another, and that constituted the sense of community, consisted of persons who underwent this process, and so forth.

In circles of increasing breadth the entire community annually underwent this comprehensive discourse of concealment and revelation, emerging within as a more solidary unit and protected from without by a strengthened redoubt no longer eroded by internal doubts. Still, as individuals returned to the strictures and strains of daily living, the pattern of duality would reform. Outside-in, suspect qualities of self would be perceived to take authentic shape within others; inside-out, the community would regard with suspicion any incursion from without its circle of familiars. Overlaying all this would be the formalism and reserve of the code of etiquette, perceived dimly as artifice – a mask that precariously hid from view the anarchy of the mummer's blank visage.

Convergence and divergence, concealment and revelation

This interpretation of mumming links one series of harmonic operations in the domain of personhood to an analogous series in the domain of collectivity. These linkages are given as analogic affinities between these two domains. But these affinities are not homologies: this addresses what I take to be a prime function of devices of inversion, one that has to do with convergence and divergence in connections among signs.

In mumming the relationship between the two domains was that of an inversion of signs, so that each domain remained a representation of what the other was not. If personhood turned itself on an axis of inside-out, then the collectivity was involuted, outside-in. Therefore these domains were not related through a simple connection of signifier to signified, of idea to image, in which one could be understood as a derivation of the other, brought into being and formed by it. This reductionist position, still not uncommon, would suggest either that personhood could be derived from collective representations or that community could be constructed as an additive collection of personae.

Instead the ongoing inversion of signs, of each domain in the other, permits a continuing relationship of 'intimate separation' among these respective domains. This maintains the autonomy and internal consistency of the respective domains. It continues to produce the integrity of the distinction between personhood and collectivity while reproducing their intimate separation. Therefore neither domain is concealed in nor subordinated by the other, although the disjunctions within each momentarily are effaced.

These points highlight an elementary principle in the logic of devices of inversion, one that I mentioned in chapter 2: the divergence of signs, their opposition that is inherent in inversion, maintains their domains of signification as distinctly separate yet intimately related. A divergence of signs in devices of inversion is to be distinguished clearly from the condition of their convergence. A convergence of signifiers erases boundaries that separate domains of discourse, enabling either their coalescence into a single domain or the subordination of one domain to the other. The most radical example of a convergence of signs and a coalescence of domains is found in the condition that Victor Turner called 'communitas', in which categorical distinctions ideally are homogenized in terms of overriding common denominators. The inclusive convergence of signs is a test for the possible presence of this condition of being.[11]

In the case of mumming, both convergence and divergence operate. Within each of the respective domains of personhood and community there is the convergence of signs, erasing disjunctions. Yet the continuing inversion of signs between domains, while convergence occurs in each, ensures their intimate separation.

Christmas mumming shows the importance of giving equal attention to both concealment and revelation in what commonly are called reversals or inversions, rather than glossing these operations. Inversion is in-version: one version is implicit within another and reverts to being subsumed by the latter. Unlike reversal, inversion is a same-space phenomenon. In mumming, inversion and reversion form a closed sequence of two phases that revolves around ideas of concealment and revelation. More generally in this sequence, inversion maintains mode of discourse. 'Reversal' does not do this since its operation does not contain its own negation, in other words, reversion. Instead, 'reversal' potentially implicates a radical overturning of social order, however this is defined in terms of magnitude, for it is open-ended and developmental, and so may really lead elsewhere. But inversion is a conservative and conservationist device that indexes reversion and so does not threaten social order. Those who speak of inversion as a seedbed of radical change are in error. Clearly the usage of inversion-reversion as a complementary set should be kept separate from that of reversal.[12]

Inversion, as I have used this term here and in chapter 2, is associated with hierarchical order, but even more so with that of hegemonic order. In turn, inversion has close ties with the idea of the dialectics of encapsulation. The subject is complicated, and I can mention here only some crude distinctions.

The simplest form of hierarchy speaks first and foremost to a rank-ordering from high to low of ideas, symbols, people, or things that are conceived in accordance with a common set of criteria but that are valued differently in terms of the latter. The control of high over low may be primarily that of scale (of resources, access to power, and so forth). Therefore levels of hierarchy may be perceived as more or less interdependent, but also as relatively autonomous of one another: lower-order levels do not depend necessarily for their very existence on higher-order ones. This is the present-day Western, democratic usage of hierarchy.

Hegemony speaks more directly to the control (potentially totalistic) exerted by higher-order levels over lower-order ones. Sider (1980: 24), in a discussion of hegemony with reference to outport Newfoundland, defines the term as 'that aspect of culture which ... most directly seeks to unify production and appropriation', and so to extend appropriation into daily life. Raymond Williams (1977: 110) refers to these relations of domination as 'a saturation of the whole process of living'. Hegemony is characterized by movement towards a unity of control of higher over lower, such that the former dictates the terms of existence (but not the very existence) of the latter. This unity of control fosters dependency, and so too a curious intimacy (often of negative valency) between controllers and controlled. In the case of Newfoundland, hegemonic domination was located primarily outside the outport, but its influence on the quality and substance of life within the community likely was forceful. The inversions of mumming were not a mere reflection of local egalitarianism but of the complex hierarchical interplay of the village and forces that lay beyond its boundaries. The arbitrariness of suspect strangerhood and coercive merchant capital probably were linked.

The most extreme form of hegemonic order is that of 'encompassment' (to whose national, symbolic dimension I will return briefly in chapter 9). Encompassment indexes a control that approaches the unity of totality: the ideas, symbols, and practices, of higher-order levels virtually imagine into existence the forms and qualities of living of lower-order ones, such that the substance of the latter is thought to derive from, or is made over in terms of, the former. Given the hegemonic control of higher-order levels, the existence of lower-order ones is ideally (and therefore potentially) produced and reproduced accordingly. Although traditional cosmologies may well work through forces of encompassment (for example, in the cosmogonic relationship between deities and humankind), its modern exemplars are totalitarian. Among the latter are death camps and concentration camps where utter control over the being of others is its own end, as Edith Wyschogrod (1985) discusses.

The phenomenon of inversion-reversion is not a function of simple hierarchy. It appears most vividly in orders that ideationally and practically have strong hegemonic features, and is less prominent in ones marked by encompassment, since the latter virtually do not admit of any lower-order independence. Inversion offers an appearance of autonomy, free and wild, yet always controlled within limits. Higher-order ideas, values, and positions are not threatened, and either there is consensus as to their worth or submission to their force. In this regard the structure of inversion-reversion translates well into the dynamic of the dialectics of encapsulation. Both strongly implicate the systematic reproduction of order. By contrast, the relative autonomy and variation of levels in a simple hierarchy may not lend themselves to this kind of straightforward involution, while the totalism of encompassment may not brook any opposition, even in pretense.

This rendition of inversion-reversion makes it an especially honed and controlled variant of re-presentation, one that begins to acquire more systemic features of self-regulation. Re-presentation has a highly permeable interface with the wider social order and a loosely-organized interior that admits high uncertainty but little control. Re-presentation through inversion has a less permeable boundary and a more controlled internal organization that strongly inhibits any momentum towards directional change. Although inversion is marked by internal self-regulation, this is in aid of simple transposition, not transformation.

An appreciation of inversion and reversion as a two-part set can open the way to a comparative semiotic of concealment and revelation and their relation to moral order through a consideration of some variants. For example, there are numerous public events that emphasize only the concealment of social personhood. Here concealment reveals an authentic replacement. Such authentic characters often channel powerful forces, frequently paranatural, from the exterior of a collectivity into its interior. Here too the authenticity of revelation is not questioned, even when its force is amoral. Examples close to this variant abound: the visits of the Japanese *Namahage* (Yamamoto 1978), Hopi 'ogres' (Kealiinohomoku 1980), Austrian village *Krampuses* (Honigmann 1977), Inuit *Naluyuks* (Ben-Dor 1969), Eastern Cherokee *Boogers* (Speck and Broom 1951), and Nova Scotia *Belsnickles* (Bauman 1972), to name a few.

These amoral characters do the work of morality because they authentically are out of place in a moral context. In the main their task is to sharpen the contrast between morality and amorality and to test community members, especially children, for these qualities. They are authentic admonitions of the dangers of amorality, and so they evoke moral responses from others. This unanimity of response provides the collectivity with a homogeneous valency in relation to the intruders, who depart still as authentic characters.

A second variant may be called 'transparent concealment'. Here the concealed is not hidden completely, nor is the revealed granted authenticity. Instead concealment and revelation, authenticity and falsity, are perceived as montage, as superimposed images in the composition of the figures. The disguise of costume often signifies that concealment and revelation will cancel out one another. Close to this variant are varieties of impersonation, like those of the carnivalesque, where one perceives as deception that which is revealed by the concealment of the social person. Given the transparency of concealment, deception is inherent in the authenticity of that which is revealed. Therefore the revelation of concealment is understood as inauthentic, and so the figure falsifies its own validity and reverts to its everyday analogue, the social person.

The inherent deception of transparent concealment underscores the morality of customary order. The initial inversion of disguise never fully places this order in doubt: the reversion to normality is built into its concealment. Transparent concealment encourages perception of an authentic reality within disguise, and so renders this surface appearance inauthentic from the outset.

A third variant is the one discussed in this chapter. Here concealment of the social person reveals an authentic alternative to what was hidden. Hence the importance of the guessing game, since the revelation of disguise must be falsified, otherwise it remains authentic. This variant uses the full set of inversion and reversion in distinct sequence. Of those mentioned here, it is the variant closest to a re-presentative and systematic renewal of moral order, especially one predicated on hierarchy. Yet this overall device of renewal, as yet unnamed and still hardly revealed, deserves careful thought lest it remain concealed within superficially similar phenomena.

Intersections

The materials for the Donkey Game were collected almost two decades ago. They reflected my conviction that social anthropology was wedded for life to the intensive immediacy of observable life, and that this reportage, whatever its format or complexity, would necessarily be small-scale. I still believe this a staple of our discipline. But the seclusion of the Donkey Game and the peripherality of its participants also reflected the marginal status of symbolism in Israeli social science, as the mere, expressive detritus of nation-building.

Since that time the shape of Israeli anthropology has reformed. The growth of ethnic awareness and identity among the most studied populations of Israel pushed anthropologists to more intensive work on the role of symbolism and meaning in particular ethnic and religious traditions, and their force in contexts of Israeli life. The rise of ethnic awareness and the growth of an Israeli symbolic anthropology have paralleled one another. Their relationship has been more than a little symbiotic. Given the often public forums for the display of ethnic and religious self-awareness, Israeli symbolic anthropology necessarily moved into the domain of public events, from local dramatic performance and assembly to the enthusiasm of mass pilgrimage.

In all of this the public occasions of the Israeli nation-state are treated as common-sensically obvious and are shoved to the edges of scholarly discourse. Yet Israel is very much a product of a utopian, twentieth century national ideology and its moral formations, versions of which are re-presented and presented through public events of this nation-state. These occasions are at the heart of Benedict Anderson's (1983: 15–6) rendition of the modern nation-state as an 'imagined community'. The following two chapters are efforts to begin to redress the imbalance noted above, by addressing occasions that are tied less to particularistic ethnic and religious ways of making meaning through public occasions, and more to the explicit and implicit claims of this nation-state. To no small degree it is within and through the enveloping claims of nation-statehood, and what Patrick

Wright (1985) calls its 'national past', that ethnic and religious groupings sharpen their conflicts and mold their accommodations with other moral and social ways of acting in the world. While it is through public occasions of different magnitude and scope, like those described in the following two chapters, that agencies of the nation-state try to integrate citizenship and national past to imagine the resolution of internal contradictions that are accentuated in daily living.

Years later, within me the existential tenor of the Donkey Game has become tempered by occasions that thrust ideology towards the forefront of consciousness. During the years I have lived in Israel the country has changed drastically, its anthropologies have struggled for different voices, and I too am not what I was nor perhaps what I hoped to become. The next two chapters are the alpha and omega of this personal shift: from little celebrations of holidays in kindergartens, that inculcate visions and feelings of citizenship, to great national occasions that to an important degree are the ideological florescence and elaboration of the former. All are versions, and so true but false, yet keeping the uncertainties of competing versions and visions at bay, and therefore holistically projecting their claims to morality and truth. I do not think these chapters polemic in tone, but I hope that the frailties and pitfalls, together with the desperate visions of hope, are there to be read.

Chapter 8 was written together with my wife. My parents embarked from Russia for North America, hers to Palestine. Lea was born and bred in Jerusalem. We live mere blocks from the street on which she was raised. Lea is a sociologist, and we work in the same university department. Much of what I learned of Israel has been through dialogue with her and Ronit, our daughter. We talk a lot, try to think through one anothers' viewpoints, and argue not a little. Lea and I also collaborate from time to time. These are all experiences of fun, mutuality, and intense satisfaction.

8   Holiday celebrations in Israeli kindergartens*

The object of education, contended Durkheim (1956: 71), 'is to arouse and to develop in a child a certain number of physical, intellectual, and moral states which are demanded of him by ... the political society as a whole'. Processes of education, he added, are among the dominant means through which 'society perpetually recreates the conditions of its very existence' (1956: 123). Durkheim conjoined two themes that are salient for the modern nation-state. That the political economy of education, especially formal education, is a crucial expression of the ideology and authority of the state. And that the reproduction of social order depends in large measure on the exercise of the power of education through the requisite apparatus of the state.

In the case of Israel the tasks of formal education were less the replication of social order than the construction of an ideological blueprint that contributed to the very creation of the state. The fusion of political ideology and formal organization, in order to influence the maturation of youngsters who were the future generation of citizenry, began in the kindergarten.[1] For example, a veteran Jewish kindergarten teacher[2] reflected as follows on the intimate ties that developed between the Jewish community, the *yishuv*, in pre-state Palestine and the kindergarten. She declared that these were bonds between a form of early-age education and 'the ideas and aspirations that lifted the spirits of those parts of the nation that rebuilt the ruins of its homeland and rejuvenated this'. The Zionist vision of returning to work the land of Israel, she added, 'brought the garden into the kindergarten' (Fayence-Glick 1957: 141). As in numerous other aspects of the nation-building of Israel, that of the kindergarten was linked closely to the practice of proto-national ideology. In this the founders of the Jewish kindergarten in Palestine were influenced directly by the civil nationalism of the kindergarten movement in nineteenth century Germany (see Allen 1986).

Very young children experience and learn the lineaments of personhood

* This chapter was co-authored by Lea Shamgar-Handelman

and world through the family arrangements into which they are born. In these contexts they are enculturated into a sense of hierarchy and status, of division of labor, and of sentiment and loyalty, through notions of kinship and familism that come to be the natural ordering of things. Only later is the child made to realize that parental domination is itself subordinate to the idea of a wider moral order; and that on numerous occasions loyalty and obligation to the collectivity transcend that of familial ties. This transition, however obvious, is essential to the reproduction of the social orders of the state. It clearly is in the interests of representatives of the state to recruit the cooperation of the family in order to achieve societal goals; and so they phrase its relationships to the family in terms of cooperation and consensus. The rhetoric of politicians commonly likens the state and its citizenry to a great family; while the idioms of kinship and familism are used in cognate ways.

Yet this relationship between state and family is fraught with tension. This is evident in times of crisis, should officials intervene in the affairs of family; and especially when they insist that organs of the state are mandated for tasks of social control and affect that the family considers its own (Shamgar-Handelman 1981; Handelman 1978). With regard to children and their maturation, state and family do have overlapping and congruent interests; but their concerns also differ and are continually negotiated.

Bluntly put, all children must learn that their parents are not the natural apex of hierarchy and authority; and that the rights of the collectivity can supersede those of familism. This is integral to the process of maturation in the nation-state. In present-day Israel the young child's entry into the kindergarten is the onset of extended periods in educational settings that are regulated and supervised by organs of the state. The youngster is moved slowly during this lengthy transition from his embeddedness within home and family until, at age eighteen, he enters the army for compulsory service. At this time he is given over wholly by his parents to the authority and service of the state. The transition is one of offspring to citizen.

With regard to this transition, kindergartens in Israel are of especial interest, since their annual round is punctuated by numerous events that on a wider scale are of import to the civil and religious orders of state and nation. In kindergartens the celebration of such occasions is presentational and re-presentational in form. The latter logic of organization is especially suitable to evoke in momentary but concentrated ways the kind of general transition to which we have referred above. Moreover, given the early ages of the youngsters, the experiencing of these celebrations often is designed in clearcut ways. Through such occasions children are involved outside their homes in focused representations that in general are thought to be of import to aspects of the nation-state. Many of these occasions explicitly celebrate versions of tradition and history of the Jewish people, of the renewal and coherence of the Jewish state, and of their integral and consensual synthesis. Scenarios emphasize the joint effort and viability of cooperation between kindergarten and parent, state and citizen, in order to inform the maturation of the child with experiences that begin to situate his personhood in relation to directives of the past and expectations of the future. On a more implicit level the 'hidden agendas' of these scenarios unearth the more problematic relationship between state and family.[3] Numerous celebrations can be understood as versions of the relationship between representations of collectivity and family, through which youngsters are shown and are encouraged to experience that the dominance of the former supplants that of the latter. This sort of exposure is especially important for children in urban locales where different spheres of living are quite compartmentalized, where settings of home and work are separated, and where the access of children to the world of adults is limited. The kindergarten is the first location where children learn of hierarchy and equality outside the home.

This chapter discusses four cases of kindergarten celebrations in relation to the symbolic loads they convey and manipulate through re-presentation. The re-presentational aspects of their scenarios are not like the more cyclical sequence of inversion–reversion discussed in the previous chapter. Instead these are linear projections of irreversible maturation that the child is expected to undergo. It is surprising how little social analysis has been done on questions of whether and how kindergarten youngsters are exposed to the focused manipulations of symbols and symbolic formations of a suprafamilial character, whether in Israel or elsewhere. Studies of kindergartens emphasize the learning of competence in daily interaction (Jones 1969; Shure 1963; Shulz and Florio 1979). Our own argument is closer in spirit to that of Gracey (1975), who contends that the task of teachers in American kindergartens is to drill children in the role of student and, by extension, to prepare them for the rigid routines of bureaucratic, corporate society. Still, work on any kind of ceremonialism in kindergartens is minimal (Heffernan and Todd 1960; Moore 1959); while there are only bare traces of such discussion on higher grades (Bernstein, Elvin, and Peters 1966; Burnett 1969; Fuchs 1969; Judith Kapferer 1981; Waller 1932; Weiss and Weiss 1976).[4]

We will take up a small number of cases from our larger corpus of descriptions of such events, for the following reasons.[5] The integrity of the event as a viable performance is violated if it is not described in and of itself. The celebration, at least in part, should become the context for its own interpretation. Moreover, detailed description enables you to form interpretations alternative to those we argue for. We hardly would insist that there are singular constructions of significance in such celebrations. It also is advantageous to have concrete examples available, perhaps as parameters of discourse for future discussion.

Nonetheless we focus on aspects of these events that are related to our argument of explicit and implicit levels of communication in versions of the interplay of collectivity and family. In particular we attend to the sequencing of enactments. Sequencing may be of signal import in cultures that, according to Lee (1959), are made coherent to their members through lineal codifications of reality. Often in public events those acts placed, for example, 'before' and 'after' implicate the logic of design of the entire sequence of enactment. In occasions of presentation, sequencing is crucial to the emergence of coherent story-lines. In those of re-presentation, sequencing signals which version of reality will supplant another, to emerge climactic or dominant. We attend also to the prominence of symbolic formations in these enactments. These formations will be related to the three categories of person – teacher, child, and parent – whose positioning in relation to one another implicates the rudimentary praxis of collectivity and family that is enacted in the kindergarten.

Kindergarten and celebration in Israel

The first kindergarten in Palestine, intended as a preparatory class for elementary school, was established in 1898. The language of instruction was German, translated into those of the pupils. The first Hebrew-speaking Zionist kindergarten opened in 1911. Unlike its predecessors it was an autonomous unit for early-age education. These kindergartens gave especial attention to the cultivation of the Zionist spirit: for example, to the values of working the land and building the nation (Fayence-Glick 1957: 141). Nonetheless there were strong continuities with the civil virtues of patriotism, citizenship, and political responsibility propagated in German kindergartens of the nineteenth century (Allen 1986: 437).

By 1919 there were thirty-three Jewish kindergartens in Palestine, with a total of over 2,000 pupils. During the British Mandate the prevalent pattern was of a variety of kindergarten frameworks, Zionist and other, that were subsidized by numerous sources. After statehood, in 1948, kindergarten education was centralized and made mandatory for children at age five. From the 1920s until the present the demand for places in kindergartens almost always exceeded those available. In 1982–83 some 250,000 children between the ages of two and five were enrolled in 2,035 kindergartens. Of those aged two, 63.6 percent were enrolled; while for those aged three and above the equivalent proportions were over 90 percent (State of Israel 1983: 654).

Throughout the period of Zionist early-age education the kindergarten was conceived of as an instrument of national purpose: one that would help to transform the child into an Israeli person different from that of his parents, who in the main were recent immigrants from diverse cultures. Writing of the Mandatory period, Katerbursky (1962: 56), a veteran educator, stated: 'The obligation of the kindergarten is to uproot bad habits that the children bring from home'. Through the child the parents too were to be resocialized. If anything, themes of inculcation intensified after statehood, with mass immigration and a more centralized educationist bureaucracy. Numerous books of instruction and advice for kindergarten teachers were published. These attest to goals of educating parents as well as children, and to enlisting the youngsters as allies in this endeavor (Zanbank-Wilf 1958: 57; Naftali and Nir-Yaniv 1974; Shemer 1966; Ministry of Education and Culture 1967).

During the *yishuv* period and after, the celebration of holidays in the kindergarten was seen by educators as a powerful medium through which to inculcate children in what was referred to as the embedding of traditional contents in new patterns (Rabinowitz 1958). Writing primarily of the *yishuv*, Fayence-Glick (1957: 141) commented that many weeks were spent in preparation for these celebrations, and that these, 'filled, and are filling today, most of the teaching year . . . and it is as if the kindergarten life is one long holiday with intermissions for pieces of secularity and intervals of reality'.

Parents were integral to these celebrations. They were lectured on the meanings of holidays; and they were taught songs and dances of the kindergarten, so that they could participate fully in the celebratory education of their offspring (Katerbursky 1962: 72). The implicit effect of these didactics was to bring parents and children together under the tutelage of teachers.

In more recent instruction books the teacher is featured as a touchstone of tradition, destroyed for parents who have undergone the traumatic dislocations of immigration. The teacher too is a wellspring of modernism in the synthesis of new patterns of celebration from different Jewish traditions (Rabinowitz 1958). No matter how naive these attitudes are, they reflect the cultural melting-pot ideology of zionism, so prominent and forceful in the early years of statehood. In these books, parents often are depicted as persons who have little information of value on ceremony in the new state. Along with their young offspring, they must be taught how to prepare the materia of ceremonialism (food, dishes, costumes, and so forth), and they must learn the symbols, songs, dances, and stories of holidays used and narrated in the kindergarten (Rabinowitz 1958). Holidays are understood by the advisors of teachers as special foci for the enculturation of the family as a whole.

In general the young child is understood, if dimly, by educators as a small-scale mediator of relationships between state and family, between public and private domains, and between paradigmatic and particularistic ideas of culture. All these relationships have built into them potentially conflicting loyalties, obligations, and rights – but these rarely are recognized by educators. Hidden in their writings is the premise that the control of the child as a resource is crucial to the reproduction of the nation-state. On the one hand the child is the citizen and culture-bearer of the future. On the other the child as parent-to-be is essential to the formation of the family to come.

Therefore serious thought is given to the planning of kindergarten celebrations; and instruction books for kindergarten teachers offer various scenarios for their enactment. These are designed less to instruct didactically or to encourage reflection. Instead emphasis is placed on the arousal of emotion through symbolic forms that evoke collective sentiments. In general there is a profusion of what Langer (1953) called 'presentational' symbolism: in her terms, media that engage the senses more than the critical faculties. Participants should experience enactments by living through their formats rather than as spectators. Instruction books note that the kindergarten child needs the emotional experience of a holiday, not a logical explanation nor historicist exposition. Ideally the celebration should be a 'common experience' that 'uplifts the spirit' and that encourages feelings of togetherness (Rabinowitz 1958).

In the views of kindergarten educators, such arousal is induced if scenarios are well-designed, their enactment left less to chance. The architectonics of celebration should be logical and holistic, with defined segments of opening, elaboration, and closure (Fayence-Glick 1948). Attention should be given to one or more major ideas or motifs, to scheduling synchronized with calendrical cycles, to the sequencing and progression of the program, and to overt symbols. Often these symbols or signs are both 'living' and 'lived through', such that the physical positioning itself of the participants creates symbolic formations. The symbol comes alive, and participants live through this both as a collectivity and as individuals. These devices powerfully invoke a metonymy of motifs of celebration and their experiencing, and a synecdoche in which each part of the collective entity replicates and signifies the coherence and unity of the whole. Educators appear well aware of this more explicit level of manipulation of symbols. But since teachers are quite autonomous in how they plan celebrations, there is a good deal of variation in enactments among kindergartens.

But kindergarten educators often deny that, at a more implicit level, symbolic formations in celebrations actively manipulate versions of relationships between teacher and parent, collectivity and family. Nonetheless, we argue that each category of participant – teacher, child, and parent – has weight beyond the immediate persons who participate in these events. The teacher is a statist figure, a 'gardener' whose task it is to cultivate, and so to enculturate, her young charges. In Durkheim's (1956: 89) words, the teacher 'is the agent of a great moral person who surpasses him: it is society . . . the teacher is the interpreter of the great moral ideas of his time'. Licensed by the Ministry of Education, and subject in part to its curricula and supervision, the teacher is the first official-like figure with whom the little child comes into continuous contact outside the home. Her structural position in no small measure is in opposition to that of parent and home. For four to five hours a day, six days a week, she is in charge of a collection of children, indeed of a small collectivity, within which each child in theory is equal in worth and status to every other, and where she has no vested interest in the particulars of any one. Her criteria of sentiment are 'objectified' in terms of more universalistic indices, like those of a child's capabilities, capacities, and behavior. Her mandate is to help mold the child, and through the youngster to affect his current family of procreation and his future family of orientation.

The child's experience and knowledge, sentiment and loyalty, derive almost wholly from the enveloping primary group of the family. In the course of years of attendance in educational institutions, he ideally will be reconstituted in the image and substance of citizen: one whose ultimate loyalties will be to the abstract idea of the nation-state. Although his attachments to family are neither attenuated nor diminished, there must occur a shift in the positional hierarchy of family and state, with the latter coming to envelop the former. This transition is also about the standardization of the biographical uniqueness of the individual and of the individual family. We believe these processes are begun in the kindergarten, and perhaps are most concentrated in its celebrations.

Kindergarten celebrations

The events to be discussed are representative of the range of holidays celebrated in Jewish Israeli kindergartens. Given the paucity of information available on such celebrations, we prefer to inform you with a sense of the variation among these occasions, rather than to limit our focus to one or two categories of holiday.[6] The first two of our cases, *Hannuka* and *Purim*, are traditional holidays, but not Days of Rest in the liturgical calendar. Both commemorate ancient victories: *Hannuka* of the Maccabees and of the rededication of the Temple in Jerusalem, and *Purim* the saving of the Jews of Shushan, in Persia, through the influence of Queen Esther. In varying degrees both are celebrated in home and synagogue, and *Purim* also in the street. Our analysis of a *Ḥannuka* celebration demonstrates the re-presentation of hierarchy, such that the family is shown to be enveloped by the collectivity. The case of *Purim* we discuss brings out an implicit premise that the maturation of children moves them from a condition closer to nature to one of civilization, and so towards their assumption of citizenship in the future. The third case, Mother's Day, is borrowed from Western popular culture, and is wholly a secular occasion of no official standing. The implications of our case are that it is the collectivity that is made to mandate the legitimacy of the family, and not the reverse that is closer to the perspective of the family. The fourth case, Jerusalem Day, is a secular state commemoration of the reunification of Jerusalem following the 1967 Six-Day War. Our analysis of this case points to the forging through symbolism of direct links between the collectivity and the child as citizen of the future, without the mediation of the family.

All of these cases offer implicit versions of hierarchical relationships between collectivity and family that should reverse the early-age experiences of the child. The re-presentations in these versions are hegemonic, sometimes approaching even that of encompassment, in the way these terms were used in the conclusion to the previous chapter. We stress that youngsters experience dozens of such celebrations during their first few years of education. Explicit themes, contents, and forms vary within and among kinds of celebrations. But the kinds of implicit relationships between collectivity and family that emerge from our cases likely have a cachet of relevance that extends to numerous other kindergarten celebrations. It is the cumulative accretion of these experiences that has pervasive effects on the child.

All the celebrations described took place on the kindergarten premises. The kindergarten is defined as 'the child's world', and the sole adult who has a legitimate place there is the teacher. Parents always are guests in the kindergarten. Nothing better exemplifies this attitude than the chairs in the kindergartens visited, where no more than one or two full-sized ones were found. As a rule the teacher sits on a full-sized chair, and at her feet as it were, the children on small chairs. When parents are invited, be it to a celebration, to a parent–teacher meeting or to their child's birthday party, they always are seated on the children's chairs. A parent in the kindergarten always occupies a child's place.

The children were given explanations in their respective kindergartens prior to a celebration with regard to the character of the holiday, its import for the people of Israel or for the children themselves (as in Mother's Day), its dominant symbols, and some rudimentary historical background. More complicated enactments by the children were rehearsed beforehand. Unless otherwise specified, all the actions described were in accordance with the explicit instructions and orchestration of the teachers.

Ḥannuka: hierarchy, family, and collectivity

Ḥannuka, the Festival of Lights, commemorates the victory of the Maccabees over the Seleucids, and their rededication of the Temple in 165 BCE. According to the *Talmud*, there was only enough undefiled oil for one day of lamp-lighting. Miraculously the oil multiplied into an amount sufficient for eight days. *Ḥannuka* is celebrated for eight consecutive days in the home, primarily by the lighting of an additional candle each day, in an eight-branched candelabrum, the *ḥannukia* (pl. *ḥannukiot*). An extra candle, the *shamash*, is used to kindle the others. *Ḥannuka* celebrates liberation from foreign domination: it is a triumph of faith, of the few over the many, the weak over the strong. In present-day Israel the martial spirit of this holiday casts reflections on the struggle of the Jewish people to create a unified national homeland.

Books of instruction for kindergarten teachers suggest that the major motif be heroism in Israel. The enactment should evoke the emotional experience of the occasion. The central signs of the celebration should be the *ḥannukia*, candles, tops[7], and the national flag. The locale of the party should be filled with light, just as the shirts or blouses of the children should be white, to create an atmosphere of joyous luminosity. The best time is late afternoon or early evening: these hours evoke the uplifting illumination of the holiday from the midst of darkness and the depths of despair; and they connect the kindergarten to the home, where candles may be lit soon after. Scenarios suggest that a central *ḥannukia* be lit by an adult; that parents light small *ḥannukiot* made by their children; that the children form 'living *ḥannukiot*'; and that parents and children dance or play games together (Rabinowitz 1958). Certain of these motifs were incorporated into the example that follows.[8]

Description: The party began at 4.30 pm. Thirty-two children, aged four to five, and their mothers sat at tables placed along three walls of the room. Only a few fathers attended. A name-card marked the place of each child. White tablecloths covered the tables. At the centre of each were a vase of flowers, bags of candies, and candles equal to the number of children at that table. Before each child stood a little *ḥannukia* make by that youngster. On the walls and windows were hung painted paper *ḥannukiot*, oil pitchers, candles, and tops, all of which had been prepared in the kindergarten. Against the fourth wall stood a large *ḥannukia*, constructed of toy blocks covered with colored paper, that supported eight colored candles and the *shamash*.

An accordionist played melodies of the holiday. The teacher welcomed those present, and at a prearranged signal her helper extinguished the lights. Each mother lit a candle and aided her child to kindle his own little *hannukia*. The room lights were turned on. A father lit the large *hannukia* of toy blocks, and recited the requisite prayers. As he did so, the teacher instructed the children: 'Remember, when father says a blessing, you must sit quietly and listen to the blessing'. Holiday songs followed.

The teacher announced: 'Now we want to make a living *hannukia*. A living *hannukia* that walks and sings, a *hannukia* of parents and children'. She arranged the mothers and their children in a straight line, so that each child stood in front of his mother. An additional mother–child pair, the *shamash*, stood some feet to the side. Each mother held a candle, and each youngster a blue or white ribbon. Each child gave one end of his ribbon to the child-*shamash*. In this formation all children were attached to the *shamash* by their ribbons, and each mother to her own child. The mother of the *shamash* lit the candles held by the others. The lights were extinguished again, the room lit by the living *hannukia* in the gathering twilight. The accordionist played a melody of the holiday, 'We came to chase away the darkness', as each mother walked around her child. The lights were turned on. The mothers returned to their seats as a group, followed by their children.

The children and mothers of one table returned to the centre of the room and were told by the teacher: 'The children will be the spinning tops. Get down, children.' They fell to their knees, bent their heads, and curled their bodies forward. Each mother stood behind her child. The teacher narrated: 'The whole year the spinning tops were asleep in their box. From last year until this year, until now. And the children said to them, "Wake up, spinning tops. *Hannuka* has come. We want to play with you."' To a background of holiday melodies the teacher moved from child to child, touching their hand. With each contact a child awakened, stood, raised his arms, and began to spin. Each mother spun her child, first clockwise, then counterclockwise. Next the mothers became the tops, spun by their children in one direction and then the other. The teacher instructed the second table: 'You'll also be the spinning tops. Each mother will spin her own child and when I give the signal, change roles. Alright? Let's start . . . The children are the spinning tops . . . the parents are the spinning tops'. Those at the third table followed.

Mothers and children held hands, formed an unbroken circle, and danced round and round the teacher. Only one father joined the circle. Singing and food followed. As 6 pm approached, the teacher gave the participants permission to leave, and the party broke up.

Discussion: This event is composed of three major segments, the overt symbolism of which is explicit. The first focuses on the serious traditionalism of the holiday, primarily through the *hannukia*. This segment brings out the connectivity between past and present. The second works through the make-believe of the spinning top, and evokes the relationship between present and future.

The initial segment proceeds through a series of candle lightings: mother helps her child to kindle the small *hannukia*, father lights the large *hannukia*, and candles are lit on the living *hannukia*. These actions and others are embedded in the melodies and songs of the holiday that tell of heroism, victory, and the illumination of darkness. These themes weave together emotion and experience to carry the past into the present. The blue and white ribbons of the living *hannukia* are the official colors of the state, and of its flag and national emblem. In the living *hannukia* ancient triumph is fused with modern renaissance.

Here the idea of family is central. The enactment replicates symbolic acts – the kindling of candles and prayers – that should take place within the home, and that delineate familial roles and an elementary division of labor. Thus it is apt for mother to help her small child, in this instance to light the *hannukia*. Moreover it is appropriate for father, the male head of household, to recite the accompanying prayers on behalf of the family. Here one father does this on behalf of the assembly. The symbolism of this enactment then re-presents and transcends the level of the family. The 'living *hannukia*' envelops all the mothers and children, while respecting the singularity of individual families, shown here by the dyads of mother and child. Each mother stands behind her child, and walks around and envelops the latter, delineating the family unit. This living *hannukia* is a collective sign that also is emblematic of collectivity; while this collectivity itself is constituted of smaller family units.

The living *hannukia* projects into the present the presence of past heroism and dedication. This is done through the living bodies of mothers and children, who themselves compose the shape and substance of this central symbol. Thus the collectivity is re-presented as living through family units, just as the latter live within and through the former. Each is made to be seen as integral to the other. However the connotation is that the collectivity is of a higher order than the individual family, since here it subsumes the latter.

In contrast to the seriousness of the first segment, the second is a playful re-presentation. Its motif is the top, a child's holiday toy that itself is inscribed with Hebrew letters that denote the miraculous. But in this segment commemoration and tradition are not marked. Instead the make-believe is evoked, slumber is shattered, and the participants act joyously in the holiday mood. Again the focus is that of the family unit, represented by dyads of mother and child. The hierarchy at the close of the first segment is kept. The teacher activates each child, and the latter performs under the direction of mother.

But in this make-believe segment, mother and child switch roles: the former becomes the sleeping top that is awakened and directed by her child. Unlike the inscription of tradition in the first segment, the playful is full of potential, as is the youngster who eventually will exchange the role of child for that of adult. As a mature adult the child will become a parent, bringing into being and controlling children of his own. This segment projects the child, as parent-to-be, towards a future in which he will replace his parents and will replicate their roles and tasks. Through the two segments past and future are joined together with a sense of the movement of generations. Whereas the first segment recreates family and collectivity in the images of tradition, the second segment shows the transitoriness of particular parents and the direction of succession. For the child the experience may evoke some feeling that his own parents are not timeless monoliths that will structure his world indefinitely.

The third segment opens with an unbroken circle dance of mothers and children who revolve around the axis of the teacher.[9] This formation is again a re-presentation of the relationship between family and collectivity. The circle dance blurs the distinctiveness of particular families and, within these, of parents and children, adults and youngsters. The delineation of family units has disappeared. Instead all are closer to being discrete and egalitarian individuals who themselves are part of a greater and embracing collectivity. This formation connotes the connectivity of present and future citizens, orientated towards an axial centre.

In this and other kindergarten celebrations the teacher is sole arbiter and ultimate authority. Children see her control parental figures before their very eyes. We argue that the teacher is a statist figure, perhaps the earliest concretization of authority outside the home that very young children encounter. In these celebrations she is not an alternative source of authority to that of parents, as she may be perceived by children in the daily life of the kindergarten. Instead she is the pinnacle of hierarchy that supersedes and that subsumes the family. Thus the whole enactment is framed by the architectonics of hierarchy that are external to, but that act upon, the family unit. All actions of such celebrations, regardless of their explicit content, are imbued with this quality of hierarchy.

The implicit messages of this *Hannuka* celebration are of hierarchy from a more statist perspective. The first segment constructs a version of the superordination of roles within the family, and then embeds the latter within a version of collectivity. The second deconstructs the centrality of family status and alters hierarchical relationships among family members. The third emphasizes equality among citizens, all of whom are orientated towards the statist figure of the teacher. In other words, through these re-presentations the family is shown to be made over into a society of citizenry.

In the first segment the child is dependent upon and subordinate to his mother in order to light the little *hannukia*. In turn, both are dependent upon the figure of the father in order to light the large *hannukia* and to recite prayers on behalf of the whole family. This series is an accurate rendition of the comparative status of elementary roles within the family. Family units then are made to constitute a formation that is emblematic of the collectivity, the living *hannukia*. The collectivity is seen to exist as a coordinated assemblage of families. Here individual families are dependent upon and subordinate to the collectivity in order to relate to one another, and in order to create an alive and enduring vision of tradition and belief. The first segment builds up the sign of the *hannukia* in increasing degrees of envelopment and hierarchy. The apex is the living of this collective emblem. Integral to this are the ribbons, in the national colors, held by the children. Thus the *hannukia* itself is imbued with the symbolism of statehood; while implicit in this more traditional emblem is a modern version.

The second segment begins with a rendition of hierarchical family roles. The dyad of mother and child outlines the coherence of the family unit. The mother directs the movements of the spinning top, her child, in an accurate depiction of status and authority in relation to her offspring. But their switching of roles is at one and the same time a re-presentation of independence and equality. The autonomy of children, and their founding of families, is expected to be an outcome of maturation.[10] Through this process children partially are freed of their subordination to their family of procreation, and thereby are inculcated in their obligations of citizenship to the nation–state. As citizens, all Israelis are the theoretical equals of one another and are subordinate to the state without the intervening mediation of the family. In the third segment, the circle dance, there is no characterization of the family unit: the unbroken circle evokes egalitarianism and common effort, and all the dancers are orientated towards their common centre. There, orchestrating their actions, stands the teacher, just as the state is positioned in relation to its citizens.

Like the *hannukia* alive, the circle dance is a living, collective formation. But each is in structural opposition to the other. The *hannukia* depends on the family and on its internal hierarchy for its own existence. The circle dance eliminates the specificity of the family unit and simultaneously relates each participant in equality to all others and to a statist apex of hierarchy that is not representative of family. In the sequencing of this celebration the unbroken circle with its apical centre supplants the cellular *ḥannukia*; just as, for children, with time the state will supersede their parents as the pinnacle of authority.

Purim: the evolution of maturity

Purim commemorates the delivery of the Jews of Shushan from the evil designs of their enemies through the persuasions of Esther, the Jewish queen of the Persian monarch. This story is read in the synagogue; and the holiday is celebrated by a festive family meal, and by the exchange of gifts of food among relatives and friends. An especially joyous holiday, it is virtually the only time in the liturgical calendar when some license in dress and behavior is encouraged. Secular celebrations take the form of dressing up in costume and attending parties.

Instruction books designate the holiday as an entertainment, with children in costume and parents in attendance. Little mention is made of the traditional import of the holiday, and scenarios for its celebration rarely are given. The explicit enactment of the example we discuss was intended to entertain and to amuse the youngsters and their mothers. But within this is a degree of implicit patterning that connotes the role of the kindergarten in the maturation of children. Of this the teacher denied any conscious knowledge.

Description: This celebration was held for three-year-olds. Some two weeks before, the teacher requested that the children be dressed in animal costumes. Her reason was that such figures were closest to the world of the child, and therefore more comprehensible to the youngsters. If this were not possible, then the child should be dressed as a clown. A few days prior to the party each mother informed the teacher of the costume her child would wear, to enable the teacher to prepare her program.

The party took place in the late afternoon, at the onset of the holiday. Mothers and children were arranged in a wide semi-circle, facing an open area in which the teacher stood. Mothers sat on the tiny kindergarten chairs, their offspring on the floor before them. Music of the holiday played in the background.

The celebration consisted of two segments, separated by an intermediate segment of an unbroken circle dance. In the first the children exhibited their costumes before the assembly in a set order of appearance. In the second, five mothers in clown costumes performed a rehearsed dance and song. The teacher, dressed as a clown, organized the showing of costumes through a simple narrative. Many years ago, she declaimed, there was a king, and she called out a boy dressed as a king. He was joined by a girl dressed as a queen. In their court, continued the teacher, there was a zoo full of animals. She called forth the inhabitants of the zoo. As each kind of character came forth a song that described its typical movements or activities was sung.

The following was the order of appearance. Five cats walked on all fours and meowed. Then three rabbits hopped out. A bear lumbered forth fiercely and was introduced as a 'teddy bear'. Three dainty dolls stepped out and were described as living in cardboard boxes. All of these dwelled in the royal zoo. The teacher told a soldier, a policeman, and a cowboy to come forward, introduced them as the 'royal guard', and marched with them around the semi-circle. This ended the narrative of the zoo within the royal court. The remaining children, all dressed as clowns, were called forth. After this, all the mothers and children formed an unbroken circle, with the teacher at its centre, and danced to the melody of a song about a little clown.

The teacher announced that the performance of the children had ended. She requested the performing mothers to sing. Each of their costumes was of a single color, and their song described the activities of clowns dressed in each of these colors. They sang in a line, with the teacher at their head. Food followed, and the party concluded.

Discussion: Unlike the *Ḥannuka* celebration, that of *Purim* was not thought to have any coherent scenario or explicit meaning. The declared intention was to have fun and to enable the youngsters to play make-believe characters. The teacher had hoped that all these characters would be animals. Faced with a mixed bag of costuming, she used a simple narrative to order their appearance. On a more implicit level this ordering is of direct relevance to our contention that kindergarten celebrations, in various ways, are engaged in the re-presentation of rudimentary socialization, in the direction of adulthood and citizenship.

The teacher recasts the kindergarten as the court of a king and queen. This role play is in keeping with the story of *Purim*, of Queen Esther and her Persian monarch. But there are no further connotations of the text of the holiday. Nonetheless, monarchy and court are emblematic of hierarchy, of moral order, and of social control. These are symbols of maturity and of statehood that exist above and beyond those of home and family. A zoo is situated within the court and is filled with characters. In Israel, zoos are institutions where wild animals, instinctive and unconstrained in their nature, are locked in cages, artifacts of civilization that place external restraints on these creatures. This is a popular view of the zoo. In the teacher's perception small children are close to the world of animals, driven by their instincts and governed neither by obligations of maturity nor by norms of civilization. In the enactment children-as-animals are placed in a zoo, itself within a court. Through these metaphors the kindergarten is made over into a locale of moral order with connotations of ultimate authority and so of statehood, and into a place of confinement for those who have yet to learn internal restraint. Is it fortuitous in this instance that the kindergarten, called in Hebrew a 'garden of children' (*gan yeladim*), is turned into a zoo, called in Hebrew a 'garden of animals' (*gan ḥayot*)?

The order of appearance of the inhabitants of the zoo intimates strongly that the more 'natural' state of the youngsters is conditional. Their sequencing projects a developmental image of enculturation, of progressing towards maturity within metaphors of hierarchy and control. The first animal to appear is the cat. Although some cats in Israel are pets, its cities are pervaded by a profusion of undomesticated alley cats, fierce, and wary of humans. Even the pet cat is seen as a comparatively independent and autonomous creature. In her narrative the teacher describes the children-as-cats as 'looking for friends'. That is, these make-believe cats desire to establish relationships, connoting their potential domestication through sociability.

The next is the rabbit. In Israel this creature usually exists in the wild, and sometimes as a pet. In either instance it is thought of as timid, passive, and docile – a vegetarian in contrast to the predatory cat. Although wild, the rabbit is more easily caged and more controllable that the cat. The rabbit is followed by a child dressed as a bear. Although the child plays the gruff bear with gusto, the teacher turns this wild and fierce creature into a 'teddy bear'. Unlike cat and rabbit, the teddy-bear is a child's plaything. A toy, it is the human product of its natural counterpart – that is, a copy. Its animalism is man-made. A product of culture, it is a fully controlled and domesticated creation, in contrast to cat and rabbit. Still, the teddy-bear retains its animal form.

The doll appears next. Again this is a child's plaything and is man-made. Yet unlike the teddy-bear it is created in a human image, and its attributes of behavior are largely those of a person. According to the narrative the doll lives in a cardboard box, its own enclosure that is somewhat more akin to a home than is a cage. Where the teddy-bear is a play upon nature, the doll is a reflection of humanity and civilization. Of all these zoo creatures the doll is the most domesticated and restrained. These controls are inherent in and emerge from its human form and its attributes of culture. They are not a shell of strictures imposed from without, as in the case of cat and rabbit, nor an intermediate being, a domesticated animal, like the teddy-bear.

Left with a soldier, a policeman, and a cowboy, the teacher makes of them a 'royal guard'. These are not inhabitants of the zoo, but stand outside it. They close and complete the framework of social control introduced by the royal figures. Like the latter the royal guards are fully human figures whose roles embody a regimentation of maturity and order. They are guardians of moral codes against the predations of more impulsive, natural beings. These associations are reinforced as the teacher takes these guardians by the arm and they march together. As she had not done with those within the zoo, the teacher identifies herself with children who, by taking on roles of control and order, play themselves as they should become in the future – as mature adults.

Wittingly or not, the teacher has created a small drama about the evolution and the enculturation of humanity and hierarchy that leads to maturity and the assumption of responsibility beyond that of the familial. Framed at the outset and at the close by human figures with statist and hierarchical connotations, the characters of the zoo are transposed from the wild to the tame, from creatures of instinct to artifacts of culture. Just as their mothers watch this encoding from the periphery, so these youngsters see their mothers watching this happen to them.

The figure of the clown was intended by the teacher as a fallback costume for the children. Clowns were not included within court and zoo, but were shown afterward. These residual figures have no logical connection to prior actions in the sequence. The clowns are simply unabashed figures of fun, in keeping with the good humor of this holiday. But these figures also are depictions of immaturity, for their costumes lack the distinctiveness of gender differences. These child–clowns contrast with the adult clowns who perform a bit later on.

The appearance of the child–clowns is followed by a circle dance of all mothers and children. As noted, the connotations of this formation are of collectivity, egalitarianism, and joint effort. Here there is no delineation of the family unit, nor of the special bond between mother and child. The teacher reunites the children with persons who first and foremost are adults, rather than mothers, after these little people have been re-presented as trained and matured in an idiom of moral and social order. This process is validated in the second segment of the celebration. The teacher and clown-mothers perform. The figure of the clown appears here as the apex of authority and maturity, with the teacher at its pinnacle. In contrast to the clown-children, the clown-mothers and the teacher are big, adult clowns. They play consciously, with a freedom of action that accrues when self-discipline is more assured – when one is well-aware that one is not that which one plays at. But the similarity of costuming of the little clowns and the big ones puts them all on the same continuum of maturation. This then parallels and replicates, through another medium, the messages of maturation in the enactment of court and zoo. In the instance of the clowns the message is that maturation takes time but that the little ones are on the right track.

The entire enactment is an extended metaphor of a process of maturation that the child will undergo in order to turn into an adult member of a wider collectivity. The children are re-presented through court and zoo, in different stages of development. The egalitarian circle dance projects the enactment towards a future in which youngsters take their place of equality alongside their parents. Overlapping these activities, the clown–children blend easily into the figures of the clown–mothers and the clown–teacher, who here are at the apex of adulthood.

Mother's Day: the creation of family and intimacy

This party was celebrated together by some forty children aged three, four, and five, from three separate classes of the same kindergarten. The explicit aim of the teacher was to have the youngsters demonstrate their love and respect for their mothers. This included the giving of gifts by the child to his mother. However the sequencing of enactment conveys a more implicit pattern: that it is the collectivity, through the teacher, that brings into being the affective bonds of the mother–child relationship.

Description: During previous days each child prepared a present for his mother: a piece of shaped dough, decorated, baked, and lacquered. Pierced, this could be hung pendant-like. Each gift was wrapped, together with a greeting card. Before the celebration, vases of flowers were placed on tables, as well as an additional flower for each mother. The children arrived that day at their usual hour; their mothers were invited for midmorning. The small chairs were arranged in a large unbroken circle. An accordionist provided music.

Each mother was seated, her offspring before her on a cushion. The teacher stood in the centre of the circle. From the outset she instructed the children on how to greet and to behave towards their mothers. In this the teacher arrogated to herself a high degree of freedom of intervention in the intimacies of the mother–child relationship. 'Come children', she cried, 'let's say a big "hello" to mother! Let's give mother a big hug! Let's sing together, "What a Happy Day is Mother's Day".' After the song each child was handed a flower. They sang together 'A Fine Bouquet of Flowers for Mother'. 'Give the flower to mother,' exclaimed the teacher, 'and give kisses to mother.' Each child turned, gave his mother the flower, and kissed her.

The mothers stood and were put in pairs. Each pair faced one another and together held their two flowers. The children formed a large circle and, holding hands, walked around all the pairs of mothers and sang. Mothers and children sat and sang together. The teacher said a few words to the youngsters on the importance of being nice to mother. The children stood, faced their mothers, and sang: 'Let's bless mother, blessings for Mother's Day. Be happy in your life, for the coming year. Arise and reach 120 years.'[11] The teacher instructed: 'Give mother a big hug and sing, "My dear mother loves only me, yes, only me, yes, only me".' After they did so, she added, 'Now smile to mother.'

The mothers closed their eyes and each child gave his mother the present made especially for her; and according to instruction, gave her 'a very warm kiss.' The children sang together, while the mothers hung the pendants on themselves. Each mother and child formed pairs and danced and sang together. The lyrics concerned physical coordination of the 'look up, look down' variety. The teacher enunciated the lyrics, so that these became instructions for movement that were followed accurately. All returned to their places. Since the day was Friday, said the teacher, she and the children would teach the mothers a song with which to welcome the Sabbath. After this the teacher pronounced the 'ceremony' completed.

One mother stood and declared: 'We want to say that it's true that we're the children's mothers. But we want to thank and to give a present to the real mother of the children while they're in the kindergarten. We want to give her this bouquet of flowers.' A youngster was handed the bouquet and presented it to the teacher, while the mothers applauded. The teacher offered snacks, and the party closed.

Discussion: The explicit scenario of this celebration is clear. The children show their affection for their mothers in order to honor them. These sentiments of emotional closeness are expressed through various media: song, dance, gifts, and numerous tactile gestures. According to the teacher the use of different media was intended to declare emphatically the strength and vitality of the mother–child bond. The sequencing of these numerous acts was not meant to convey any hidden agenda. Instead their purpose was to lengthen the celebration, and so to give the children many opportunities to demonstrate their appreciation.

But there is a more implicit patterning in this sequence: one that projects the creation of the familial bond out of collective formations, under the supervision of the teacher. The major formation consists of an outer circle of mothers, an inner circle of children, and the teacher in the centre. Each concentric circle constitutes a category of person – that is, mother and child. The child is situated between mother and teacher. Although each child is placed close to his mother, the expression of affect in this dyad is orchestrated wholly by the teacher.

The enactment initially delineates the social category of motherhood. Mother is welcomed first as something of a 'stranger', and the youngsters are told exactly how to show her affection ('Let's say a big "hello" to mother! Let's give mother a big hug!'). Such instruction may be necessary to coordinate the actions of participants, especially when half are little children. Yet these directives also impress that an acquaintanceship is being formulated, that the category of children is being introduced to that of mother. It is as if, within the kindergarten, the abstract category of mother is being made real to the child. The intimacy of the mother–child bond, that of course antedates the kindergarten experience, is made over here as the creation of the teacher.

The first gift follows: a flower given the child by the teacher, that he in turn presents to his mother. This gift is standardized for all of the mothers. Like gifts generally, its doing establishes a relationship. Of common value, this gift forges the same kind of relationship between each child and each mother. This rather impersonal gift mediates into existence the category of mother and articulates it to that of the child. This gift accords motherhood to each woman, through the proof of her status – her child who is the giver of the gift. In contrast to the developmental cycle of the family, here it is the alliance of teacher and child that forms and activates the category of motherhood. But the source of the gift is the statist figure of the teacher, and so the category of mother and its articulation to that of the child is shaped at her behest.

Subsequent practices support this line of interpretation. After the first gift the seamless circle of seated mothers is fragmented. The mothers form pairs: each couple holds jointly their gifts of flowers, and is connected through these. Through the medium of the gift each mother is re-presented and transposed: from being a member of the category of mother to becoming individuated, a person and a mother in her own right. As such she stands for the motherhood and nurturance of a family unit. Moreover, connections between families as discrete entities are delineated, as mothers jointly clasp their gifts. But these particular families are still denied children of their own. The youngsters are kept in their categorical formation that encircles these mothers. This implies that, from a more collectivist perspective, person-hood develops within categorical boundaries: that, first and foremost, people are members of social categories, and only then are they accorded the status of persons with their own unique attributes.

The participants resume their original formation. The children stand as a category, face the mothers, and sing their blessings. They then sing, 'My dear mother loves only me, yes, only me, yes, only me'. This act marks the onset of a transposition whereby each child is told to recognize the particularly intimate and affective bond between himself and his mother. This re-presentation is realized through the personalized gift that each child had prepared especially for his mother. The second gift mediates the creation of a unique relationship between a particular youngster and mother. Previously the mother was accorded personhood in her own right. Now too is her child. The category of child is fragmented; mother and child are united, and the family unit is delineated.

This intimate bond is further demonstrated as the concentric formation breaks up, and as each mother and child form pairs and perform together. Each pair, like each family, is a separate and distinct entity. Still its unity depends on the teacher, who tells each pair exactly how to coordinate their movements in unison. The special bond that is crucial to the existence and reproduction of the family is under her control. This is underlined as teacher and children teach the mothers a song with which to welcome the Sabbath. The occasion of welcoming the Sabbath within the home on behalf of family and household is exclusively the domain of the wife and mother. Her expertise, should she practice this, likely is garnered from sacred texts and from having watched her own mother. No external intervention is required. Here she is treated as one ignorant of liturgy basic to the integrity of the traditional home. Instead it becomes incumbent on a representative of the collectivity in alliance with its wards, the children, to impart such knowledge to mother and home.

There follows an addendum to the planned party, decided on by some of the mothers. This complements well the preceding sequence. One mother on behalf of the others thanks the teacher, calls her 'the real mother of the children while they are in the kindergarten', and presents her with a gift of flowers, via a youngster. Motherhood, the special bond between mother and offspring, is returned through the figure of a child to its source in the enactment, the teacher. She is described as a mother and, by extension, the kindergarten becomes akin to the home, a locus of socialization that prepares the child for adulthood. Yet on this occasion it is through the kindergarten that the home is shown to come into existence. And through this final gift it is to the kindergarten, embodied in the figure of the teacher, that this right is returned. The teacher is a representation of collectivity, and it is to this wider entity that authority is arrogated to mold these youngsters.

In other words, motherhood is delegated to the collectivity by a representative of the mothers attending the party. In Hebrew the words 'state' (*medina*) and 'motherland' (*moledet*, literally, land of birth) take the feminine form. Phrases like, 'I gave my child to the state' or 'I sacrifice my child for the good of the motherland' are common in referring to the

relationship of family and collectivity. Against this background the delegation of motherhood to a representative of the collectivity gains in depth of
resonance.

From the perspective of family and home the implicit patterning of the
whole event upends and recasts the normal progression of the domestic
cycle: for here it is the collectivity that creates the family. The usual view of
parents, and one that the little child first experiences, is that in the beginning
there is the family; that into this nexus the child is born and within it
matures; and that with time he leaves and establishes his own home. But
here the progression through re-presentation is as follows: first the collectivity exists and is composed of social categories. Links are forged between
categories, and from these there emerge discrete social units, or families.
These are accorded the right to bear and raise children; and from this there
emerges the special bond between mother and child. In this process the
rights of, and obligations to, the collectivity are shown to be paramount.

Jerusalem Day: statehood and citizenship

Jerusalem Day was promulgated as a civil, state holiday to commemorate
the reunification of the capital of Israel following the 1967 Six-Day War. It
is celebrated primarily through official receptions and other functions, that
presently include a festive, mass march around the perimeters of the city.
The major thoroughfares are decorated with the national flag and with the
banner of Jerusalem, a golden lion (the emblem of the ancient kingdom of
Judea) rampant on a white field with blue borders. Jerusalem is the central
place of the Jewish nation-state, and at present of most varieties of Judaism,
from those that are pillars of nationalism and its state religion to those who
are ambivalent about, or who oppose, the existence of this state on religious
grounds. From 1948 until 1967 the city was divided into western and
eastern sectors, the former within Israel, the latter controlled by Jordan.
Within the eastern sector is Mount Moriah, the Temple Mount, site of the
first temple built by Solomon, and of the second, destroyed by the Romans
in 70 CE. This defeat is reckoned as the customary onset of the Diaspora,
the widespread dispersion of the Jews into exile from ancient Israel. The
only parts of this temple complex to survive are remnants of its outermost
ramparts.

A short section of the western rampart is called the Wailing Wall, known
in Israel as the Western Wall. Previously a place of popular worship, since
1967 the Wall also has been made the most dominant symbol of the state
and of its organized religion. The Wall has become evocative of a nation
whose florescence as a state awaited the return of its people, of a continuity
that is perceived to have endured throughout the absence of Jewish

sovereignty for close to 2,000 years. As does no other single physical presence in present-day Israel, it is perceived to condense the glory and then the desuetude of the past and the national redemption of the present. We raise these points because much of the symbolism of this kindergarten celebration is focused on this motif, discussed further in chapter 9, in the context of Israeli state occasions.

Description: Three classes of three-, four-, and five-year-olds, totalling some sixty youngsters from the same kindergarten, participated on the morning of Jerusalem Day. Parents were not invited. The open courtyard of the kindergarten was decorated with national flags and with cutouts of the lion of Jerusalem. As requested, most of the youngsters were dressed in blue and white clothing. Each was given a lapel pin that depicted the lion. Each class was seated along one side of the courtyard, the teacher in the centre and an accordionist nearby.

The occasion opened with songs whose respective themes were: the ancient kingdom of Israel, rejoicing in Jerusalem, and the rebuilding of the temple. In a brief peroration the teacher declared that Jerusalem was the eternal capital of Israel; that this Day marked the liberation of East Jerusalem and the reunification of the city by the Israel Defence Forces; and that this Day was celebrated throughout the land.

Four five-year-olds recited a lengthy poem that told of two doves who dreamt of the arisal of the people of Israel. The doves flew to Jerusalem and alighted on the Wall. The closing lines stated: 'The children of Israel are singing a song; next year the city will be rebuilt.' The assembly then sang of the ancient longing of the Jewish people to return to Jerusalem. As this melody continued, six of the four-year-olds danced, each holding blue and white ribbons. During the dance each child gave the ends of his ribbon to two others. As their performance ended the children were joined by the ribbons in the form of a six-pointed Shield of David (the *magen david*, commonly translated as the Star of David), the central motif on the national flag.

The teacher told a story taken from a booklet of legends about Jerusalem. The narrative spoke of a lonely wall, dark with age, and laden with the memories of the great temple and of the free nation that dwelled here. Enemies burned the temple and drove out the Jews. Although they tried to destroy the wall, their tools broke. But the gentiles used the wall as a rubbish heap in order to obviate its presence. For centuries in their hatred of the Jews they dumped garbage about the wall, until it disappeared from sight.

One day a diaspora Jew came to see the wall at a time when gentiles ruled the land. All denied its existence. He found a great mound of rubbish and there learned of the custom of obliterating the Jewish wall. He swore to save it. A rumor spread that precious metals were buried there. The populace swarmed to sift through the garbage, found some coins of value, and uncovered the top stones. The next morning another rumor spread that treasure was buried at the base of the mound. People excavated the rubbish and gradually the whole of the wall was revealed. No treasure was found except for that of the Jew – the Wall itself. The Wall still was filthy, but clouds gathered and rains poured, cleansing and purifying the Wall. And the Jew gave thanks for this salvation.

Dancing and carrying toy blocks, the three-year-olds built a wall of roughly their own height. All the other youngsters formed a circle, held hands, and revolved singing and dancing around this edifice.

Discussion: Unlike the previous three celebrations, in this one no reference is made to the family. The relationship between nation-state and citizen is direct, immediate, and hierarchical. Here the family not only is superseded but is rendered irrelevant to the nation-state. The nation is depicted as the redeemer of the state, and the state as the protector of the nation. Both depend on the faith and loyalty of the citizenry.[12]

The courtyard is decorated in emblems of statehood, and acquires the semblance of an official locale. The dress of the youngsters is standardized through colors that shape these children into living emblems of the state. Their bodies are inscribed with signs of citizenship, of membership in the collectivity. Each child appears as a small part that embodies the greater whole, itself composed of many such parts. The ideal relationship between citizen and collectivity is one of synecdoche. This relationship is not manipulated during the occasion, but is re-presented in various ways.

The event consists of a preamble of song and speech, followed by formal enactments. The preamble enunciates themes and sentiments that are repeated and elaborated through performance. The opening songs connect past, present, and future. The words of each have references in common to verities that are held eternal. The first tells of King David, who made Jerusalem the capital of ancient Israel. The second rejoices in Jerusalem eternal. The third relates that the Temple, a metaphor of the nation in its reborn homeland, will be rebuilt. The words of the teacher situate these sentiments within constructions of reality in present-day Israel. The assembly celebrates the reunification of the eternal capital of this nation-state, accomplished by citizens in the people's army, in which these youngsters will serve on their completion of high school. Collectivity and citizenship are made interdependent.

The enactments begin with a poem that evokes prophecy. The doves dream that the renewed people of Israel will rebuild the city around the central focus of the eternal Wall. In Israel the dove is an emblem of peace that harks back to the biblical story of Noah's Ark and the dove that returned with an olive branch, signing an end to God's wrath. The next song expresses the longing of the people to return and carry out this endeavor. The sense of prophecy is mated with feelings of deepest desire.

In turn, prophecy and desire are realized as six youngsters shape a living Shield of David. This is a complex, multivocalic motif used by the Zionist movement to encode rejuvenation and attachment to a national homeland (see Scholem 1971). We note again that it is a preeminent emblem of the State. Thus children who first sat in a loose assemblage create the precise, coordinated pattern of this emblem. As in other symbolic formations, just as they bring the emblem into being through their collective efforts, so its shape ties them to one another and incorporates them within a greater, enveloping design. The aesthetic and emotive effect is one of a symmetrical blending of part and whole, of the blue and white coloration of dress and of connecting ribbons. The implication is that the citizens of the future will continue together to carry through the design of this emblem, one that connotes the actualization of the collectivity.

The primary message of the narrative of the rediscovery of the Wall is that the Jews must defend their patrimony, otherwise they will lose this. The tale is an allegory: the world of Israel, of the Wall, must be demarcated clearly from that of non-Jews who threaten its integrity and viability. This also is the logic of the modern, precisely demarcated nation-state, one that resonates strongly with aspects of the historical Jewish experience. In terms of nationhood or peoplehood, one either is a Jew or one is not. In terms of statehood, one either is a citizen or one is not. In the ideology of the nation-state these axes of inclusion-exclusion become almost isomorphic. The outer boundaries of the permissible are set by the collectivity, to which the desires of the citizen are subordinate. This is perhaps the highest level of contrast between 'inside' and 'outside' that is set for the Jewish citizen of modern Israel. Moreover it is a lesson that youngsters will have reason to learn in numerous contexts beyond that of the family in years to come. At this level of contrast the hierarchy, values, and relationships of the family always are of lesser relevance.

The tale posits a series of contrasts between Jew and gentile that derive from a simple postulate: that the Wall, and by analogy the nation and state, are indestructible despite all the depredations of enemies. This is its internal and eternal truth. By comparison all else is transitory. The Jew who returns to his source, across the gap of generations, is motivated by ideology. His is the wisdom of spirituality. The gentiles who try to destroy his roots are driven by materialism. He uses their cupidity to reveal his truth. In the context of the celebration the qualities of Wall and Jew are those of the nation-state and its citizenry. The attributes of the gentiles are associated with all those who would deny to the Jews their homeland. The tale is at once a metaphor of renewal and a parable on boundaries of national salvation that in the present-day world the state views itself as best able to uphold.

The closing enactment brings the message of the story into existence through the cooperative efforts of the children, just as the living Shield realized the prophecy of the doves. The youngsters build the Wall from the ground up, just as modern Israel is redeemed through the joint efforts of its citizenry. The simulated labors of the children show that which will be expected of them upon adulthood. The children dance in an unbroken circle around the completed Wall. Again their formation evokes egalitarianism, connectivity, synchronization, and perhaps the outer boundary of statehood that must be protected by its citizenry. Once more the centre of the circle is filled, here by the edifice of the Wall – an emblem that is hierarchical, authoritative, and nationalistic.

Conclusions

In the world of the little child the kindergarten celebration is among the few categories of occasion when the order of things that structures the wider social world directly intersects with and dominates that of the home. This is evident through explicit symbolism. But more profound in their impact are the architectonics of enactment. Their influence derives from the very ways in which persons in unison are mobilized and synchronized in social formations in order to do the more explicit scenarios of celebration. The lineal progressions of such formations constitute their own implicit sets of messages, and it is these that we have addressed.

These celebrations, and numerous others like them, make extensive and intensive use of living formations. Some of these forms are shaped explicitly, like the *hnnukia* and the Shield of David. Others, like the unbroken circle and the dyad, stay more implicit. In either instance these are powerful media. Through them the meaning of things is turned into the shape of things. The shape of things is graspable through the senses, as is the case of icon and emblem. Yet in the latter instances these shapes still are largely external to the human body, to the source of emotions and feelings. But the shape of things in living formations is grasped by living through them. This is a more sensual experience, one that engages the senses more fully to create a holistic experiential environment. Architects and others sometimes refer to haptic space, of coming to know the shape of space and the feelings this engenders through the sense of touch. Through living formations the visual, the auditory, the tactile, and perhaps the olfactory senses are all 'touched' by the shape of things. The meaning of form and the form of meaning become inextricable.

Re-presentation through the sequencing of formations, in keeping with premises of linearity, are at the experiential heart of the kinds of enactments we have addressed. As noted, they are intended to touch the heart of the little child, and so to impress upon his being lessons that otherwise may remain more exterior to his sense of self. In particular we have stressed themes that will be adumbrated for the child in numerous ways and contexts in the years to come: for example, the relationship between hierarchy and equality. The interior hierarchy of the family is supplanted by and is subsumed within the collectivity. The collectivity, the nation-state, is superior to each of its citizens; yet they compose it, and it exists only through their cooperative efforts. As citizens they in principle are the equals of one another. So too as children grow, they will succeed and replace their parents, as heads of family and as citizens. These processes depend on the proper outcome of that of maturation. Here the kindergarten sees its role to infuse the child with internal restraint and with feelings of responsibility towards the collectivity and its parts. In turn, all of the above seems to evoke elementary patterns of social boundedness, and of the categories and entities that these demarcate and define. Thus boundaries between people, as members of categories and as persons, between family and collectivity, and between the nation-state and whatever lies without, are re-presented and constructed anew.

This kind of re-presentation is a way of projecting desired and expected futures of linear, irreversible development. In this it has some superficial similarity to modelling. But obviously these futures are not actualized in the course of kindergarten celebrations. The logic of these occasions is other-wise; and so they contain no rules of, nor procedures for, transformation. But in additive fashion these occasions do help to remake the biographies (and retrospectively, perhaps the autobiographies) of little children, during a time when these personalized narratives of self are embryonic. And this from another perspective of power – that of the nation-state.

The messages outlined above are essential to the production of moral order, and to the reproduction of social order in terms of this. In kindergarten celebrations they are communicated in ways easy to grasp for the little child. Youngsters are full of feeling, but they have yet to develop the critical attitudes that buffer personal choice against the demands of group pressure and the inducements of collective sentiments. Enculturation through celebration, as instruction books for kindergartens note, is first and foremost an appeal to the emotions of little children. Moods and feelings about centricity, control, collectivity, and cooperation are communicated early on to these Israeli youngsters. These sentiments were crucial to the periods of the *yishuv* and the early state, years of self-defense for survival and growth. Still we should inquire whether the emphasis today on these and related values survives primarily as an ideological tool, and through the inability of the apparatus of education and polity to check the viability of its own involution. The quality of life of this nation-state may depend as much on the teaching of critical perspectives and personal choice as it does on values that continue to close the collective circle.

Intersections

Even more than the little kindergarten celebrations of the previous chapter, the grand state occasions of chapter 9 are easily accessible to observers. But the latter, too, are given short shrift by scholars. Ignoring these and similar public events demonstrates a misplaced bias against phenomena that, if not before our faces, are merely round a few corners. Perhaps in their nearness they are not imbued with an otherness that excites imagination. Yet it is the preparedness of anthropologists to adopt prismatic perspectives, to privilege the cast of otherness in the most mundane, that propels much of the creative power in anthropology.

Unlike the other case studies of this book, the following chapter was written in direct response to the typology of chapter 2, with the claims of events-that-present the world in mind. But the idea of looking seriously at national events originated long before, during the years that Elihu Katz and I taught together a course on public events and media events at The Hebrew University. We also collaborated on this chapter.

I corrected the page proofs of chapter 9 during Israeli Remembrance Day 1989. The evening before, in the opening ceremony, the President lit the beacon at the Western Wall in memory of the war dead. Trailing him was a figure I had not seen before in the open spaces of this ceremony – young, alert, looking in all directions, and ignored by the TV commentator. Mr non-person, an absent presence, had the mannerisms of security personnel. A sign of worsening times. Support for my argument that the action in such occasions is mainly at the interface of event and social order.

The ceremonies to be discussed are the productions of a vigorous parliamentary democracy. Yet with modifications they could serve visions of ultra-nationalism that would welcome pluralism only within a citizenry made utterly homogeneous in terms of peoplehood and religion. The danger is not unreal, but the battle will be fought outside the ceremonies.

9 State ceremonies of Israel – Remembrance Day and Independence Day*

Daughter:	Why did Herzl write *The Jewish State*?
Mother:	Because he thought the Jews should have a state of their own.
Daughter:	Why is it [Mount Herzl] next to the soldiers' cemetery?
Mother:	Because many people were killed in order to get our state, and here [she points to the cemetery] is where the ceremony for Remembrance Day takes place.
Daughter:	So why, Holocaust Day?
Mother:	That is there [she gestures towards Yad Vashem, over the rise], and the remembrance of Holocaust Day takes place there.

(Mount Herzl, Saturday, 21 March 1987)[1]

Like many nation-states of the modern era, Israel designated a particular date to remember those who sacrificed their lives for the existence of the state, and another to commemorate its coming into being. The first is named Remembrance Day (*Yom Hazikaron*), and the second, Independence Day (*Yom Ha'atzma'ut*). Each is opened by a central state occasion, referred to as a 'ceremony', that is televised in its entirety.

Each ceremony is one in which this nation-state, through official agencies, intentionally presents something of its self-understood purposes, and their foundations, aspirations, and apprehensions. Each ceremony presents a version of moral and social order that contrasts with the other. Each version, suitable to its occasion, stands on its own, valid in and of itself. However, as we will discuss in detail further on, these two ceremonies deliberately are articulated with one another. Taken together, through the sequence of their scheduling, these versions of this nation-state become segments in a dramatic narrative that encodes temporality, and therefore, history. In turn, it is this history, or more accurately, these versions of history, that inform and infuse the overall story with deeper significance.

Although these ceremonies have undergone changes since their inception, their basic formats have remained quite stable for over a decade. However, our purpose is neither to do a historical account of such changes, nor to

* This chapter was co-authored by Elihu Katz

191

summarize in detail the histories of these ceremonies. Such aims are beyond the scope of this chapter, and must await future attention. Here our purpose is more structural, and is addressed to the interpretation of state ceremonial in the modern era.

We first address why it is that these two opening ceremonies demand discussion in common. We then show, in a preliminary manner, how their respective Days came to be scheduled as they are. This forms the basis for our thesis that these ceremonies together come to constitute a narrative structure. This is followed, first by an interpretation of the ceremony that opens Remembrance Day, and then of that which opens Independence Day, in order to delineate their respective versions of moral and social order. The concluding section returns to the kind of narrative structure that we think is found through the sequence of these versions, and to the encoding of a rhythm of temporality that, in a broad, cultural sense, is formative and informative of this.

The unit of comparison: sirens and fireworks

From its inception the State adopted as its own the rhythm of the Jewish cycle of holy days and holidays (in distinct contrast to the efforts of certain other revolutionary states to radicalize the cultural ordering of temporality: see Zerubavel 1985: 27–43). Only one new holiday, in the full sense of a 'day of rest' (*shabbaton*), was instituted. This was Independence Day. Moreover the period of observance of State Days became that of all Jewish holy days and holidays: all begin with darkness, as the stars appear, and end with darkness.

The few studies there are on Israel's Independence Day (including references to its opening ceremony) treat it as a separate and wholly autonomous occasion. The sorts of questions asked in these works highlight the sparse attention given by scholars to state ceremonial in Israel, especially in relation to its logic of composition. Kamen's (1977) analysis of survey data asked about the degrees of enjoyment experienced on Independence Day by different social categories of Israelis. More recently, Virginia Dominguez argues that Israelis do not seem to ask themselves what it is that they are celebrating. That is, which aspects of the 'collective self' are marked, expressed, and perhaps formulated through this holiday.[2] Don-Yehiya (1984) discusses how early Independence Day celebrations expressed the impress of a 'statist' polity during that period (see Liebman and Don-Yehiya 1983, on this variety of 'civil religion' in Israel).

Israel is unusual among modern nation-states in that its Remembrance Day is scheduled for the twenty-four hour period that immediately precedes Independence Day. This articulation is intentional; and official announcements of the program of Remembrance Day, published in the daily newspapers, list the last occasion of this Day as, 'Conclusion of Remembrance Day and opening of Independence Day celebrations by Knesset Speaker at Mount Herzl'. That is, the official ceremony that opens Independence Day includes, as its initial segment, the closing of Remembrance Day. However, unlike Independence Day, Remembrance Day is not a 'day of rest.' Still, during the eve of Remembrance Day all public places of entertainment and fun are shut.[3]

Unlike Independence Day, Remembrance Day begins with a singular and shocking sound that penetrates and simultaneously synchronizes the different worlds of everyone in the country. On the appointed minute, and for one minute's duration, siren blasts shriek in every village, town, and city in the land.[4] Human life stands still: people stop in their tracks, vehicles stop in mid-intersection; all is silent, yet all silent space is pervaded by the fullness of the same wail. These sirens also announce crisis and the activation of emergency procedures. The sole difference is not of intensity nor pitch of sound, but of modulation: to announce crisis, the wails rise and fall; to declare bereavement their note is steady and uniform. On the morning of the morrow, again simultaneously throughout the country, the same enactment is repeated, this time for two minutes. The sound synthesizes mourning and action, absence and presence.

The opening ceremony of Remembrance Day has something of the singular and monotonic qualities of the siren's keen, and of the stillness of the land. The next morning, the siren's wail signals the beginning of memorial services at military cemeteries and memorial sites throughout the country, in memory of the fallen of different corps, regiments, and other units of the armed forces, and of geographical localities, sometimes down to the neighborhood level. By contrast, Independence Day expands out of its opening ceremony into a variegated and colorful multitude of activities, planned and informal. On the eve of Independence Day there are open-air stages where popular entertainers perform, dancing in the streets, games of chance (otherwise illegal) in city centres, and bonfires and singing, as well as private house-parties. On the morrow there are special services in synagogues, the opening of selected military bases to the public, and official receptions. If the weather is good, as it usually is in the late spring, Independence Day is marked by a host of family outings and picnics. As the opening ceremony of this Day ends there are sustained bursts of fireworks in the dark sky. Their expansion in space, brilliantly lighting the night in diverse shapes and brightly-colored hues, is an apt metaphor for the meaning of this Day. Each ceremony provides a key to the tenor of activities that constitute the bulk of each Day.

As Dominguez remarks, these two Days form a 'neat conceptual set' of comparison and contrast. But this set is not a construct of the scholar (as is, for example, Da Matta's [1977] interesting comparison of Brazilian carnival and Independence Day). As noted, it is an artifact of deliberate design. This design is seen with the greatest clarity in the articulation of the opening ceremonies, and in the implicit narrative structure that is invoked by their sequencing. Therefore any symbolic analysis that does not relate to these ceremonies as a unified set, and then that does not treat this set as diachronically encoded, simply will miss much of their significance. These ceremonies are a semiotic set: they make meaning together.

The dating of days, the shaping of space: aspects of Zionist cosmologic

That these events make meaning together should tell us immediately that their calendrical scheduling, and so their sequential ordering, are neither 'natural' nor inevitable. As Eviatar Zerubavel (1982: 288) comments, 'Temporal arrangements are closely related to group formation, since a temporal order that is commonly shared by a group of people and is unique to them functions both as a unifier and as a separator'. Moreover, the chronological coding of temporality, as 'before' and 'after', is the produc-tion of history (Lévi-Strauss 1966: 257–60). Time and the temporal vision are essential to Zionist cosmology, as they are to that of Judaism (Yerushalmi 1982). So too is the temporal rhythm implicit in this, as well as the rhetoric and sentiments of a unique people, beleaguered in the world (cf. Gertz 1984).

In fact, Israeli Jews accept the contiguity and continuity of these dates as morally correct, even though the immediacy of transition from mourning to celebration is felt as especially heartrending. Thus, a bereaved father, interviewed on television before Remembrance Day 1986, remarked on the lack of any intervening period between the two Days. But he insisted on the justness of this intimate linkage, stating: 'This is the price [bereavement], and this is what you have [independence]'.[5] One may well contend that this suddenness of transition is felt as morally just, precisely because it is so difficult. The transition should be hard, for its abruptness encodes tempor-ally the minute differences in chronological time between the establishment of the State and its War of Independence. This war was well under way before independence was declared, but intensified greatly with that declara-tion. For Israeli Jews the two were identified indelibly, and perhaps still are. The difficult experience of abrupt transition between the two Days mirrors the reality of experience in the establishment of the State.

However fitting this temporal flow is felt to be, it exists only because decisions were taken as to which dates to mark, and in which order.

Nation-states choose their significant dates according to different semiotic and temporal codes; moreover they may experiment with different calendrical arrangements (Zerubavel 1985). Thus the French promulgated Bastille Day as their 'founding day' only in 1880, following the formation of the Third Republic; while French governments shifted the public focus given to prominent calendrical markers in accordance with prevailing political conditions. So, in 1920, the government combined the fiftieth anniversary of the Third Republic together with the solemnities for the fallen of the Great War – and chose a date other than Bastille Day for this (Rearick 1977: 456). In the instance of Australia, its memorial date, Anzac Day (the date the Anzacs landed at Gallipoli in 1915), has developed as the major marker of Australian nationhood, rather than Australia Day, which commemorates the landing of the first convict settlers from England in the eighteenth century. According to Kapferer (1988), the reasons for the different valencies given to these two dates are intimately related to the formation of Australian national cosmology.

In the Israeli case, a number of dates hypothetically could have been chosen to mark the autonomy of independence, but then each would have given its own thrust of meaning to the new state. So 29 November, the date in 1947 when the United Nations decided on the partition of Palestine, a decision that gave international legitimation to the founding of a Jewish state, would have emphasized the role of foreigners (and gentiles) in the creation of the state. Or, an arbitrary date to mark the end of the War of Independence (that, formally, produced only armistice agreements) would have highlighted the decisive role of armed struggle in achieving independence. Or, the date that marked the election of the first Knesset, the parliament of Israel, would have stressed the values of parliamentary democracy, and so forth.

The date chosen for Independence Day in 1949, apparently with no disagreement, was 15 May. In 1948 independence was declared on 14 May, that then became the eve of Independence Day. A further decision, over which there was some argument, adopted the date in the Hebrew calendar, the 5th of *Iyar*, that corresponded to 15 May of that year.[6] The Hebrew and Gregorian calendrical cycles are independent of one another. Although the date of Independence Day has a fixed and stable location in the annual Jewish ceremonial cycle, it varies from year to year by a matter of weeks in the Gregorian calendar. This was no small matter, since according to the Hebrew calendar, Independence Day falls permanently only thirteen days after the end of Passover. In Judaism, Passover is perhaps the quintessential 'festival of freedom', celebrating the exodus of the Israelites from Egypt. The festive family meal, the *Seder*, on the eve of the holiday, 'is a symbolic enactment of an historical scenario whose three great acts structure the

Haggada that is read aloud: slavery – deliverance – ultimate redemption'
(Yerushalmi 1982: 44; see also Fredman 1981).[7] The metaphysics of the text
of the *Seder*, the *Haggada*, insist on the annual 'fusion of past and present'
(Yerushalmi 1982: 44), and on the identification of each and every Jew with
that ancient attainment of freedom. 'In each and every generation let each
person regard himself as though he had emerged from Egypt', reads the
Haggada. Passover is a holiday beloved of Israeli Jews, secular and religious
alike; and one may say that the great majority celebrate the occasion.

The identification of Independence Day with Passover was speedy. Just
as Independence Day was referred to as the onset of a new period in the
history of the nation, the People of Israel (*Am Yisrael*), so it was perceived in
continuity with holidays of national freedom, but especially with Passover.
And just as Independence Day was seen to sign the rebirth and redemption
of the Jewish nation-state, so too it was compared to the exodus from Egypt
(Don-Yehiya 1984: 10–11). Of all Jewish holidays, Passover had the greatest
influence on the perception of this Day.[8]

Like the scheduling of Independence Day, that of Remembrance Day
required an arbitrary decision, since there was no traditional date to
commemorate the fallen in war. The need to memorialize the war dead was
felt early on. Thus during the Knesset debate in 1949 on the law to
promulgate Independence Day, Shmuel Dayan of the centrist Mapai party
stated: 'Happiness is a universal human matter. Still, there is a special Jewish
tone to happiness. Once it was customary that at the time of the happiness
of a wedding, people would go to the cemetery to invite the dead to
participate in the festivity ... we have to remember those who with their
blood bestowed upon us arisal and independence'. At the outset, memorial
ceremonies were part of Independence Day, but were decentralized, the
initiative for their observance taken locally (Levinsky 1957: 495ff.). By
1951, the Ministry of Defense began to experiment with a separate
Remembrance Day, the day prior to Independence Day. In 1954, the
Ministry stated that this linkage and sequencing had not aroused contro-
versy; and the Minister of Defense commented that he viewed as 'organic'
this attachment of Remembrance Day to Independence Day.[9] The law that
formalized this schedule was passed in 1963. Unlike Independence Day,
Remembrance Day was not opened by a central ceremony until 1967.

During the period between the end of Passover and Independence Day,
the State scheduled a third date as a national day – Martyrs and Heroes
Remembrance Day, (usually referred to as Holocaust Day) – again according to the Hebrew calendar.[10] Holocaust Day (*Yom Hasho'a*) is discussed in
this section because it is integral to the calendrical sequence of Days
scheduled by the State. Holocaust Day precedes Remembrance Day and
Independence Day in this sequence. Therefore, its timing is integral also to

the kinds of narrative that this sequence evokes. Nevertheless, Holocaust Day and its opening ceremony are beyond the purview of much of this chapter. Instead, the positioning of this Day will be glossed here, to be retrieved again in the concluding section, when the relationships between these Days and national cosmology are discussed.

The eve of Holocaust Day falls on the 26th of the Hebrew month of *Nissan*, five days after the last day of Passover. As its name indicates, this Day commemorates the catastrophe of the Holocaust, the murder of 6,000,000 Jews by the Nazis, the destruction of Jewish culture and community in Europe, and the heroism of Jews who rose in armed struggle against their Nazi oppressors. Like Remembrance Day, Holocaust Day is not a day of rest, but again all public venues of entertainment and fun are shut during its eve. The opening ceremony of this Day is held at Yad Vashem, the memorial and archival centre of the Holocaust in Jerusalem, and is televised live. In its identification with the tragic destruction of Jews in the diaspora (one that is fated, to no small degree, in the Zionist vision), Holocaust Day in most years is perceived generally as of less immediate relevance to the founding, the commemoration, and the celebration of the State, than is Remembrance Day. Indeed, the scale of this Day, and usually of public response to it, is more modest than that of Remembrance Day. So, synchronized sirens do sound throughout the land on Holocaust Day, but only once. Nonetheless, our concern here is not with the manner of meaning made at the interface of the event and wider social order, but with the emergence of a legislated cosmology that has direct bearing on the relationship between Remembrance Day and Independence Day.

The scheduling of Holocaust Day once more is not fortuitous. This Day is identified explicitly with the anniversary of the uprising of the Warsaw Ghetto in 1943, that became the exemplary instance of Jewish armed struggle against impossible odds during World War II. On 19 April of that year, German troops came to strip the Ghetto of its remaining Jews, to ship them to the death camps, and armed resistance began in earnest. 19 April 1943 was the eve of Passover in that year. It was not possible in Israel, for various reasons, to schedule a remembrance day for the Holocaust on Passover eve. Judaism interdicts mourning during Passover. Instead, the commemoration date was made to coincide with the extinction of the Uprising, on 2 May, the 27th of *Nissan* in that year, according to the Hebrew calendar.[11] The German command itself dated the end of armed resistance to 16 May when the great synagogue was blown up: 'This act of destruction was meant to symbolize the end of the ghetto' (Krakowski 1984: 211). (In fact, fighting continued into July.) However, the acceptance of such a date, which actually extended and enhanced the duration of Jewish armed struggle, would have scheduled Holocaust Day almost a week after Independence Day, according to the Hebrew calendar. Whether by design or not, the eve of Holocaust Day, the 26th of *Nissan*, falls seven days before the eve of Remembrance Day, the 3rd of *Iyar*. This period of seven days corresponds to the traditional period of Jewish mourning following death, the *shiva* (literally, 'seven').[12] We note the implicitness of this association, since it is not marked – nonetheless, it is embedded in this temporal sequence. On the one hand, Holocaust Day, the catastrophe of diaspora Jewry, is distanced from Remembrance Day and Independence Day, occasions of the arisal of nation-statehood. On the other, Holocaust Day is scheduled near to and prior to these occasions, and so is linked intimately to them. This scheduling of what may be termed 'close distance' is itself an apt metaphor for the often ambivalent relationship between diaspora Jewry and the Zionist State.

On the basis of the calendrical sequence of these three Days, we offer here a preliminary reading of its temporal design, to be honed in the conclusion to this chapter. The destruction of European Jewry was followed by the War of Independence, during which the State of Israel was created, and through which the state kept its freedom, as it has ever since through the mortal sacrifices of its citizenry. Given the utter tragedy of the Holocaust, it is appropriate that its Day be followed by a period of separation (or 'mourning', as it were) from the subsequent Days. However the sacrifice memorialized on Remembrance Day led to the revival of the Jewish state and the redemption of the Jewish people. Therefore the celebration of Independence Day is an immediate and fitting response to the commemoration of Remembrance Day.

This semiotic sequence also conveys the following. The utter degradation and despair of the Holocaust finally harvested the inevitably bitter sowing of Jewish seed in the lands of the gentiles. The diaspora was the dead end of Jewish existence. Even so, the Holocaust also kindled sparks of resistance among this downtrodden and humiliated people. The snuffing of these heroic sparks (the Jewish partisans, the ghetto and camp uprisings) are mourned, but also are celebrated on Holocaust Day. For in Palestine, amongst independent and proud Jews returned to their own land and once more battling against seemingly insurmountable odds, these sparks flamed into ramified armed struggle. The outcome was the Jewish State. In Zionist visions, these developments became the only creative response to the Holocaust. In these readings, the sequence of the three Days recapitulates a theme of 'death and the regeneration of life' on a grand scale (cf. Bloch and Parry 1982).[13]

The scheduling of these three Days is a construct of the nation-state, but one that is neither haphazard nor merely instrumental, in any simple way. This sequencing is accepted as natural and appropriate by Israeli Jews, however it is interpreted. It is a statist version of modern Jewish history, but one of cosmological, temporal harmonics that are embedded in Zionist ideology. These relationships were enunciated with clarity by Prime Minister Levi Eshkol, in his address on Holocaust Day, 1964: 'The Martyrs' and Heroes' Memorial Day falls between the ancient Festival of Freedom [i.e. Passover] and the modern Day of Independence. The annals of our people are enfolded between these two events. With our exodus from the Egyptian bondage, we won our ancient freedom; now, with our ascent from the depths of the Holocaust, we live once again as an independent nation.'[14] In its modern, nationalist interpretations, the narrative structure of the sequence of Days is easily identifiable with certain of the overt, processual motifs of Passover: of slavery and oppression, of exodus and arisal. Passover itself corresponds to that which Yael Zerubavel (1986: 5) calls the 'basic conflict formula' of the present-day celebration of many Jewish holidays. In turn, this facilitates the identification of the sequence with the Jewish struggle against oppression that is embedded in other Jewish holidays.

Yet, in one important respect the scheduling of the three Days is more in keeping with the romantic and rationalist reckonings of modern European nationalism than it is with the annual ceremonial cycle of Judaism. In the traditional cycle there is only a limited correspondence between the order of occurrence of holidays and their location in a chronology of historical reckoning (Y. Zerubavel 1986). The ordering principles of the traditional, annual cycle are cosmic and mythic, and not those of chronological history. However, these three Days of national reckoning synthesize their order of sequence and the chronological order of temporal occurrence that this sequence indexes. In other words, the sequence of Days is one of modern history; but one that is harmonized with the rhythms of time in traditional cosmology.

We surmise that it is this synthesis of ontological rhythms of time, the traditional narratives that these enable, and their encoding of modern chronological history that makes the sequence of Days so experientially acceptable to Israeli Jews. These themes are addressed more substantially in the concluding section.

The temporal articulations among these three Days are produced and reproduced topologically. In August 1949, the remains of Theodore Herzl, the visionary of modern Zionism and the founder of the World Zionist Organization, were brought from Vienna and reinterred in Jerusalem, on the summit of the mountain named in his memory. Mount Herzl, perhaps the highest location within the city, affords a vista of 360 degrees of Jerusalem and its environs. Previously, during the War of Independence, the lower reaches of this mountain had become the military cemetery of

Jerusalem. His black, polished basalt tombstone bore the simple inscription, HERZL. Without contextual qualifiers his presence was made more eternal and less historical.[15] Encircled by flower beds, Herzl's tomb stands alone at the apex, separated by broad, open spaces from the graves of others. Mount Herzl is a cemetery wherein Zionist history is encoded topologically, through the spatial locations of ancestors and their descendants.

The spatial layout of gravesites on Mount Herzl is as close as secular Zionism has come to inscribing itself topographically as a pantheon. Radiating outwards from Herzl's tomb, at different levels and in different quadrants of the downslope gradient of the mountainside, are clusters of graves. At a distance from, and lower than, Herzl's tomb, is that of another Zionist visionary, Vladimir Jabotinsky, the founder of the revisionist movement, and those of members of his immediate family. At the same level, in another quadrant, is the cluster of graves of members of Herzl's immediate family and of the presidents, the inheritors, of the World Zionist Organization, and their wives. These widely distanced clusters are themselves set apart from the rest of the cemetery by a horizontal border that follows the contours of the mountainside and that intersects its downslope gradient. Thus, on the highest reaches of the mountain are the graves of modern prophets of Zionism who created the movement in its aims of returning all Jews to the land of Israel, and the graves of those who nurtured and sustained this vision. At their pinnacle and centre lies Herzl. With the passage of time, the visionary figure of Herzl (and to a lesser extent, that of Jabotinsky) has become the depoliticized representation of Zionism as the encompassing ideology of Jewish national resurrection and renewal.

Returning to the border, it is traversed by a gateway that leads further downslope to a cluster of gravesites reserved for the 'Greats of the Nation' (*Gedolei Ha'uma*) and their spouses. These are the presidents and prime ministers of the State of Israel, and speakers of the Knesset, the first citizens and political leaders of the nation-state itself.[16] Without any further demarcation, these graves are close to and virtually continuous with those of the military cemetery which continues downslope and covers the bulk of the mountainside.

The upper slopes of the mountain are carpeted with lawns, shrubs, and flower beds; and resemble most a park dotted here and there by groves of trees and clusters of graves. The military cemetery, although dense with graves, is heavily forested. The overall composition likely derives in part from nineteenth-century European romanticism (see Mosse 1979).

Thus the highest reaches of the mountainside signify the source, genesis, and deeds of the Zionist movement, which culminated in the creation of the nation-state. Further downslope are buried the elected leaders of the State, whose graves are higher than, but continuous with those of the citizen-soldiery who gave their lives to buttress the zionist mountain. On the morning of Remembrance Day, a memorial service is held in the military cemetery. That evening, as it has since 1950, the opening ceremony of Independence Day is held on the summit of this mountain of Zionism, with Herzl's tomb as its spatial centrepiece.

In 1953, a lower spur of Mount Herzl, at some distance from the main massif, but still high above the valley floor, was named the Mount of Remembrance (*Har Hazikaron*). There Yad Vashem was built. As noted, the opening ceremony of Holocaust Day takes place there. Unlike the gateway that internally connects the upper reaches of Mount Herzl to the 'Greats of the Nation' and to the military cemetery, one must leave this Mount to enter Yad Vashem.

In the terms introduced by Erwin Straus (1966: 34), the articulation between the sites of Yad Vashem, the military cemetery, and the summit of Mount Herzl is that of 'historical space', whose direction acquires a 'dynamic momentum'. For the temporal sequence of ceremonialism is matched with, moves through, and infuses space with meaning. Holocaust Day and the tragedy and heroism of diaspora Jewry, are marked on a lower and more distant spur of the Zionist mountain, just as this Day is distanced temporally from those that commemorate and celebrate the nation-state. On the morning of Remembrance Day, the heroism and sacrifice of the citizen-soldiers of the nation-state are commemorated in the military cemetery, on the lower reaches of the main massif itself. That evening the venue climbs to the summit of the mountain, to the tomb of the Zionist visionary and ancestor, to celebrate Independence Day. The heights are scaled spatially in the temporal order of Days, from destruction, through the struggle for renewal, to the pinnacle of triumph, that also is the source of the vision and the annual enactment of its viability. The practice of this ceremonialism integrates axes of space and time in Zionist cosmology and history. This integration of time and space is evident again in Levi Eshkol's speech, from which we quoted above: 'The very struggle against the adversary [the heroism and sacrifice of the Holocaust] and the victory which followed [the War of Independence] laid the foundations for the revival of our national independence [the creation of the state]. Seen in this light, the Jewish fight against the Nazis and the War of Independence were, in fact, a single protracted battle. The geographical proximity between Yad Vashem and Mount Herzl thus expresses far more than mere physical closeness'.[17]

This sequence of ceremonialism is enacted to the present day. However, the addition of a central ceremony at the Western Wall to open Remembrance Day has interposed refractions, likely radical ones, within this vision of the progression of secular Zionism from its antecedents to the present.

Opening Remembrance Day: closing ranks and the struggle for renewal

The setting is the great earthen plaza that abuts the Western Wall in the Old City of Jerusalem. The topographical and physical contrasts with Mount Herzl are striking. In place of vast, open vistas of West Jerusalem and the Judean Hills, of wide expanses of softly contoured greenery, the plaza and its surroundings are severe, rectilinear enclosures in the built environment, bordered by looming structures that evoke a host of (often conflicting) associations. To the west, the heights of the Jewish Quarter. To the east, the Wall itself, abutting the bulk of Mount Moriah (the ancient site of the First and Second Temples) on which stand the silver-domed mosque of al-Aqsa and the golden Dome of the Rock. Further east, in front of the ramparts of the Mount (themselves part of the ancient Wall), archeological excavations that expose the skeletons of buildings dated to the Second Temple period. To the north, the edge of the Muslim Quarter. Immediately before the Wall, the fenced-in prayer area, paved with flagstones, and divided into a large section for males and a smaller one for females.[18]

Not only has the Wall been made into a central, public venue of state religion in Israel, but numerous occasions of the civil state are now held in its plaza.[19] One must appreciate the singular, centripetal attraction that the Wall has exerted for so many sectors of Israeli Jewish society, since the reunification of Jerusalem under Israeli rule in 1967. The reasons for this kind of attraction are complex and involve, among other factors, nationalism and historicity (cf. Aronoff 1986; Schwartz et al. 1986; Bruner and Gorfain 1984). The most immediate of associations evoked in Zionist Israel by the Wall is that last period of Jewish statehood, and so of its modern revival. However, if one so desires, through a series of epistemological transpositions the Temple can be linked to the giving of the *Tora* on Mount Sinai, following the exodus from Egypt – in other words, to the very beginnings, as this is understood, of Jewish peoplehood. The Wall also may be perceived as a sign of the centricity of place (and of the place of Jerusalem and Israel in this) in varieties of Judaism and in modern Zionism. So it often is referred to as a 'witness' to the endurance of this centredness of nationhood, awaiting the return of the people from their millennia of diasporic exile. As in other major national or quasi-national symbols of Israel, it may be very difficult to disentangle signs of statehood attributed to a symbol from those of peoplehood, and those of peoplehood from those of religion.[20] Here the synthetic role of memory is pervasive (Paine 1983).

The ease with which such associations can be, and are made, speaks both to the banality of their cultural common-sensicality and to the profundity of feeling that they evoke. The Wall, of blank, stone frontage and of

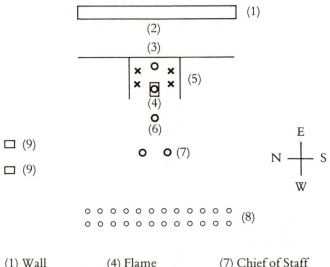

Figure 7 The opening ceremony of Remembrance Day, spatial layout

temporality that is perceived as continuous, is a powerful synthesizer of sentiment and symbol, of the present making the past. It is a *symbolon* in that original Greek sense: that part of the whole that remains, and that evokes its absent completion.

The hour is night. At the siren's moan, the ceremony begins. The plaza is in semi-darkness, the Wall lit. All stand at attention, gazing towards this illumination.[21] The spatial focus is the Memorial-Heroism Beacon, in a small, rectangular enclosure located just outside the fenced-off prayer area (see figure 7). The beacon itself is encased in a squared conus, made of dressed stones that evoke those of the Wall. Within the enclosure stands an honor guard of four young soldiers. The flagpole, the national flag at half-mast, is aligned linearly with the beacon, between the enclosure and the prayer area. Facing the enclosure, standing at a marker on the ground, is the President of the state. He is flanked by two high-ranking officers, one of whom is the Chief-of-Staff of the IDF, the Israel Defense Forces. Well behind these three stand invited members of the bereaved families, and behind them, to the borders of the plaza, other spectators. On the northern side of the plaza are two small rostra, that of the invited speakers and that of the announcer. On the southern side, a large honor guard closes off and completes the rectilinear space of the ceremony.

Apart from these solitary markers of presence, the large plaza is a place of space filled by emptiness and still shadows. Only the flag moves, fluttering fitfully in the quiet breeze. The moan of the siren dies, the ceremony proceeds in silence. The three figures walk forward at a measured pace. To the north of the enclosure, two female figures appear, one a bereaved mother (or alternatively, a war widow), the other a young female soldier bearing a lit torch. The two officers stop at a second ground marker, the President continues forward alone. At the entrance to the enclosure he meets the two women. The soldier hands the torch to the bereaved mother. She in turn gives it to the President, who advances the few paces into the enclosure and lights the memorial flame. A bugle sounds. The President communes a moment before the flame. The bereaved mother and female soldier reenter the shadows. The President now makes his address before the enclosure, facing the flame. His words, like all those on this occasion, are brief. In recent years he has spoken of the unification of the People of Israel in remembrance of the fallen; of the 'bereaved family' (*mishpaḥat hashhol*), and their sons, the fallen; and of the necessity of sacrifice and its memory. His words have referred to the location of the ceremony as 'this holy place', and to the Wall as 'witness to the destruction of two thousand years ago', and now, 'witness not to destruction, but to revival'.[22] Escorted by the two officers, the President takes his seat next to his wife, at the northwestern edge of the plaza, in the first row of bereaved families, and next to the speaker's rostrum. Seated, the presidential couple now are flanked by the two officers.

From this moment, the focus of activity shifts to the speaker's rostrum, and to speech, reading, and prayer. During these utterances, the central area of the plaza remains completely empty, a lengthy expanse separating the bereaved families and speakers from the memorial flame, where the flickering of fire and fluttering of flag are the only motion, against the serene, still, backdrop of the Wall.

The Chief-of-Staff speaks, and addresses his remarks to the bereaved families. This is followed by the single, secular reading of the occasion – in 1984, from the work of a noted Israeli Jewish author, on the theme of dead soldiers gazing down at those left behind, and apologizing for the sadness of the latter; but they, the dead, were obliged to do battle. And God receives them as His sons.[23] The chief rabbi of the IDF reads from the Book of Psalms. A bereaved father recites *kaddish*, the mourner's prayer, that praises the greatness of God.[24] And the IDF cantor sings 'God, full of compassion . . .' (*El malei raḥamim*), the prayer that asks God to take the soul of the departed into his keeping. The assembled rise, and are asked to remain in place until the President exits. On their way out, he and his wife converse with members of the bereaved families. The opening ceremony has lasted some fifteen minutes.

Much of the power in numerous events of presentation is focused in the evocation of mood, in large measure through their symbolic, spatial formations and through their rhetoric. This is so in this ceremony. The spareness and simplicity of the program, and of its enactment, are striking. So too are the stillness and darkness, the vacant spaces, the constrained and restricted movement. These aspects reflect and reinforce one another, and are echoed in rhetoric to evoke a focused cast of mind, mood, and sentiment. The ceremony is composed all of a piece, its unity of symbolism not to be broached. The occasion is characterized by a high degree of symbolic synthesis of person, position, performance, and place, from which variation and individualism are quite effaced. On the other hand, signs of collectivity and of collective endeavor are prominent.[25] Although the ceremony is brief in linear time, it also calls forth a sense of eternality – of a version of moral and social order pervaded by a recurrent and everlasting problematic, that of heroism and death, for which there is no solution save sacrifice. Clearly the occasion is neither causal nor transformative in any teleological sense. Nonetheless, it is intended to be poignantly expressive of the duties of person and collectivity, of obligations that give profound meaning to death in the service of the nation-state. Here metaphors of sacrifice do have intimations of transformation and transcendence, though these stay wholly connotative. Thus the transformation of heroism into powerful death happened elsewhere, on the battlefield. Here that transformative power is remembered.

This reading of sacrifice is one of presence turned into absence in exchange for a strengthened, national collectivity. The agency of exchange is a certain kind of death, that of heroism. One whereby living members of the collectivity willingly surrender their lives so that others, and the collectivity itself, may live. Thus, in his 1969 speech on this occasion, President Shazar stated: 'in the name of the whole House of Israel we elevate the memorial candle to the souls of all our dear ones who gave their life for our freedom and [the] release of our souls . . . and their pure sacrifice will be accepted, forever and ever'.[26] The acts of sacrifice in the modern nation-state are far from causal models of sacrifice in traditional societies, yet the logic of ideas that motivates the former may not be that distant from the latter.

This occasion evokes presence from absence. Just as, through Holocaust memorialism, the dead of that catastrophe are named 'martyrs' and are given 'remembrance citizenship' in the nation-state, so this ceremony is one of re-membering the fallen in the greater collectivity of living and dead of the nation-state, which of itself must then have connotations of eternality.

In this opening ceremony of Remembrance Day, the living momentarily reach out to touch the dead, to sign their presence out of absence, but then to draw back, to address them from afar. This is done at the very outset of the ceremony, in two ways: in the kindling of the flame by the figure at the apex of the civil hierarchy, and by the semiotic alignment of symbols during those moments.

The memorial flame is brought into being by the living in memory of the dead.[27] The rising flame signs the metaphoric presence of the dead, of their re-membering among the living. Through this juncture the living rearticulate the memory of the dead by collectively remembering them. Therefore the kind of collectivity in which their membership is reasserted is crucial to an interpretation of this occasion. Here the alignment of symbols, during and immediately after the kindling of the flame, is pivotal. Four symbols then are aligned linearly and continuously, in increasing magnitudes of rank and, to a degree, of encompassment: president, memorial flame, flag, and Wall. This requires further discussion.

In Israel, the office of President is formally that of head of state, the highest in the land, although one of limited powers that often are of a ceremonial character. Elected by the Knesset, encumbents are expected to be aloof from the hurly-burly of politics. In large measure, the presidency is depoliticized by design, and presidents are expected to be figures of moral stature who uphold principles and values of import to the collectivity. Although often little more than a figurehead, the President may be also an agent of moral mediation. Popular presidents have had qualities of the father-figure about them. Noteworthy too in this regard is the absence from active participation in this ceremony of the partisan, political leadership of the country – its prime minister and cabinet.

The head of the nation-state, on behalf of its citizenry, remembers the sacrifice of the heroic dead by lighting the flame, and so re-members them in the greater collectivity of the living and dead.[28] This unity is a greater encompassment, yet not only because of its increased magnitude. Whether understood in terms of the sacred, with reference to spirituality, or simply as memory, the dead are beyond the living, recast as closer to valued ideals.

Together, the living and the dead constitute the nation-state as both an actual and a historical entity. But the nation-state, here signed by the national flag, is again a greater encompassment. The nation-state is not merely the sum of its citizenry. The state is assumed to exist independently of the particular categories of membership that compose it. It is to the nation-state that all the dead and the living give their allegiance, and from which they accept their obligations.

This lineal alignment of symbols of increasing magnitude and encompass-ment is itself encompassed by the Wall. 'This holy place', as the President called it, an unyielding 'witness' to history, has stayed rooted throughout the ebb and flow of ancient destruction, exile, return, and sovereignty once more. As the Wall endured all tribulations, so too in Zionist mythos did the Jewish people, and so will they continue to endure the loss in battle of their offspring. On this occasion the Wall signs the people, from whose enduring memory of themselves, in Zionist vision, Jewish sovereignty and statehood were recreated in the present. Therefore that which the Wall signifies is given fresh vigor and strength through the trials and victories of the nation-state. In increasing orders of encompassment, the sign of flame nests within that of flag, as both then nest within the symbolism of the Wall. The concept of 'encompassment', one that builds on Louis Dumont's (1972, 1979) discussions of hierarchy, describes this nesting. Encompassment implies that ideas embedded in higher-order levels contain within them-selves those of lower-order levels; and therefore that higher-order ideas have the capacity to generate, or to reproduce, lower-order ones. We return shortly to these relationships.

Yet there are two qualities of ambivalence here. The first likely was more subdued or absent when Mount Herzl was the major focus of memorialism on Remembrance Day, prior to 1967. For the Wall, as signifier of the Jewish people, also may be understood as the people encompassing the State; and this contradicts the Zionist ideal (at least as this was constituted in the early years of statehood). The Zionist vision (that still survives in numerous variations) was one in which all Jews of the world would move to the Jewish state to become its citizenry. At the end of this process, state and nation would become coterminous, but the authority of the Zionist state would encompass and subsume its citizens, the people. The state would be the culmination and fulfillment of the national endeavor. These ideals are fully consistent with Remembrance Day memorials on Mount Herzl, at whose summit lies the prophet of modern Jewish statehood, and with the transition there from Remembrance Day to Independence Day. But the Wall projects more ambiguous versions of the state/people relationship, ones that may be more in keeping with other religious-nationalist trends that have accelerated their momentum since the 1967 war.

The second note of ambivalence in this ceremony relates to the incipient dualism of a social order divided into military and civilian sectors – of those in uniform and those who are not, with the added implication that each sector is ordered by often antithetical principles. However, this incipient opposition is stabilized and unified by two factors. One is the sequencing of discursive action in the ceremony; and the second is the spatial hierarchy that characterizes the major symbols of the occasion. Both factors are discussed below.

Following the lighting of the memorial flame, there are six discursive acts, in the following order: the President's speech, the Chief-of-Staff's speech, the reading by a civilian, the reading of psalms by the IDF rabbi, the recitation of *kaddish* by a bereaved father, and the recitation (in cantillation) of 'God, full of compassion', by the IDF cantor. The obvious point about this sequencing is that its action alternates between civilian and military roles. Less obvious, is that this sequence falls into three parts, each composed of a civilian and military figure, and each given over (roughly speaking) to a somewhat different discursive genre. Thus the President and Chief-of-Staff do speeches, the civilian and IDF rabbi do readings, and the bereaved father and IDF cantor do recitations. Through this alternation and pairing there is a vivid expression of partnership and synchronization between the civilian and military sectors, in their common task of commemoration. The ceremony, and the versions of moral and social order it conveys, depend on the full cooperation of these sectors. Yet the civilian sector is dominant: the President begins this sequence, and the first slot of each pair is filled by a civilian figure.[29]

The second factor that stabilizes the incipient civilian–military dualism in this ceremony is that of hierarchy. The demonstration of hierarchy, that includes the subordination of the military to the civilian sector, is most evident in the spatial alignment during the kindling of the flame and the President's speech, before he sits among the bereaved families.

In fact, this spatial alignment during these moments is more extensive than we have noted. In its first minutes, the entire thrust of the ceremony is laid out spatially along its east–west axis, in a formation that essentially is lineal. Along this axis, from east to west, are aligned the following: the Wall, the flag, the memorial flame, the President, the Chief-of-Staff of the armed forces, and then at the plaza's western edge, bereaved families (those rank-and-file of the citizenry who have participated most directly in the sacrifices of the fallen), and behind them those persons who have come to watch. Flame, flag, and Wall are imbued with qualities of eternality. The flame separates the eternal from the transiency of the living. Flame, flag, and Wall nest within one another. The concept of 'encompassment' describes this nesting. As we implied, the idea of peoplehood (signed by the Wall) generates the nation-state (signed by the flag). The idea of the nation-state generates that of soldier-citizens who sacrifice their lives for the state (signed by the flame). In the reverse direction, these soldier-citizens are encompassed by the nation-state, as this is encompassed by the people.

On the side of the living, these more complex relationships of encompassment become the simpler ones of degrees of rank. So the President, the head of state and first citizen, is ranked higher than the Chief-of-Staff, who is first a citizen and second the commander-in-chief of the armed forces. The latter, at whose command the fallen sons entered combat, ranks higher than the bereaved families. On this occasion, in their sacrifice of their sons, the bereaved families exemplify the highest of virtues among the rank-and-file of the citizenry, those who stand behind them in the plaza. During these minutes, the entire length of the east–west axis is constituted through principles of hierarchy, first of encompassment and then of rank-order, that are reproduced on the ground. On the side of the living, this elongated, spatial alignment vividly shows the hierarchical relationship between the civilian and military sectors, that then is continued through the alternation of discursive practices.

In lighting the memorial flame, the President articulates the living to the realm of eternal verities. This we referred to as the moment when the living reach out to touch the dead. At the close of the President's address, in front of the enclosure of the flame, the lineal hierarchy is severed at the point of juncture between the living and the eternal. The President sits among the bereaved families. The first among citizens is the first among mourners. From this point on the focus of activity shifts to the northern edge of the plaza. For the remainder of the ceremony the centre of the plaza remains dark and vacant, separating the living from flame, flag, and Wall. In terms of spatial formation, the living have drawn back from the eternal. Subsequent activity is more distant from the memorial flame, and conveys an atmosphere of reflection and contemplation on duty, heroism, loss, and afterlife.

On the side of the living, the civilian figure of the President is integral both to the spatial alignment of rank-order and to the beginning of the sequence of discursive acts. This figure keys and shifts the spatial alignment of hierarchy into the discursive sequence, such that, as we discussed above, discursive action continues the rank-ordering of the civilian and military sectors through alternation and pairing.

The most evident feature in the composition of this ceremony is its monolithic depiction of unity through singularity. The singularity of theme is self-evident: architectonics, actions, and utterances highlight the same consistent focus of sacrifice, loss, mourning, and the meaning of this kind of death for the continued existence of the nation-state. But singularity is prominent too in the ceremony's ensemble of categories. In the main there is but one of each: one Wall, one flag, one flame, one president, one chief-of-staff, one rabbi, one cantor, one bereaved male, one bereaved female, one female soldier (and the one language, Hebrew, is used throughout).

Each of these categories signifies a multitude of members in its typification, but each is one. At the risk of continuing this monotone, we point out that the Wall signs all of the people, the flag all of the nation-state, the flame all of the fallen, the President all of the citizenry, the Chief-of-Staff all of the armed forces, the bereaved male all bereaved males, the bereaved female all bereaved females, the female soldier all female soldiers. Therefore each signed multitude is as one, a multitude of equivalences within each category. Moreover, none of these categories undergoes any change of character during the ceremony: the attribution of each is consistently homogeneous within itself, and in relation to the others, as is the multitude that each category contains.

This 'oneness' of symbolic condensation is profound in its logic of organization, for it returns us again to the principles of hierarchy (encompassment and ranking) that inform the ceremony. This 'oneness' suggests once more that, albeit not perfectly, these categories logically can be collapsed, accordian-like, into one another in increasing orders, first of magnitude and then of encompassment, without any principled contradictions. Through this extreme condensation, the nation-state stands as one. In part, this logic of organization stems from the inclusion of characters who can neither be duplicated nor varied: there is only one president, one chief-of-staff, and so forth. Nonetheless, other signs (like flag and flame) and participants (the bereaved mother/widow and bereaved father, the female soldier) easily could be multiplied, either in kind or in accordance with cultural codes of showing variation on a common theme. Yet, throughout the ceremony there is the decisive symbolic equation between 'oneness' and unity. Therefore there is little or no recognition of horizontal variation within categories of persons or symbols.

The ceremony is produced by the Ministry of Defense, and its constitution owes much to this provenance. Indeed, the maximal, lineal ordering of symbols and participants during the lighting of the flame does have substantive affinities to military conceptions of ranked order and chain of command.[30] Yet this hierarchical ordering is predicated not only on a conception of difference (higher and lower) in ranking, that is similar to the military mold, but also on the capacity of higher-order symbols to absorb those of lower order, and so to reproduce the latter. As we have argued, the symbolic hierarchy here is a lineal, sequential arrangement that depends in part on rank-ordering in the realm of the living, and in part on encompassment in the realm of the eternal, such that the latter also encompasses the former.

The version of moral and social order that is presented through this ceremony is marked by a sparseness and singularity of roles and symbols, by a homogeneity of membership, by a single-mindedness of intention, and by a oneness of being – of everything in its place, in a continuous hierarchy of heritage and legacy. An extremely holistic unity, in which each component imparts its sense of purpose to the one beneath, with little strain, competition, or conflict.[31]

The ceremony imparts a sense of order in the nation-state that may be summarized best by the metaphor of 'family' (and moreover, the family at home). We note that especially in times of national crisis [and in its memorialism] both the people of Israel and the citizenry of the state often are referred to as a 'family'. At memorial services and festive gatherings alike, past and present members of a particular branch of the armed forces together may be referred to as a 'family'. On Remembrance Day, either the people or the citizenry may be called 'the bereaved family'. The metaphor has powerful associations: of common ancestry, of a close relationship between kinship and membership, of the warmth and support of kin relations, of the oneness and protectiveness of family spirit, of the relatively small number of kin roles that family structure offers, and of a hierarchical internal structure that is intergenerational and therefore that projects itself into the future.

This atmosphere of familism is implicated in the lighting of the memorial flame. The fire is lit by the President, who structurally is something of a father-figure in this nation-state. He is aided by a bereaved mother or war widow. Together, the couple tend to kindling the memory of their dead sons. The older woman is escorted by a young, female soldier doing her national service. In terms of age and task, she fits the position of daughter or younger sister of the deceased. The flame itself is protected by an honor guard of four young male soldiers doing their national service. They fit the position of younger sons or brothers of the deceased. Behind the father-figure of the President stand the two senior officers. They fit the position of older brothers of the deceased. In other words, a tightly-knit group within which the 'parents' together procreate the memory of their fallen offspring, of the past in the present, surrounded by living offspring with the potential, as it were, to procreate the future into being (that may make of them the sacrifices of future wars). And, following his address, the President sits next to his wife for the remainder of the ceremony, among the bereaved families. They, together with the others, are the 'bereaved family'.[32] And at this time the bereaved family is homologous to a high degree with the citizenry of the nation-state.[33]

Is this 'family' a Jewish one? Not an idle question, this, since national ceremonies not only inform us on how the modern nation-state, through its leadership, perceives itself, but also where and on which grounds the boundaries of the collectivity are drawn. In this case the answer is equivocal. In principle there is no exclusivity: the occasion is one of national mourning for all those who fell in the wars of the State of Israel, and these include Israeli Druze, Bedouin, and Circassians. The major symbols (flag, flame, president, chief-of-staff), with one ambiguous exception (the Wall), are statist. However, the forms of mourning (prayers and reading of psalms) are those of Jewish liturgy.

This ambiguity is highlighted, for example, in an announcement of the Ministry of Defense for Remembrance Day 1979. This calls on 'citizens' to mark the occasion, adding that on this day the 'People of Israel' (*Am Yisrael*) remember their fallen, and requesting that all of the 'House of Israel' (*Beit Yisrael*) light a memorial candle at the time the President kindles the flame in the opening ceremony. The term, citizen, is unambiguously statist. That of the People usually is reserved for the nation of Jews. The House of Israel (that has strong familial connotations) can be used to refer either to the state (and so to the whole of its citizenry) or to the Jewish people.[34]

In comparison to the opening ceremony of Independence Day, that of Remembrance Day is a closed, inward-looking, contemplative affair, reserved for members of the immediate family, however this is understood in a given year.

The major events of Remembrance Day itself are smaller-scale renditions of the opening ceremony. Early that morning, at an appointed hour, a memorial flame is kindled in military cemeteries. At that time, memorial services are held in synagogues. In midmorning, again at the appointed hour, sirens moan throughout the country for two minutes. This signals the beginning of memorial services in military cemeteries. At the same time, members of youth organizations pay their respects to the fallen at numerous memorial sites and markers. In this multitude of ceremonies, that replicate the singular thematics and general symbology of the opening occasion, the dead are re-membered through their more particularistic affiliations: by region, community, and locality, and by military unit. Allowing for local variations and emphases, the occasions of Remembrance Day evince the remarkable degree of extreme unification of this nation-state that was evident in the opening ceremony.

Opening Independence Day: the glories of pluralism

The ceremony that closes Remembrance Day and opens Independence Day is held at Herzl's tomb, on the summit of the mount that bears his name. The architectonics of this ceremony are radically distinct from those that opened Remembrance Day. We begin with a discussion of space, since its organization (like that of the Remembrance Day ceremony) encodes the version of moral and social order that is elaborated through enactment. We then discuss the ceremony itself, which falls into three segments. The first

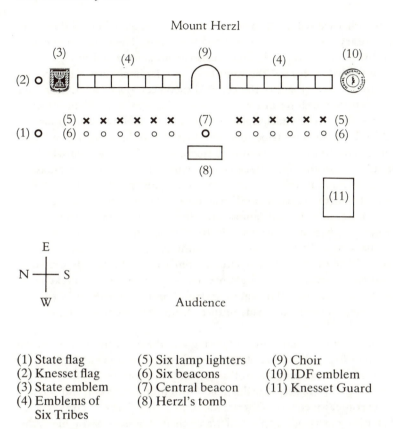

Figure 8 The opening ceremony of Independence Day, spatial layout

(1) State flag
(2) Knesset flag
(3) State emblem
(4) Emblems of
    Six Tribes
(5) Six lamp lighters
(6) Six beacons
(7) Central beacon
(8) Herzl's tomb
(9) Choir
(10) IDF emblem
(11) Knesset Guard

segment closes Remembrance Day. The second, composed of readings, songs, and the address of the Speaker of the Knesset, constitutes a brief period of transition between the two Days. The third, composed of the lighting of beacons and a military tattoo, celebrates the beginning of Independence Day. The entire ceremony lasts some forty minutes. Through our exposition this ceremony is compared to that which opens Remembrance Day.

One proviso: not all the spatial features we discuss are evident to onlookers (especially television viewers) at the outset of the occasion, since this ceremonial ground stays darkened in the main, until the end of Remembrance Day. Then the shift from darkness to light is a condensed recapitulation of both Days, and is indexical of their relationship.

The spatial layout is orientated in relation to a centre, Herzl's black, basalt tombstone, encircled by flower beds. Before the tombstone is an open area that we will refer to as a plaza. This is bounded on all three sides by temporary bleachers for some 2,000 spectators. These routinely constitute a diverse audience, including tourists from abroad and foreign diplomats. Immediately behind the tombstone is a large circular, unlit beacon (see figure 8). To each side of this central beacon is a row of six smaller, unlit beacons. Behind each set of six beacons are the painted emblems of six of the tribes of ancient Israel, again twelve in all. Below each emblem is inscribed the name of its tribe. Between these sets of beacons and emblems, behind and to the east of the central beacon, is a half-shell within which the choir stands. On the upper arch of the half-shell is inscribed a phrase or motto that enunciates the theme of that year's Independence Day. To the north of the northerly set of emblems is the official emblem of the State (the *menora*, or seven-branched lampstand). Immediately north again of this emblem is the flag of the Knesset. In front of this flag is that of the State, now at half-mast. To the south of the southerly set of tribal emblems is the official emblem of the IDF. The circumference of the plaza is decorated by national flags, and there may be other iconic embellishments. Next to the national flag is a small IDF honor guard. Announcements of what is to occur in the ceremony are made in three languages: Hebrew, English, and French.

To this point we note the following on these architectonics. In the pantheon of Israel, the figure of Herzl was given a prominent place, that of prophet of the modern, Zionist state, and that of the founder of the movement created to actualize this vision. But his figure is not, and was not, one of encompassment, as this term was used earlier. Herzl's figure is closer to that of a nexus of people and state, than it is to one of hierarchy. Similarly, the other major signs and symbols of the ceremony take their orientation from his tomb, but more in a formation of centricity and semi-clustering, than one of linear, ranked hierarchy. In this formation, the tomb is more pivot than apex, and so any sense of hierarchy is more flattened than it is vertical.[35] Therefore the same holds for the central, east–west axis of the ceremony (tomb, central beacon, motto). Balanced to each side of the central axis, are equivalent sets of signs of the citizenry (the beacons) and of the people (the ancient tribes). Similarly, all twelve beacons are equivalents of one another, as are all twelve tribes.

At its northern and southern edges, this ensemble is framed and contained by explicit signs of the state: to the north by its emblem, knesset flag, and national flag, that signify political autonomy and legislative authority, and to the south by the emblem of the IDF, that signifies legislated might. From this perspective the implicit design is one of the state containing that which constitutes it, its citizenry and people.

We also note that the north–south axis (beacons, tribal emblems, signs of the state) is an expansion, elaboration, and specification in breadth of the values encoded in the central east–west axis (tomb, central beacon, motto). If one looks at this patterning of semiotic space from the air, and therefore on the ground, so to speak, it has the shape of a broad, flattened triangle, anchored at its base by the signs of legislative authority and legislated might, and at its apex by the tomb of the visionary founder. The content of this horizontally inclined triangle is very much what this ceremony, this version of the nation–state, is all about. Here the composition of space depicts frontally a sense of breadth rather than of length, in contrast to the ceremony that opens Remembrance Day. The heterogeneity of symbols in this ceremony, including that of the composition of the audience, point to the comparative openness of the boundaries of this occasion, in comparison to the inwardly focused 'bereaved family' of Remembrance Day.

The announcer declares the ceremony open, locating it with reference to Herzl's tomb (by stating, for example, that the assembled are 'facing the tomb of the visionary of Israel'). The lighting is indirect, the plaza dark and empty. The Knesset Guard (*Mishmar Haknesset*) enters, fills the central space in close-order drill, and takes up position in serried ranks at the southeastern edge of the plaza. The Guard is under the command of the Speaker of the Knesset (in Hebrew, he is entitled 'chairman'), and is charged with security, protection, and order in the Knesset compound. The Guard's transposition to Mount Herzl is a signal index of major themes in this ceremony.

The Speaker enters the plaza, escorted by two, flanking, senior IDF officers. The three sit just in front of the first row of spectators at the western edge of the plaza, facing the tomb, but rise immediately as a soldier marches forward to tell the Speaker that the ceremony is at the ready, and to ask his permission to proceed. The Speaker assents.

The ceremony is enacted under the auspices of the Speaker. Elected by the Knesset from among its membership, the Speaker is the head of this assembly, charged with setting the agenda of legislation, with keeping order during parliamentary proceedings, with adjudicating infringements of Knesset norms by its members, and so forth. Although a representative of a political party (in practice, the one with the largest parliamentary representation), upon election he is expected to become largely apolitical, in keeping with his crucial functions of mediation among the political parties in the assembly. Of the 120 Knesset members, who in principle are the structural equivalents and equals of one another, he is the first among equals. Just as the President officially is the first citizen of the state, so the Speaker is the first citizen of its democratically elected parliament. There also is a direct structural link between the offices of President and Speaker. Should the President be unable to carry out his duties, the Speaker becomes President *pro tem*. In this ceremony, through the agency of Speaker and Guard,

Knesset values of legislative democracy and egalitarianism are transposed to Mount Herzl. Again, the partisan, political leadership of the country is conspicuous by its absence from active participation.

The recitation of the *yizkor* memorial prayer follows. This asks the people of Israel to remember their war dead.[36] The prayer constitutes the final utterances of Remembrance Day, and its note of civil rhetoric is unlike that of the ritual liturgies recited during the ceremony that opens this Day. Thus this prayer shifts the focus from the level of the eternal to that of humankind and the celebration of nation-statehood.

To the accompaniment of bugling, the state flag is run to the masthead, and the announcer declares the end of Remembrance Day. The shadowy sadness of darkness lifts as the plaza is illuminated, and the full panoply of varied and colorful signs and symbols comes fully into view. Some seven minutes of the ceremony have elapsed.

There follows that which we call the second segment of this occasion, although there is no enunciation of its distinctiveness during the enactment. This segment consists of alternate readings and songs, and closes with the address of the Speaker. In recent years there have been three readings, and these tend to convey a mood of historical transition, that within the ceremony parallels the shift from one Day to the next. So the first reading typically is from the biblical books of the Prophets, giving voice to the ancient tie between the people and the land. The following readings take up that which is understood as the modern legacy and continuation of ancient longings, the Zionist prophecy of the ingathering of the exiles, the return of the people to their land. The songs, spirited and tuneful, are a mixture of provenance and theme, but can be subsumed under the rubric of modern folk-songs (often called in Hebrew, 'songs of the people'). The choir itself is always an amateur group: that is, composed of persons whose song is vocation rather than profession. They are perceived as persons who sing out of affection for such genres of music and the freedom and love of the land that these express. These values of free choice and vocation characterize all of the civilians who hold centre stage during this ceremony.

These readings and songs are best summarized as mood-shifters between the two Days. The few minutes of their performance are the sole acknowledgement of, and accommodation to, the existential difficulty of switching abruptly from mourning to celebration. This brief period also starts to move the focus of occasion in another way. Remembrance Day is preoccupied with the severity of duty to the nation-state (even if this is entered into willingly), and with the obligation to remember the fallen. But this period of reading and song begins to introduce the spirit of voluntarism, and its centrality to the free and independent citizenry of this nation-state. Readings of biblical prophecy, fated and deterministic, give way to the free-spirited pioneering of nation-building. Above all, to the desire of those who chose freely to return, echoing the romanticism of Herzl's most quoted of words: 'If you will it, it is no dream'. As the ceremony moves into Independence Day, the embrace of citizenship as vocation comes to the fore, giving full expression to the architectonics of this occasion, and leaving behind those of verticality and determinism.

This intermediate segment is closed by the address of the Speaker, standing next to the tomb. This is the sole niche in either ceremony in which a participant is quite free to express himself as he wishes, as citizen and individual. Perhaps something of this holds for the President's address, but the latter is more constrained by the formulaic rhetoric of bereavement and mourning. At least in recent years, Speakers have treated their address as a stocktaking of the moral condition of the nation-state during the previous year. Some of these addresses have been openly critical (as well as complimentary) of trends in Israeli society. So in 1982 the Speaker attacked factionalism and social problems, and spoke of the need for their solution in order to redeem the good name of the State. In 1986 the Speaker scathingly denounced increasingly blatant evidence of racism, violence, and other dangers to democracy, and demanded tolerance and respect for others.

The opening ceremony of Remembrance Day is monolithic and singular in its thematics and enactment, deliberately evoking a monochromatic mood of reflection and contemplation on the subordination and sacrifice of the individual for the sake of the whole. No doubts or questions are raised, nor even intimated. Moral and social unity are presented as harmoniously continuous from top to bottom, without seams of conflict nor even cracks in opinion. The ceremony that opens Independence Day demands unquestioned allegiance to the integrity of the nation-state (for example, the *yizkor* prayer), but it then proceeds to enumerate various aspects of the body politic, like and unlike, sometimes showing their integration to be imbalanced and imperfect. The Speaker talks as a concerned citizen, the first among equals, close to his fellows, and often with a minimum of ritualized rhetoric. The message tends to be one of the individual responsibility of every citizen for a society that is continuously in the making, changing in its contours and concerns from year to year. The design of this ceremony has the potential to evoke greater reflexivity towards moral and social order, and this is most evident in the Speaker's address.

The Speaker's summarizing discourse on the past year signals that the ceremony has moved fully into the present, and into its third segment. At the close of his address he declares the beginning of Independence Day celebrations, and proceeds to kindle the central beacon. The lighting of the twelve beacons (plus one, the Speaker's) is usually perceived as the highlight and climax of the occasion. The entire ceremony sometimes is referred to as that of 'the lighting of beacons on Mount Herzl', and the twelve beacons, led by that of the Speaker, have been kindled on this mount since 1952 (Levinsky 1957: 501; Don-Yehiye 1984: 15). The number of beacons is identified explicitly with the twelve tribes of the ancient people, and is enunciated as such by the announcer. In the first years of the state, the beacons were lit by twelve new immigrants (called *olim*, in Hebrew; literally, 'those who ascend') from different countries. They embodied the Zionist 'ingathering of the exiles', the movement from the foreboding darkness of the diaspora to the light of Israel, on the mountain top, kindled anew by the efforts of those pioneers and new citizens who ascended there (i.e. immigrated to Israel).

It must be stressed that the template of twelve tribes, twelve beacons, is essentially a horizontal, plural formation, whose available niches (the beacons) will translate any categories of content that fill them into an egalitarian vision of social order. This is in distinct contrast to the vertical, singular formation of the Remembrance Day ceremony, one which admits of little variation. This Independence Day formation plays on what Nathaniel Tarn (1976: 28–9) considers a basic process of detotalization and retotalization. As we will indicate, here these two aspects are combined in presentation – the whole and its parts are simultaneously on view and open to inspection, continually constituted through one another in the vision of viewers.

The motif of the twelve tribes is a key to the logic whereby this ceremony expands out of the monochromatic singularity and hierarchy of Remembrance Day. As this commonly is understood, the twelve tribes were the offspring of the Sons of Jacob: that is, the people were divided into twelve different units of affiliation, that in principle were more or less the equivalents of one another. Similarly, these units could be added together to form the entire people. Nonetheless, each tribe had its own characteristics (as its emblem in the ceremony implies), different from those of the others. Therefore the twelve included diversity within their egality, heterogeneity within their equivalency. The imagery of the tribes, cast into the distant past, presents the entire people in the mold of pluralism and equality. So too, the analogy of the tribes to the modern people of Israel also casts the latter in the same mold, while retaining their mythic relationship of forebears and descendants. The nation-state is cast here in the mold of egalitarian pluralism, through the arrangements amongst its component parts. The harmonization of analogies within this metaphor perhaps was most evident in the early years, when twelve *olim* often were the lamplighters, each the symbolic equivalent of the others, and together the 'ingathering of the exiles'.

In keeping with its emphasis on relative diversity within the nation-state, this ceremony is keyed as well to a dominant theme that is chosen annually. This theme is enunciated in the motto, is evident to a degree in the Speaker's address, but is highlighted especially in the choice of the lamplighters. The theme is chosen by a committee of public figures and educators. Every second year the choice of theme is coordinated with one being promoted in the country's schools by the Ministry of Education. As in the past, the ceremony is intended as didactic (Don-Yehiya 1984: 12). And, in contrast to the 'eternality' of Remembrance Day, this opening ceremony is made comparatively dynamic, and is attuned to changing national moods. Thus the theme of the celebration may be intended to advance trends perceived as positive, or to counter destructive ones. For example, the motif of the 1986 ceremony was the Advancement of Democracy, in response to the increasing blatancy of racist utterance and action in relations between Jews and Arabs, which the Speaker attacked in his address.[37]

The twelve persons who kindle the twelve beacons are chosen (again, by committee) because their lives, deeds, or affiliations are thought to exemplify or to embody the motif of that year's celebrations. As noted, the Speaker lights the central beacon, next to Herzl's tomb. His action delegates the others to follow suit. The first among equals passes the torch of renewal to citizens who are the full equals of one another. The beacon lighter is flanked by a young male soldier who holds a lit torch, and by a young female soldier who holds out a microphone. The lighter, on a podium, is raised above the flanking military pair. Before each kindling, with stirring music in the background, the lighter dedicates the beacon in terms of the thematic motif of that year's ceremony. The dedication itself is formulaic: 'I [full name of the lighter], the son/daughter of [the names of his/her father and mother], [followed by the title, position, or dwelling-place of the lighter], am honored to light this beacon, to the [numbered] year of independence of the State of Israel, in honor of [there follows the recitation of social categories, sectors of population, institutions, regions, deeds, and so forth, that the lighter is representing], and to the glory of the State of Israel.' The lighter accepts the torch from the male soldier, lights the beacon, and the focus shifts to the next.

The following points emerge from this description. The Speaker, the elected first among equals, represents the Knesset of 120 elected members (including himself), just as they together are the legislative body of the entire citizenry. Analogously, each of the twelve lamplighters is here the 'first among equals' of that segment of the population he or she represents in the ceremony. Together, the lamplighters represent the entire citizenry, as it is organized categorically by the theme of that year's Independence Day. In the ceremony, the speaker plus the twelve lamplighters are the metaphor for the elect of the Knesset in the daily life of the state. Thus it is worth noting that the first words of the formulaic dedication of each beacon (I, [name of lighter], the son/daughter of [name of father and mother]) are similar to the first words of the swearing in of a new Member of Knesset.

As is frequent in Zionist cosmology, signs of presence in the present are made to play on and be evocative of that which is perceived as the ancient past. In Zionist cosmology, the recent and distant pasts are 'hot chronologies', 'those of periods where in the eye of the historian numerous events appear as differential elements' (Lévi-Strauss 1966: 259). These are the periods pervaded by occurrences of national import. Since the distant past is perceived as something of a spiritual ancestor and spatial precursor of the present, the metaphors of their temporal continuity are quite elaborated.

Continuing for a moment with such temporal analogies, one of the meanings of the word, *knesset*, for example, is that of 'The Great Knesset' (*Knesset Hagedola*), the Council of Sages, 120 in number, and ruling body of the people during the period of the *Talmud*. The parliament of Israel, the Knesset, takes the number of its members from this ancient body. Another meaning of the word, *knesset*, is that of the 'Great Assembly of Israel' (*Knesset Yisrael*), that during the talmudic period was used analogously to the 'Whole of Israel' (*Clal Yisrael*), a term that in turn was equivalent to the People of Israel (*Am Yisrael*). In the present day, deliberately echoing these textual sources, the Speaker represents the parliament of Israel, the Knesset, that represents the People of Israel in their, as it were, modern reformulation as the citizenry of the State, the whole of Israel. Similarly, the twelve lamplighters represent the citizenry of the State, again the whole of Israel. Therefore, the symbolism of beacon lighters and Speaker resonates strongly with one another, as do the collectivities they respectively represent, the citizenry and its Knesset.

In turn, the lamplighters recall the twelve tribes, with whom they are paired and whose emblems stand behind the former. The twelve tribes were the primeval people led out of ancient Egypt in the exodus, to become the People of Israel in Sinai. In a later era, the People were governed by the Council of Sages, 120 in number . . . Such temporal cross-references clearly are teleological in their sentiment, chronological in their historicity. Their intent is not to recreate primordiality, but instead to sound the 'hot' past for recurring echoes of the present, and so to anchor the absolute historical progression, the 'march of history', from the former to the latter. Therefore in this symbolism there is the deliberate knotting together of timelines and place markers. This encourages the collapsing of temporality, and so both the identification of present with past in the same space, and the elongation of temporality to draw out the long strands of continuity between present and past, again in the same space. The relationship between now and then is metaphorized as being so very lengthy and yet, immediate. Seemingly paradoxical, this relationship is less so, when the rhythms through which time is encoded are taken into account, in the next section.

But foremost the lighting of beacons brings to the fore relationships whose referents are primarily in the present. There is here the metaphoric delegation of citizenship and representation, from Herzl (the modern vision) to the Speaker (the democratic parliament), to the twelve lamplighters (the free and independent citizenry) who reflect continuity with the ancient twelve tribes (ancestry and history). This vision is inherently pluralistic in its organization.

The dedication itself of beacons spells out the plural version of moral and social order by articulating personhood, a sector of society, and the 'glory' of the state. Lamplighters identify themselves by name, parentage, and location in society.[38] Each is not only a citizen, but also a named individual with his or her own personal history and idiosyncracies; one who appears in ceremony not only dutifully but also voluntarily. This individuation of the beacon lighters is signalled also by their dress. In contrast to the uniform dress of the soldiery, the Guard, and the choir, the lighters dress as they please or as they are accustomed. That of the men often varies from open-necked shirt or sweater and trousers to suit and tie; that of the women from fancy dresses to blouses and slacks. Through their self-adornment, they inscribe on themselves their own individuality and, as it were, personality (although sometimes this reflects stereotypically the sector of society to which they belong). Thus the state is shown as composed elementally of autonomous individuals, each of whom stands for more than his or her self, and each of whom in their own way is dedicated to a common goal (the theme of that year) and to the greater good of the state.

At the very least, this parcellation of diversity (textually, figuratively, and iconically) out of simple multiplicity has the greater capacity to arouse a reflexive stance in onlookers, than does the severe singularity of the Remembrance Day ceremony. But more than this, depending on choice of theme and lamplighters, the vision of the ceremony also may be one of the societal integration of a complex heterogeneity of identities that at times are at odds in the social world beyond the occasion. The theme of Independence Day 1984 was that of a United Israel. The kindling of beacons brought together a diversity of persons who, in the usual course of living, would have little or nothing to do with one another. Their number included a kibbutznik, a resident of an economically depressed new town, a Druze soldier, two rabbis (one *Sephardi*, the other *Ashkenazi*), the wife of a Yemenite rabbi, a Muslim Arab teacher of Arabic, and new Jewish immigrants from Iran, Ethiopia, the Soviet Union, and the United States. Without dwelling on this, the lines of actual and potential cleavage among all of these marked identities approached the exponential. Yet, visually and

rhetorically, within the pluralistic mold of figurative and spatial equivalences, these seemed to merge and submerge in the common cause of
kindling the beacons.

We asked of those assembled for the opening of Remembrance Day
whether they constituted a Jewish 'family'. Similarly here we note the
potential confusion of citizenship, nationality, and religion when a non-
Jewish lamplighter stands in front of an emblem of an ancient Israelite tribe,
while lighting a beacon to the glory of the state. What is the lamplighter
then? A mediator of shifting conceptions through time of nationhood and
citizenship? Momentarily an 'honorary Jew' in the Jewish state? Or merely
a powerful magnet for conflicting claims that divide the country outside of
the occasion?

So discord may threaten to intrude within the ceremony. Thus one of
the lighters chosen to embody the 1986 theme, the Advancement of
Democracy, was the chairman of the municipal council of a large Arab
town. This selection was decried by a Jewish Knesset member representing
an ultra-nationalist party, on the overt grounds that several residents of this
town were under arrest at the time, suspected of murdering a Jewish soldier.

The lighting of beacons next to Herzl's tomb is the climax of the
ceremony. Until the early 1970s, apart from the singing of the national
anthem and the display of fireworks, this also ended the occasion. At that
time a military tattoo was grafted onto the ceremony. The foci of the tattoo
are the official flags of the State and the IDF. For the preceding year these
had been entrusted into the keeping of one branch of the armed forces.
During the tattoo, these flags are given over for the coming year to the
safekeeping of another branch.

In this closing phase the nation-state is summarized in its most popular of
signs, the national flag, given over wholly to the protection of the armed
forces. The tattoo is colorful and full of disciplined, rapid movement in its
maneuvers and formations. The music is martial, the armed forces dominant. This reflective moment fills the plaza between tomb and audience.
This shift to the tattoo effaces the reflexivity of the diverse citizenry that the
beacon kindling brought to the fore. This is replaced by the regimentation
of difference (the colors and uniforms of the participating units) and closure
of ranks. The composition of the nation-state is again homogenized and
stratified, its external boundaries hardened once more.[39] As such, this
closing is somewhat at odds with the tenor of the entire ceremony, as it
moves from mourning to the utopic climax of independence. Put otherwise, the addition of the tattoo to this ceremony has juxtaposed two
alternative endings to the overall narrative sequence of Holocaust Day,
Remembrance Day, and Independence Day. The one still the most popular
perceives the beacon lighting as climactic, and the tattoo more in the order

of a colorful show. Still, these versions of this country – pluralistic democracy or nation-under-arms – have interacted continuously since its inception to inform, gladden, bewilder, and frighten its citizenry.[40]

The ceremony ends formally with the national anthem, *Hatiqva* (The
Hope), that is not sung at the close of the opening ceremony of Remembrance Day, but only at the conclusion of both. This indicates again that
both ceremonies should be treated as a single unit of analysis. Further
evidence of such framing is in the use of fire as ceremonial punctuation.
Before the grafting of the tattoo onto the Independence Day ceremony, the
climactic coherence of the latter clearly pivoted on the beacon lighting.
Therefore, just as the Remembrance Day ceremony begins with the
kindling of a single flame, so that of Independence Day climaxes or closes
with the lighting of multiple flames. Given the polysemic qualities of fire
and light, these flames sign the common source of both national sacrifice
and national rebirth, with each shifting without contradiction in the
direction of the other.

In the spirit of its opening ceremony, Independence Day offers an
elaborate variety of activities, planned and informal. We briefly mentioned
some of these earlier. Like its opening ceremony, this Day tries to offer
something for the great majority of citizens, among which, given their
interests and predilections, they can pick and choose, or ignore altogether.
Among these activities are an international bible quiz for youth and the
awards of the Israel Prizes. Both are televised live. The Prizes, initiated on
the fifth Independence Day (Don-Yehiya 1984: 14), are the highest, public
accolade that the State offers to the contributions of its living scholars,
writers, and public-spirited citizens. This Day highlights and celebrates the
excellence of achievement of named individuals through the competition of
youth and through the capping of careers. To the close of this Day, the
nation-state is cast in the plural and egalitarian vision, here of the diverse,
humanistic achievements of mind and motive. And, just as the monolithic
singularity of Remembrance Day is opened by the President, so too the
closing occasion of Independence Day, the awarding of the twelve Prizes, is
held in his presence. The vision of each Day keeps its integrity, just as the
two are joined in their completion.

National cosmology and the encoding of time

At the outset of this chapter we commented that the lineal encoding of time
created a certain narrative structure, one that is sequential, generating story-
lines that are cumulative and climactic. In other words, these story-lines are
progressions, similar to those we call 'history'. In this section we argue that
the common-sensical acceptability for Israeli Jews of the sequence of

Holocaust Day, Remembrance Day, and Independence Day, and the story-lines this sequence can generate, are elementally grounded in and gather their power from axioms of time in general, Jewish culture. These axioms are rhythmic. They pulsate an impetus through Jewish cultural time, without of course forming or even formulating the contextualized interpretations and meanings attributed to temporality, whether as 'history' or as 'myth'.

We begin with properties of time that are self-evident to Israeli Jews. We turn then to a further interpretation of the dramatic narrative of this nation-state, whose enactment we claim receives especial elaboration through the sequence of these three Days. Our subsequent argument is that this narrative can encode the story-lines it does because its sequencing reproduces experientially the rhythmics of time we referred to above as axiomatic of Jewish culture. Therefore we discuss this rhythm, and some of the units of duration through which it is encoded and reproduced. In conclusion, we return to the sequence of the three Days, and to time as the blueprint of history.

The encoding of time that is self-evident in Zionism is summarized succinctly by Lewis (1985: 138–9). He comments that the Zionist prescription for social action derived from ideas of European nationalism, but that 'its existential thrust is deeply rooted in the ethno-history of the Jewish people. In this, it adopts a conception of time implicit in the Bible, a view that suggests that the meaning of the Jewish people is intimately bound up with the working out of Jewish history.' The rhetoric of Levi Eshkol's speech, from which we quoted earlier, is exemplary of modern Zionist references to time endowed with such impulsion. Religious thought in Jewish culture commonly links the ingathering of the exiles to the onset of redemption for the collectivity of the people, and to the enhancement of their spiritual perfection. In turn, this is to increase the likelihood of God's intervention in history to end time, to begin a utopic condition of Being. Zionist time adopts and adapts the idea of the ingathering, and makes the viability of nation-statehood contingent on this. Nationalism is the means to the physical and spiritual unification of the people and to their moral purification and renewal in the modern world. Nationalism and rationalism will bring about the redemption that Ben-Gurion called, 'a model people and a model state'. Nonetheless, the attainment of this condition of Being depends still upon an ontologic of Becoming: of exile, leading to return, culminating in redemption. The achievement of utopia denies and yet embraces a temporal rhythm of Jewish cultural time, to which we return shortly.

The encoding of time as an ontologic of Becoming is essential to the comprehension of Holocaust Day, Remembrance Day, and Independence

Day. Just as these Days are ordered in temporal sequence, so they are to be experienced in temporal progression. Although we concentrated on the latter two Days, please keep in mind that Holocaust Day is integral to this progression. Therefore, we again refer shortly to the narrative structure conveyed by the full sequence of the three Days.

The opening ceremonies of Remembrance Day and Independence Day contrast most blatantly in their surface expression of mourning and celebration. In this regard each ceremony stands on its own, suitable to and meaningful for its own occasion. Yet their structural articulation also is temporal; and this constitutes not only the passage through time, but is suggestive also of its meaning. To give meaning to time is to generate history. In the context of these ceremonies, history evokes the temporal continuity within which they become phases. Therefore the mourning of the fallen and the celebration of statehood are not sufficient to account for the significance generated by the temporal sequence of Days. Instead, as we have done, there must be recourse first to the structuring of meaning in each ceremony, and then to the meaning of their temporal ordering, that then incorporates the former. Given our earlier delineation of contrasting versions of nation-statehood in these ceremonies, we now hone the narrative encoded by the full sequence of three Days – then turn to the cultural rhythm of time that enables this sort of narrative structure and that is reproduced through its impulsion.

Holocaust Day, the first of the sequence, commemorates the horrific destruction of European Jewry, a terror that in explicit Nazi intentions towards the whole of Jewry was utterly indiscriminate and totally final. More abstractly, the Holocaust signifies the disconnection from one another of all vital values, the uncoupling of all essential relationships, the dismemberment of all community and collectivity, of social body and human body, leading inevitably to the denial of humanity and to death. Through its absolute negation of the human, the Holocaust is ramified disorder on the cosmic scale. For Jewry, it is the experience of the extinction of cosmos, of primeval chaos.

The opening ceremony of Remembrance Day exemplifies the polar opposite of chaos, and so its utter negation. The nation-state replaces the diaspora. The ceremony presents the nation-state as the moral order of ramified hierarchy. Every element of sociality has its proper place, and indeed is located there, while all are interrelated in principled ways within rigid, inward-looking borders that distinguish clearly between who belongs and who does not. The hallmark of the ceremony is unity, but more than this, a unity that verges on encompassment; and encompassment, in its primordial, mythic agency speaks to the creation of cosmos from chaos in Judaic cosmogony. This ceremony is a statement of severely-bounded integration, of a total cosmos of extreme order rescued from primordial chaos through self-sacrifice, itself the encoding of presence from absence, creation from extinction.

The opening ceremony of Independence Day celebrates the fruits of the Zionist cosmos. That is, once the work of ordering cosmos (akin to its creation) is done, the Zionist cosmos comes fully to life in the idiom of fruition, that of the Jewish nation-state. On the basis of its exacting certainty and ordered solidity, the external boundaries and internal strictures of cosmos are relaxed; integration is decentralized; pluralism is extolled; variance in ideology and ways of living are more tolerated; individual will and creativity are encouraged.

In a roughly analogous manner, this enactment of 'cosmogony' echoes Zionist allegories of biblical and liturgical process: exile, the ingathering of the exiles and their battle for freedom, the way to utopic redemption. This is a story-line of Becoming that is elemental to Zionist credo, its outline taken for granted and encountered over and again in public and private discourse and action, as a schema for making sense of the world. But this, of course, is what any principled ideas of cosmologic are about. Here their force is accentuated by their embeddedness in the cosmology of nation-statehood, that modern imagination of power enshaped (Anderson 1985). For this narrative structure is encoded and reproduced, as we have argued, in the scheduling of the Days, in their topological inscription, and in the ceremonies that activate and unify these matrices of time and space as chronological history. The expression of this cosmology of nation-statehood is characterized by extreme redundancy, of the same set of messages encoded through numerous media.

At the outset of this section, we suggested that these three national days can encode narratives like that of the 'cosmogonic', offered above, because their sequencing reproduces experientially an elementary rhythm of time in Jewish culture. What is this rhythm we have alluded to? Writing of the Jewish week, Eviatar Zerubavel (1985: 115) comments that this unit of duration is characterized by a peak day, the Sabbath, that imparts a 'beat' to the week. He continues: 'The experience of beat is essentially a sensation of a throbbing pulsation'. The Jewish week is a unit of cultural time that pulsates in accordance with a certain beat, or impulsion.[41]

This is a deceptively simple yet profound observation, for this rhythm of temporal pulsation is deeply embedded in numerous units of time in Jewish culture. This pulsation may be described as a beat or impulsion from lower to higher, from ordinary to extraordinary. The rhythm is climactic, but more so, for this pulsation also implies movement from the less valued to the highly valued. For reasons not dwelt on here, this pulsation also may be identified with movement from fragmentation to integration, unity, and holism. In keeping with this climactic pulsation, the abstract formation of time in Jewish culture is, generally speaking, that of directional development and that of collective Becoming. In the distant past this climactic pulsation was divorced in part from natural cosmic rhythms, and therefore from ideas of the eternal character of processes of 'becoming'. As Zerubavel (1985: 11) notes of the Jewish week, it had to be based on an 'entirely artificial mathematical rhythm'.

As important for our purposes was the idea that the movement of time, and the fixing of times, be imbued with the moral valuation of the human condition (Kaufmann 1972: 73). Then Becoming is in the first instance (and in the last) a moral problem; and therefore that time, the medium of 'becoming', is necessarily the moral ordering of existence. Put otherwise, the pulsation of Jewish time was and is the encoding of the impulsion of moral order, through different durations.

Should one need reminding, in the biblical myth of cosmogenesis the creation of time, the separation of light from darkness, day from night (Genesis 1: 3–5), is almost isomorphic with the onset of cosmic creation, while the whole creative process is encoded by consecutively numbered days, culminating in the seventh, which God blessed and made holy. As the medieval philosopher Maimonides (1956: 171) stated, 'Even time itself is among the things created'. Whereupon he added (albeit for purposes of his own argument) that the 'true and essential condition' of time 'is not to remain in the same state for two consecutive moments'. In other words, that time is inherently processual.

That time has a special status in Jewish thought is not in question. Heschel (1951: 8) writes that, 'Judaism is a religion of time ... The main themes of faith lie in the realm of time.' The nineteenth century Orthodox thinker Hirsch (1985: 41) stated that 'The catechism of the Jew consists of his calendar'. Once time is created, everything else (with the exception of the Creator) happens within and during continuous time. Heschel (1951: 100) argues that 'it is within time that we are able to sense the unity of all beings'.

This evokes a crucial characteristic of such cultural time. Time is continuous with the cosmos, yet more than this, it is the one matrix of cosmos that never falters, that never loses its continuous self-coherence, integrity, and unity. Time is not entropic. By contrast, space is alienated (by expulsion) and fragmented (by destruction). Desired space is often at best the promise of time: elsewhere, and attainable only through the coherent continuity and integrity of time. People are perceived over and again to dissipate their moral virtues, to shatter their collective endeavors, to become dislocated in space, and so to suffer some form of dispersal. Thus it is within and through the pulsating rhythms of time, encoded as a moral order of becoming, of progression, that all strivings for utopic perfection and for the unification of people and place occur. The eschatological visions of traditional Judaism, of God intervening in time to end time, and so to begin an eternity of perfection, point precisely to the essential integrity of this matrix. We may say that in these views time ends when it is no longer necessary – when its processual shepherding of Becoming is completed.

The matrix of time (and texts that document 'times' and 'timing') holds everything together in the Jewish phenomenal world.[42] As Newton–Smith (1980: 88) comments, 'relative to our system of beliefs, non-unified time is a much more outlandish possibility than non-unified space'. In secular Zionist discourse, ethno-history has pride of place rather than time. Yet, to appreciate how this ethno-history is ordered, one must recognize that its 'sensible' interpretations are harmonics that resonate continuously with rhythms of cultural time, whether the latter are perceived in secular or religious terms. In a phenomenology of Jewish life, time is a root metaphor that is expandable into three dimensions of Becoming, in other words, of existence.

In the abstract, time expands into the continuous totality of the world, one that never shatters nor loses its resilience or integrity. This view of cultural time is somewhat akin to what Wittgenstein termed 'logical space' – it determines nothing, but does suggest which combinations of elements are possible. Second, time signifies movement towards (and away from) the actualization of various sorts of moral unities or completions within this totality. Third, this movement often is encoded in terms of the rhythmic pulsations of duration that we sketched earlier.

Our delineation of Jewish cultural time is broad and unqualified, and we have not the space to take up its limitations. Our primary interest has been to contextualize any further discussion of rhythms of time, in relation to the Days and ceremonies of this chapter, on the premise that these rhythms are the intimates of lived experience. Nonetheless, this rhythm of pulsation – from low to high, from morally inferior to morally superior – is evident through different durations of Jewish time, from the short to the lengthy, as we indicate briefly, below.

Consider the pulsation of the Jewish twenty-four hour day. In the phrasing of Genesis (1: 5), 'And the evening and the morning were the first day.' The Jewish day begins in darkness and moves into light. Generally speaking, light has the more valued connotations of morality and capability, than does darkness. In a simple yet ever-continuing way, this night-day, as Hirsch (1985: 42) calls it, condenses and recapitulates the momentum of cosmogonic and existential movement.

Consider the pulsation of the Jewish week. It moves through six ordinary days to peak at the extraordinary seventh, that Heschel (1951: 14) calls 'the climax of living', and that has its own distinctive, superior character

(Zerubavel 1985: 113). In the biblical text, at least, 'the Sabbath commemorates the creation' (Kaufmann 1972: 117); and so, one may surmise, again implicates that elementary momentum.

Consider the pulsation of holidays like *Purim*, Passover, and *Ḥannuka*. Purim is preceded by a fast day that commemorates the period of trepidation and repentance, when the lives of the Jews of Persia were under dire threat. On the eve of the holiday the story of their salvation is read. The following day is one of celebration and jubilation. Passover is preceded by a fast day that commemorates the time of trial when the firstborn of the Egyptians were slain, whilst those of the Israelites were protected. On the eve of the holiday the story of the exodus is read. *Ḥannuka* too is a tale of trial and triumph. The beat of all these holidays moves from the low of tribulation to the high of triumph. But the peak of these occasions, like that of the Sabbath, is always celebrated during their eves, in darkness. In these instances the reversal of the usual night-day significance serves to usher in their special climactic beat, when metaphors of darkness are eclipsed and are turned into those of the height of light.

Consider rhythms of longer duration. Every Sabbath service includes a reading from the *Tora* (the *Pentateuch*) that is concluded with a reading, called '*haftara*' (literally, 'conclusion'), usually from the books of the Prophets. Exegeses tend to link the meanings of these sets of readings, of a given Sabbath. Consider the rhythmic pulsation of the readings, in Ashkenazic tradition, for six Sabbaths that fall in sequence between the end of the Hebrew month of *Shevat* (February-March) and Passover (March-April).[43] Here we review this implicit rhythm in brief, without discussing substantive details (texts and commentaries are easily available in Hertz 1938).

The first of these Sabbaths is called *Shekalim*. The *Tora* reading tells of the obligation of every Israelite to contribute a half-shekel towards the upkeep of the Temple. This has been interpreted as an annual renewal of collective membership (Hirsch 1985: 323; Vainstein 1953: 139). The associated *haftara* tells of revolt against foreign idolators, of the enemy within and of their destruction (Hertz 1938: 954). The second, called *Zaḥor* ('remember'), precedes the holiday of *Purim*. The *Tora* reading recalls the unprovoked and vicious attack of Amalek on the Israelites, following the exodus. The *haftara* tells of Saul's extermination of the Amalekites. Both readings relate to the destruction of the enemy without. Haman, the arch-enemy of the Jews of Persia, who is destroyed at *Purim*, commonly is assimilated as a descendant of Amalek.

The third of these Sabbaths is called *Para* ('heifer'). Its readings are on themes of purification, bodily and moral, and of renewal of the nation from within, preparatory to the fruition of the desolate land (Hertz 1938: 961). The fourth is *Haḥodesh* ('the month'). Its *Tora* reading describes preparations for Passover, the festival of the exodus. The *haftara* is part of a prophecy of the New Jerusalem, to arise when exile is ended. The fifth, *Shabbat Hagadol* (The Great Sabbath), is the Sabbath prior to Passover. The *haftara* concludes with a vision of the coming of the Prophet Elijah, in religious tradition the herald of redemption who would appear at Passover-time (Hertz 1938: 967). The sixth of these Sabbaths falls during Passover itself. Its *haftara* is Ezekiel's great vision of the dry bones returned to life, of resurrection and redemption: 'I will open your graves, and cause you to come up out of your graves, and bring you into the land of Israel' (Ezekiel 37: 12).[44]

The sequence of these Sabbath texts encodes crescendo, one that includes the peaks of *Purim* and Passover. The sequence begins with the corruption from within, its expulsion, and the renewal of collective identity. It continues with the collective response to evil from without; and then with themes of purification and cleansing from within. The subsequent texts relate to visions of the end of fragmentation and exile, and to the onset of reunification and perfection, climaxing during Passover, itself identified with the primordial coalescence of the Israelites in their collective deliverance from oppression.

Consider the period of fifty days (seven weeks of seven days, plus one), called 'Counting the Omer' (*Sefirat Ha'omer*). This begins on Passover and continues until the holiday of *Shavuot*, identified with first-fruits and often with the giving of the *Tora*, the voluntary surrender of freedom in contractual relationship with God. This period is one of quasi-mourning, broken once by the holiday of *Lag B'omer*. In traditional exegeses, this sad period has assimilated numerous catastrophes, most recently that of the Holocaust (through the timing of Holocaust Day). However the Chief Rabbinate proclaimed Independence Day, that occurs during this duration, a time of rejoicing, thereby likening it to *Lag B'omer* (Vainstein 1953: 156–60). Thus time beats in diminuendo, rising to the minor peak of *Lag B'omer*, and then to the climax of Shavuot.[45] The sequence of Passover (the struggle for freedom) to *Shavuot* (the contractual surrender of freedom) has its own analogies to the sequence of Remembrance Day (the struggle for freedom) and Independence Day (the voluntary, contractual relationship between citizen and state).

Consider the lengthiest of durations of Jewish religious time, the eschatological. Whether conceived of as progressive or apocalyptic, time pulsates towards the climactic and utopic, towards the moral unification and perfection of the cosmos.

In sketching some durations of this ethno-logic of time, we have avoided discussion of specific cultural substance, of whether this logic is peculiar to Jewish (and Western) cultural rhythms, and of whether time can be ordered, lived, and anticipated otherwise (the likelihood is that it can). We addressed a certain ordering of time and one of its prominent rhythms, that of climactic pulsation through various durations that nest within one another, and that overlap and reproduce one another. There is change in the particular referents and interpretations of time. But its elementary rhythm, and the experience of living this, remain – whether for secular, traditional, or orthodox Jewry.[46]

This rhythm of time – pulsating and climactic, morally encoded, lineally moving from low to high, holding within itself impulsions from fragmentation to unification – shares much in common with the progressive visions of secular zionism. The proviso is that here, as in secular Western life more generally, time is not perceived as teleological. These secular visions of progress are perhaps old-fashioned in an uncertain, shattering postmodern era, but still operative common-sensically, for all that. Remember that the State of Israel officially adopted the Hebrew Calendar, the Hebrew Sabbath as the weekly day of rest, and much of the annual cycle of holidays. Secular Zionists sloughed off the strictures of religious tradition, its way of life, and its teleologic of 'frozen history'. Yet they still have in common the rhythmics of time we discussed, and so too what constitutes a proper narrative structure.

The sequence of Holocaust, Remembrance, and Independence Day, reflects the importance accorded to the encoding of cultural time in Israel, and a plethora of examples could be adduced. The cosmology of Zionism (as of Jewish culture, more generally) depends in no small measure on its control and elaboration of time. It is in part through temporal rhythms that national history is generated, and it is within this ethno-history that this nation-state is legitimated in large measure to itself. This hegemony of ethno-history constitutes a moral economy of time, one keyed to innumerable injunctions to remember, and so to re-member.

Since the ordering of Days likely is a product of the cultural rhythms of time, this sequence is itself constituted to encode other durations, themselves the products of these rhythms. Thus the narrative structure of the Days and their ceremonies enables the encoding of the meaning of Zionist temporality on different planes of abstraction and scales of time.

The most abstract plane is the encoding of cosmological process, of an implicit narrative of creation, as we have outlined this, from chaos to cosmos. Its temporal scale is grand and mythic, approaching that of a cosmic root-metaphor. The temporal momentum of this plane is one of unidirectional coalescence and progression.

The second plane, in keeping with Zionist 'hot' chronologies, encodes time as modern history. Its scale is roughly the twentieth century. This plane explicitly retells the narrative of the Holocaust, of egress from the extinct era of diaspora, and of ingress to statehood, within which people-hood is again made viable; and of progress towards the fruition of the utopic vision of Zionism. Its temporal momentum is again one of unidirectional progression. One that distinguishes itself from cosmologic, yet echoes it.

The third plane encodes time as a more immediate, still shorter duration. Its temporal scale is that of Israel from independence through the present. Its markers of chronological division are those of that which Kimmerling (1985) calls 'the interrupted system' – of war and peace, crisis and relative normalcy. By Israeli reckoning, Israel has fought six wars since the declaration of independence. Each of these (with the exception of the deep cleavages of opinion over the Lebanon War of 1982) is characterized consensually as a war of defense. Each demands the mobilization of the citizenry. Every mobilization requires the shift from a plural vision of society to a singular one, from personal autonomy to duty and obligation, from free will to the constraining intimacy of a 'family' atmosphere, from egalitarianism to hierarchy. Every crisis footing evokes the vision of the extreme unification of order that informs the opening ceremony of Remembrance Day; while relative normalcy evokes the pluralism of that of Independence Day. On this plane of encoding, the narrative of Days is that of the relationship between a closed and an open society, and of the dependence of the latter on the former. The alternative is the descent into chaos, and Holocaust Day forever lurks in the background. The significance of Holocaust Day is that of 'Never Again', and its presence undoubtedly conditions the relationship between Remembrance Day and Independence Day. On this plane, temporal momentum is asymmetrical (since it depends on the chronology of war) and oscillating. This momentum of oscillation is embedded deeply in Israeli perception and sentiment, but it is not a necessary feature of this cosmology: rather it is an emergent property of Israeli experience understood through cosmology. Most of Israel's major wars are, in a way, a moment of creation, since the conditions of viable national survival are put to the question, and since the alternative is seen as akin to the annihilation of the Zionist cosmos.

Each of Israel's major wars has evoked the temporal logic of the planes of lengthier duration. Yet the emergent, oscillatory momentum of this temporal plane also has threatened to encode a sense of circular inevitability into the relationship between crisis and normalcy, although this kind of determinism generally is absent from zionist cosmologic. This coding of temporality is dangerous, since it begins to change the valencies of its poles of oscillation. In the Zionist, linear reading of history, it is Independence Day and its democratic and humanistic values that signify the higher climax and culmination of temporal progression, and not the values of Remembrance Day. Yet, coded as oscillation (with its implicit dialectical thrust), the values of Remembrance Day are elevated to a status that is symmetrical to those of Independence Day, and, therefore, so too is the autarchic vision of the former.[47]

The fourth plane encodes this temporality most overtly, in a still shorter duration, that of the year. Here the temporal momentum is annual and cyclical. In terms of this plane, the Days monitor more immediately this nation-state in close dialogue with itself about the meaning of its own temporality, its history, and the relationship of this to the present that ceaselessly is becoming the uncertain future. In this plane, Holocaust Day reflects on the chaos that was, and warns against present-day dangers that may again presage such a descent into nihilism. The boundaries of the people are illuminated once more. Remembrance Day reflects on the battles to create and to keep the nation-state. The boundaries of the nation-state are affirmed. Independence Day celebrates the fruition of this temporal progression, the present condition of the nation-state.

The encoding of national history on these different temporal planes has two important consequences for national cosmology. First, the narratives encoded by ceremonial can telescope into and out of one another with little contradiction. This is so, since all the sorts of narrative we have discussed are harmonics of, and so resonate with, analogous pulsations and orderings of temporal rhythm. Second, together these planes encode narrative through various modalities of time – linear, oscillating, and cyclical. Together, resonance and modality enable the multidirectional cross-indexing and cross-referencing of lengthily separated periods and events. The result is a complex temporal grid of the mastery of time, a blueprint that helps shape the meanings of national history and that interprets ongoing, national existence through the perception of such temporal processes.

Intersections

I like to believe that serendipity is parent to the imagination – the unexpected confluence that procreates thought before we are aware of its momentum, heading in directions yet unknown. While at Pittsburgh in 1978, I received a manuscript from Pnina Werbner of the University of Manchester, analyzing Pakistani weddings in Britain. One of the characters of these occasions, a clownish conundrum, sent me reading further. In the figures that anthropologists name ritual-clowns there is some kind of special composite, of qualities of play and not-play. Finding these together within a single figure was a treat that forced me continually to juxtapose their opposition, and so to relate to them as a unity. Until then, play and not-play had clashed more than coalesced, in my thoughts.

But how to think coherently about this unity of fluff and gravity? Stumped, I talked about this with Janet Dolgin, who had taught anthropology at The Hebrew University. Janet made a succinct suggestion: why not look in the dictionary. Yes, indeed. In the etymology of 'clown' I found hints of qualities of processuality that dissolved integration and integrated dissolution. Later on, in another form, this reappeared as the relationship between transformation and uncertainty, that informs chapter 3, and that later still influenced thoughts on modelling in chapter 2.

The year before, passing time in the Tel-Aviv University bookstore before teaching a class, I came across a single copy of a book by Richard Grathoff that was unknown to me. For all I know, it was then the only copy in Israel. Now, fighting to hold together the fluidity of qualities within the figure of the clown, I was given the container through Grathoff's concept of 'symbolic type', and its peculiar interaction with social situations. Bruce Kapferer found Grathoff at about the same time. Much of the thinking on how symbolic types affect context, that in my view is crucial to comprehending processes of progression within many public events, is Bruce's.

This whole mix of ideas – mishmash, is more accurate – resonated deeply with my personal condition. I was struggling to stand upright, trying to recover through many months from a chronic, incapacitating, back problem. I was extremely worried, but at times absurd to myself: standing, I felt lumpish and cloddish; but flat on the floor, light and airy. And as I tottered and teetered, up and down, I felt the equilibrated instability in the clown.

Searching for physical relief and functioning, I tried to learn techniques – one more existential, the other more mechanical – that accentuated self-regulation in discipline, while holding out ideal goals of self-transformation. My formulation of the clown as a symbolic type came to include features akin to these. In a way the clown type became a prototype for events-that-model the world, with their systemic qualities of transformation. And so this book at its end, returns to the formulation of its beginning.

10 Symbolic types – clowns

In earlier chapters I argued that public events have logics of design that encourage particular operations to be done through them and that inhibit others. Here this premise is carried into the interior of a particular character, the symbolic type of the clown, a denizen of certain traditional public events. The clown's logic of composition is keyed to, and enables the enactment of these occasions. To make this argument I will draw out affinities between this type and other aspects of such occasions. In the course of the chapter, three ethnographic examples are adduced: a phase in a Pakistani wedding, segments of Hopi sacred occasions, and the Dance of Man of the Tewa.

Detailed descriptions of the clown's place in public events are scarce. The examples chosen provide better than usual descriptions on the sequencing and progression of activities in which clowns appear. This is important, since I argue that there are strong affinities between ideas of 'process' in sacred occasions and the internal composition of the clown as a symbolic type. I suggest further that there are affinities between clown types, and ideas of 'process' and 'boundary'; and that these are opposed to deity figures and to 'anti-structure'. These terms, including that of symbolic type, are clarified as the analysis proceeds.

There is no universal character called 'clown' or 'ritual clown'.[1] My reference is to figures that combine contradictory features in their composition, more particularly the playful and the serious, and that appear in special contexts that often are summated as 'ritual'. There is overlap here with figures called 'fool', 'trickster', and 'picaro' (cf. Ricketts 1966; Zijderveld 1982; Gilhus 1984), although the usage of the two latter terms refers more to contexts of myth and narrative. There are of course other self-contradictory characters whose composition contains little or no playfulness. These I do not address.[2]

The clown type is an ambivalent figure of enticement and danger, hilarity and gravity, fun and solemnity. But the contexts of its presence are often those of sacredness, truth, and the authenticity of experience. This matrix of contrast and clash is crucial to the appreciation of affinities between the clown type and ideas of process and boundariness, and their opposition to anti-structure. The paradoxical placement of the clown type is related also to the resolution of these opposed affinities through the sequencing of particular events.

The major concern of other studies of 'ritual-clowns' is to pinpoint how their behavior within sacred contexts contributes to mundane order. These studies do not unearth how clowns actually make the occasions of their presence work. If clown activity is always present in certain occasions then this action is integral to them. Therefore a parsimonious interpretation of the presence of clowns should look first to the constitution and texture of the event itself. I am not saying that clown behavior in events does not have implications for the conduct of mundane life. However, I argued in chapters 2 and 3 that certain public events are self-reflexive and self-regulative in their organization. This kind of problem opens to discussion only when the clown type is related to the working of those occasions in which it is sited. The sequencing of these events must be considered, before summating their clowns as figures that, for example, simply enable persons to behave or think in otherwise forbidden ways, work that is done with equal competence by other self-contradictory characters.

So Honigmann (1942) and Charles (1945) suggest that the harmless burlesques of the ritual-clown make familiar and reduce the repressed anxieties engendered by living. Steward (1930) maintains that this clowning reflects the cultural interests of a given people, and so reinforces these concerns. Crumrine (1969) argues that clowning casts social structure into atypical combinations that arouse cognitive awareness, and so make learning through ritual more effective. For Makarius (1970) the *raison d'être* of the ritual-clown is the violation of taboo. She concludes that this figure exists solely to evoke that which must be suppressed.

In most of these and other studies there is a lingering scent of the hoary axiom of 'comic relief'. Let me say only that this antedates social-science, and that its assumptions of psychic catharsis and ritualized rebellion were put well by a fifteenth-century theologian from Auxerre who advocated the Feast of Fools. Welsford (1935: 202) writes that he 'explained that wine barrels break if their bung-holes are not occasionally opened to let in the air, and the clergy being "nothing but old wine-casks badly put together would certainly burst if the wine of wisdom were allowed to boil by continued devotion to the Divine Service"'.

My major criticism of expositions of clowns in public events is that with few exceptions they ignore how these figures relate to the public occasions of their appearance. Yet here is where much of the power of these characters is concentrated. My exposition begins with a phase in a Pakistani wedding in Britain. This instance points to the affinity between a clownish figure and the processuality of the occasion, and will aid the delineation of clowns as a symbolic type, in the following section.

'In process': the clown at a Pakistani wedding

The wedding consists of distinct phases through which the bride is separated from her family of procreation and her age mates; is changed internally from a state of 'weakness' to one of 'strength', and from sexual innocence to sexuality; and is united magically with her groom. The cultural intentionality of the entire sequence is clearly one of transformation, as this term was used in chapter 2.

During the phase called *mhendi*, a bizarre, clown-like figure appears, and communicates the condition of the sequence itself. The figure endows the event with a degree of reflexivity through which it is enabled to comment to itself about its ongoing progression. Previously in the sequence the bride was tied still to her natal family. She wore old clothes and was passive and tearful. Wedding songs described the match as loveless and the groom as ugly. Joking behavior enacted the grudging reluctance of the bride's family to surrender her.

In the *mhendi* phase the bride's hands and feet are decorated with a henna mixture, one of a number of anomalous, medial markings that separate the bride and that change her into an in-between condition of being.[3] She is made to stand out between her previous being of an innocent child and that of her coming one as wife and sexual partner.

The onset of *mhendi* is similar in mood to the previous phase. Dressed in old clothes, the bride sits crying on the floor, surrounded by her girlfriends. The songs of the older women mourn the loss of their daughter. Then the bride is decorated with henna. Thus it is when she is in her 'coldest' condition that the mood of the occasion changes (P. Werbner 1986: 238). The young girls sing songs of love and romance. They perform wedding dances and give gifts of explicit eroticism to the bride (P. Werbner 1986: 240).

Then 'a girl or young woman enters, dressed as an old man. In one wedding this "man" dressed in old clothes with a long beard danced an exaggeratedly romantic tango with one of the girls dressed as an older woman. In another ... the "old man" his face wrinkled by wet chapatti flour, wearing an old hat and carrying a cane, attacked the mother of the bride with his walking stick and tried to embrace her' (P. Werbner 1986: 240). In these instances the 'old man' is mocked about the virility he projects.

What is the significance of this figure? It appears at a point when the henna decoration of the bride is advanced; when she has been separated from her female kin and age mates; but before she is joined to her groom. In her 'coldest' condition, the bride incipiently is 'heated' and 'cooked' (P. Werbner 1986: 239). Werbner (1986: 241–2) comments: 'The clownish figure of the old man combines opposing elements for it is neither man nor woman, neither young nor old, but a grotesque combination of all these qualities in one . . . despite its dishevelled appearance, it is not an arbitrary figure, but a well-defined, well-contained one'. She adds that as an 'old man' this figure also is authoritative, and that this attribute permits the girls to break taboos on the expression of sexual desire. Werbner's published account implicates a point of importance for the study of clowns in public occasions: that the figure embodies the in-between condition of the bride and comments on this (although my interpretation of this commentary differs from Werbner's).

The wedding formulates an in-between figure that is analogous to the changing, in-between condition of the bride. The 'old man' is a nubile female, sexually aggressive, but of uncertain virility. The figure is a peculiar composite that is moving in the right direction, in terms of the causal progression of the occasion, but one that is not completed. Forgive me the same pun twice, but the figure is 'half-baked', an ill-designed, playful composite.

The figure comments on the following: the bride's movement towards separation (to becoming sexually mature and aware), her ongoing disjunctive condition (she is yet an ill-figured composition), and the direction in which she is headed (towards intimate union with a male). Misshapen, the figure is in flow from one condition to another, without its final state specified clearly. Unable to stabilize its own conflicting attributes of identity, the figure combines paradoxical imagery, sentiments of transition, and metaphors of transformation.

The figure performs while the bride is hennaed and heated incipiently. The juxtaposition of bride and 'old man' is harmonic, such that the latter resonates with and reflects upon what the bride has become. But the bride is in-transition, changing within herself, and the internal composition of the 'old man' is fantastic and impossible. This figure is not a final index of the bride's being, but only an intermediate one – an analogue of the bride, showing to all what has/is happening, the unstable condition she has reached, and the direction of her becoming. That this figure is one of play, absurdity and fun, within the context of processes of transformation, implicates its indeterminacy as that of intermediacy. Engrossed in these transformations, the participants are confronted suddenly and dramatically with a summatory reflection of the temporary condition of their own creation. This dimension of reflexion monitors the processual progression of the occasion. Clownlike figures are well-suited to perform as reflexive agents, for they are sited often at the boundary of occasions (cf. Welsford 1935: 72) – an ideal vantage from which to comment on the ongoing event.

Within the *mhendi* phase the clownlike figure also embodies something that is related especially to liminal contexts. This is mentioned here and returned to. 'Liminality', writes Turner (1974: 53), is 'the state of being in between successive participations in social milieux dominated by social structural considerations ... [it is] betwixt and between the categories of ordinary social life'. Liminality summates qualities in the interstices of mundane order and discourse. The existence of diachronic order depends on temporal discontinuity: 'if there were no intervals, there would be no structure' (Turner 1969: 201). In Leach's (1976: 35) phrasing, liminal phases are 'abnormal, timeless, ambiguous, at the edge, sacred', and are bracketed by zones of space-time that are 'normal, time-bound, clear-cut, central, and secular'. The ambiguity and indeterminacy that are internal to liminal phases are especially congruent with those contexts of processuality that are the hallmarks of events of modelling and transformation.

In the transformation of mundane order no intermediate station may be mistaken for the final destination. The validity of these stops is necessarily contingent. Such events exist through conditions of 'in-process', from outset to end, since these boundaries are accorded a kind of ultimate validity. Here reflexivity is in part a monitoring of the journey between these points of anchorage; and in part it enables this voyage to proceed. This quality of orchestrated flux permits the arisal of that which Turner called anti-structure, to which I return. The composition of the clown type discussed in this chapter has particular affinities with the idea of 'in-process': thus this type is especially well-suited to communicate to occasions of transformation that their condition is indeed that of in-progress.

The clown as a symbolic type

My contention is that this clown type has an internal logic that is related to ideas of reflexivity and process. In this regard the etymology of 'clown' is enticing. The word 'clown' appears in English in the second half of the sixteenth century (as *cloyne, cloine,* or *clowne*). According to the Oxford English Dictionary (1933/II: 532), the word 'clown' originally derived from words that meant 'clod', 'clot', and 'lump'. Among its usages is that of a 'fool or jester, as a stage character'. Glosses of 'clown' suggest that this character and the 'fool' were analogous in character.

'Clod' and 'clot' were long synonymous, according to the OED. Among the meanings of 'clod' are: 'a mass formed by the coagulation of anything liquid' and 'a lump of earth or clay adhering together' (OED 1933/II: 511).

Among the meanings of 'clot' are: 'a mass, lump, rounded mass: esp. one formed by cohesion or congelation'; 'a semi-solid lump formed of coagulated or curdled liquid, or of melted material'; and 'of fluids, as blood, cream, gravy: To coagulate, curdle, run into clots' (OED 1933/II: 521).

In putting together the meanings of 'clown', 'clod', and 'clot', one gets a vivid vision of the clown as a figure that is somehow unfinished or incomplete in the logic of its internal organization; an entity that hangs together in a loose and clumsy way. The clown is torn out of context, and its outline is blurry. It is 'lumpish' in its imperfect, but congealed and adhering fusion of unlike attributes. And it has a quality of 'frozen movement' or of 'congealed liquidity' that is strongly reminiscent of a condition of 'in-process'. The clown has an affinity to the medieval fool, for whom Welsford (1961: xii, 223) noted the tendency to 'dissolve' the solidity of the world. The clown type combines, subsumes, and decomposes unlike attributes in its composition – and therefore remains in-between all of them. This type is doubly anomalous: in its morphology, and in its denial of morphological stability.[4]

The word 'fool' (OED 1933/IV: 298) derives from the Latin *follis*, literally 'bellows', but also used in the sense of 'windbag'. The term 'buffoon', with connotations similar to those of 'fool', is cognate with the Italian *buffare*, 'to puff'. In the derivation of the word 'fool' there are qualities of movement, motion, and lightness; but also that of the generation of movement and process (cf. 'bellows'). Weekley (quoted in Willeford 1969: 11) carries further the derivation of 'fool': 'from the Latin *follis*, which he defines as "bellows, windbag, but probably here in the specific sense of scrotum; . . . cf. It. *coglione* . . . lit. testicle; also L. *gerro*, fool, from a Sicilian name for pudendum"'. Added to the qualities of 'fool' is that of a generating force with connotations of fertility and regeneration.

Given the probable affinities between clown and fool, there is in the clown a figure that is uncertainly and clumsily integrated, that adheres to itself with a strong, incipient momentum of internal movement or of frozen motion, and that has connotations of the generation of fertility and process. Therefore it is not surprising that in medieval Europe the fool was present at folk festivals associated with seasonal changes in the agricultural cycle (Welsford 1935: 70–3; Willeford 1969: 85, 90; Swain 1932: 66–9). In related dramas the folk fool frequently was the character killed and resurrected. Swain (1932: 66) comments that here the fool was considered indispensable, perhaps as a sign of life itself. In some of these occasions the folk fool acted as prologue or epilogue, as a kind of master of ceremonies. (Welsford [1935: 73]; see also Shulman [1985: 200–13] on a somewhat similar complex of attributes that delineate South Indian folk-clowns; and Kligman [1981: 28–9, 33–4] on an analogous character in Romanian peasant festivities). These folk fools, festival fools, holy fools and rural clowns embody many of the characteristics intimated by the etymology of the words 'clown' and 'fool'.⁵ One way of summarizing these qualities of the clown type is to say that it is continuously 'in-process' within itself – its internal logic is pervaded by the uncertainties of process.

Zucker (1969: 77) insists that 'Self-contradiction . . . is the clown's most significant feature. Whatever predicate we use to describe him, the opposite can also be said, and with equal right'. These clowns are divided against themselves: they are 'clots' or 'clods', often 'lumpish', that hang together in seemingly ill-fitted and disjunctive ways. The interior of this clown type is composed of sets of contradictory attributes: sacred/profane, wisdom/folly, solemnity/humor, serious/comic, gravity/lightness, and so forth. This type is neither wholly one attribute of a set nor another. Given this quality of neither-nor, this type can be said to subsume holistically, albeit lumpishly, all of its contradictory attributes.

In and of themselves, these contradictions within this type are never resolved (although they may be altered by the sequential progression of a public event; that is, by meta-context, as in the Hopi and Tewa instances to be discussed). Instead, regardless of that attribute the clown type is showing, its complementary but contrary aspect always is imminent. Thus the opposing attributes within the type continuously oscillate, so that each attribute brings to mind its clashing complement.

Given its internal oscillation, this clown type can be said to subsume a boundary within itself, that it straddles and through which it moves, back-and-forth in a never-ending pattern, so long as it is true-to-type. This clown type is paradoxical: neither wise nor foolish, but both, yet never wholly one or the other. Therefore this type evokes inconsistencies of meaning, referential ambiguities, and inconstancy and uncertainty. The type is a design of incompleteness, yet whole (a lump), that is transformed from one condition to another (congealing), but that is out-of-place (a clod), yet pregnant with generative force or power (scrotum, pudendum).

The clown type subsumes paradoxes that are self-referential, like the paradox of play discussed in chapter 3. The type is full of play, and replete with not-play. Both coexist simultaneously at the same level of abstraction within the type. Formulations like true/false, or within/without, are equivalences within the type, since either proposition can neither subsume nor negate its contrary. Both are conjoined and neither transcends the other. Constituted internally through paradoxes of self-reference, and therefore through uncertainty, this clown type does two things of importance. It reifies itself as autonomous to a high degree, from the contexts of its appearance. This quality it shares with symbolic types that are constituted quite differently. But within itself it moves between alternative realities without solving these paradoxes of transition (from seriousness to play, and the converse), and without invoking a meta-message like, 'This is play', to override paradox. Instead, the type is its own meta-message of reified paradox. In turn, this quality links the clown type to the idea of boundary.

The internal oscillation of this symbolic type suggests that it exists within an ongoing condition of self-transformation. Objectified, it often appears as an ill-formed unity. But internally it is unstable, fluctuating, in-transition. Its qualities are those of movement and fluidity. The type holds itself in precarious equilibrium. Its external stability depends upon the continuing oscillation of its internal composition. Its appearance is a product of its deep instability.

Like events of modelling and transformation, that necessarily are in-process from outset to end, I would summate the internal organization of the clown type as that of 'in-process': in motion, but unfinished and incomplete. If the exterior of this type is a summation of its interior qualities, then the type as a whole is a powerful device of uncertainty. The type is a consistent solvent of strata of reality, and its essence seems to be that of process. And though the type is externally stable, on another stratum it is melting within itself. The problem of 'process' is discussed further in conjunction with that of anti-structure.[6]

Let me return to the clownish figure of the *mhendi* phase. The internal composition of this figure constitutes a logic of complementary opposition: youth/age, female/male, pre-sexual/post-sexual. The figure also projects a logic of progression that resolves these oppositions. The oppositions within the figure bracket the kind of person that the bride will become. The being that she should acquire is projected somewhere in the 'middle' of the figure, between its clashing sets of attributes. She is to become someone between youth and age, between pre-sexuality and post-sexuality, to unite with a male.

This figure oscillates within itself, projecting into its middle-ground that hypothetical person the bride will become as a mature woman. The figure generates this projection because its interior composition is in flux, in-process. And the middle-ground of the figure – its hypothetical median of creative imagery – matches the in-between, liminal condition of the bride. But this middle-ground also signs a 'boundary' for the bride. Transformed, she will become a mature, wedded woman. Therefore the fleeting imagery of a projected maturity signals the outcome or boundary of the transformation, and the dissolution of the figure. It projects its own demise. The liminality of the bride and the interior flux of the clownlike figure lead in tandem to the boundary of a new state of being, within which the uncertainty of the clown has no space. That the figure generates and contains this incipient border (the median of maturity) also brings out the affinity between the clown type and the idea of boundary.

The event comments upon itself as it progresses, encouraging participants to reflect upon its movement and direction. In its presence, the clownlike figure is as incomplete as the serial transformation of the bride at that juncture. A summatory index of progression, the figure is a commentator on transformation, with intimations of predictive self-regulation for the event.[7]

Throughout this chapter I have referred to the clown as a symbolic type. Let me explain what is intended. This usage concentrates attention on the effects that these types (of which the clown is but one) have on context. The concept of symbolic type is adapted from that of Richard Grathoff (1970). Grathoff contrasts it to the role type, or role in conventional social science discourse. Roles in interaction are constructed through one another. Roles are constituted and depend upon the mutual tending of one to another. Therefore each contains attributes of the other, and their perspective and composition shifts with interpersonal negotiation, with the give and take of living. This follows from George Herbert Mead's idea of 'taking the role of the other' in the development of 'self' and 'other' through interaction. Similar processes constitute personae through interaction. Roles in mundane order are determined to a high degree by context, whether this is understood as a confluence of roles in concert or as a definition of the situation through which roles are coordinated and synchronized. The ordering of context concerts roles with one another in mutual modification, and their coherence depends on this kind of synthesis in social life.

By contrast, the symbolic type is delineated by the following attributes. Its prominent features are its closure to negotiability, its lack of mutual tending, and the relative absence of give-and-take in its relationship to roles, to personae, and to context. Instead the symbolic type is consistently and wholly true to the logic of its own internal composition, however this is constituted. At one extreme are symbolic types whose internal composition is not only heterogeneous but also profoundly inconsistent and perhaps paradoxical. Trickster and fool types, as well as that of the clown, likely make their home here. At the other extreme are types whose internal composition is highly synthetic, unitary, homogeneous, and consistent. At both poles, its radical impenetrability to mutual modification distances a symbolic type from the flexibility and constraint of give-and-take in mundane interaction.

Although figurative in form, the symbolic type often is perceived as a relatively autonomous being, one that introduces limits in keeping with the logic of its composition. Put otherwise, there are two elementary ways in which roles and their personae can interact with a symbolic type. The definitions of reality projected by the type are rejected, and persons refrain from relating to the type. Isolated, the type nears the in-human. This is the state of the Mad in the everyday. Or, the definitions of reality, of context, projected by the type are accepted. Then the type is related to, but only on its own terms of context that follow from the logic of the type's composition. Given the type's closure to mutuality, no other relatedness is possible. This is the state of Prophet or Saviour in the everyday. The type becomes more super-human, dictating the terms of context to others. In either instance, the composition of the type nears the paradigmatic, given the totalism of context that it projects into its environs. Whatever their fate, symbolic types have far greater autonomy from context than do roles and personae, since the former carry within themselves the totality of their own reality.

The major implications are, first, that the symbolic type is reified above context and, second, that it contains the routine capacity to form or to deform the coherence and consistency of the social contexts of its presence.[8] The symbolic type is radical among human figures in its capability to mold context to the logic of its own composition (Handelman and Kapferer 1980), so that context and attendant personae and roles become reflections of the logic of the type. This is not to argue that symbolic types are wholly autonomous of context, or free to determine it. The point is that these types are so powerful in relation to context precisely because they themselves are so overdetermined. In social life the symbolic type is comprehended more incisively as a 'set of concepts' rather than as a character or personality, as Claire Farrer (1979: 11) has noted for an analogous figure.

Should symbolic types appear in public events (and this would have to be established in each case), their presence is keyed to the design of the occasion, and thereby controlled by this. The design constitutes one or more meta-contexts that generate the contexts of its enactment. It is on these lower-order contexts, and on their sequencing, that the compositions of types have their effects. In the instance of clowns that appear in Pueblo Indian sacred occasions, the processuality of their type destabilizes and dissolves context. On the other hand, most of the deities in these events are thoroughly unitary, homogeneous types that reify the stability of context. The interplay among types enables these events to progress from outset to end.

The clown type and the boundary

Let me expand briefly on the affinities between the clown type and ideas of 'boundary'. A boundary may be thought of in two elementary ways: as discontinuity and as paradox. In either instance there is a clear affinity of the clown type to an epistemology of the boundary. It is common to regard the boundary as a discontinuity that divides and separates, just as it links and orders the phenomena that it compartmentalizes. Boundaries enable the existence of discrete phenomena. Mention of discontinuity necessarily brings continuity to mind. Between boundaries, or through boundaries that are more permeable, the relationships among phenomena are continuous. That is, phenomena are brought into conjunction through analogy and metaphor that mute difference and accentuate similarity.

Yet in a universe constituted of analogies, of related, continuous grada-tions, there are also more rigid boundaries whose character is 'digital' rather than analogic. These boundaries (of which the play frame is one example, and that of the sacred perhaps another) tend towards an absolutism of difference that is less easily breached by metaphor. That is, these boundaries insist more on a hegemony over interpenetration: something is definitively inside the boundary or outside, true or false, and so forth. This sort of boundary is a point of discontinuous, digital decision in the universe of analogic continuities. It functions something like a simple digital 'switch', labelled no/yes, out/in, relevant/irrelevant. Thus in Rappaport's (1979: 187) terms, the presence of 'ritual' is that of 'digital brackets'. The question is then one of the manner of operator that triggers the switch to permit passage.

One answer is that the operator must have the requisite expertise. Another (and it is likely there are many more) is that an operator in harmony with the boundary can key or manipulate its opening. One method of harmonics is to construct the operator's internal composition as akin to a boundary, as something that separates and yet conjoins. This is closer to the structuralist idea of a composition that mediates between oppositions. It is often evident, for example, in shamanic initiation, when the novice is reconstituted as a being who partakes of different levels of cosmos and so is able to move among them, as well as in the relationship between microcosm and macrocosm. Similarly, the clown type internalizes an idea of boundary, and this embodiment is integral to its constitution. Within itself it operates both sides of the boundary. Therefore the type subsumes and masters this kind of digital reality: the contained fluidity of the clown dissolves the absolutism of rigid boundaries.

Another way is not to think about a boundary as a 'thing', and so not to focus on the substance of that which lies on either side (cf. Stewart 1979: 87). Instead, if perception shifts to the internal constitution of a boundary, it becomes evident that this divider may be ambiguous and even paradoxical. The boundary itself is of a different property from whatever it divides, since it is an amalgam of whatever adjoins it. Then a boundary may be seen as composed of contradictory sets of attributes: top/bottom, known/ strange, inclusion/exclusion, and so on. Paradoxically, if a boundary is of the inside, then it also is of the outside, like a moebius strip. These contraries are not resolved, in and of themselves: instead their figure-ground relationship continuously shifts. If the internal constitution of a boundary is paradoxical, then the paradox (and therefore the boundary) is self-referential, closed, and impenetrable. For the solution to paradox, in its own terms, is a search for logical exit that returns to itself, and so that sets off its contrary manifestation.[9]

This sense of boundary is that of the in-between or the 'middle' of what is separated and combined. Like that of the clown type, its internal composition is in a condition of oscillation among its unlike properties. The interior of the boundary is fluid, plastic, and in-transition. This interior matches that of the clown type. As a figurative analogue of the boundary, the clown type holds the idea of boundary within itself. The type is an ambulatory manifestation of boundariness. In phenomenal terms, the internal paradoxicality of boundary is overcome by treating it as a homogeneous unity – as an artifact of perception that is portentous for the moral security of the mundane.

Yet in numerous public events it is precisely the discontinuity of the boundary that must be erased, to bring people into contact with the paranatural, to imbue the collectivity with sacred qualities, and so forth. This may be done either by treating the boundary as a digital switch, or by focusing on its internal composition – thereby changing perception of it from the solidity of the mundane to that of the fluidity of transition. Then the reified, uniform valence of boundary is replaced by one that is multiform and ambi-valent – one whose discontinuities are become questionable, uncertain, and problematic. The clown type is one key to this alteration.

In the etymology of 'clown' and 'fool', these terms were associated with qualities of power and regeneration. Douglas (1966) notes a connection between 'boundary', 'dirt', and 'power'. She comments that: 'dirt is matter out of place'; and Leach (1976: 62) adds that power, 'resides in the interfaces ... in ambiguous boundaries ... hence that power is located in dirt.' This power changes the shape and meaning of cosmos: if boundaries are altered, then so is the relationship between those parts that these borders order. Clown types are out-of-place on either side of a border, and in-place in neither. They have affinity with dirt (Makarius 1970: 57), primarily through their ability to turn clearcut precepts into ambiguous and problematic ones. Therefore, if there is an affinity between boundary, dirt, and power, and one between the clown type, boundary, and dirt, then there likely is an affinity also between the clown type and that sense of power that inheres in the alteration of borders and in the dissolution of mundane realities. So it is not surprising that this type often is perceived as highly dangerous.

I differ with the insistence that the most prominent work of the clown is the breaking of taboo (cf. Honigmann 1942; Charles 1945; Makarius 1970; P. Werbner 1986). The type does not 'break' sacred precepts – it erases the border between this domain and that of the mundane, thereby altering the order of relationship between them. So too, the fool (or clown) is not the enemy of the boundary (cf. Willeford 1969: 132). The type is rather 'of the boundary', whether as a digital key to its permeability, or harmonically attuned to its self-referential paradoxicality. In either instance the clown type is an embodiment of uncertainty, and so a device for the dissolution of boundaries – whether that between sacred and mundane realms, or those that separate from one another the phases of progression in a public event.

Attributes of Pueblo Indian clowns

In the following sections the affinities drawn between the clown type and the idea of in-process are extended to ideas of anti-structure and process, more generally. Discussion relates to segments of Hopi sacred occasions and the Dance of Man of the Tewa (Laski 1959). No student of clownlike types can ignore the Pueblo Indian data that, although scanty and uneven in quality, are enticing with regard to the interpretations offered in this chapter. There seems to be no full description of clowns within the phases of an entire Pueblo sacred event, but Laski's reconstructed account will serve. I begin with relevant features of Pueblo cosmology and clowns. Those of the Tewa are discussed further on.

All Pueblo peoples set clearcut boundaries to their worlds, in terms of cardinal directions and cosmic levels. The idea of a centre or middle to the cosmos is highly elaborated. The centre may be an earth navel or an entire community: 'Usually there are many different centers because sacred space can be recreated again and again without ever exhausting its reality' (Ortiz 1972: 142). The major orientations of space and motion are inward looking: 'all things are defined and represented by reference to a center' (1972: 142).

Cosmic rhythms are governed by the movements of nature, particularly by changes of the seasons. The winter solstice, the end and outset of the calendrical cycle, is a period of extremes marked by inversions of roles and identities and by 'ritual' license. Unlike the emphatic contrasts of the winter solstice, the summer solstice is characterized by a fusion and lack of differentiation of cosmic material. 'When the sun stands still in the middle of the sky . . . man can enter into a period of pure sacra, when time past and time future are fused with time present. There is no winter nor summer, cold nor heat.' (1972: 160) This 'middle' of the calendrical cycle is also the 'middle' or juncture of contrary elements. In counterpoint, the equinoxes are periods of gentle moderation.

All elements whose natural location is external to the Pueblo world are, 'defiling, dangerous, or the opposite of normal . . . It is probably no coincidence that the pueblos . . . place the kachinas [deities themselves, and representatives of more abstract cosmic principles] just at or just outside their world when thinking of them as occupying horizontal space' (1972: 154). Pueblo conceptions of boundariness are strong, rigid, and impermeable.

The sun is conceived as the cosmic agency of fertilization, the earth as mother. Clowns often are 'children of the sun'. They tend to be initiated during the equinoxes, periods of the combining of opposites (as against their separation during the winter solstice and fusion during the summer one). Ortiz (1972: 155) calls the clowns 'those permanently equivocal and liminal characters'. The clowns are referred to as the 'fathers' of the deities (*koko, kachina*) or as their caretakers (Parsons 1917: 202); and they routinely accompany the deities during public sacred occasions (Bunzel 1932: 950).

The creation myths of Pueblo clowns include hints of their inner composition, in terms somewhat akin to my discussion of the *mhendi* 'old man'. The Zuni *koyemci* were the offspring of an incestuous union. Called by 'names of mismeaning', the character of each was the opposite of that which his name connoted (i.e. the bow-priest warrior who was a coward). They had the semblance of men, but were impotent. They were silly, yet wise as the deities. They spoke of things 'seen of the instant', yet were oracles. They were 'inconstant as laughter', but grave in the presence of dieties. Their names meant 'husbandmen of the koko' and they were called 'sages of the ancients': they became the attendants and interpreters of the dieties, and were precious in the eyes of all (Bunzel 1932: 948ff.; Hieb 1972: 173ff., after Cushing). However, he who touches *koyemci* goes mad, for they carry a sacred butterfly in their drums that compels persons to follow them. The flighty fluttering of butterfly wings is an apt metaphor for the interior motion of the clown type.

The first Zuni *newekwe* clown was generated from skin-rubbings: this child 'was never still. He talked all the time. What he said was all the same to him; he did not care about the effect' (Parsons 1917: 229ff.). The first *kachale* clown (of Acoma and Laguna Pueblos) was placed on a rainbow, 'so he could play over it, back and forth'. In these instances there are attributes similar to those adduced for the clown type: an uneasy union of contraries, a memorable rhythm of oscillation, and the uncertainty of in-process.

The creation myth of the *kachale* hints that this internal oscillation is not resolvable, in and of itself. Before the world was completed, the *kachale* were led astray by a wizard who taught them 'jugglery' – the taking of things out of the mouth. In other words, they altered their interior composition by removing attributes of themselves. In punishment, their mother 'shut them up for four years during which time they drank and ate their own ordure' (Parsons 1917: 233). By consuming themselves they became wholly true to their own type, keeping intact their unlike interior attributes, and becoming beings independent of their environment. They became permanently liminal.

Pueblo clowns are paradoxical beings whose dress and demeanor reflect their interiors. Their appearance is that of lack of form or that of clashing contrasts. The faces of the *koyemci* seem turned inside out: clod-like and formless, they are 'literally lumps of clay with the potential for creation' (Hieb 1972: 181, 175; cf. Bunzel 1932: plates 23ff.; and Highwater 1977: 124). The *newekwe* have sharply delineated black and white body and facial markings; while the Tewa *kossa* are horizontally striped. The *koyemci* are potency enchained, their penises tied with cotton (Parsons 1917: 237), and like children they remove their breechcloths (Bunzel 1932: 947). Without shame, they are pregnant with potential power. According to Hieb (1972: 187), 'The koyemci represent a return to a state of being free of distinctions ... they are characterized as being "innocent" in terms of the Zuni creation myth.' The clowns are preoccupied with materia of transition, like excreta, and in differing ways the *koyemci* and *newekwe* embody 'dirt' (1972: 191). Pueblo clowns behave in flighty, aimless, confused, witless, and volatile ways. They cry out loudly and run about without direction (see Stephen [1936] and Stevenson [1904: 254ff.], respectively on Hopi and Zuni clowns).

Pueblo clowns are feared and revered: the *koyemci* must not be denied anything (Parsons 1917: 235). Bunzel (1932: 947) adds: 'The Koyemci are the most dangerous of all the Katcinas'. But too, 'the Koyemci are the most valuable of all the gods' (1932: 955). The clowns are innocent but dangerous: true-to-type they seem the very stuff of motion and flux, of the potential for dissolution.[10] Pueblo clowns regularly appear during the 'interludes' between sacred dances of the *kachina*. Titiev (1972: 255) writes of the Hopi, 'It's strange that the clowns should be said to have ritual value ... Clowning occurs only during the least important part of serious rites.' But the 'interlude' has that in-between, median quality to which the clown type has strong affinities.[11]

Hopi clown and *kachina*: opposition and reconciliation

The symbolic type of the clown is imbued with processuality. Other symbolic types, like the *kachina* who appear together with clowns, are imbued with solidity and stability. The opposition of types is informative of the relationship between process and anti-structure in these events. The materials used are from Hopi occasions of the summer solstice, in which the motif of clash is striking. This section serves as a prelude to the Dance of Man, in which themes of clowning, boundariness, opposition and reconciliation, are subtly interwoven.

The Hopi *niman* concludes occasions of the summer solstice, bidding farewell to the *kachina* until the advent of midwinter. The *niman* is translated as 'Go Home' (Stephen 1936: 493) or 'Homegoing' (Titiev 1944: 227). Like most Hopi events of this period the *niman*'s concern is with rain and fertility. Among the different clown groups in Oraibi on Third Mesa are the *paiyatamu*. According to their myth of origin, they settled there in exchange for protecting the outermost limits of the community (Titiev 1971: 327). The *paiyatamu* are called 'fathers' of the *kachina* and perform primarily in the *niman*.[12]

During the *niman*, as the *kachina* dance in the plaza, these clowns do 'a circuit of the village as if patrolling . . . in fulfillment of the promise' (Titiev 1971: 327). Their bodies decorated in alternating stripes of yellow and black, the clowns surreptitiously approach the plaza from its periphery, climbing on housetops behind the spectators. Four times they jump up, yell, and hunch from sight (cf. Simmons 1942: 187). Clowns and *kachina* are arranged spatially in their respective affinities: the *kachina* in the sacred centrality of the plaza; the clowns tracing the boundary, then to pierce abruptly the imagery of truth and stability of the *kachina*.

The clowns infiltrate the plaza and form a motley group, parallel to the beautiful and stately *kachina*, as if unaware of the latter. The clowns discover the *kachina*, play with them, and dissolve their synchronized performance. Thus the clowns carry the solvent of uncertain fluidity into the sacred centre, which they commandeer. The parallel stances of clown and *kachina* incisively show their contrast.

The *kachina* retire from the plaza. The clowns build their ash-house (cf. Simmons 1942: 188), eat like gluttons, drink urine, and enact burlesques of marriage and intercourse. This so-called interlude is the dissolution and reordering of the sacred centre in the clownish idiom of movement, motion, and transition. Context is unformed. The gravity of centricity is turned into the inconstancy and vitality of process. Deities and clowns clash like matter and anti-matter. As essential representations, the two are incompatible. The mode through which to unite them is not yet available in the occasion's progression.

As the clowns gambol, a *kachina* (often an owl) warns from a housetop that their behavior portends their destruction. In response the clowns boast of their own strength, force, and imperviousness. On its fourth warning the clowns seize and maltreat the owl, who returns to the plaza with a mixed group of *shoyohim kachina* armed with whips and weapons. The clowns seek shelter in their ash–house, but are tracked down. The *kachina* destroy the ephemeral refuge, drench the clowns with water and urine, and whip them.

This drama enacts the interplay of two elementary principles: each by itself is incomplete and ineffectual; together they are highly generative. The *kachina* warn the clowns that their self-consistency dooms them. True-to-type, the clowns mock these admonishments. The clash of opposing principles of order and energy intensifies. The clowns mistreat the owl. The *shoyohim* forcibly subdue and thrash the clowns. The principle of stability, of enduring verities, begins to control that of uncertain, unbound vitality. But as yet there is neither harmony nor complementarity in this forced union of opposites.

Before concluding the place of clowns in the *niman*, I turn briefly to segments of two other events of the summer solstice, enacted prior to the *niman* on First Mesa during the 1890s: these are performances of the duck *kachina* and of the *shoyohim*.

The clowns enter the plaza near the end of duck *kachina* dancing. There are forceful exchanges between the clowns and an owl *kachina*. More *kachina* enter, tie and pile the clowns in a heap, and drench them with water. Later these *kachina* return bearing gifts of food that they proffer to the clowns. With hesitation the clowns shake the hands of the *kachina*. But before the clowns can claim their gifts, the *kachina* 'seized upon one of the clowns in a forcible way, but not in hostility ... [The *kachina*] then insisted upon the clown dancing his typical sidelong shuffling dance' (Stephen 1936: 480), and made each clown tell a scatological tale: one advised the assembled men to ravish a neighboring Hopi community. Another told of a Hopi who in copulation used a cannon in place of his penis, and so his wife gave birth to 'young firearms'. But the discourse of the last clown was emphatically moral. He related that in bygone times of hunger his father told him of the coming days of plenty, and so it had come to pass: 'He spoke in a grateful tone, edifying to his hearers ... [the *kachina*] made him continue his discourse for some time' (1936: 481).

The performance of the *shoyohim* elaborates on the clash between clown and *kachina*. During a two-day period the following set was repeated some seven times. The clowns are playing in the plaza when the *shoyohim* enter.

'They [the *kachina*] strolled through the trees and when they had approached quite close to the clowns, these feasting squatters sprang to their feet and promptly each of them took from a tree a long string or old frayed lariat, at the end of which was fastened the stuffed skin of a prairie dog, and this stuffed skin they cast toward the group of *kachina* who showed great fear and drew back in alarm and finally fled in panic before the clowns, who launched their strange weapon against the *kachina* with great hilarity' (1936: 449). Four times in this set the *kachina* enter and are driven off. On the fifth the *kachina* 'come in assumed anger, seize the clowns, tie them hand and foot, fling them in a huddle, lash them with the willow and yucca, and drench them with water' (1936: 449). Sometimes the *kachina* are deferential, explaining that they lash the clowns so that rains will come (1936: 454, 462).

The *kachina* leave, later to re-enter, 'this time in gracious mood, anxious for reconciliation and bearing gifts in their hands'. The clowns are distrustful, but finally acquiesce (1936: 450). In their reconciliation, 'it is common for one kachina and one clown to stand about twenty yards apart, facing each other with extended arms. As they advance together, at first quite slowly, each moves his arms up and down like a semaphore and when they come close they run into each other's arms and embrace' (1936: 451). As the sets progress, the beatings by the *kachina* increase in severity, and the tone of the occasion becomes more intense. On their fifth entry in the seventh set, 'they slash the clowns with tremendous severity. Several of the clowns are bloody on face, breast, back, and limbs; this is the severest punishment of the whole celebration, as it is the culmination' (1936: 462).

The concluding interchange between clown and *kachina* in the *niman* is similar to those of duck and *shoyohim* enactments. After thrashing the clowns the *kachina* return with gifts. But the clowns receive these only after each performs under the direction of the *kachina*. Then the clowns leave 'in a fashion similar to that in which kachinas are sent off' (Titiev 1971: 330).

The symmetry of increasing moderation in the clash of clown and *kachina* is evident in all these examples. In each the volatility and uncertainty of the clowns is tempered and molded by the gravity and enduring stability of the *kachina*. In the duck performance the humorous, scatological tales of the clowns give way to the sober moral discourse of the last of their number. This final clown, the closing note in the overtures of clown and *kachina*, narrows their gap. His tale reaches forth, as the *kachina* did previously, and matches their stable stance. *Kachina* and clown then resonate to the same complementary rhythm, and their interaction ends in close harmony.

Stephen commented that the clowns are thrashed with increasing severity by the *shoyohim*, conveying a feeling of 'culmination'. Generally to be whipped by the *kachina* is thought to engender good health. But in lashing the clowns the *kachina* are disciplining and molding the vital energy of uncertainty, a necessary component in the equation of fertility that transforms and revives cosmic order and that gives the sun strength to continue the journey to his winter home.

In these occasions there is the sequential adumbration of themes in the contact of clown and *kachina*. Initially separated – clowns at the boundary, *kachina* in the sacred centre – their dress, demeanor, and movement are in vivid contrast. The clowns dart and gambol erratically, full of play. The *kachina* are grave and stately in demeanor, harmonious in movement, and quite alike and interchangeable in appearance. As symbolic types the clowns are full of flighty uncertainty, the *kachina* homogeneous and deeply stable.

These essential representations clash: a universal solvent versus the bedrock of the world. The clowns dissolve the context of solidity evoked by the *kachina*. But throughout there is the feeling that these types need to join together within a sacred centre – for these locations open to and connect all strata and areas of the world. These are nodes of articulation through which the cosmos is infused with strength and harmony as an organic unity. By bringing the pueblo boundary to the sacred centre, the clown type dissolves distinctions of structure and context. The way is opened to the reaffirmation of the world as a unity of interdependent principles and parts. Yet should the clowns triumph at its centre, the world would teeter precariously on its 'edge', as it were, full of the vitality of uncertainty but without direction.

The *kachina* subdue the clowns. Their vitality is given fertile aim, to bring rain, in keeping with generic pueblo ideals on the harmonic ordering of cosmos. Nonetheless the subjugation of the clowns leaves these occasions incomplete. Cosmic harmony depends on the smooth mesh of principles, and less on their forced conjunction. So the final contacts between types are marked by reconciliation. *Kachina* and clown exchange attributes of type through tale, embrace, and gift. In the duck performance the risqué clowns become grave; the sober *kachina* enjoy the scatological tales; and the clowns receive gifts that likely sign the generative union of order and energy. The types interact fully, each becoming more similar to the other while retaining its own typification. Perhaps a meta-type of fruitful unity emerges in the sacred centre to guide this conjunction. In any case, the idea of a vital impulse, of 'process', is bent voluntarily to that of order, so that each is integrated harmoniously with the other. The clown type, the solvent of stable centricity, is itself remade once the work of separating principles of process and structure is done.

Anti-structure and process

In chapter 3, I argued for the affinity of the idea of uncertainty to that of conditions of liminality. In this chapter I suggested the affinity of the clown type to the idea of boundary. Together these affinities possess that fluid cluster of qualities summated as a condition of in-process. Imbued with qualities of uncertainty, liminality is an excellent medium (a word that originally meant 'in-between') through which generic versions of mundane order can be shaped. The anti-structural version not only arises within the medium of liminality, but it may constitute an 'essential' version of structure. That is, its premises relate to elementary values and precepts of how the world should be constituted. Thus anti-structural forms often are associated with metaphors of sacred centrality.

Within the liminal medium the mundane order is reconstituted in essentialist versions of structure, in other words as anti-structure. The most complex form of anti-structure is that organized according to premises of modelling and their controlled, predictive capacity to transform mundane order. Then the operations of anti-structure may rejuvenate or regenerate cosmic and social order. In these events of modelling, anti-structure evokes the imagery of enduring and valid truths, of a unity of interdependent parts monumental in that which it subsumes, and of the *punctum indifferens* that stabilizes and anchors cosmic edifices.

Still, a vital complement is missing from this formulation. Mundane order is an ongoing fusion of ideas that connote 'structure' and 'process'. If anti-structure is separated from social structure within liminal media, then what are the causal energizers of anti-structure? May there not be ideas of energy and vitality within the liminal medium that are the essential, processual complements of anti-structure? Cannot the essential qualities of anti-structure and process be modelled as separate within the liminal medium – there to be joined again in causal and generative union? Then is not anti-structure returned to mundane order as the renewed fusion of the stability of 'structure' and the volatile power of 'process?'

These two ideas or principles likely are opposed in their ideal or essential conditions within the liminal medium, since their respective constitutions are so distinctive. The essence of process, uncontrolled by structure, flows forth in fluid eddies, its uncertain currents fragmenting or displacing points of rest. One would expect it to be transitory and energetic, but unpredictable, without direction.

If an idea of anti-structure dominates the spatial centre, then where would its complement of processuality be located? I would look to the periphery for manifestations implicated as processual. The clown type with its affinity to the boundary, its vitality and energy in demeanor, and its internal condition of in-process, frequently conveys this idea of process. The type may be summated as an embodiment of uncertainty and processuality that is opposed to anti-structure. Stated baldly, this formulation may seem crude; but I think it also substantive, in accordance with the attributes and affinities of the clown type.

According to this formulation, deity types are often the cornerstones of anti-structure in sacred occasions. I would expect to find clowns and deities opposed to one another when they appear together. But in events of renewal I would expect these types to be reconciled or reunited with messages of fertile union. In the Hopi examples this is done by narrowing the distance between deities and clowns, and through their exchange of attributes. Something similar occurs in the Dance of Man.

The Dance of Man: clown, boundary, process, and anti-structure

This section brings together themes developed throughout this chapter: the symbolic type of the clown, the idea of boundary, and ideas of process and anti-structure. The context is that of the Dance of Man of the Tewa, a sacred event of the autumnal equinox.

The spatial ordering of the Tewa cosmos is set and orientated by sacred places organized as a series of largely interchangeable tetrads (Ortiz 1969: 21). Each set of tetradic locations encompasses the Tewa world from its outermost limits (the tetrad of sacred mountains and their earth navels) to its centre (the tetrad of dance plazas within the community). One of these plazas is called the 'earth mother navel middle place', or the 'centre of centres'; and Ortiz comments that it is a condensation of all other sacred locations. All blessings and good things issue from this central location into the Tewa world. The other tetradic locations catch these bounties and direct them inward again, back towards the community. Therefore he argues that in this cosmos, 'we seem to have an opposition between sacred and sacred ... there is no simple opposition between the center and the periphery' (1969: 22). All entry into the Tewa world is immediately that of the sacred, without any waxing or waning of sacrality as one moves towards the centre or away. The deities are located at or just outside the Tewa world (1969: 91, 129, 149). Beyond this world are those 'whom the Tewa did not recognize as people' (1969: 172). And, 'anyone who leaves the Tewa world for any reason has to be debriefed and ritually purified before he can take his normal place in society again' (1969: 173).

The Tewa cosmos is conceived as a self-sealing, self-encapsulating unity: it is seamless. The paradoxical corollary is not that this world is boundaryless, but that its boundaries are everywhere. If representations of centrality are ever-present then so is boundariness. Although this reinforces conceptions of sacred centrality, it also requires that this centricity of the world be sealed and protected. Ideas of centre–periphery relationships may not be relevant to the Tewa cosmos, but those of centre and boundary are.

The Tewa are structured by moieties of Summer People and Winter People. Each moiety is headed by a chief (and by his society of assistants) who is responsible for the organization of roughly half of the calendrical ceremonial cycle. The chiefly societies, together with those of the clowns and those of four other categories of people, constitute the Tewa category of the Made People, or those who were 'finished' during the Tewa creation and the emergence from the underworld. The Made People are mediators between spiritual and human existence: their general task 'is to keep the seasons progressing normally and to concern themselves with peace and harmony in social relations' (1969: 73). All the groups of Made People, with the exception of the chiefly societies of Summer and Winter People, together form a category called, 'of the middle of the structure' (1969: 36). The moiety chiefs and their societies stress the dual, structural division of Tewa order. The other categories of Made People, who are recruited from both moieties and partake of the qualities of both, mediate these cleavages. Therefore they are 'of the middle of the structure'.

Among the Made People are two societies of clowns: the *kossa* and *kwirana*. According to one variant of the Tewa myth of creation, during the Emergence the people were full of sadness and sorrow. The clowns were created to make 'fun', and then 'the people began to laugh and to grow glad again' (Parsons 1929: 147). In another variant, many of the people sickened and died on their journey. The clowns were created, painted in stripes, and told: 'The way you have to do is to make fun, so that people will be happy ... The sick people came out to see them and began to laugh and get well ... The kossa made fun as they went, and the people moved on fast' (1929: 148). In these myths the clowns again connote qualities of buoyancy, motion, and the energy and potency of rejuvenation.

The *kossa* are 'warm' clowns, the *kwirana* 'cold' ones. The deities (*oxua*) are differentiated also into 'warm' and 'cold' ones, while those 'of the middle' share the qualities of both. Like the moiety chiefs, the clowns are associated with changes of the seasons; and like the chiefs the clown societies alternate during the year in their assumption of sacred tasks.[13] One of their functions is to bring the deities to sacred events. In moiety-specific occasions this task may be done by the chief, but in those of the entire community it is primarily that of the clowns.[14]

There are other hints that the clowns are related to the vitality of life-giving forces. The *kossa* are called 'children of the sun' (the father), a virile force. They pray to *Fatege eno*, a 'youthful fire-god' (Parsons 1929: 129, 267;

Laski 1959: 87); and his ashes enable them to perceive the approaching deities. Their ash-house is used to recruit through 'trespass' (Parsons 1929: 128; see also Ortiz 1969: 86; Laski 1959: 12). And Laski (1959: 87) comments that 'fire' and 'ashes' may be metaphoric of renewal.

The Dance of Man is held between the autumnal equinox and the winter solstice (Laski 1959: 25; Ortiz 1969: 35–43). It is done within the *kiva* on two nights, four days apart. On the second night the *oxua*, or *kachina*, come. During the first night all groups of Made People appear in the *kiva* to perform their prayer dances to the deities. The purpose of the whole Dance of Man is to obtain the blessings of the deities for the entire community, acts that are crucial to Tewa well-being. The occasion's logic of organization is likely that of modelling and transformation.

The second night begins with enactments by the groups of Made People. The men then recite the Smoke Prayer (Laski 1959: 39), an enunciation of anti-structure. In this are described the attributes of the *kachina* and their relationships to their children, the Tewa. Particularly striking is a phrase that appears also in prayers that precede the occasion and that index its closure: 'May we all catch up with that for which we are always yearning' (1959: 85). The initial framing of the occasion is that of transition: the border between mundane and sacred is not yet dissolved. The phrasing, 'May we catch up' may be an index of anticipation, of movement into liminality, when the mundane world is suspended and the people can attain that for which they are always yearning – the essential lineaments of their moral order. That is, they can partake of that which the Tewa conceive of as a blessed state of goodness, when 'structure' and 'process' are modelled and separated: for these principles are indivisible in their regulation of mundane exigencies.

Two clowns (presumably *kossa*) enter the *kiva*, and behave as if in a strange environment (1959: 40). They continue the distancing of the mundane world from that of the enactment. Their behavior is imbued with uncertainty and is highly reflexive. The clowns dominate the sacred centre of the *kiva*: they stroll about and examine the participants with curiosity, but without apparent purpose or predictability, joking and playing with sexual themes (intercourse, adultery), and poking fun at the onlookers. They say the opposite of what they intend, and continue to free the assembled from their mundane bonds. In-process, they do not constitute any stable focus as a replacement. Their *métier* is the dissolution of boundaries that segment routine roles and personae, and that divide this realm from the sacred. They create a fluid context that will be highly amenable to reordering by the *kachina*.

The joking and play of the clowns correlates with shifts, organizational and experiential, from one phase to another within the event. These shifts index the capacities of the clown type to dissolve boundaries within the event itself. Here the clown type controls the sequential unfolding of the occasion, and so too its instrumental progression. Laski calls the clowns 'masters of ceremony', and their play also controls the self-reflexive pauses, or 'interludes', of the event. In this early phase the play of the clowns dismantles taken-for-granted aspects of the mundane, and so makes the participants reflexive towards the occasion.

The clowns summon the deities to the *kiva*. Being 'of the boundary', the clowns are eminently suited to this task. Moreover, they themselves decide when to do this, by declaring something like, 'Now, let's get down to business'. The clowns 'shout the emergence path' to trace the journey of the deities (Ortiz 1969: 40). Peering into a cloud of ash, the clowns break up their search for the deities with sporadic jokes. They rock the participants back and forth through different and still unstable realities of perception, as they transform one phase into the next. But soon they gravely describe the deities and their attributes at length and in earnest.

The *kachina* arrive silently in the *kiva*, behind a screen of blankets. By now, 'the clowns have stirred up everybody's feelings to the utmost . . . all are waiting tensely, tingling with excitement' (Laski 1959: 47). The deities enter amidst deafening sounds, welcomed happily by the people. True-to-type, the clowns first recoil in fear and huddle together, and then rush to the entrance to greet the *kachina*. The clowns continue their reflexive work, switching from fear and awe to joy, emotions that likely are experienced also by the assembled. One by one the *kachina* enter amidst prayers of rejoicing. Each deity is greeted by a clown who leads the *kachina* to the chief of the Winter People (who sponsor the event). The deity hands the clown a sacred watermelon, that he deposits before the moiety chiefs.

This welcome is marked by clown behavior analogous to that found in Hopi events of the summer solstice. As each deity appears a clown rushes towards him with open arms, crying something like, 'Yes, Great Ones! Let us be friends!' The deity responds by striking the clown, who jumps back in pain, but who repeats his entreaty. The deity relents and gestures his acceptance of the clown. These enactments are repeated for each *kachina*.

Unlike the clowns the deities are not reflexive: they unequivocally deny the oscillating realities of the clown and insist on their own. These are profoundly solemn and majestic types who will be reconciled with the clowns, but only in terms of their own deep stability. Through their own uncertain processuality, the clowns had engendered conditions of ideational and emotional plasticity in the *kiva*. Now they are disciplined and subordinated by the deities. That is, representations of process and anti-structure initially are separated and opposed, but then are reconciled, albeit in a forceful way.

The clowns are the interpreters of the deities, who do not speak except to utter their characteristic calls. So as the chief *kachina* comes to the moiety chiefs, it is a clown who asks: 'Yes, yes, O Great One. I think you have something on your mind, something you want to say, don't you?' (1959: 50). The chief deity signs that they have come to speak with the moiety chiefs. Thereupon a clown motions to a young man to stand, and introduces him as a moiety chief. The deity violently shakes his head. The second clown then gestures to both moiety chiefs to stand. Still reflexive, the clowns offer a stripling in place of a moiety chief. The deity, insisting on the verities he embodies, rejects this ruse. The clowns acquiesce once more. Thus the clowns continue to test the validity and stability of the deities, and the latter prevail. But the clowns have raised the question of who are the moiety chiefs. And in turn, of who are the deities. Uncertainties raised by the clowns are stabilized emphatically by the deities. Yet anti-structure and process are still in uneasy conjunction.

The deity communicates to the moiety chief the concern of the deities that the people have not followed their precepts. The moiety chief assures the deities that the Tewa are living together in peace and harmony and will try to continue so. He signals to the deities that they may return to their dwelling-places. Both clowns reiterate this in detail.

One by one the deities are led out by the clowns. Each deity performs the Blessing Rite of fertility and abundance: each reaches out to the six directions to take in the 'Great Goodness' and offers this to the people who take it in, mumbling, 'Let it be so' (1959: 52). The clowns echo this refrain. The deities exit as solemnly and majestically as they entered. But then one clown exclaims, 'Thank goodness, they are gone, those troublemakers!' Once more the clowns disrupt the fabric of sacred verities: a moment before they were grave and enrapt in the blessings of the deities; now they are flighty and inconstant. Once more they question who and what the deities are. So too they transform one phase of the occasion into another through their internal processuality.

Silently there enters a strange deity not yet seen. He is called *Yeng sedo*, the Silent One. Ortiz (1969: 166) notes that he has this name because 'he alone has no distinctive call and, indeed, makes no oral sounds whatsoever when he appears.' Parsons (1929: 153) translates his name as, '"Restless" old man ... always in motion'. He is 'a kind of clownish raingod, he wears a funny mask with a crooked mouth ... He walks like an old man' (Laski 1959: 52). Ortiz (1969: 93) adds that this deity is also known as 'Temples male elder'. He comments that this deity is 'difficult to characterize ... so equivocal is he ... But the reference to "temples" indicates a lack of intelligence and other "human" faculties on his part' (Ortiz 1969: 166). He is known by numerous other names that include, Deer Hunter (he carries a bow and a quiver of arrows), He of the Mountain Top (according to Parsons, he always walks on the mountains), Rabbit Belt (he carries a string of rabbits), and the Flowerman. Ortiz (1969: 166) remarks that for both moieties he is 'a humorously attired figure who shuffles in last during Tewa ritual dramas, and who, after sustaining considerable verbal abuse from the kossa, has ritual intercourse with four young virgins'.

Hence the Silent One, a paradoxical deity-type: old and virile, wise and foolish, solemn and comic, a deity but restless. Unlike the homogeneous constitution of the other deities, the internal composition of this one is of contradictory attributes. He is associated explicitly with the elemental potency of fertility. His composition and demeanor respectively connote qualities of motion or oscillation, and a summary feeling of process. As a symbolic type the logic of his reflexive composition is much closer to that of the clowns. The clowns recognize his contradictory attributes and their affinity to him. One asks the other whether this figure is that of a 'tramp'. Scrutinizing the deity the second exclaims: 'Oh, it is our Great One! Are you our Great One?' – to which the deity nods assent (Laski 1959: 53, 87). As this occasion nears conclusion, clown and deity seem to draw closer to one another, their clash muted. Instead the affinity of deity and clown is emphasized as they progress towards a rejuvenation of the unified cosmos.

The Silent One signals to the clowns his desire for a virgin, outlining a small female form with his hands. Still true-to-type the clowns offer a young boy, whom the deity vigorously rejects. The clowns call forth a young girl and escort her to the deity. They take her shawl, adjusting it before her in female shape. Through humorous byplays the Silent One instructs the clowns that the girl should spread her legs further – and they stretch the ends of the shawl. The deity does the Blessing Rite: he catches the 'goodness' from the six directions, brings it all out of himself, and 'takes all this goodness and strength and blessing and, by clapping his hands, shoots it at the girl who stands silent and embarrassed' (1959: 55). He repeats this with three other young girls, and does the Blessing Rite for all the assembled.

Laski (1959: 62) comments that *Yeng sedo* 'never runs and never stops; he walks and walks about the kiva ... This constant motion seems to be a symbol of the creative power of itself'. Taking from the virgins their pure but static state, he potentiates, activates, and sets into motion the fertile union that the other deities have indexed in a more general way. In comparison to the clowns the Silent One is a more harmonious composition of the unity of sacred anti-structure and process. But his constitution also shows their own elemental force: the transformative powers of uncertainty when controlled by and united with the verities of anti-structure.

There are a series of progressions during this occasion – from oscillating clowns, to stable deities, to their integration in the Silent One, and the fusion of his power with the collectivity – that implicate how the components of this model of cosmos are added and activated to generate renewal. In my terms the clowns are embodiments of process, of uncertainty that is essential to transformation. The stable, homogeneous deities are embodiments of anti-structure, of eternal verities that contain the potential of dynamism. Through their blessings this potential is projected onto the community. The Silent One contains and subsumes qualities of clowns and deities both. He is paired with a virgin who embodies the pure community, full of the potential for fertility. This the Silent One activates.

In this occasion the Silent One is the highest-order symbolic type to appear. He totally makes over sacred context in terms of his own composition. Within himself he integrates and unifies all previous contradictions among principles and types. The Silent One likely is a meta-type of properties of encompassment that subsume (and so that can recreate) all contraries. As this cosmic unity, he stabilizes and energizes simultaneously. This is the operation of the mundane cosmos. In the Dance of Man it is made to work by unpacking and relating certain of its components in dynamic conjunction. Put otherwise, the event builds up hierarchical levels of encompassment that culminate in the Silent One, the apex of cosmos within the occasion, but the source of its totality in the outside world. It is this totality that is reconstructed and regenerated in controlled and predictive ways within the event. And it is this integrated totality of cosmos that the Silent One embodies.

The Silent One leaves. The clowns humorously imitate the sounds and gestures of the deities. Then they break into pieces the sacred melons brought by the *kachina*, and distribute these in collective communion. Though the clowns seem still to oscillate, after the advent of the Silent One it is more likely that their contrary tendencies no longer are paradoxical. Instead these contradictions exist harmoniously within the cosmos, as they do within the symbolic type of the Silent One. No longer the independent-minded guides of the deities, the clowns become integrative extensions of the harmonious fusion of principles of order and energy. Their reflexivity now embodies different aspects of a unitary vision of the Tewa cosmos.

On their initial entry into the *kiva* the clowns made fun of the people, whose reflectiveness about themselves was heightened. This contributed to their separation from mundane reality and to the approach of the deities. Now the clowns distance the people from sacred reality by making fun of the deities. The clowns also open the aperture for their own exit, as one says to the other, 'Let's get out of here'. Before leaving they too do the Blessing Rite for the assembled. In its closing phrases they say, 'May you be loved and liked . . . and may you die immediately'. This utterance is the obverse of the formulaic phrasing. But I understand it to reflect consistencies in meaning among different principles, as these were encompassed and unified in the advent of the Silent One.

The moiety chiefs lead the people in the Thanksgiving Prayer, within which there reappears the theme of 'to catch up with that for which we are always yearning'. It is as if during the liminal occasion the people had indeed 'caught up': separated, purified, and invigorated once more. Now they are phased back into the mundane, and the theme is again of relevance to the condition of the collectivity.[15]

Conclusion

More comprehensively, the symbolic type of the clown is related to ideas of comedy. In a seminal essay, Susanne Langer (1965) discusses comedy as the sheer vitality in the celebration of life. The work of comedy is in 'restoring a lost balance, and implying a new future' (1965: 127). The essential comic feeling, Langer concludes, 'is the sentient aspect of organic unity, growth, and self-preservation' (1965: 140). Langer's discussion has much in common with the resonances of play, uncertainty, and transformation, taken up in chapter 3 and in this one. So too the processuality of the clown type resonates deeply with this sense of comedy, and with those events wherein the energy and vitality of play/comedy thrums in the doing of transformative change. In these occasions this symbolic type contributes to the feeling of 'a whole world moving into its own future' (1965: 138).

But the clown type cannot be delineated as wholly comic, and this is its special power. The anti-theses within the type encourage it to slip among paradigms in creating syntagmatic sequences of meaning – and this slippage may be a matrix of humor and laughter (Milner 1972). Its internal composition enables the type to dissolve paradigms, thereby to make uncertain the relationships among those parts ordered by such boundaries. So the type breaks down context, and 'shakes up' reality on a number of levels, from the cosmic to the visceral. This formulation especially complements the discussion of self-monitoring and self-regulation in events of modelling – in particular that of *chisungu* in chapter 2, but also to a degree that of the Sienese Palio in chapter 6. During events of modelling the monitoring of progression in transformation is crucial, sometimes to make that very progression continue to happen in the right direction. The clown type's deformation of context is also a kind of systemic self-correction in the Dance of Man. For it gestures to an impetus of design within the event to alter and to reorganize itself into something else – that is, into its next phase. Participants who are enrapt in the flow of action may be more unlikely or unable to distance themselves enough, either to appreciate cumulative accretions of meta-meaning, or to break the embrace of context and move into the next phase.

However, the capacities of symbolic types to do this kind of work is a function of their internal composition. Types that are unitary in composition likely cannot comment upon the ongoing, changing progression of an occasion. So too, their effect on context is different. Their homogeneous constitution reifies and stabilizes context (Handelman and Kapferer 1980), to engender sentiments of its certainty and verity. However, types that are self-transformative not only shift an event through its design of progression, but also continually comment on this and on its cumulative accretion of meaning. So the *mhendi* clown comments on the half-baked condition of the bride. The Pueblo clowns, as they shift between hilarity and gravity, comment upon the relationship between the mundane and the sacred. Types that are said to function as 'masters of ceremony' in events of transformation are likely to be heterogeneous, reflexive, and self-transformative in their logic of composition.

I have adopted the heuristic stance that deity-types tend to be homogeneous and non-reflexive. Yet clearly there are numerous other instances that are worth considering in terms of the formulation of homogeneous and heterogeneous types: thus Indic, Orphic, and Gnostic deities who may be ludic at times. The reflexive capacities of the 'comic spirit' in Zen Buddhism (Hyers 1974) may be looked at in this way. Let me offer one brief example.

Salteaux 'conjuring' (Hallowell 1942) is held to obtain from spirits the answers to problems of members of the audience. The shaman calls the spirits to be present. Always there is the spirit of *mikinak*, the Great Turtle.[16] He is one of the few spirits understood without translation. Moreover he translates the messages of other spirits to the audience. He is a messenger, travelling long distances to discover the information requested by participants. *Mikinak* is something of a mediator between spirits, shaman and audience, and among different planes and locales of the Salteaux cosmos. He is a key figure in the progression of this event.

But *mikinak* is also given to witticisms, jokes, and pranks during a performance (1942: 45–50). Within this deity are conjoined attributes of gravity and hilarity, and he oscillates between these qualities throughout the occasion. As mediator and prankster, *mikinak* combines the features of a master of ceremony with those of a comic. He dissolves boundaries between protagonists, and among cosmic domains. As he oscillates between the serious and humorous, he likely casts protagonists into changing relationships with one another, and so brings the audience to reflect upon the nature of spirits, upon their own, and upon the character of the reality within which they coexist. *Mikinak* is the only spirit in the event who is so endowed, thereby making the conjunction of mediation and playful, uncertain oscillation within this character all the more enticing for problems of transformation and reflexivity in public events.[17]

Similarly, the clown type (and the uncertainty it generates) highlights the significance of play in public events. Imbued with play and gravity, this type is a shifting kaleidoscope that is completing itself continuously, but that is unfinished permanently. Serious attention to the ludic reveals this existential mode to have extensive and intensive properties of phenomenal transformation. Then an emphasis on the frivolity of play, as (psychic and social) cathartic relief, may well be the shallowest way of thinking about this entire subject, culturally and cognitively.

The clown type makes its home most comfortably in events of modelling, since these do change under controlled conditions. I argued that this requires the introduction of uncertainty and the engendering of inconsistencies. Here symbolic types like that of the clown seem designed culturally to create inconsistencies and to open the way to their resolution. In events of re-presentation, these self-contradictory types are more problematic, since such occasions do not work through systemic premises of control over their own operations. Then these types may accentuate and accelerate conflict and clash that can spill over the interface between event and social order, spreading inconsistency and disruption. But in events of presentation there is no room for these types, just as there is little space for self-contradiction. If contrary characters are there in force, then this probably is an index of severe conflicts in social order that are remaking the event through their own overwhelming dynamics.

Epilogue: towards media events

Television is used increasingly to bring national and international occasions to the populace of the modern state. Therefore the study of public events, as I have discussed this, opens towards the fluid composition and rigid framing of the television screen. Although this shift is complicated, it is important, and so a few words in conclusion on certain of its premises and implications.

The conditions of the modern state seem increasingly pervaded by a failed centricity. In part this is due to the failure of systemic premises to actualize perfectible social order, and in part to their over-determination of order. Responses to the uncertainties that imbue social life are also contradictory. On the one hand there is more of an 'incredulity toward metanarratives' (Lyotard 1984: xxiv), and their capacities to integrate and legitimate formulaic progress. On the other there is the search for the moment or occasion of significance, one that is said to make a difference in the quality and direction of living. The first response is itself a byproduct of the tendency of systemic organization to rationalize the authenticity of experience, and thereby to diffuse and to lose its special qualities. But the second response claims that systemic organization can refine qualities of experience in heretofore unknown ways. Both forces are consequential in their impact on public events of the presentday.

Incredulity towards metanarrative is linked to the successes of systemic technologies of mass reproduction. Mechanical reproduction has made populist the singular, and so has made the question of authenticity both problematic and irrelevant. The message is an artifact of the medium, while the medium itself has no correspondence to the natural world, but only to abstract theories about the latter. Therefore the copies of phenomena produced by mechanical technologies are freed of the requirement to present or to represent the phenomenal world naturalistically. Yet this very autonomy of phenomena made more fluid also opens them further to conscious manipulation on the part of their makers, and to mass production in accordance with the criteria of market economies.

Information in the modern state commonly is transmitted as images of

266

images, copies of copies. Stories of living, about living and for living, tend systemically to lose their beginnings and endings. Story-lines merge and diverge in often interchangeable ways. Authoritative origins and definitive versions have little endurance in systems of information-processing that specialize in remaking the unknown by making it visible and accessible.

In consequence, copies of phenomena enter domains into which the originals could not go (Benjamin 1969: 220). The systemic transmission of phenomena joins contexts of living that were otherwise separate and distinctive. In turn this likely adds to an overall sense of the amorphous, of 'stories' without beginnings and endings, that characterizes the ongoing macroscopic processing of information.

Television necessarily refracts and distorts. Like any public-event discussed in this book, the images and sounds of televised, live occasions are selected, and selectively integrated. This selection contextualizes the televised event as a whole. But for the television viewer this must be accompanied by the suspension of disbelief. The picture, the copy, must be accepted as authentic. Otherwise the image is the artifice of fantasy, and so again a story without end. But if one accepts the authenticity of the copy, then one is vulnerable to a twice-told artifice – that of the composition of the live occasion, and that of its purveyors and transmitters. Once more, reality and fiction blur and blend. Thus viewers of television are opened to being remade in the images of copies of phenomena – copies that are bound no longer by the natural strictures of these phenomena in the indigenous settings of their occurrence. Raymond Williams (1975: 5) comments that 'drama, in quite new ways, is built into the rhythms of everyday life'. The unceasing dramatization of living, of copies that intersect and merge with other copies, other versions, is now an internal rhythm and a habitual experience (Williams 1975: 7).

Commentators on American culture note that a sense of historicity is shifting away from singular stories that are forever true – away from story-lines that are hero-orientated and confrontational. There are fewer authentic moments of 'catastrophic time' (Braudy 1982). Instead, perceptions are conditioned by continuous stories, always evolving – by the endless narratives of 'soap-opera time' that continually recycle themselves. This world is one of ongoing stories that reinforce 'the endless interconnection between plots rather than any simplistic casualties' (Braudy 1982: 490) – a world of many small victories and defeats, but few absolute or final resolutions. History becomes constituted of shifting trends, predictions, and retrospections, of equal value and without sharp edges. In this vision there are virtually no public events, only occasions that blend without end. An ironic byproduct of this reduction of narrative through certainties of systemic communication is the loss of social and personal centricity, and so the spreading pervasiveness of uncertainty, generated within systems that are intended to eradicate the latter.

Through telecasts of live, singular occasions that are said to mark authentic turning-points or major transitions in the flow of living, television strives periodically to return to metanarrative (such events include, for example, the first moon-landing, Sadat's trip to Jerusalem, Pope John Paul's first visit to Poland, the royal wedding of Charles and Diana). Katz and Dayan (1985) call these occasions 'media events'. They are attempts by television to create the singular occasion of especial significance – the marker of 'catastrophic time', of the making of history that is done because it is seen to be done, and is not diffused in the revolving circuitries of stories without definitive climax.

Media events intensify systemic premises to make known the unknown, to encode phenomena through commonplace systems of available information. Media like television are ahistorical in that their workings connect domains that otherwise would remain separate in space and through time. As Benjamin noted, the copy can go anywhere, anytime. The telecast does.

In earlier times the power and achievement of the state was made known to the populace in part through events in squares, plazas, stadia, and streets. People en masse met the presentations of the state in public places, in loci largely dominated by state authority. When people battled this power, then they did so also in the street. The events-that-present of the state (or of other authorities) permitted the populace to witness and to bear witness to the demonstrativeness of power, although knowledge of its operations often were denied them. The contexts of participation chosen by the authorities tended to be those that stressed inclusion and exclusion: anyone was permitted in some, only elites in others. As well, one could rarely stay home and also bear witness to triumph, grandeur, a sense of occasion, and so forth.

Via live television, the media event overturns the indigeneous identity of play, space, and occasion. The viewer is simultaneously in two locations, and which of these contextualizes the other remains a crucial question. One is at home to oneself, to one's family and friends with whom one views, and with the Pope in Poland or with an astronaut on the moon. The apex of hierarchy greets the living-room; the corridors of power end at the family sofa; outer space is mapped out within that most inner of social spaces, the family domicile. Two distinct and opposed sets of premises are conjoined: on home grounds the distant abstractions of hierarchy and power intersect with the relations and sociality of kin and community.

Not only are such intersections unique in reality, but the populace also becomes privy to information generally denied them in events-that-present. Viewers are taken on guided tours of the interiors of palaces, cathedrals, and spaceships, where transformations are said to be happening. In contrast to a presence at events-that-present, often in some kind of linear or mass formation, being in one's living-room is a friendly, chummy experience. Viewers rarely sit in ranks or in other linear formations before the television set, but perhaps in a cosy half-circle. One's attention even need not be focused on the televised proceedings: the familiarity of the home domesticates the event. Thus there may be conversation, commentary, and reflectiveness within the home while the occasion is in progress.

The television audiences of these occasions are 'mass audiences' only in magnitude, not in quality. They are not massed with regard to the relative anonymity of individuals. Media events become home-centred occasions. The total audience is massive in magnitude, yet the units of reception are constituted as familial – and this, in no small measure, is a re-constitution of the vector of the individual in relation to systemic, bureaucratic organization.

This linkage between events and television may be profound in two directions. First, media events reinsert the significant occasion, the moment of momentum (whose longer-term outcome is as yet uncertain) back into the repetition of 'soap-opera' time. The sense of closed systemics is diminished; simulation is not yet complete. The lived-in world is more open once again to a feeling of wonder. The commonplace discourse of the mass media, of stories that endlessly recycle and replicate themselves, is changed into one that is said to presage change.

Second, media events address family and household, kin and community, in ways that are most rare on the more abstract levels of the modern state. This likely is not intentional. Yet it speaks to the potential for family occasions that stand in opposition to the individuating systemics of bureaucracy – to a kind of intimacy and sharing of monumental, politicized experience within the elementary circles of demographic and cultural reproduction.

But just as 'The mass media infinitely heighten the knowledge people have of what transpires in the society .. [so too] .. they infinitely inhibit the capacity of people to convert that knowledge into political action' (Sennett 1977: 283). Like events-that-present, media events are affective rather than effective. The media event is one response to postmodern uncertainties. But even more distinctive and pronounced is the seeking of refuge in the kind of ethos that is called 'religious', and that in turn tends to engender public events of systemic closure, control, and prediction – events whose premises resonate more with those of modelling. Postmodern incredulity is an anti-systemic response to crises in systemic organization. Yet most ironically, both the media event and a return to traditionalism seek solutions to incredulity through premises of the systemic.

Notes

Chapter 1 Premises and prepossessions

1 This photograph is reproduced in black-and-white in Kapferer (1983).

2 Courtesy of Louis Chiaramonte. This photograph is reproduced in Sider (1986).

3 In England these events were thought of as 'triumphs' that continued those of ancient Rome (Kipling 1977: 39), although these forms of occasion had little in common. On the Roman Triumph see Versnal (1970).

4 This metaphor of mirror plays on the idea that these surfaces often are thought to reflect an essence of things, while ignoring the optical tricks that mirrors play (Fernandez 1980: 31–2). Thus the metaphor plays up the presentation of ideals of rulership and power in the royal entry, but plays down its qualities of 'lived topical allegory', through which the planners of the occasion tried to persuade monarchs of the political concerns of the former (Montrose 1977: 24–6). In this vein, the monarchical style of participation was interpreted as indexical of the future policies of rulers (Kipling 1977: 38, 44, 54). Nonetheless, the mirror image projected by a royal entry could only be a version of social order, and I will emphasize this point throughout. For even the mirror image has autonomy as a version of reality. As Eugen Fink (1968: 27) writes of a tree, reflected on the surface of water: 'What is the mirror image? As an image it is real – it is a real reflection of the original tree existing in reality. But a tree is also represented in the image; this tree appears on the surface of the water, yet in such a way that it exists only through the medium of the reflections and not in reality. An illusion of this kind is an autonomous category of Being and embraces something specifically "unreal" as a constitutive element of its reality'. But the mirror image also attributes symmetry to the phenomena it reflects; and symmetry may signify boundedness, formality, and order (Weyl 1952: 16).

5 These discussions of public events rely in the main on writings of anthropologists. This is not to make light of substantive works in comparative religion (cf. Frankfort 1948), folklore (cf. Glassie 1975; Abrahams 1977), sociolinguistics (cf. Sanches 1975; Bauman and Scherzer 1974), history of theatre (cf. Yates 1969; Hardison 1969; Taylor and Nelson 1972), and social history. Yet few in these disciplines have developed concepts or schema that are of direct relevance to social science thinking in the domains discussed in this book. Each discipline continues to maintain its own contours of relevance.

The case of social and cultural history is especially interesting, since in recent years not a few historians have been influenced by anthropological thought (cf. Davis 1982; Schmitt 1983; Darnton 1985; Price 1986). For anthropology the return has been one of studies of period, place, and people that we, as ethnographers, can read with recognition and enjoyment, but that have added little to conceptualization in our discipline (as most of us understand this). So the historian, Maurice Agulhon (1985: 177–8), begins an article on 'Politics, images, and symbols in post-revolutionary France', by stating that 'cultural history had to learn to present itself as a kind of retrospective ethnology in order to escape the contemptuous label of "little history".' One paragraph further along, he exclaims: 'But enough abstractions! Historians have their own responsibilities, quite distinct from devising a theory of signs – responsibilities that should precede such theorizing'.

Of these historians, Peter Burke (1987: 3–7) is most explicit in delineating a 'historical anthropology'. This approach is qualitative in method, microscopic in focus, pays serious heed to cultural symbolism, strives to interpret activity in relation to a society's own 'norms and categories', and is informed by social and cultural theory. The first four of these features read much like pronouncements of modern ethnography. The fifth in practice is more of an additional compass of terminological orientation, than of conceptual substance. With regard to public events a similar position is enunciated by Hammerton and Cannadine (1981: 144–5), in their discussion of Queen Victoria's Diamond Jubilee in Cambridge. They comment that an understanding of a 'ceremonial occasion' depends less on analyzing the event itself, and theorizing on this, and more on the social context within which the event is situated. Like Burke and historians generally, they emphasize that the constitution of context only makes sense through time. However valuable these projects, they eschew the development of concepts for public occasions. Their stress is on method, not theory. And they deflect any effort to grapple with what in chapter 2 I call the 'logics of design' of public events. Therefore these projects also evade considering whether such designs have any effect on what it is that public events may do in relation to social order. When historians do relate to social theory, their focus shifts more to conceptions of society, and away from the logical status and internal constitution of inter-mediate phenomena like public events. This they share with anthropologists.

6 An anonymous reviewer of the manuscript of this book suggested that the profusion of concepts and names for public events in anthropology was less an index of confusion than one of interest in this domain. The two, of course, are not in contradiction, especially so long as conceptualization in anthropology stays closely tied, inductively, to that kind of knowledge we call ethnographic description.

7 See, for example, Swiderski (1986) for an opposite view, in the spirit of Bhaktin.

8 The transposition and translation of occasion into 'memory' and 'myth', alters and extends its existence. This is beyond the scope of this book. But see Straus' (1966) discussion of 'memory traces', and Ohnuki-Tierney's (1981a) incisive delineation of 'memory codes' and 'analogy codes', and their complementarity

in the analysis of symbolism. The relationship between memory and public events stays latent in all the case studies of this book, but is raised more substantially in chapter 9.

9 The conceptualization and documentation of emergent events, like that generally of processes of 'emergence' (see Handelman 1977a), remains minimal. Grimes (1982) writes of 'nascent ritual', Schechner (1985) of the 'restoration' of behavior (of 'strips' of behavior arranged in innovative, and perhaps emergent patterns), and Gutowski (1978) of the 'protofestival', although his usage refers to prototypes of institutionalized 'festival' occasions. See also Ludwig (1976).

10 As I noted, there is little documentation on that which I call proto-events. What there is, refers often to work settings, perhaps because of modern sensibilities about the alienation of labor from means of production. See for example, Ludtke (1985) on 'horseplay' in late nineteenth century German factories. Schwartzman's (1981) valuable study of 'dancing' during meetings in a formal organization is closer to the sense of the emergence of protean form through face-to-face interaction, as this is used here. Other references are found in part II.

A study unusual in its attention to the fleeting significance of a protean workplace occasion is Darnton's (1985: 75–104) discussion of the 'great cat massacre' in an eighteenth century Parisian printing shop. In relation to the coming paragraphs of this chapter, Darnton's case is of interest as a one-time occasion that first was turned into a pantomime, was then enacted a number of times, and latterly inscribed as a text.

11 Gananath Obeyesekere (1981) propounds a psychologistic view on the invention of 'personal' symbols and their becoming public ones, that relates to my argument on the creation and practice of proto-events. The following are major points in his exposition. In the psyche there is freedom of fantasy to invent personal symbols, through the interaction of intrapsychic processes and cultural context. Personal symbols that are made public are the end product of individual motivation. As a private symbol is conventionalized, as it emerges into the public domain, 'it loses its inherent ambiguity', and so too 'its capacity for leverage and maneuverability' (1981: 51). The same symbolic idiom or form operates simultaneously on intrapsychic, interpersonal, and cultural levels (1981: 99).

Obeyesekere privileges the psyche in the invention of culture, and reduces cultural context to an arena for the expression of intrapsychic conflict. 'Culture' is reduced to the conventionalized expression of psychic process. This view of context smothers in simplicity the capacities of emergent symbolic forms to comment on the perceived realities of their creators, that the latter live in concert. That these commentaries operate differently at various levels of social life is obscured, as is their capacities to reorganize social life and its significances through their own emergent forms, and the experiences these engender. This is a prime message of my argument for proto-events. It is the more inter-mediate forms of social life (including public events) that reproduce 'culture' on the one hand, and that innovate this on the other. Intermediate forms have their own logics of design, constraint, and freedom. The formation of social form is not reducible to the dualism of 'culture' (or 'society') and the individual. Similarly, symbols receive their ambiguity from intermediate forms that formulate this in keeping with their own formation, tensions, and dynamics. Each intermediate social form is a source of creativity through individuals, but one that hardly is controlled by their personal motivations, as such.

Chapter 2 Models and mirrors

1 Argument over the status of belief and its consequences among different peoples is hoary in anthropology. Sir James Frazer (1951: 222) contended that magic was a kind of inferior science, calling it the latter's 'bastard sister'. Horton (1973) and Skorupski (1973), as well as others, have engaged in lengthy interchanges on epistemological problems in comparisons of 'religion' and 'science'. My own concern, as I indicate further on, is with segments of human activity that are perceived (particularly, but not only, by their practitioners) as 'transformative' in their logics of operation, and therefore as consequential in relation to themselves. Here 'modelling' may be a useful point of start for comparison.

2 The best, concise, critical overview of these and related issues is that of Evens (1982).

3 This is why, regardless of the extent of its internal complexity and elaboration, the relationship of model to lived-in world is one of reduction, so long as that world is the basis for the model. This view becomes blurred when, as is often the case, such articulations are understood to open into cosmic time and space. Nonetheless, the active control over, or the influencing of cosmos, require its principled reduction through modelling.

  In terms of information theory, Conant and Ashby (1970) argue that a regulator of a system must itself be a model of that system. Then, assuming for the moment that social orders are themselves systemic (of which I am far from convinced), one could hypothesize that a public event whose controlled output acts on that order in predictive ways would be organized as a model of that system.

4 One may well argue, for a given culture, that a similar logic of operation in reverse would make a sick person of a healthy one. In other words, its progression would approach a logic of that which anthropologists would call 'sorcery', or a related term.

5 Many of the occasions that scholars call 'rites of passage' are not organized in terms of what I call 'modelling'. But the label of 'passage' serves to cover a multitude of design. Some of these occasions merely mark and legitimate a change in status and in the rights and obligations that accrue to the initiated. Others have a design that is 'looser' and more modular than that of the systemic, and tend more to a pedagogy of enculturation. Writing of the Ommura peoples of Papua New Guinea, Johnson (1981: 474) states that their male initiations are articulated by particular genres, such that 'initiation events and instructions are presented in random order, can be omitted or substituted and new content is frequently incorporated provided that it conforms to the conventions of a particular genre'. The metaphor of passage has been extended even to the lengthy study of Latin by Renaissance boys, that Walter Ong (1959) likens to a 'puberty

rite'. My concern is only with those 'rites of passage' that are organized systemically to do transformative work.

One further example of how terminology can obscure design will suffice here. Meyer Fortes (1968) addresses a type of occasion, the 'installation ceremony', through which persons are inducted into high office. Fortes discusses a variety of occasions of this kind, from those of West African kingship to that of the present-day British monarchy (see Shils and Young 1956). Following Hocart (1927), Fortes treats the morphological and functional commonalities of royal installations, and thereby misses their radically distinctive processual designs. According to the data Fortes (1968: 15–18) gives, some African royal installations (for example, those of Yoruba and Mamprussi kingship) are without doubt events of transformation, through which both the being and status of the king are changed radically. These events also contain 'ordeals' (1968: 10) that introduce uncertainty, and that can be understood as devices of testing and self-regulation in these occasions – since failing the ordeal would lead to the cessation of the event (because the candidate would die). By contrast, the installation of a modern British monarch contains little of the radical reconstitution of the ruler through a logic of transformation. Instead the monarch is re-presented during the coronation, in the ideal images and idioms of rulership. This point is taken by David Cannadine (1987: 18): 'In many traditional societies, coronation ceremonies made a man into a king and into a god, who thereby linked the earthly and heavenly hierarchies. But in Britain in 1953, very few people believed that making a woman a queen meant making her a goddess, or that the coronation somehow connected the terrestrial and the cosmic order.'

6 This formulation restricts transformation to totalistic change, in both the being and the categorization of the phenomenon undergoing alteration. At first sight this appears overly constrictive. In modern, Western society are not weddings and court trials transformative through their doing, in the decisiveness of their impact on the categorization of protagonists? This, even though there may be no expectation of immediate transformation in the being of protagonists; but rather that this will accrue through time, as newlyweds and convicted felons enact their lives in new contexts. But the matter is more complicated. The judicial process of court trial does seem to be organized systemically to introduce uncertainty into the classification of the accused, and to resolve this contradiction in controlled, predictive ways. But the public event of trial can be bypassed entirely by the bureaucratic device of plea bargaining. This questions the special status of the trial as a venue of transformation, and lays the onus for systematicity on the institutions of the entire judicial process, rather than on the public event. This shift is in keeping with my arguments in the last section of chapter 3, on the relationships between types of event and societies.

The wedding is again another matter in which this common-sensical label can obscure what it is that such occasions do, not in terms of their social function, but in terms of their own logic of process. To take two extreme examples, both covered by the label, 'wedding'. Civil marriage is in essence a bureaucratic procedure that merely shifts protagonists from one column of a ledger to another by the powers of change and accountancy vested in the state. Whether these persons really are transformed (in their own perceptions, and in those of others) is less a function of the wedding ceremony itself, and depends more on the interaction of the variable capacities of the newlyweds and the new situations within which they become sited. But a wedding whose fulfillment depends on proof of consummation, in which the groom takes the virginity of the bride, not only changes her status but also transforms her very being in an irreversible way. This proof of consummation, a kind of negative feedback, makes it likely that this variety of wedding occasion is organized more through premises of systemic organization than is that of civil marriage – although the bureaucracy that does occasions of civil marriage, unlike such events themselves, probably will be organized systemically. Like the language of 'rites of passage', that of 'wedding' can hide quite different logics of design, and so too the intentionalities built into these.

7 Rappaport (1979: 209) comments that in terms of information theory, 'information' is defined 'as that which reduces uncertainty'. Therefore, given the comparatively invariant character of much 'ritual' liturgy, 'this contains no information because it eliminates no uncertainty'. This formulation is essentially that of Wallace (1966). Rappaport takes it in directions other than those pursued here. However, its relevance for modelling is quite the converse of the above inference: the logic of an event of modelling is that, first uncertainty is created within the event and then it is eliminated. The rubric of 'ritual' is again more one of obfuscation than of elucidation.

8 All extended discussions of the ethnographies of others are my own reanalyses of those materials, and therefore my responsibility. Reanalysis has long had an honorable role in modern anthropology, and I refer to it again in the 'intersections' to chapter 4.

9 Somewhat analogous relationships among growth, sexuality, fertility, and maturity in girls' initiations among the Ndembu peoples of Zambia are rendered evocatively by Edith Turner (1987: 58–81).

I also should note that Father Corbeil (1982: 10), in his discussion of fired pottery figures used in *chisungu*, comments that these are not made over and again for each such occasion, but are stored in a secret riverbed location, to be retrieved and decorated anew. He (1982: 8) seems critical of Richards' description of *chisungu*, however his reasoning is not explicit. His own discussion is not relevant to my own, since his is limited to the didactic meanings of images, prefigured by his Christian belief, and he does not address *chisungu* as a substantive, systemic occasion in its own right.

10 This seems to have been a premise of certain major, public occasions in the civilizations of the ancient world. These would benefit from a rereading as events of modelling. See, for example, Fairman (1974) on Egypt; Heesterman (1984), Johnson (1980) and Smith (1986) on Vedic India; Schipper and Wang (1986) on Taoism; Frankfort (1948) on Egypt and Mesopotamia. For a critical view of Frankfort's analysis of occasions of the New Year in Mesopotamia, see Black (1981).

11 In Firth's terms, such symbolic affirmation is a hallmark of that which he calls 'ceremony', in contrast to those 'ritual procedures' that act to change social

situations. His usage is roughly similar to Gluckman's distinction between 'ceremonial' and 'ritual' (Gluckman and Gluckman 1977: 233).

12 As I will indicate shortly, my argument is not that events of presentation are inconsequential in their effects on social order, but that these sorts of occasions do not make change happen within the design of their enactment. Therefore the event, in relation to itself, does nothing. Its effects, whatever their impact, are worked out through interaction with the wider social order. Events of presentation may mobilize, reinforce, evoke, demonstrate, cohere, and give direction to sentiment and emotion. But their effects on social order also may be quite contrary to the expectations of their organizers.

In the case of Nazi rallies, *Mein Kampf* is explicit on the power Hitler attributed to collective, demonstrative force. But as Albert Speer's memoirs tell us, the totalitarian design of a Nuremberg Rally set it in its entirety as a given, one intended to heighten and to accentuate sentiments already held by participants. George Mosse (1975: 202) writes that Hitler (like Mussolini [Melograni 1976: 228]) was strongly influenced by Gustave Le Bon, 'and followed the dictum ... that the leader must be an integral part of a shared faith, that he cannot experiment or innovate. His own experimentation and innovation consisted only in heightening the meaning of what was already widely accepted, in introducing a Manicheanism which transformed his words into deeds.' In these rallies (and elsewhere), Hitler perceived himself as a symbol, part of an ensemble of symbols orchestrated as the collective occasion. The entirety of the ensemble was the evocation of an internally consistent and homogeneous reality, one not opened to question or doubt. Thus, a powerful evocation of that already known by participants, of that endlessly enunciated elsewhere and elsewhen – but so much more concentrated in the Rally, in the intensity of desire and commitment it evoked. Speer's description of the physical planning of such occasions tells us that the chords Hitler thrummed in his speeches were also the sinews that coursed through all of its aspects, including that of material props, and the positioning and movement of participants. Hitler preached to the converted, to those who already partook of his odious vision.

Nazi public events reflected and extended an epistemological obsession with the aesthetics of the production of power that pervaded numerous domains of German existence. Its intentionality was to subjugate human subjectivities to social forms, so that the former would reflect and ornament the latter (see Rabinbach [1976] on the aesthetics of industry in the Third Reich).

I've cited these materials on Nazi rallies to show to you the internal consistency of events of presentation. Yet as I wrote this note, and quoted Burden in this chapter, I was filled with loathing. So it is on every rereading. There are no alternative readings of this within me.

13 In these sorts of events their official conceptions and definitions bar entry to alternative or contradictory visions. These events are most like mirrors the more these efforts succeed. Counter-visions and the media of their expression exist in the wider social order, and compete with official versions. This tension may be perceived as creative and elaborated, or as subversive and suppressed. But in

events of presentation, unlike those of modelling, this tension inevitably focuses attention at the interface of event and social order.

14 Hughey's (1983: 109–23) critique of Warner points out that in the interest of highlighting sentiments and functions of community unity and solidarity in Memorial Day commemorations, Warner largely ignored profoundly divisive developments in Newburyport. Hughey argues that such public occasions were arenas within which conflicting perspectives, interests, and resources interacted. The commemorations (like the tercentenary pageant) bolstered the waning prominence of the old middle-class business interests. Though Hughey's criticisms are pointed, he (like Warner) conflates the interface of event and social order (what went into the making of these events, and their 'functions' for social order) with the programatic enactment of the event itself. In turn this points to the continuing influence of Durkheimian perspectives, in a variety of guises. To reiterate, my points are that the pageant itself (like the commemorations) presented a unified, conflict-free vision of social order; that this could be only a version of social order; that this version had a particular logic of organization; and that outside the event this version could not be construed as, nor confused with, the constitution of social order. Therefore the interaction of event with social order, and its effects on the latter, were unpredictable and indeterminate.

15 Events of presentation in modern, Western nation-states are obsessed with the feeling-states of participants, with expressiveness, and so with the capacity of an event to affect. Perceptions of the success of such occasions depend on this to a high degree. In turn, this indicates a profound dualism in these societies between ethos and instrumentality, that in its own way refracts the dualism of mind and body. The minds of the citizenry (their spirit and emotion) are to be affected and moved on special occasions (albeit often through their bodies), while their bodies are to be effected and controlled in mundane realities through routine bureaucratic forms. This division of labor is most evident in fascist and other totalitarian regimes, as I indicated in note 12, this chapter. Only under totalistic conditions of utter subjugation (concentration and labor camps, deprivation and torture) is the dualism of affect and effect thought to become integrated fully, as proof of the power and control of the state (cf. Wyschogrod 1985; Gregory and Timerman 1986).

In the public events of modern democratic states, affect also is understood as effect, but as different from the instrumentalities of actually making and molding social order. Consequently discussions of public events by Westerners, scholars and others, are preoccupied with 'functions' that primarily are ones of emotion and aesthetics. Similarly the discourse of these events so often is taken up with rhetoric, pageantry, and historicity.

Influencing the feeling-states of participants may indeed imply goals of transformation to such occasions. Nonetheless, these events do not constitute causal schemes of modelling, as I discussed these; consequently their 'effects' are unpredictable; and affect largely is divorced from instrumentality, and thereby made relatively marginal in the making, changing, and control of social order. In the last section of chapter 3, I suggest that the causal schemes of modern societies often are perceived as imbedded in the mundane workings of social order itself.

Only functionalist perspectives, necessarily preoccupied with the 'output' of public events for social order, could blithely clump together events of modelling and presentation under the same or similar rubrics. The designs of events of modelling frequently attribute functions to their own doing that are to be distinguished from the attribution of function by the analyst. To conflate the intentionality embedded in these events with the analyst's attribution of social function is to conflate also the logic of internal operation of an event with interaction at the interface. But numerous events of presentation mirror versions of social order, and so the substance of their enactment is more continuous with social order. Then the internal intentionality of occasion may be quite isomorphic with the analyst's attribution of social function. So an emphasis on solidarity within the event, or on the suppression of conflict, may well be continuous with and equated to its function of solidarity for social order. The perspectives of native and analyst coincide more easily, unlike their greater divergence in relation to events of modelling.

16 A useful example of inversion and its potential for overflow at the interface is Keith Thomas' (1976) discussion of 'barring-out' – the barring of headmasters from their schools by pupils at the end of term, in early modern England. Initially a sort of inversion of highly repressive school regimes, barring-out flared at times into violent rebellion that eventually was tamed once more, this time as convivial inversion, as 'celebration' in accordance with accepted conventions.

17 Bruner (1986) discusses changes in ethnographic narratives about American Indians – from earlier ones that characterized Native Americans in terms of cultural disorganization and assimilation, to more recent ones that emphasize cultural resurgence.

18 There are numerous instances that exemplify this problem. See, for example, Davis (1982), Goldberg (1978), Lavenda (1978a, 1980).

19 So MacAloon (1984b) discusses nested frames of 'spectacle', 'festival', 'ritual', and 'game' that interact with one another in the Olympic Games. A variant of ramification is the event that is created in response to another, and that builds on and comments upon the latter. See, for example, Lawrence's (1982) study of the Doo Dah Parade and the Tournament of Roses in Pasadena. See also Fernandez (1984), for an interesting study of ironies generated by incongruities within a public event.

20 In the typology, the problem of assuming a division of roles into performer and spectator is avoided. Were this addressed, my question would be whether such a structural distinction is built into the organizational logic of a public event. In other words, whether spectators are necessary to enactment (the relevance of spectators to the success of enactment is another matter). And, if so, whether 'spectator' is best treated as another variety of participant, varying between degrees of activity and passivity, or between different modes of activity. See, for example, Kapferer (1984b), and Schieffelin (1976).

21 I am lumping together media with profound differences (and consequences) for the organization of the senses, and therefore for phenomena they structure, while doing justice to none. Nor is it my intention to do so here. Of these media, rhetoric and oral narrative have had pride of place in analyses of enactment. This

preoccupation with words reflects anthropology's overriding concern with speech as action, and as validation of action. (Thus, this speaks also to the validation of the anthropological enterprise itself, given the high value placed on our own competence with words. In turn, this valuation of words reflects the academic and class contexts of much of our work.) Still, some work is being done on sensory modalities and social order (cf. Almagor 1987).

22 The problem of 'meaning' within public events has been posed most abruptly (with a deliberate contentiousness) by Frits Staal, a logician and sanskritist, based on his studies of Vedic 'ritual'. Staal (1979: 3) argues that, 'A widespread but erroneous assumption about ritual is that it consists in symbolic activities which refer to something else. It is characteristic of a ritual performance, however, that it is self-contained and self-absorbed', obsessed with the ruledness of orthopraxy.

For Staal, 'ritual' is all rule and no meaning. Semantics are not relevant to the syntactic-like structuration of 'ritual' rules (Staal 1986: 193). Rules exist for their own sake in the world of Vedic 'rites'. Ironically, Staal does not address how rules are constituted as a structure of intentionality, and so perhaps of causality. For there are numerous indications that Vedic 'rites' can be used for various purposes, and hints that these occasions are put together through attributes of modelling (cf. Heesterman 1984; Hocart 1927: 217–18, 223–4; Oguibenine 1983: 168); and that they contain degrees of feedback and self-regulation (for example, the role of a category of priest in ensuring that correct procedures are followed exactly. Geertz [1964] mentions an analogous function of 'quality control' in Balinese Hindu orthopraxy). Such an occasion may be organized as a systemic structure that is symbolic, in that it purposively leads elsewhere in ruled and controlled ways to do transformation, although exegeses vary on what this may consist of.

However, Jan Heesterman (oral communication, April 1988) comments that the historical evolution of Vedic ritual, and its emphasis on the perfecting of this ritual milieu, did away with 'uncertainty' within the design of such occasions. Thus the mechanics of Vedic ritual were rendered impotent, unable to effect any change in the wider world beyond the event.

Chapter 3 Precariousness in play

1 This case has been put cogently and thoughtfully, for aspects of South-Indian Hindu cosmology, by David Shulman (1980), and for a cognate Sinhalese–Buddhist cosmology by Kapferer (1983). See also Handelman (1987b).

2 This is put forward with conviction in Bateson's (1958) pioneering discussion of schismogenesis. See also Evens (1975).

3 The phrase, 'betwixt and between', was used by Hocart (1927: 213) to refer to paradoxical self-negating conditions.

4 The uncertainties of the Western postmodern period are quite another matter. Here uncertainty is felt to burgeon in social order. Losing its centredness, reality becomes pluralistic, and people then may reenact nostalgically the coherence of lost or imaginary worlds, as if these existed – that is, playfully (cf. Fine 1983) – 'precisely like the play theologian plays as if God existed' (E. Cohen 1985: 300).

Nonetheless, since the postmodern view exists through lacunae of meaning, and since it is not part of cosmologies that enshrine (and so, control) uncertainty, the 'as if' substitute is fictive. Therefore this substitute decentres itself, and so denies to itself the likelihood of long-term commitment on the part of adherents.

5 In his autobiography (vol. 1, pp. 147–51), Bertrand Russell describes his struggles to solve paradoxes similar to that of Epimenides the Cretan, who stated that all Cretans were liars.

'At first I supposed that I should be able to overcome the contradiction quite easily, and that probably there was some trivial error in the reasoning ... It seemed unworthy of a grown man to spend his time on such trivialities, but what was I to do ... Throughout the latter half of 1901 I supposed the solution would be easy, but by the end of that time I had concluded that it was a big job ... The summers of 1903 and 1904 we spent at Churt and Tilford ... Every morning I would sit down before a blank sheet of paper. Throughout the day, with a brief interval for lunch, I would stare at the blank sheet ... the two summers of 1903 and 1904 remain in my mind as a period of complete intellectual deadlock ... it seemed quite likely that the rest of my life might be consumed in looking at that blank sheet of paper. What made it the more annoying was that the contradictions were trivial, and that my time was spent in considering matters that seemed unworthy of serious attention.'

6 Or, to reverse this premise, by paraphrasing Heisenberg's Principle of Uncertainty: the imperceptible may be perceived only if one is uncertain about its imperceptibility. See Fischer (1985: 53) for an alternative formulation.

7 The ongoing work of Jean Briggs (cf. 1983) on Inuit enculturation, through play, into an existence perceived as inherently unstable and continually changing, promises to clarify the essential role of uncertainty in a particular cultural world.

8 The reader interested in instances of Ik laughter and 'play', will find them on the following pages of Turnbull (1973a): 49, 59, 110, 112, 113, 123, 135, 153, 163, 164, 165, 204, 205, 216, 218, 223, 226, 240, 260, 261, 271, 273.

9 Minneapolis Star and Tribune, 1 July 1983.

Chapter 4 The donkey game

1 The areas from which these workers emigrated included Morocco, Tunisia, Serbia, Turkey, Georgia, Syria, Kurdistan, Iran, and Yemen.

2 The operation of the welfare department, and the processes through which clients became dependent on welfare assistance are discussed in Handelman (1976, 1980).

3 Anthropologists usually study formalized games, in terms of their relationship to cultural traditions. This is so as well for the extensive literature on joking (as distinct from jokes) that need not be cited here. Even where more spontaneous play forms are studied in Western settings, the tendency is to analyze them along the lines of joking relationships suggested by Radcliffe-Brown (1952). See Bradney (1957), Sykes (1966), and Lundberg (1969). An attempt to break out of

this conceptual trap is found in Handelman and Kapferer (1972). Nonetheless, as I noted in chapter 3, spontaneous adult play rarely is addressed substantively by social scientists. Examples of 'play' in work settings, some brief, others more detailed, can be found in the following: Homans (1950: 60–1), Street (1958), Coser (1959), Lupton (1963: 36), Cunnison (1966: 213–15), Emerson (1969), Haas (1972), Kapferer (1972: 229), Westwood (1984: 111–28). In this regard the recent research of Helen Schwartzman (1981, 1984), on the constitution of serious activity in a formal organization in part through forms of play, is a radical and fruitful alternative to most of the studies cited above.

4 From my knowledge of the lives of the men, they seldom saw one another outside the workplace. Therefore their contacts in the shop were the substance of their relationships with one another.

5 The game ended when Shlomo was transferred to another workshop. This move was due to manpower needs and not to the game, whose existence was unknown to the administration. In retrospect, Shlomo, the inventor of the tail, was even more a key to the game than I thought at the time. In his absence the other players returned more frequently to the other modes of play described earlier. In his new workshop, Shlomo tried to introduce the tail. But there a different order was evolving, and his actions were seen as mere foolishness.

Chapter 6 The Palio of Siena

1 For an overview of the connotations of 'festival' for the renewal of social order, see Caillois (1959: 98–102).

2 Anthropological studies of community in Italy often mention the bell tower as a point of orientation and metaphor for local centrism and solidarity (see Pratt 1980: 37). One suspects that in terms of the ideology of public culture, bell towers would be identified with a version of community characterized by predominantly 'male' qualities.

3 Edmund Leach (personal communication, 12 March 1985) likens the Campo to a metaphoric womb, and the conjoining sites of Campo and tower to the symbolism of generation. According to the coming analysis, this potential is embedded in the *comune*, and is activated through the festival model.

4 Relations between *contrade* often are dyadic: each has its arch-enemy, its friends and its alliances with other *contrade*. These relationships have been stressed the most by other scholars, and they are all important from the viewpoint of the *contrade* themselves. But from the viewpoint of the *comune* within the festival model, their dyadism is secondary although highly visible.

5 Though this is a radical shift in organization, it must be emphasized that continuities with aspects of the everyday are prominent, as one would expect in part-whole relationships. Although Siena is located in Italy's Red Belt, local politics are dominated by Palio-related concerns, rather than by the polemics of party politics and their broader issues (Silverman 1985: 9).

6 See for example, Silverman's (1985) discussion of the Ceri Festival of Gubbio. This festival is based on a form of competition that in my terms is devoid of any transformative capacities. In fact the Ceri is closer to an occasion that presents or

mirrors an aspect of the social world of Gubbio, a point that is visible only when the logic of the event is considered.

7 I have found no independent support for the claims of Dundes and Falassi regarding these connotations of duality in folk perceptions of the Madonna. In Christian theology this dualism is lodged in two distinct but complementary figures, for example the Virgin and the Magdalene, of whom Marina Warner (1978: 235) writes: 'The Church venerates two ideals of the feminine – consecrated chastity in the Virgin Mary and regenerate sexuality in the Magdalene.' Early Christianity had a vigorous tradition of female saints who were former harlots (see Waddell 1946: 173–201; Bullough 1982: 38–41).

Turner and Turner (1978: 156) note the complementary opposition between the figures of Mary and Eve. A figure of redemption, Mary is contrasted with Eve, 'through whom mankind, represented by Adam, fell into original sin . . . But Mary is not merely the Antithesis of Eve . . . she is also her advocate, who will restore her to her pristine state'. This complementarity has a long history in Christian theology (see Graef 1985, Pt. 1: 39–40, 75–6). See also Pina-Cabral (1986) on views of Mary and Eve in a Portuguese peasant community. Connotations of an earthier Madonna were present in some strands of Christian theologies (see Graef 1985, Pt. 2: 28, 75); and are present in the implicit attitudes of some religious brotherhoods to holy female figures (Driessen 1984: 89, and personal communication, December 1987), as well as in certain epithets used by men of the circum-Mediterranean (Anton Blok, Henk Driessen, personal communications, December 1987). See also Muir (1981: 137–53) on the fate of a great festival dedicated to the Virgin Mary in late-medieval Venice, and scheduled during the carnival season.

I am indebted to Sydel Silverman who, some years ago, provided a detailed critique of many of the materials in this chapter. Silverman (personal communication, 1 August 1980) writes: 'I haven't seen a shred of evidence that supports . . . any notion of harlot-virgin contrasts [in the Palio].' It is interesting that Maureen Giovannini writes that the category of 'woman' in a Sicilian town subsumes six female figures. Among these are the 'virgin' and the 'whore'. The virgin figure synecdochically represents her family as a viable unit with its boundaries intact. By contrast, the whore conveys internal divisiveness within the family. She notes further that in the male view there is an ambiguity associated with the female figure, one that focuses particularly on the dualism of virgin and whore (Giovaninni 1981: 412, 420, 423–4). See also Blok (1981) on the symbolism of gender in this region.

Also worth noting is the renaissance humanist tradition in Italy that tended to merge qualities of the Madonna (i.e. chastity) within the figure of Venus, goddess of love (see Wind 1958: 74, 127; Graef 1985, Pt. 2: 3). The great fourteenth century, Middle-Dutch story of Beatrice (Geyl 1927) is instructive here. The protagonist, a devoted nun, is struck by Venus and deserts her calling for her lover who awaits her beneath an eglantine (the sweetbriar or 'wild rose', a symbol of Venus, often contrasted with the domesticated rose of the Virgin Mary). She leaves her habit on the altar of the Virgin, and the key to the sacristy nearby. For seven years she lives in sin, bearing two children, and for seven years more she earns her bread as a prostitute, but praying daily to the Virgin. Returning to the convent after fourteen years, she discovers that no one has missed her, for the Virgin had excellently filled her place. I am indebted to Ria Jansen-Sieben for bringing this work to my attention. On the one hand this story exemplifies the medieval view of the Madonna as the protectress of sinners who are devoted to her (Graef 1985, Pt. 2: 5; Bynum 1982: 137). But on the other, it is clear that the Virgin and Venus are linked hierarchically, and that the protagonist moves within their cosmic framework, from one to the other, all the while keeping her ultimate fealty to the Virgin.

Future work may indicate whether there is substance to the contrast of spiritual and earthy aspects within the Madonna figure; and it still remains for anthropologists to address this topic in seriousness.

8 Turner and Turner (1978: 156, 171) comment that Mary often represents the Church, while Eve represents mankind outside the Church; that in both instances there is the implicit metaphor of woman as the container or encloser of a human group, but that it is through the motherhood of Mary that the fallen children of Eve are transformed.

9 The articulation of the Madonna, as a wellspring of continuity and regeneration, to the 'male' city in the Palio model may be understood in the context of the Turners' (1978: 199) argument that in patrimonial orders, 'attachments through women ... come to stand for the seamless unity of the whole community', while paternity and masculinity are associated with rules, rights, and property.

10 This distinctive but complementary pattern of the universal and the particular divided among the two Palio cycles seems to surface in a variety of guises, recently in the artists chosen to paint the respective Palio banners. In the past few years the artist chosen to do the banner for the Palio of 16 August has been one of renown and repute, while the artist chosen for the banner of the 2 July Palio has been local, a Sienese (Falassi and Catoni 1983: 22).

11 The motifs that by regulation are required to appear on the banner are weighted heavily in favor of the higher level of social structure. In addition to the image of the Madonna and the emblems of the competing *contrade*, the required motifs include the emblem of the *comune* and that of the current head of the municipal council (Falassi and Catoni 1983: 21).

12 An additional connotation is related to the *partiti* (sing. *partito*) – machiavellian arrangements between *contrade* to increase their chances of winning, or to prevent their enemies from doing so. One meaning of '*partito*' is marriage contract, with its connotation of a virgin bride. But in an older idiom the phrase, '*femina di partito*' referred to a harlot.

13 The distinction between sacred and secular does appear to have validity in the Italian experience, rather than being solely an analytical construct. For example, 'The Italian lives in two worlds, one profane, imperfect, disunited, and the other sacred, perfect, harmonious' (Crump 1975: 23). Crump adds that these worlds interact continuously at the human and superhuman levels.

Silverman (personal communication, 1 August 1980) questions whether the Palio should be considered a 'sacred' occasion in any sense of the term, and she rejects the cognitive, affective, or functional linking of Palio to Madonna. She writes: 'The fact that the race is held on a festive day related to Madonnas is only to say that all festivals are geared to the church calendar, even football games. The fact that the race is theoretically in honor of the Madonna has very little to do with anything about it.' Silverman adds: 'I would say quite certainly that I don't think there is anything at all "sacred" in the palio, unless you want to talk about the most Durkheimian view of sacred as isomorphic with society; then there is still nothing I would see as a contrast between sacred and secular.' I would reiterate only that such isomorphism is a characteristic of the particular design of an event that models the world, and as such has a limited relationship to everyday social order. To fully equate the logic and working of a model to that which it models would demand a reconsideration of the validity of the entire idea of modelling.

14 Dundes and Falassi (1975: 212) state that in the past Palios sometimes were run with prostitutes in place of horses. Then harlot, horse, and the earthy aspect of the Madonna would be clear functional equivalents. But they offer no citation of these Palios. See also Heywood (1904: 20–2).

Silverman (personal communication, 1 August 1980) finds no evidence that the horses are 'feminine'. In conversation (April 1979), she commented that neither stallions nor thoroughbreds were used, since such powerful animals running within the narrow confines of the track, very close to stands packed with spectators, could cause grave injuries. Granting the exclusion of such animals in the past on functional grounds, one would want to know whether, over time, other meanings were attached to the animals that were used, giving them symbolic import. As Silverman (1979: 428) is careful to note in another context, the relationship between the politics of the Palio and its form and symbolism is quite problematic.

15 Other examples of the dissolution of boundaries by the horse involve the bringing into contact of sacred representations (Holy Wine or a priest) with the buttocks of the horse or those of a contrada official responsible for the animal's performance (Dundes and Falassi 1975: 192–3).

16 A nineteenth century report indicated that if the horse were a mare, 'she' would wear a white cap inside the church, since women were not permitted entry with head uncovered. As well, in an older tradition, following its victory the horse would be given bread and wine as a form of communion. In these examples the horse was treated as more than a mere animal (Dundes and Falassi 1975: 96).

17 Pratt (1980: 39) writes of Tuscany that local elections are termed 'administrative' rather than 'political', and that politics are perceived ideologically as disharmonious – as disruptive of local unities whose solidarity is based on metaphors of belonging to a territory, the interdependence of social parts within that territory, and family. This ideal is exemplified by the upper tier of the festival model, just as its converse is epitomized on its lower tier by the incessant, conflictual politicking among *contrade*. However, within a *contrada* the converse holds once more, thereby pointing again to the replicability of city and *contrada*.

18 But by the 1980s these six riders followed the *comparse* of the seven *contrade* not participating in the race, and preceding the triumphal chariot. As well, the seven horsemen representing the *contrade* not competing, who had accompanied the

chariot, apparently were no longer part of the parade (Falassi and Catoni 1983: 69).

19 Of course, for the *contrada* the finishing order of its arch-enemy and that of the other *contrade* is of great import.

20 As a fairly recent innovation (Silverman 1979), marchers may suck on pacifiers, hang giant rubber nipples around their necks, or carry baby bottles on this grand tour (Dundes and Falassi 1975: 138; Logan 1978: 57).

21 These include Peter Burke, Edmund Leach, Bruce Lincoln, and Sydel Silverman.

22 This relates to the question of how it was that the Palio apparently did not become a vehicle for sentiments and actions of unrest and uprising that characterized so many urban 'festivals' and 'carnivals' of early modern Europe. Was this just a matter of policy of 'divide and rule' implemented through the *contrade*, or had it something to do with the logic through which the Palio was put together?

Chapter 7 Christmas mumming in Newfoundland

1 For their comments on the original version of this chapter I am especially indebted to Raoul Anderson, Louis Chiaramonte, Rex Clark, Tom Nemec, Robert Paine, and George Story.

According to Gerald Sider (1976: 109), outport mumming was indelibly associated with the onset of the family fishery, roughly from the mid nineteenth century. Here fishing was organized along lines of kin and community, and fishermen sold the products of their labor rather than the labor power itself. Therefore they controlled their social relationships of production, although not the external, hierarchical and dominating conditions that gave these relationships their particular, poignant form.

2 This form of mumming differed from its urban counterpart in Newfoundland. Urban mumming was constituted through public parades and through performances by lower-class men in upper-class homes (Sider 1976). It was pervaded overtly by a symbolism of hierarchy and by distinctions of religion and ethnicity, and like similar carnivalesque forms in Europe it became a vehicle for social protest (Burke 1978; Scribner 1978). Urban mumming virtually ended when all such activities were banned throughout the island in 1861, although the practice of its outport form continued (Story 1969: 179).

3 Conceptions of selfhood, personhood, and community derive from my reading of ethnographies of outports and were not part of a predetermined scheme of analysis intended to use these materials. These distinctions are said to be common in Western thought, but my first concern is to decipher how outports implicate themselves through mumming. Therefore it is not incumbent upon me to discuss whether outports are distinct in this regard from other Western collectivities.

4 Available data outline how outport men perceived one another. Yet there are hints that the perceptions of women were not necessarily different. Indirect evidence comes from the design and placement in the home of hooked rugs

made by outport women. Pocius argues that rugs with a symmetrical and geometrically repetitive pattern were those with a community-wide provenance. Rugs of such standardized designs were used in the main in the kitchen, the spatial interface between household selves and community personae. Such rugs, like persons, were perceived as equal in quality and worth to one another, and so were interchangeable in a community-wide sense. Rugs with innovative or idiosyncratic designs were used solely in the inner recesses of the home, particularly in the parlor. Here guests of high status, who were not substitutable for one another, were received. And here the household revealed aspects of its individualistic and creative selves that were not interchangeable with those of others. Like the self, 'the innovative rug kept in the front room was rarely seen, although its existence was acknowledged' (Pocius 1979: 284).

5 The relationship between person and self hardly was unitary in outport culture. Alternative versions of this relationship are found, for example, in the '*cuffer*' (Faris 1966), in the craftsman–client contract (Chiaramonte 1970), and in the '*scoff*' (Sider 1984). The *cuffer* is a tale of licensed exaggeration based on a core of truth, told by men before a male audience, usually in neutral public settings, and argued over by the participants. The *cuffer* temporarily encourages the suspect self to emerge when moral constraints of etiquette are relaxed but are buffered by messages of play. The *cuffer* validates the relationship between person and self in the image of selfhood. That is, personhood is constructed here as a version of selfhood, but one whose validity is actively disputed, if in fun.

The *scoff* is a festive meal enjoyed by a few couples who are friends. The food for the meal is '*bucked*' – that is, taken surreptitiously from the stores of other families in the same village without the victims' knowledge. The *scoff* accentuates the validity of the suspect self across family lines. Unlike the *cuffer*, where the validity of the suspect self is disputed, suspicious selfhood is made the basis of cooperation for the victimization of others through the *scoff*.

By comparison, the contract between craftsman and client is negotiated with a view to establishing trust and sincerity between these persons in order to accomplish a clearly defined, instrumental goal (for example, the building of a boat). This trust depends on the validation of the relationship between self and person in the image of personhood. Here selfhood is constructed as a version of personhood. Only then can the parties rely fully on one another to fulfill their respective obligations over a lengthy duration.

In contrast to all of the above, the device of mumming operated not to construct selfhood and personhood as alternative versions of one another but to efface their incipient dualism. I am indebted to Robert Paine for bringing *cuffer*, *scoff*, and contract to my attention in this context, although the interpretation is my own.

6 Ingressive speech – talking while inhaling – obviously disguises voice. However the direction of its vocality connotes the inverse of sociable communication. The respiratory rhythm of speech encourages the impression that the speaker reaches out to others. Ingressive speech inverts this, closes off the self from others, and nullifies sociality.

7 Nonetheless it is worth noting that one of the highlights of community and

familial solidarity during the Christmas season was mediated through a figure of masked and licensed strangeness. Some outports chose one of their members to be Santa Claus for one night, and to redistribute presents between familiars, and indeed between family members, before the entire collectivity in a public location. Like stranger and mummer, Santa Claus was an ambivalent, even feared, figure (especially for children) who accompanied his redistribution of gifts with insult and sexual innuendo (Faris 1972: 160–1). Thus this most extensive public demonstration of reciprocity and mutuality was done through an ambiguous figure who conjoined a beneficient exterior and something of a suspect self.

8 There is a fascinating 'cultural catch' in the guessing game. Through the game the outcome of the program of mumming was left indeterminate, since revelation was not assured – although in practice the interaction of participants likely raised the probabilities of unmasking the mummers. Nonetheless the dependency of successful mumming on this game suggests an implicit cultural recognition on the part of villagers of the contingent character of their community.

In seminars and discussions it was put to me that such a contingent reconstruction of community is not unusual. I agree with regard to events of modelling, but not with regard to those of re-presentation. Events of modelling have correct outcomes that control uncertainties built into their texts or programs, although disputes or errors of practice can destroy or circumvent such outcomes on particular occasions. In mumming the program is contingent while practice must overcome this. Events of modelling, like the Palio of chapter 6, are rigged contests in which a proper outcome is built into the premises and program of the event. But hypothetically the premises of mumming imply that numerous households, and so too the community, could fail the test of the guessing game, producing a highly negative version of community for villagers, one that would reduce the village to a collection of solitary and alienated households.

9 Although I summarize the everyday self in the above manner, this is intended to highlight aspects of personhood and selfhood that are of especial relevance to this interpretation of mumming. This summation is not intended to take in all predispositions of perception and behavior among outport people (see note 5, this chapter).

10 The interplay of concealment and revelation in connecting selfhood and personhood, community and strangerhood, likely had wider ramifications that through inversion related the home to the community. In many of these small villages, households were closely related, and wives tended to be taken from outside the community, and therefore were strangers. The interior of the home was regarded largely as a female domain. Homes too were strangers to one another, for each contained a privatized interior that was hidden to familiars. The intimate and solidary tie between husband and wife implies that this elementary relationship, on which the home rested, also was imbued with strangeness in the perceptions of others. From the perspective of familiar personhood and community, the collective self of the household was covert and authentic but strange and therefore suspect.

The aggressive intrusion of mummers, their roaming through the interior of the home and their rough housing with women of the house, unmasked the strangeness of the household to others and made it more known and familiar. In a similar vein, wives-as-strangers who controlled the interiors of homes were made more known to familiars. In other words, homes also were turned inside-out. The authentic collective self of the household was revealed in a positive light, and in turn this revelation contextualized those of the mummers. Thus householders and ex-mummers were on display before one another, and open to inspection. I owe these points to a discussion with Jane Guyer. Although I am not certain that the insights she had are clear to me, my gratitude to her is.

11 I began to understand the role of signs of convergence and divergence in extending Bateson's analysis of *naven* behavior among the Iatmul (see Handelman 1979). In *naven* activity, inversion enables particular roles to maintain their distinctive contours when situational conditions increasingly signify their convergence and the effacement of their differences. A complementary point, phrased in quite different language, seems implicit in Buechler's (1980: 348) discussion of *naven*.

12 See Smith (1970) for an example of textual rhetoric apparently couched in terms of inversion, but that lacks any phase of reversion. Indeed Smith interprets this example, the apocryphal Acts of Peter, as a call of revolt.

Chapter 8 Holiday celebrations in Israeli kindergartens

1 In both the pre-state and state periods there is no especial distinction between nursery school and kindergarten. Youngsters may be in kindergarten by age two, and at age six continue on to elementary school.

2 The Hebrew word for kindergarten teacher, in the feminine gender, is *gannenet*. Its meaning is literally that of 'gardener'. As in English, the connotations of the terms are those of one who is an active agent in the processes of growing, of cultivating, and of taming. The word likely is a translation of the German, *kindergärtnerin*, a gardener of children, and is distinguished clearly in Hebrew from 'educator' (fem. *m'ḥaneḥet*) and 'teacher' (fem. *mora*). The Hebrew term for kindergarten, *gan yeladim*, again is a translation from the German.

3 Our usage is analogous to that of 'hidden curriculum' (Gearing and Tindall 1973: 103), although we stress more the contested relationship between parents and state that is implicit in the maturation of youngsters, from offspring to citizens. In a similar vein, the at times conflicted relationships between 'nation' and 'state' in the hyphenated nation-state (Handelman 1986) are not made explicit in such scenarios.

4 These comments hold as well for social science in Israel. The major exceptions are the studies of kindergarten birthday parties by Doleve-Gandelman (1987) and by Shalva Weil (1986). These events emphasize more the development of the child as a certain kind of social person. The cases in this chapter relate more to the implicit figuration of a statist view of moral and social order. Therefore birthday parties are excluded from our discussion.

5 Descriptions of daily life and of celebrations in kindergartens were collected during the course of a seminar conducted by Lea Shamgar-Handelman at The

Hebrew University. The ethnographers were supervisors employed by the Ministry of Education. They observed kindergartens that they themselves supervised, and so with which they were conversant. Their observations and responses, and those of the teachers they reported on, convinced us that the distinction between explicit and implicit agendas of celebrations was a valid one. These educators consistently understood such events in terms of the obvious occasions that were celebrated; and in terms of that which they perceived as the cooperation between teacher and parent in the establishment of a consensus on the education of the child. They did not acknowledge that the form and substance of celebratory enactments in the kindergarten implicitly conveyed a statist perspective. However they did agree that the task of the teacher was to educate not only the child but also the parents. This is discussed in the following section.

All the kindergartens observed belonged to the secular stream of state education in Israel. All their classes consisted of both boys and girls; although for the sake of convenience we use the masculine gender to refer to the child in categorical terms. These kindergartens operated six days a week, four to five hours a day.

6 We do not discuss an example of holy days, the Days of Rest, like Passover and the weekly Welcome of the Sabbath (*kabbalat shabbat*). These occasions are celebrated primarily within the family. In the kindergarten they are done as rehearsals for family celebrations rather than as enactments in their own right. Their performance in earnest is permitted only in accordance with the liturgical calendar, and associated texts of sacred standing.

7 On each of the four sides of the Hannuka top is inscribed the first letter of each of the Hebrew words, '*Ness Gadol Haya Po*' (There was a great miracle here). Spinning the top is a popular children's game. Regardless of which side remains uppermost when the top topples, its letter signifies the integrity and unity of the whole message, as does the top in its circular spinning.

8 The *hannukia* is distinguished from the *menora* (the seven-branched candelabrum) that appears as the official emblem of the State of Israel, that once stood in the Temple, and that was relit for eight days following the victory of the Maccabees. Hence the eight branches of the *hannukia*.

9 The circle dance became popular during the period of the *yishuv*, as a form through which to show the egalitarianism and dynamism of enduring bonds between persons who, through their collective efforts, forged the embracing collectivity of which they were a part.

10 This switching is a variety of inversion, but one that differs in a major respect from those discussed in previous chapters. Even though the latter are devices of temporal extrapolation, their intentionality is synchronic. Ideologically their reversion is final, and therefore timeless. There ideology and devices of enactment are homologous. However the inversion of this example, although clearly followed by reversion, projects a future condition that will come to fruition in all legitimacy. Therefore the intentionality of this kind of inversion is diachronic. Paralleling this, there is some contradiction between ideology and this device of enactment.

11 The age to which, tradition has it, Moses lived; and a customary salutation of well-wishing.

12 Other such celebrations involved the family in the scenario. Fathers reminisced about their experiences as soldiers fighting for Jerusalem; or parents told of life in Jerusalem under siege during the War of Independence. In these instances the stress was on the obligation, transferred from parents to children, to serve the country under any circumstances.

Chapter 9 State ceremonies of Israel

1 Mother and pre-teen daughter are in a family group of five, that include father, younger daughter, and baby in pram. They park the pram under a tree, sit on a stone fence, and unpack a snack lunch. Then daughter asks mother . . . We thank Lea Shamgar-Handelman for this record.

2 In her forthcoming book on Israel (untitled, as of this writing).

3 Each ceremony is organized by a different official body. That of Remembrance Day by the Section for Perpetuating the Memory of the Fallen, of the Rehabilitation Department of the Ministry of Defense. And that of Independence Day by the Information Centre, presently attached to the Ministry of Education.

4 See Vogt and Abel (1977: 174–6) for a device of national simultaneity that begins Mexico's Independence Day.

5 Interview on the television program, *A New Evening*, 13 May 1986.

6 Argument centred on whether the presentation of the new state should focus more outward, to the world, or inward. The issue was prominent in other discussions of national symbolism at that time (Handelman and Shamgar-Handelman 1986a). With regard to the Knesset debate over the law to promulgate Independence Day, Y. Idelson of the socialist Mapam party, argued for the Gregorian date of 15 May, for example, as follows: 'This holiday is not only for us', he contended, for 'we want to turn it into one of the important international dates'. If the Hebrew date were promulgated, Independence Day would 'be celebrated every year at a different time', according to the Gregorian calendar.

Responding for the government, the Minister of Education and Culture (and a future president of the state), Zalman Shazar, insisted that only within the Hebrew calendar would Independence Day have meaning for Israeli and diaspora Jewry. 'The thought is . . . to incorporate this celebration within the system of Israeli life, to make it customary for the Hebrew child and the Hebrew diaspora of the whole world to realize the idea that a great event happened in Israel . . . I can't imagine how it is possible to introduce this holiday according to a different system and a different spirit and concepts different from those to which we are accustomed to celebrate the Israeli holidays' (*Knesset Record*, Arisal [Independence] Day Law, 1949, pp. 394ff.). No dissenting votes were cast on this legislation.

7 Michael Walzer (1985: 133) has argued that the biblical story of Exodus became paradigmatic for revolutionary politics in the West. In the concluding section of

290

this chapter we indicate that the exodus narrative is itself ordered in accordance with a Jewish, cultural rhythm of time. And, that it is this rhythm that enabled and encouraged the identification of Independence Day with Passover, to which we point in the following paragraph of the text.

8 For example, the armed forces commissioned a *Haggada*, to be read at a festive Independence Day meal, which paraphrased the Passover text, to wit: 'We were slaves of the gentiles in all lands and in all states'. The Independence Day text recounts the return of the exiles, the pioneers, and their triumph over tribulation, culminating in the founding of the State.

9 Correspondence between the legal advisor of the Ministry of Defense and the government secretary, 17 March 1954, 1 April 1954, 13 April 1954.

10 Laws established Holocaust Day and Yad Vashem, the Remembrance Authority of the Holocaust (see note 11). Among the aims of Yad Vashem was to award 'remembrance citizenship' in the State of Israel to every one of the Holocaust dead. To this end, the names and personal details of the dead were compiled at Yad Vashem (*Yad Vashem Bulletin*, 1957, no. 1, p. 40). The dead were to be incorporated into the nation-state, that, in accordance with zionist vision, would incorporate eventually all of the Jewish people. 'Remembrance citizenship' finally was bestowed on the Holocaust dead by the President of the State, during the opening ceremony of Holocaust Day, 1987.

11 The decision to commemorate the Holocaust on the 27th of *Nissan* was made in 1951. Much of the present forms of commemoration were set by law in 1959. The legislation establishing Yad Vashem was passed in 1953. It should be noted that the entry into the Warsaw Ghetto of Nazi forces on the eve of Passover, 1943, was not coincidental. Nazi experts on Jewish affairs were fully conversant with the Hebrew calendar, and Nazi actions against the Jews were scheduled for Jewish holy days and holidays. Thus the mass expulsion of Jews from the Warsaw Ghetto began on the eve of the 9th of *Av* (the calendrical date of religious mourning for the destruction of the First and Second Temples) in 1942, and on the day of the 9th of *Av* the gas chambers of Treblinka began operation (*Yad Vashem Bulletin*, nos. 4/5 1959, p. 2).

12 We are indebted to Lea Shamgar-Handelman for this observation. In varieties of Judaism, following the exemplar of biblical creation, the arithmetic unit of seven is thought to sign completion, closure, and unity. Implicitly, in this instance, the seven days between Holocaust Day and Remembrance Day, and the implications of this number for the completion of a basic duration of mourning, may point to the closure of the diaspora chapter of Jewish history, in accordance with zionist visions of the period.

13 In present-day Israel this rhythm continuously encodes the relating of the Holocaust to independence. One example will suffice. In 1981 the World Gathering of Jewish Holocaust Survivors convened in Jerusalem for four days. The program of this occasion was constituted as follows. The first day, opened at Yad Vashem, was dedicated to the 'remembrance' of the Holocaust. The second, dedicated to 'rebirth and achievement', was given over to visits to kibbutzim founded by Holocaust survivors. The third was dedicated to the children of survivors. The fourth, convened in the name of 'lest we forget', was concluded

in ceremony at the Western Wall. The temporal and topographical trip from Yad Vashem to the Wall virtually recapitulated the kind of sequence we are writing of. So too, the rhetoric of the closing ceremony. Menaḥem Begin, then Prime Minister, spoke of the momentum, 'from the depths of the pit to the peak of independence', and Elie Wiesel stated, 'If Auschwitz marks the end of man's hope, Jerusalem symbolizes its eternal beginning.'

14 *Yad Vashem Bulletin*, no. 16, 1965, p. 62.

15 His will requested that the dates of his birth and death, and the names of his parents, also be inscribed. These details were added later, but in small script on one side of the tombstone, almost unseen unless one looks carefully.

16 Ben-Gurion, the first Prime Minister, is buried at Sde Boker in the Negev, where he lived after leaving government, in keeping with his call to settle the desert. Ḥaim Weizmann, chemist and first President, is buried on the grounds of the Weizmann Institute of Science, that bears his name.

17 *Yad Vashem Bulletin*, no. 16, 1965, p. 63.

18 Before 1948, space for prayer before the Wall was extremely constricted. After the 1967 War, a small Muslim quarter was bulldozed, its space used to form the plaza. The area was given over to the jurisdiction of the Ministry of Religious Affairs, that enforces present-day standards of modesty in Judaism in plaza and prayer area. At best a place of popular veneration during previous periods, without any formal standing in Jewish religious law, the Wall since 1967 has emerged as an official, Jewish holy place of powerful attraction; although some see its elevation and veneration as iconophilia and idolatry. Webber (1981: 10) refers to the Israeli capture in 1967 of the Old City of Jerusalem as a 'founding event' in a cosmological sense – one that provided traditional religion with numerous points of penetration into secular, national symbolism.

19 The plaza is now the venue for the swearing-in ceremonies of new recruits to many army units. During these occasions the recruit swears the oath of allegiance on a bible. Events held here inevitably have been skewed by religious strictures, as these are interpreted by religious authorities. So the closing ceremony of the Gathering of Jewish Holocaust Survivors (mentioned in note 13), held in the plaza, was to have featured an address by a member of the Knesset and heroine of the Warsaw Ghetto uprising. She was prevented from speaking because of her gender.

20 See, for example, Handelman and Shamgar-Handelman (1986a, 1986b) on the choice of Israel's national emblem; and Aronoff (1986) on the present-day cooptation and nationalization of remnants defined as ancient. A substantive analysis of the role of archaeology and folklore studies in Zionist nationalism has yet to be done.

21 For this description, and that of the opening of Independence Day, we have used videotapes of these ceremonies from the years, 1982, 1984, and 1986. As we have mentioned, both this ceremony and the one that opens Independence Day are televised in their entirety. Both ceremonies are set-pieces, but neither is characterized by mass, public participation. Therefore television has become the medium of bringing these occasions to the public. The influence of telecasting

likely is profound, and includes technical decisions about the placement of cameras, close-ups and long shots, montage, and so forth. The telecasts also contextualize these occasions for viewers, by offering selected sketches on history and symbols, and of the biographies of participants. In other words, television interprets these events to viewers. In certain respects these occasions are similar to those that Elihu Katz and Daniel Dayan (1985) call 'media events'. But television probably has not influenced the composition of these state ceremonies on the ground.

The first ceremony to open Remembrance Day was held in 1967 (before the Six-Day War) at President House in Jerusalem. In 1969 the ceremony was moved to the Wall. The first telecast of this ceremony, and of that which opens Independence Day, were done a few years later.

22 Such rhetoric is usual in this ceremony. In the first Remembrance Day opening ceremony at the Wall, in 1969, then-President Shazar began his address with the words, 'In this holy place for all the generations, next to the remnants of the House of Our Delight [i.e. the Temple]' (from a voice recording in the archives of the Israel Broadcasting Authority).

23 Religious tradition is respected in this reading. Judaism forbids the utterance of the name of God, and so the reader pronounces the Hebrew name, *Elohim*, as *Elokim*, which is permissible.

24 *Kaddish* (literally, 'sanctification') makes no mention of the dead, but praises the unfathomable wisdom of God, of the cosmic order. This prayer has a sense of closure, for in its different variations it is recited at the end of a section of the prayer service, and at its conclusion, as well as by mourners.

25 These comments are echoed in Aviva Aviv's study of memorial booklets on their dead soldier sons, published by bereaved parents, in which the individualism of the dead is constructed in accord with societal ideals and duties. Her unpublished paper is entitled, 'Symbols and myths in Israeli society'. More generally, the national imagery of fallen soldiers, and the typification of heroic death, is discussed in Shamgar-Handelman (1986).

26 The purest sacrificial offering of ancient Judaism was that which was wholly consumed by fire, the '*korban olah*' (literally, the 'sacrifice that ascends'). Ideas of sacrifice and purity were intimately related. Although Shazar uses the words, 'their pure sacrifice' (*korbanam hatahor*), his phrasing seems to partake of the metaphoric relationship between total sacrifice and highest value.

27 Fire and light have manifold connotations in Judaism, many of which are associated with junctures between heaven and earth, God and man, as well with a host of associated values. Don-Yehiya (1984: 14), for example, lists the following: good, beauty, belief, hope, freedom, redemption, bravery, growth, awakening, revival, unity, eternal rebirth. As well, there are numerous connotations of fire and light in European romanticism and rationalism, including reason, progress, and of course, enlightenment.

28 Not long after writing 're-member' into this text, we came across a somewhat parallel usage by the late Barbara Myerhoff. Barbara used this phrasing to refer to the recollection of selves and others in one's personal past. Most relevant here,

Barbara commented that re-membering, 'is a purposive, significant unification
... Re-membered lives are moral documents and their function is salvific,
inevitably implying, "All this has not been for nothing"' (Myerhoff 1982: 111).

29 This sequence also may be understood as composed of halves: the first of secular
actions (speeches and reading), and the second of religious actions (psalms,
kaddish, and 'God, full of compassion'). Nonetheless, primacy here still seems
that of the secular domain, since its representatives begin this sequence of
discursive action, and since the President and Chief-of-Staff are the figures of
highest stature in this ceremony.

30 Thus, Willner's (1976: 411) contention that military 'rituals themselves encode
and reiterate a very few basic messages of military life.'

31 Nonetheless, as Jan Heesterman has put it to us, the strict and monolithic
character of the occasion, of every element in its place, papers over deep
divisions in this nation-state, including those between secular and religious Jews,
which we cannot pursue here. A recent example of how easily such cracks may
surface is in Wright's (1985: 135–59) discussion of Remembrance Day in Britain.

32 In keeping with this metaphor, before and during Remembrance Day, members
of bereaved families are highlighted in the media, and in other remembrance
gatherings. They become spokespersons for, and interpreters of, the sacrifice. As
such, their status is enhanced temporarily (Shamgar-Handelman 1986).

33 The metaphor of 'family' includes in its unity both the civilian and the military
sectors. One complement of this metaphor is the common Hebrew expression
that, 'the whole people are an army' (*kol ha'am tsava*). That is, the total unity of
moral and social order also can be constituted metaphorically through the
military, through the transposition of unities of order. The military version of
order is the not so hidden obverse of the civilian. This points again to the
significance of hierarchical integration, in space and sequencing, in this Remembrance Day ceremony.

The use of metaphors of kinship in national occasions deserves further
attention. Driessen (n.d.) analyzes Spanish occasions during which figures of
nationhood are joined through metaphors of marriage to an emblem of the state,
their union entrusted to the keeping of the military.

34 Nonetheless, this ambiguity is muted within the ceremony itself, if only since
alternative or competing versions of order have no place there, in keeping with
the claims made for events of presentation in chapter 2. In the wider society of
Israel, this ambiguity is given the full voice of contradiction and conflict. Some
16 per cent of the citizenry are Arab in culture. The great majority do not serve
in the IDF. Until 1965 the Israeli Arab sector was governed by the military, as
are the occupied territories since 1967. The status and future of the large
Palestinian-Arab population of the latter is unclear, to say the least. Thus this
ceremony, and that of Independence Day, are versions of order that must not be
confuted with the so much more complex realities and visions beyond the
ceremonial borders.

35 This flattening of hierarchy holds for this version of the Zionist vision on the
summit of the mountain, the culmination of the struggle for statehood.
Therefore it does not obviate the hierarchy of struggle in climbing the mountain

itself, as this is encoded in the ceremonial sequence of Yad Vashem, military cemetery, and Herzl's tomb.

We note also the spatial sense of 'assembly' conveyed by the arrangement of clusters of graves on the upper reaches of Mount Herzl. To approach these clusters (the Jabotinsky family, the presidents of the World Zionist Organization, the Greats of the Nation) one walks roughly from east to west; while one approaches Herzl's tombstone most frontally by walking roughly from west to east. Although these clusters are not visible from Herzl's tomb, the implicit effect of this layout, if one pays attention, is that the clusters 'face' Herzl's tombstone, in the arrangement of an 'assembly' over which he presides.

36 The wording of this *yizkor* prayer is a modification of its conventional form, that asks God to remember the dead. Hebrew terms for 'memory' (*zeḥer*/ *zikaron*) have connotations both of identity and of its active retrieval. Thus the term, '*zeḥer*', is used in the Bible as a synonym for 'name' (*shem*). Among the connotations of 'memorial' or 'remembering' are those of the enactment of memory, for example, 'An act deliberately performed with the purpose of preserving something in the heart' (Dinur 1957: 8–9).

37 Naomi Tadmor examined the themes of the period 1963–84. She concluded that there have been broad changes of emphasis in the choice of themes, from ones of national consensus and challenge, that brooked little multiplicity of views, to ones that brought forth a greater diversity of social categories, but so too, the cleavages amongst them. This tendency was accentuated following the rise to power of the Likud coalition, in 1977, in keeping with its emphasis on legitimating ethnicity and traditional religion in national life, as well as its own ultra-nationalist ideology, which had become intimately identified with both. Her paper, 'The ritual of lighting the beacons on the eve of Independence Day', was prepared in 1984, for coursework at The Hebrew University of Jerusalem.

38 The lamplighters also are individuated and personalized through the mass media before Independence Day. And at the beginning of the telecast the lighters are shown to the viewing audience and something is told of their backgrounds.

39 This is a mild exaggeration. Although the shift is to a version of regimentation, the military presence here is itself more pluralistic: the tattoo is composed of soldiers of both sexes, the emblems and flags they carry represent numerous corps and units; and the Knesset Guard also participates.

40 In counterpoint to note 39, the overall role of the armed forces in this ceremony is ambiguous. Until the tattoo the military presence is small, and belongs primarily to the Remembrance Day segment of the ceremony. As noted, each beacon lighter is assisted by two soldiers who aid the former's performance. But the lighter is elevated above the soldiers. Therefore the interdependency here is complex.

The participation of the armed forces in this ceremony increased as their prominence in the overall celebrations of Independence Day diminished. In earlier years there were two large-scale demonstrations of military might and prowess during Independence Day. Both were highly popular with the citizenry, who attended en masse. One was the Night Tattoo, during which the flags were passed. The second was the military parade that alternated yearly among the three largest cities in the country. In 1968, the Night Tattoo was attached to the military parade. But the parade itself was virtually cancelled soon after. In the early 1970s, the tattoo, greatly abbreviated in size and duration, was grafted to the close of the Mount Herzl ceremony.

41 Zerubavel (1985: 115) contrasts this unit of temporal pulsation to 'the astrological model of a seven-day non-pulsating cycle'. It may be instructive to contrast lengthy durations of Jewish time to those of classical Indian thought. In the latter, pulsation may be of entropy, cyclicity, the eventual return to points of start, and so to re-start (Nakamura 1981). Complementing these rhythms are modes of belief and action that theoretically can enable the individual to break free utterly of these toils of time (Pocock 1964). Such disjunctions and contradictions in temporal logic generally seem absent from Jewish time.

42 Traditional Jewish thought, so sensitive to chronicle, seems to be unreflexive about the nature of time itself. Perhaps its unfaltering coherence and continuous linearity did not encourage time, as Johannes Fabian (1983: 13) comments, 'to be a variable independent of the events it marks', and therefore to be separated reflexively from history.

43 The first four Sabbaths of this sequence are explicitly accorded a special status in traditional Judaism. Their temporal rhythm is accentuated if one adds to this sequence the readings from Prophets of the two subsequent sabbaths. We are indebted to Shlomo Fischer for bringing this sequence to our attention.

44 The upward impulsion of this sequence continues through the *haftara* from Isaiah, that is read both on the last day of Passover and (as an addition, following independence) during the special prayer service of Independence Day (Vainstein 1953: 159). This reading contains the vision of a perfected cosmos, in which wolf and lamb, leopard and kid, and so forth, will dwell together in harmony (Isaiah 11).

45 Other, lengthier durations that are endowed with this rhythm of pulsation could be adduced – thus, the seventh, sabbatical year and the hypothetical fiftieth year of the Jubilee.

46 The sources used to discuss rhythms of Jewish time are embedded in liturgical texts and schedules. But the penetration of these rhythms into mundane living was, and in certain ways still is, necessarily pervasive. Therefore these rhythms are not easily subsumed wholly within the rubric of ritual time, in contradistinction to that of mundane time, as Bloch (1977) would have it. Our view is closer to that implied in Peacock (1978: 220–2): that cultural formations likely differ in how they inform living with senses of proper time and processuality.

47 Then not only is peace perceived as unattainable, but itself becomes identified with forms of chaotic disruption. So there are contentions that peace would encourage internal cleavages to explode, wracking social order from within; or, that peace would lead to cultural subversion by the Arab world from without.

Chapter 10 Symbolic types – clowns

1 Critiques of the typing of clowns insist that these figures have only intra-cultural significance (Hieb 1979: 185), or dismiss typing as an artifice of 'traditional

realism' in ethnography (Little 1986: 63). Treating clowns as cultural artifacts does have drawbacks: existential issues of creative innovation in performance are ignored, as are the meanings these personae have for performers. On the other hand the designs of many public events do make types of some of their characters by overdetermining them, and clowns certainly are among these. Then the relationship between event, character, and progression of enactment must depend on a comprehension of the logic of type. My more general argument for typing is given in chapter 2. See also Grottanelli (1983) on the trickster as type.

2 In the original, published version of this chapter I discussed Mayo Indian 'ritual' figures whom ethnographers call 'clowns' (Parsons and Beals 1934; Crumrine 1969). These figures are indeed contradictory in their composition, but on reflection there is little play, humor, or amusement in their constitution. Rather, they oscillate between poles of terror and righteousness, disorder and order. With reference to this chapter they are not clowns. More generally, the application of this term to them is misleading.

3 Henna combines 'cold' and 'hot' qualities. It undergoes changes in color after application, from dark brown to red. Alterations in color are indexical of changes that are made to happen in the being of the bride. Initially henna is considered extremely cold, separating the bride from the profane 'heat' of the mundane world. As it turns red it exposes the increasing heat that is caused to occur within the being of the bride. The process is more complex than this, since it also depends on the application and ingestion of other substances, and on protecting the bride through a balance of 'hot' and 'cold' elements (P. Werbner 1986: 37–40).

4 On the concept of anomaly, see the comprehensive discussion in Ohnuki-Tierney (1981b: 119–29).

5 Writing of the appearance of medieval fools, Willeford (1969: 16) comments: 'This lumpishness suggests chaos registered by consciousness as mere, crude fact: the audience is confronted with something relatively shapeless, yet material . . . [this] implies a rudimentary differentiation of the primal lump, the guise that chaos assumes when attention is paid to it: it consists of particolored bits and pieces'.

6 The interior of the clown type can be conflated with the phenomenon of inversion, but their logics of composition are distinct. In chapters 2 and 7, I noted that inversion commonly is recognized as unusual and temporary. The alterations of inversion are internally incomplete and externally unstable, and so are falsifiable. Inversion commonly breaks down and reverts to its normal analogue. But instabilities within the clown type are complete in themselves, and the type is transformative without leaving its own borders. While inversion points elsewhere, to its normal analogue, the clown type points inward, sealing itself into itself.

7 The clown type of this chapter differs from circus clowns in Western traditions. Bouissac (1976: 164) maintains that the usual circus-clown act consists of at least a dyad. One is the whitefaced clown, an epitome of 'culture', formal, elegant, authoritative, and somewhat overcivilized. The other is the crude, rude, lumpish

'*auguste*', the anti-thesis of whiteface and 'champion of nature' (see also Fellini 1976: 124–30).

Together, these two clowns bracket boundaries and play across them. The two circus-clowns are viable only in tandem (Little 1986: 52). Their relationship to boundaries is an exterior one: so that the hypothetical boundary between nature/culture would run somewhere between the two figures. By contrast the clown type's affinity to boundariness is interiorized. Therefore this figure dissolves boundaries by itself, rather than merely manipulating them. Each circus-clown is stable internally, and they play with boundaries only as a dyad, in which each supplies a pole of contrast. But the clown type interiorizes its poles of opposition, and so is internally unstable and self-transforming.

Peacock's (1967) useful study, of clowns and transvestites in Javanese *ludruk*, relates categorical distinctions between characters within the same event to ideological differences.

8 This holds as much, or more, for persons who are constituted (or who constitute themselves) as symbolic types in mundane life. In this regard I found useful Eva Gobey-Bogan's unpublished paper, 'Joking behavior and the fool in an agricultural work setting', on such a character in an Israeli community. A copy is in my possession. See also Zijderveld's (1982: vii–viii, 163–9) discussion of Peppi, the caretaker of an apartment house in Vienna. Smadar Lavie (1984, 1986) has developed the idea of 'allegorical type', adapted from that of symbolic type, and used it with insight to discuss the effects of temporary typing on mundane social situations and on cultural identity among Bedouin of Southern Sinai.

9 The message 'This is play', for example, is not self-referential and therefore overrides the paradox to enable passage through boundaries. But the clown type is a solution that elaborates on self-reference.

10 Pueblo clowns are intimates of boundaries, as will become clearer further on. Here I mention only recruiting to clownship. During their performances the clowns may site their sanctuary (an 'ash-house' among Zuni and Hopi) within sacred space. Anyone crossing this border is recruited to clownship. Or, one may be dedicated to clownship through recovery from illness. In either instance there are intimations of a paradoxical or transformational passage via a contrary condition of being.

11 To denigrate the 'interlude', as Titiev does, is to distort the English term. The English Interlude originally was a brief morality play whose messages were communicated through comedy. Where these comic Interludes were featured within sober morality plays, there was often a jarring incongruity between them (Rossiter 1950: 102). This kind of alternation is integral to the Pueblo materials (see Ortiz 1972: 148). I know of no evidence that the 'interludes' of Pueblo sacred occasions are less important than other segments. Many of these events are particular blends of the moral and comic. One need only review the numerous examples of clown burlesques of Pueblo customs, of the Catholic mass, and of American officialdom to recognize how intertwined here are morality and comedy.

12 The prevalence of clowning within the *niman* is not clear. In his description of the *niman* on First Mesa, Stephen makes no mention of clowns. Edward

Kennard (personal communication, March 1978), with lengthy and intensive fieldwork among Hopi, does not recall the appearance of clowns during the *niman* (see Earle and Kennard 1971: 41–5). Louis Hieb (personal communication, May 1978) also has no recollection of their appearance during this occasion. Hieb properly notes that the *niman* occurs somewhat prior to the summer solstice. For the sake of convenience I continue to refer to it as a solstice occasion. The point here is that Hopi had and have a cluster of events within which clown and *kachina* were brought into opposition.

13 The sacred work of the *kwirana* has become minor, compared to that of the *kossa* (Ortiz 1969: 167). The *kossa* appear between the autumnal equinox and the winter solstice; and one would expect the *kwirana* to appear during that other period of intense Tewa sacred activity, between the winter solstice and the vernal equinox. Instead, 'fake' *kossa* appear during the latter period.

14 Among the Made People, only the clowns and moiety chiefs alternate positions according to seasonal changes; and the clowns are the only categories among those 'of the middle of the structure' to do so. The chiefs are at the apex of the Made People, and signify the structural stability of Tewa social order. The clowns are close to the middle of the Made People, and are intimates of boundariness and transition. The *kossa*, the more dominant of the two clown groups, rank either third or fourth (depending on the season) among the seven categories of Made People (Ortiz 1969: 81). Therefore the *kossa* are sited very close to the middle of the Made People. Moreover, during any given period either the *kossa* or the *kwirana* do rank fourth among the seven categories of Made People.

In the hierarchy of Made People the Summer and Winter Chiefs (and their societies) are counted as a single group, presumably because they are equal but alternating in the authority they share. But according to the Tewa myth of Emergence, the moiety chiefs were not the first Made People; and although the chiefs were created during a single phase of the Emergence, they were not made simultaneously (1969: 14). If the Summer and Winter People are counted as two separate groups, there are eight groups of Made People. Then the *kossa* and *kwirana* alternate between positions four and five – and both clown groups are 'in the middle' of the Made People. I suggested that in the Tewa cosmos there is a close association between sacred centrality and boundariness. The possible positioning of the two clown groups exemplifies this association, and makes of them sacred mediators par excellence. On the other hand, the apical moiety chiefs are more distant from centricity and transition, and so can signify more the stability and less the transformation of Tewa order. Whether there is any value in these suppositions I leave to scholars of the Tewa to decide.

15 Towards the close of the Hopi and Tewa cases, the clowns become more of a reflecting surface for the verities of the deities. As the transformational work of these occasions ends, the oscillation of the clowns is stilled.

The place of clowns in the Dance of Man resembles somewhat that of the *koyemci* at the great Zuni occasion of *shalako*. Here the clowns announce the coming of the deities, and are instrumental in closing this event. Towards its end, 'the character of their dancing changes, becoming more solemn. They do not indulge in their usual obscenity' (Bunzel 1932: 945, 953). The clowns then visit each dwelling in the community to bring their blessings (see also Parsons 1916: 395ff.).

16 Should *mikinak* not come, then Little Jack Fish does – and this spirit has comic attributes similar to those of the Great Turtle.

17 There are numerous ways, apart from that of symbolic types, of evoking reflexivity in public events. Thus the organization itself of an occasion can evoke different foci and varieties of reflexivity at various junctures.

Bibliography

Abrahams, Roger D. 1977. Toward an enactment-centered theory of folklore. In *Frontiers of Folklore*, ed. W. R. Bascom, pp. 79–120. Boulder, Westview Press.

Agulhon, Maurice. 1985. Politics, images, and symbols in post-revolutionary France. In *Rites of Power: Symbolism, Ritual, and Politics Since the Middle Ages*, ed. Sean Wilentz, pp. 177–205. Philadelphia, University of Pennsylvania Press.

Allen, Ann Taylor. 1986. Gardens of Children, gardens of God: kindergartens and day-care centers in nineteenth-century Germany. *Journal of Social History*, 19: 433–50.

Almagor, Uri. 1987. The cycle and stagnation of smells: pastoralists–fishermen relationships in an East African society. *Res*, 13: 106–21.

Anderson, Benedict. 1983. *Imagined Communities: Reflections on the Origin and Spread of Nationalism*. London, Verso.

Anderson, Alan Ross and Omar Khayyam Moore. 1960. Autotelic folk models. *Sociological Quarterly*, 1: 203–16.

Aris, Rutherford and Mischa Penn. 1980. The mere notion of a model. *Mathematical Modelling*, 1: 1–12.

Aronoff, Myron J. 1986. Establishing authority: the memorialization of Jabotinsky and the burial of the Bar Kochba bones in Israel under the Likud. In *The Frailty of Authority*, ed. M. J. Aronoff, pp. 105–30. New Brunswick, N.J., Transaction Books.

Babcock, Barbara A. 1978a. Too many, too few: ritual modes of signification. *Semiotica*, 23: 291–302.

Babcock, Barbara A., ed. 1978b. *The Reversible World: Symbolic Inversion in Art and Society*. Ithaca and London, Cornell University Press.

Barbour, Ian G. 1974. *Myths, Models, and Paradigms: a Comparative Study in Science and Religion*. New York, Harper and Row.

Bargatzky, Thomas. 1984. Culture, environment, and the ills of adaptation. *Current Anthropology*, 25: 399–406.

Barth, Fredrik. 1966. *Models of Social Organization*. London, Royal Anthropological Institute (Occasional Paper No. 23).

1974. On responsibility and humanity: calling a colleague to account. *Current Anthropology*, 15: 99–103.

1975. *Ritual and Knowledge Among the Baktaman of New Guinea*. Oslo and New Haven, Universitetsforlaget and Yale University Press.

Bateson, Gregory. 1956. The message 'this is play'. In *Group Processes*, ed. B. Schaffner, pp. 145–241. New York, Josiah Macy Foundation.

1958. *Naven* (2nd edition). Stanford, Stanford University Press.

1972. A theory of play and fantasy. In *Steps to an Ecology of Mind*, pp. 177–93. New York, Ballantine.

Bauman, Richard. 1972. Belsnickling in a Nova Scotia community. *Western Folklore*, 31: 229–43.

Bauman, Richard and Joel Sherzer, eds. 1974. *Explorations in the Ethnography of Speaking*. Cambridge and New York, Cambridge University Press.

Beeman, William O. 1982. *Culture, Performance and Communication in Iran*. Tokyo, Institute for the Study of Languages and Cultures of Asia & Africa, Tokyo University of Foreign Studies.

Beidelman, T. O. 1966. Swazi royal ritual. *Africa*, 36: 373–405.

Bell, Catherine. 1987. Discourse and dichotomies: the structure of ritual theory. *Religion*, 17: 95–118.

Ben-Dor, Shmuel. 1969. The 'Naluyuks' of Northern Labrador: a mechanism of social control. In *Christmas Mumming in Newfoundland*, ed. H. Halpert and G. Story, pp. 119–27. Toronto, University of Toronto Press.

Benjamin, Walter. 1969. *Illuminations* (ed. H. Arendt). New York, Schocken.

Bergeron, David M. 1971. *English Civic Pageantry, 1558–1642*. Columbia, University of South Carolina Press.

Bernstein, Basil, H. L. Elvin and R. S. Peters. 1966. *Ritual in education*. Philosophical Transactions of the Royal Society of London, Series B, no. 772, 251: 429–36.

Bezucha, Robert J. 1975. Masks of revolution: a study of popular culture during the Second French Republic. In *Revolution and Reaction: 1848 and the Second French Republic*, ed. R. Price, pp. 236–53. London, Croom Helm.

Bhaktin, Mikhail. 1968. *Rabelais and His World*. Cambridge, MIT University Press.

Binns, Christopher A. P. 1980. The changing face of power: revolution and accommodation in the development of the Soviet ceremonial system, II. *Man* (N.S.), 15: 170–87.

Black, J. A. 1981. The new year ceremonies in ancient Babylon: 'Taking Bel by the hand' and a cultic picnic. *Religion*, 11: 39–59.

Black, Max. 1962. *Models and Metaphors: Studies in Language and Philosophy*. Ithaca and London: Cornell University Press.

Bloch, Maurice. 1974. Symbols, song, dance and features of articulation. *European Journal of Sociology*, 15: 55–81.

1977. The past and the present in the present. *Man* (N.S.), 12: 278–92.

Bloch, Maurice and Jonathan Parry, eds. 1982. *Death and the Regeneration of Life*. Cambridge and New York, Cambridge University Press.

Blok, Anton. 1981. Rams and billy-goats: a key to the Mediterranean code of honor. *Man* (N.S.), 16: 427–40.

Bohm, David. 1985. Fragmentation and wholeness in religion and science. *Zygon*, 20: 125–33.

Bouissac, Paul. 1976. *Circus and Culture: A Semiotic Approach*. Bloomington, Indiana University Press.

Bourdieu, Pierre. 1977. *Outline of a Theory of Practice*. Cambridge and New York, Cambridge University Press.

Bradney, Pamela. 1957. The joking relationship in industry. *Human Relations*, 10: 179–87.

Braudy, Leo. 1982. Popular culture and personal time. *Yale Review*, 71: 481–98.

Briggs, Jean. 1983. Le modèle traditionnel d'education chez les Inuit: différentes formes d'expérimentation face à l'inconnu. *Recherches Amérindiennes au Québec*, 13, no. 1: 13–25.

Bruner, Edward M. 1986. Ethnography as narrative. In *The Anthropology of Experience*, ed. V. W. Turner and E. M. Bruner, pp. 139–55. Urbana and Chicago, University of Illinois Press.

Bruner, edward M. and Phyllis Gorfain. 1984. Dialogic narration and the paradoxes of Masada. In *Text, Play, and Story: The Construction and Reconstruction of Self and Society*, ed. E. M. Bruner, pp. 56–79. Washington, D.C., American Ethnological Society.

Bryant, Lawrence M. 1986. *The King and the City in the Parisian Royal Entry Ceremony: Politics, Ritual, and Art in the Renaissance*. Geneva, Librairie Droz.

Buechler, Hans C. 1980. *The Masked Media: Aymara Fiestas and Social Interaction in the Bolivian Highlands*. The Hague, Mouton.

Bullough, Vern L. 1982. The prostitute in the early Middle Ages. In *Sexual Practices and the Medieval Church*, ed. V. L. Bullough and J. Brundage, pp. 34–42. Buffalo, Prometheus Books.

Bunzel, Ruth. 1932. Zuni Katcinas: an analytical study. *Annual Report of the Bureau of American Ethnology*, 47: 837–1108.

Burden, H. T. 1967. *The Nuremberg Party Rallies, 1923–39*. London, Pall Mall Press.

Burke, Peter. 1978. *Popular Culture in Early Modern Europe*. London, Temple Smith.
   1987. *The Historical Anthropology of Early Modern Italy: Essays on Perception and Communication*. Cambridge and New York, Cambridge University Press.

Burnett, J. H. 1969. Ceremony, rites and economy in the student system of an American high school. *Human Organization*, 28: 1–10.

Bynum, Caroline Walker. 1982. *Jesus as Mother: Studies in the Spirituality of the High Middle Ages*. Berkeley and London, University of California Press.

Caillois, Roger. 1959. *Man and the Sacred*. Glencoe, The Free Press.
   1961. *Man, Play, and Games*. Glencoe, The Free Press.

Cannadine, David. 1987. Introduction: divine rites of kings. In *Rituals of Royalty: Power and Ceremonial in Traditional Societies*, ed. D. Cannadine, pp. 1–19. Cambridge and New York, Cambridge University Press.

Caws, Peter. 1974. Operational, representational, and explanatory models. *American Anthropologist*, 76: 1–10.

Chaney, David. 1983. A symbolic mirror of ourselves: civic ritual in mass society. *Media, Culture, and Society*, 5: 119–35.

Charles, Lucille Hoerr. 1945. The clown's function. *Journal of American Folklore*, 58: 25–34.

Chiaramonte, Louis J. 1969. Mumming in 'Deep Harbor': aspects of social organization in mumming and drinking. In *Christmas Mumming in Newfound-*

land, ed. H. Halpert and G. Story, pp. 76–103. Toronto, University of Toronto Press.

1970. *Craftsman–Client Contracts: Interpersonal Relations in a Newfoundland Fishing Community*. St. John's, Institute of Social and Economic Research, Memorial University of Newfoundland.

Clayre, Alasdair. 1974. *Work and Play: Ideas and Experience of Work and Leisure*. London, Weidenfeld and Nicolson.

Cohen, Abner. 1981. *The Politics of Elite Culture: Explorations in the Dramaturgy of Power in a Modern African Society*. Berkeley and London, University of California Press.

1982. A polyethnic London carnival as a contested cultural performance. *Ethnic and Racial Studies*, 5: 23–41.

Cohen, Erik. 1985. Tourism as play. *Religion*, 15: 291–304.

Conant, Roger C. and W. Ross Ashby. 1970. Every good regulator of a system must be a model of that system. *International Journal of Systems Science*, 1: 89–97.

Corbeil, J. J. 1982. *Mbusa: Sacred Emblems of the Bemba*. Mbala, Zambia, Moto-Moto Museum.

Coser, Rose Laub. 1959. Some social functions of laughter. *Human Relations*, 12: 171–82.

Crump, Thomas. 1975. The context of European anthropology: the lesson from Italy. In *Beyond the Community: Social Process in Europe*, ed. J. Boissevain and J. Friedl, pp. 18–28. The Hague, Department of Educational Science of The Netherlands.

Crumrine, N. Ross. 1969. Čapakoba, the Mayo Easter ceremonial impersonator: explanations of ritual clowning. *Journal for the Scientific Study of Religion*, 8: 1–22.

Cunnison, Sheila. 1966. *Wages and Work Allocation*. London, Tavistock.

Da Matta, Roberto. 1977. Constraint and license: a preliminary study of two Brazilian national rituals. In *Secular Ritual*, ed. S. F. Moore and B. Myerhoff, pp. 244–64. Assen, Van Gorcum.

Daniels, E. Valentine. 1984. *Fluid Signs: Being a Person the Tamil Way*. Berkeley and London, University of California Press.

Darnton, Robert. 1985. *The Great Cat Massacre and Other Episodes in French Cultural History*. New York, Vintage Books.

Davis, Natalie Zemon. 1982. *Society and Culture in Early Modern France*. Stanford, Stanford University Press.

Davis, Susan, G. 1982. 'Making night hideous': Christmas revelry and public order in nineteenth-century Philadelphia. *American Quarterly*, 34: 185–99.

1985. Strike parades and the politics of representing class in antebellum Philadelphia. *Drama Review*, 29, no. 3: 106–16.

Dinur, Benzion. 1957. Problems confronting 'Yad Vashem' in its work of research. *Yad Vashem Studies*, 1: 7–30.

Doleve-Gandelman, Tsili. 1987. The symbolic inscription of Zionist ideology in the space of Eretz Yisrael: why the native Israeli is called tsabar. In *Judaism Viewed From Within and From Without: Anthropological Studies*, ed. H. E. Goldberg, pp. 257–84. Albany, SUNY Press.

Don-Yehiya, Eliezer. 1984. Festival and political culture: the celebration of Independence Day in the early years of statehood. *State, Government and Internation Relations*, 23: 5–28 (in Hebrew).

Douglas, Mary. 1966. *Purity and Danger: An Analysis of Conceptions of Pollution and Taboo*. London, Routledge & Kegan Paul.

    1968. The social control of cognition: some factors in joke perception. *Man* (N.S.), 3: 361–76.

    1982. *In the Active Voice*. London and Boston, Routledge & Kegan Paul.

Driessen, Henk, 1984. Religious brotherhoods, class and politics in an Andalusian town. In *Religion, Power and Protest in Local Communities: The Northern Shore of the Mediterranean*, ed. E. R. Wolf, pp. 73–92. Berlin, Mouton.

    n.d. Ceremonies of the national flag. Unpublished Ms.

Dufrenne, Mikel. 1973. *The Phenomenology of Aesthetic Perception*. Evanston, Northwestern University Press.

Dumont, Louis. 1972. *Homo Hierarchicus: The Caste System and its Implications*. London, Paladin.

    1979. The anthropological community and ideology. *Social Science Information*, 18: 785–817.

Dundes, Alan and Alessandro Falassi. 1975. *La Terra in Piazza: An Interpretation of the Palio of Siena*. Berkeley and London, University of California Press.

Durkheim, Emile. 1956. *Sociology and Education*. Glencoe, The Free Press.

Earle, Edwin and Edward A. Kennard. 1971. *Hopi Kachinas*. New York, Museum of the American Indian.

Eco, Umberto. 1985. At the roots of the modern concept of symbol. *Social Research*, 52: 383–402.

Emerson, Joan P. 1969. Negotiating the serious import of humor. *Sociometry*, 32: 169–81.

Evens, T. M. S. 1975. Stigma, ostracism, and expulsion in an Israeli kibbutz. In *Symbol and Politics in Communal Ideology*, ed. S. F. Moore and B. G. Myerhoff, pp. 169–209. Ithaca and London, Cornell University Press.

    1982. On the social anthropology of religion. *Journal of Religion*, 62: 376–391.

Fabian, Johannes. 1983. *Time and the Other: How Anthropology Makes its Object*. New York, Columbia University Press.

Fairman, H. W. 1974. *The Triumph of Horus: The Oldest Play in the World*. Berkeley and Los Angeles, University of California Press.

Falassi, Alessandro and Guiliano Catoni. 1983. *Palio*. Milan, Electa.

Faris, James C. 1966. The dynamics of verbal exchange: a Newfoundland example. *Anthropologica* (N.S.), 8: 236–48.

    1968. Validation in ethnographic description: the lexicon of 'occasions' in Cat Harbour. *Man* (N.S.), 3: 112–24.

    1969. Mumming in an outport fishing settlement: a description and suggestions on the cognitive complex. In *Christmas Mumming in Newfoundland*, ed. H. Halpert and G. Story, pp. 129–44. Toronto, University of Toronto Press.

    1972. *Cat Harbor: A Newfoundland Fishing Settlement*. St. John's, Institute of Social and Economic Research, Memorial University of Newfoundland.

Farrer, Claire R. 1979. Libayé, the playful paradox: aspects of the Mescalero Apache ritual clown. Annual Meeting of the American Anthropological Association.

Fayence-Glick, S. 1948. Ḥannuka in the kindergarten. *Oshiot*, 2: 28–39 (in Hebrew).

    1957. Kindergartens in Eretz Yisrael. In *The Book of the Fiftieth Anniversary of the Teachers' Union*, pp. 132–44. Tel-Aviv, Histadrut Hamorim b'Eretz Yisrael (in Hebrew).

Fellini, Federico. 1976. *Fellini on Fellini*. New York, Delacorte.

Fernandez, James W. 1980. Reflections on looking into mirrors. *Semiotica*, 30: 27–39.

    1984. Convivial attitudes: the ironic play of tropes in an international kayak festival in northern Spain. In *Text, Play, and Story: The Construction and Reconstruction of Self and Society*, ed. E. M. Bruner, pp. 199–229. Washington, American Ethnological Society.

    1986. The argument of images and the experience of returning to the whole. In *The Anthropology of Experience*, ed. V. W. Turner and E. M. Bruner, pp. 159–87. Urbana and Chicago, University of Illinois Press.

Fine, Gary Alan. 1983. *Shared Fantasy: Role-Playing Games as Social Worlds*. Chicago and London, University of Chicago Press.

Fink, Eugen. 1968. The oasis of happiness: toward an ontology of play. *Yale French Studies*, 41: 19–30.

Firestone, Melvin M. 1967. *Brothers and Rivals: Patrilocality in Savage Cove*. St. John's, Institute of Social and Economic Research, Memorial University of Newfoundland.

    1969. Mummers and strangers in Northern Newfoundland. In *Christmas Mumming in Newfoundland*, ed. H. Halpert and G. Story, pp. 63–75. Toronto, University of Toronto Press.

    1978. Christmas mumming and symbolic interactionism. *Ethos*, 6: 92–113.

Firth, Raymond. 1967. *Tikopia Ritual and Belief*. London, Allen and Unwin.

Fischer, Roland. 1985. Deconstructing reality. *Diogenes*, 129: 47–62.

Fortes, Meyer. 1968. Of installation ceremonies. *Proceedings of the Royal Anthropological Institute*, pp. 5–20.

Foucault, Michel. 1979. *Discipline and Punish: The Birth of the Prison*. New York, Vintage Books.

Frankfort, Henri. 1948. *Kingship and the Gods: A Study of Ancient Near Eastern Religion as the Integration of Society and Nature*. Chicago, University of Chicago Press.

Frazer, Sir James George. 1951. *The Golden Bough: A Study in Magic and Religion*, part I, vol. 1. New York, Macmillan (3rd edition).

Fredman, Ruth Gruber. 1981. *The Passover Seder: Afikoman in Exile*. Philadelphia, University of Pennsylvania Press.

Friedman, Jonathan. 1979. Hegelian ecology: between Rousseau and the world spirit. In *Social and Ecological Systems*, ed. P. C. Burnham and R. Ellen, pp. 253–70. London and New York, Academic Press.

Fuchs, E. 1969. *Teachers Talk*. New York, Doubleday.

Gearing, F. O. and B. A. Tindall. 1973. Anthropological studies of the educational process. *Annual Review of Anthropology*, 2: 95–105.

Geertz, Clifford. 1964. 'Internal conversion' in contemporary Bali. In *Malayan and Indonesian Studies Presented to Sir Richard Winstedt*, ed. J. Bastin and R. Roolvink, pp. 282–302. Oxford, Oxford University Press.

1973. *The Interpretation of Cultures*. New York, Basic Books.

1976. 'From the native's point of view': on the nature of anthropological understanding. In *Meaning in Anthropology*, ed. K. Basso and H. Selby, pp. 221–37. Albuquerque, University of New Mexico Press.

Gertz, Nurit. 1984. The few against the many. *Jerusalem Quarterly*, 30: 94–104.

Geyer, R. Felix and Johannes van der Zouwen. 1978. Introduction. In *Socio-cybernetics: An Actor-Oriented Social Systems Approach*, vol. 1, ed. R. Felix Geyer and J. van der Zouwen, pp. 1–13. Leiden and London, Martinus Nijhoff.

Geyer, Felix and Johannes van der Zouwen, eds. 1986. *Sociocybernetic Paradoxes: Observation, Control and Evolution of Self-Steering Systems*. London and Beverly Hills, Sage.

Geyl, P. (tr.) 1927. *The Tale of Beatrice*. The Hague, Martinus Nijhoff.

Giesey, Ralph E. 1985. Models of rulership in French royal ceremonial. In *Rites of Power: Symbolism, Ritual, and Politics Since the Middle Ages*, ed. S. Wilentz, pp. 41–64. Philadelphia, University of Pennsylvania Press.

Gilhus, Ingrid. 1984. The Gnostic demiurge – an agnostic trickster. *Religion*, 14: 301–11.

Giovannini, Maureen J. 1981. Woman: a dominant symbol within the cultural system of a Sicilian town. *Man* (N.S.), 16: 408–26.

Glassie, Henry. 1975. *All Silver and No Brass: An Irish Christmas Mumming*. Bloomington and London, Indiana University Press.

Gluckman, Max. 1954. *Rituals of Rebellion in South-East Africa*. Manchester, Manchester University Press.

1962. Les rites de passage. In *Essays on the Ritual of Social Relations*, ed. M. Gluckman, pp. 1–52. Manchester, Manchester University Press.

Gluckman, Max and Mary Gluckman. 1977. On drama, and games and athletic contests. In *Secular Ritual*, ed. S. F. Moore and B. G. Myerhoff, pp. 227–43. Assen, Van Gorcum.

Goffman, Erving. 1961. *Encounters: Two Studies in the Sociology of Interaction*. Indianapolis, Bobbs-Merrill.

Goldberg, Harvey E. 1977. Rites and riots: the Tripolitanian pogrom of 1945. *Plural Societies*, 8: 35–56.

1978. The Mimuna and the minority status of Moroccan Jews. *Ethnology*, 17: 75–88.

Goldstein, Robert J. 1984. Political funerals. *Society*, 21, no. 3: 13–17.

Gourevitch, Aron I. 1975. The comic and the serious in religious literature of the Middle Ages. *Diogenes*, 90: 56–77.

Gracey, Harry L. 1975. Learning the student role: kindergarten as academic boot camp. In *Lifestyles* (2nd ed.), ed. S. D. Feldman and G. W. Thielbor, pp. 437–42. Boston, Little, Brown.

Graef, Hilda. 1985. *Mary: A History of Doctrine and Devotion*, parts 1 and 2. London and New York, Sheed and Ward.

Grathoff, Richard H. 1970. *The Structure of Social Inconsistencies: A Contribution to a Unified Theory of Play, Game and Social Action*. The Hague, Martinus Nijhoff.

Greenwood, Davydd J. 1977. Culture by the pound: an anthropological perspective on tourism as cultural commoditization. In *Hosts and Guests: The Anthropology of Tourism*, ed. V. L. Smith, pp. 129–38. Philadelphia, University of Pennsylvania Press.

Gregory, Steven and Daniel Timerman. 1986. Rituals of the modern state: the case of torture in Argentina. *Dialectical Anthropology*, 11: 63–72.

Grimes, Ronald L. 1982. Defining nascent ritual. *Journal of the American Academy of Religion*, 50: 540–55.

Grottanelli, Cristiano. 1983. Tricksters, scapegoats, champions, saviors. *History of Religions*, 23: 117–39.

Gudeman, Stephen and Mischa Penn. 1982. Models, meanings and reflexivity. In *Semantic Anthropology*, ed. David Parkin, pp. 89–106. London and New York, Academic Press.

Guetzkow, Harold. ed. 1962. *Simulation in Social Science*. Englewood Cliffs, N.J., Prentice-Hall.

Gutowski, John A. 1978. The protofestival: local guide to American folk behavior. *Journal of the Folklore Institute*, 15: 113–32.

Haas, Jack. 1972. Binging: educational control among high steel ironworkers. *American Behavioral Scientist*, 16: 27–34.

Hagen, Everett. 1961. *On the Theory of Social Change*. Homewood, Ill., Dorsey Press.

Hallowell, A. Irving. 1942. *The Role of Conjuring in Salteaux Society*. Philadelphia, University of Pennsylvania Press.

Halpert, Herbert. 1969. A typology of mumming. In *Christmas Mumming in Newfoundland*, ed. H. Halpert and G. Story, pp. 35–61. Toronto, University of Toronto Press.

Hammerton, Elizabeth and David Cannadine. 1981. Conflict and consensus on a ceremonial occasion: the Diamond Jubilee in Cambridge in 1897. *The Historical Journal*, 24: 111–46.

Handelman, Don. 1973. Gossip in encounters: the transmission of information in a bounded social setting. *Man* (N.S.), 8: 210–27.

　　1976. Bureaucratic transactions: the development of official–client relationships in Israel. In *Transaction and Meaning: Directions in the Anthropology of Exchange and Symbolic Behavior*, ed. B. Kapferer, pp. 223–75. Philadelphia, ISHI.

　　1977a. *Work and Play Among the Aged: Interaction, Replication and Emergence in a Jerusalem Setting*. Assen, Van Gorcum.

　　1977b. Play and ritual: complementary frames of metacommunication. In *It's A Funny Thing, Humour*, ed. A. J. Chapman and H. Foot, pp. 185–92. London, Pergamon.

　　1978. Bureaucratic interpretation: the perception of child abuse in urban Newfoundland. In *Bureaucracy and World View: Studies in the Logic of Official Interpretation*, by D. Handelman and E. Leyton, pp. 15–69. St. John's, Institute of Social and Economic Research, Memorial University of Newfoundland.

1979. Is Naven ludic? Paradox and the communication of identity. *Social Analysis*, 1: 177–91.

1980. Bureaucratic affiliation: the moral component in welfare instances. In *A Composite Portrait of Israel*, ed. E. Marx, pp. 257–82. London and New York, Academic Press.

1981. Introduction: the idea of bureaucratic organization. In *Administrative Frameworks and Clients*, ed. J. Collman and D. Handelman. Special issue of *Social Analysis*, 9: 5–23.

1983. Shaping phenomenal reality: dialectic and disjunction in the bureaucratic synthesis of child-abuse in urban Newfoundland. *Social Analysis*, 13: 3–36.

1985. Charisma, liminality, and symbolic types. In *Comparative Social Dynamics: Essays in Honor of S. N. Eisenstadt*, ed. E. Cohen, M. Lissak, and U. Almagor, pp. 346–59. Boulder, Westview.

1986. Comments on state and religion in Israel. Annual Meeting of the American Anthropological Association, Philadelphia, December 3–7.

1987a. Play. *Encyclopedia of Religion*, 11: 363–8.

1987b. Myths of Murugan: asymmetry and hierarchy in a South-Indian Puranic cosmology. *History of Religions*, 27: 133–70.

Handelman, Don and Bruce Kapferer. 1972. Forms of joking activity: a comparative approach. *American Anthropologist*, 74: 484–517.

1980. Symbolic types, mediation and the transformation of ritual context: Sinhalese demons and Tewa clowns. *Semiotica*, 30: 41–71.

Handelman, Don and Lea Shamgar-Handelman. 1986a. Shaping time: the choice of the national emblem of Israel. Conference on Symbolism Through Time, Wenner-Gren Foundation, Fez, January 12–21.

1986b. Imagining the nation-state: visual composition in the emblem of Israel. Annual Meeting of the American Anthropological Association, Philadelphia, December 3–7.

Hardison, Jr., O. B. 1969. *Christian Rite and Christian Drama in the Middle Ages*. Baltimore, Johns Hopkins Press.

Heesterman, Jan. 1984. The ritualist's problem. In, *Am.tadhārā: R. N. Dandekar Felicitation Volume*, ed. S. D. Joshi, pp. 167–79. Delhi, S. Balwant, Ajanta Publications.

Heffernan, Helen and Vivian E. Todd. 1960. *The Kindergarten Teacher*. Boston, D. C. Heath.

Heisenberg, Werner. 1960. The representation of nature in contemporary physics. In *Symbolism in Religion and Literature*, ed. R. May, pp. 215–32. New York, George Braziller.

Hertz, J. 1938. *The Pentateuch and Haftorahs*. London, Soncino.

Heschel, Abraham Joshua. 1951. *The Sabbath: Its Meaning For Modern Man*. New York, Farrar, Straus, and Young.

Hesse, Mary B. 1966. *Models and Analogies in Science*. Notre Dame, Ind., University of Notre Dame Press.

Heywood, William. 1904. *Palio and Ponte*. London, Methuen.

Hieb, Louis A. 1972. Meaning and mismeaning: toward an understanding of the ritual clown. In *New Perspectives on the Pueblos*, ed. A. Ortiz, pp. 163–95. Albuquerque, University of New Mexico Press.

1979. The ritual clown: honor and ethics. In *Forms of Play of Native North Americans*, ed. E. Norbeck and C. R. Farrer, pp. 171–88. St. Paul, West Publishing.

Highwater, Jamake. 1977. *Ritual of the Wind*. New York, Viking.

Hirsch, Samson Raphael. 1985. *The Collected Writings*, vol. II. New York and Jerusalem, Feldheim.

Hobsbawm, Eric J. and Terence Ranger, eds. 1983. *The Invention of Tradition*. Cambridge and New York, Cambridge University Press.

Hocart, A. M. 1927. *Kingship*. Oxford, Oxford University Press.

Holy, L. and M. Stuchlik, eds. 1981. *The Structure of Folk Models*. London and New York, Academic Press.

Homans, George C. 1950. *The Human Group*. New York, Harcourt, Brace.

Honigmann, John J. 1942. An interpretation of the social-psychological functions of the ritual clown. *Character and Personality*, 10: 220–6.

1977. The masked face. *Ethos*, 5: 262–80.

Horton, Robin. 1972. Ritual man in Africa. In *Reader in Comparative Religion* (3rd ed.), ed. W. Lessa and E. Z. Vogt, pp. 347–58. New York, Harper and Row.

1973. Paradox and explanation: a reply to Mr. Skorupski. *Philosophy of the Social Sciences*, 3: 231–56, 289–314.

Hughey, Michael W. 1983. *Civil Religion and Moral Order: Theoretical and Historical Dimensions*. Westport and London, Greenwood Press.

Huizinga, Johan. 1970. *Homo Ludens: A Study of the Play Element in Culture*. London, Paladin.

Hunt, Lynn. 1983. Hercules and the radical image in the French Revolution. *Representations*, 2: 95–117.

Hyers, M. Conrad. 1974. *Zen and the Comic Spirit*. New York, Rider.

James, Mervyn. 1983. Ritual, drama and social body in the late medieval English town. *Past and Present*, 98: 3–29.

Jasper, Patricia A. 1980. 'To the beat of a borrowed drum . . .': the Bonus March of 1932. In *Folklore Papers of the University Folklore Association*, no. 9, ed. K. F. Turner, pp. 77–92. Austin, Center for Intercultural Studies in Folklore and Ethnomusicology, University of Texas.

Jenkins, Richard. 1981. Thinking and doing. In *The Structure of Folk Models*, ed. L. Holy and M. Stuchlik, pp. 93–117. London and New York, Academic Press.

Johnson, Ragnar. 1981. Order or disorder in Melanesian religions? *Man* (N.S.), 16: 472–5.

Johnson, Willard. 1980. *Poetry and Speculation of the Ṛg Veda*. Berkeley and London, University of California Press.

Jones, N. Blurton. 1969. An ethological study of some aspects of social behavior of children in nursery school. In *Primate Ethology*, ed. D. Morris, pp. 437–63. New York, Doubleday.

Kahler, Erich. 1960. The nature of the symbol. In *Symbolism in Religion and Literature*, ed. R. May, pp. 50–73. New York, George Braziller.

Kamen, Charles S. 1977. Affirmation or enjoyment? The commemoration of independence in Israel. *Jewish Journal of Sociology*, 19: 5–20.

Kapferer, Bruce. 1972. *Strategy and Transaction in an African Factory*. Manchester, Manchester University Press.

    1983. *A Celebration of Demons: Exorcism and the Aesthetics of Healing in Sri Lanka*. Bloomington, Indiana University Press.

    1984a. Postscript. *Social Analysis*, 1: 192–7.

    1984b. The ritual process and the problem of reflexivity in Sinhalese demon exorcisms. In *Rite, Drama, Festival, Spectacle: Rehearsals Toward a Theory of Cultural Performance*, ed. J. J. MacAloon, pp. 179–207. Philadelphia, ISHI.

    1986. Performance and the structuring of meaning and experience. In *The Anthropology of Experience*, ed. V. W. Turner and E. M. Bruner, pp. 188–203. Urbana and Chicago, University of Illinois Press.

    1988. *Legends of People, Myths of State: Violence, Intolerance, and Political Culture in Sri Lanka and Australia*. Washington, D.C., Smithsonian Institution Press.

Kapferer, Judith L. 1981. Socialization and the symbolic order of the school. *Anthropology and Education Quarterly*, 12: 258–74.

Katerbursky, Z. 1962. *The Ways of the Garden*. Tel-Aviv, Otsar Hamoreh (in Hebrew).

Katz, Elihu and Daniel Dayan. 1985. Media events: on the experience of not being there. *Religion*, 15: 305–14.

Kaufmann, Yehezkel. 1972. *The Religion of Israel*. New York, Schocken.

Kealiinohomoku, Joann W. 1980. The drama of the Hopi ogres. In *Southwestern Indian Ritual Drama*, ed. C. J. Frisbie, pp. 37–69. Albuquerque, University of New Mexico Press.

Kimball, Solon T. 1960. Introduction. In *The Rites of Passage*, by Arnold Van Gennep, pp. v–xix. London, Routledge & Kegan Paul.

Kimmerling, Baruch, in collaboration with Irit Backer. 1985. *The Interrupted System: Israeli Civilians in War and Routine Times*. New Brunswick, N.J., Transaction Books.

Kinser, Samuel. 1986. Presentation and representation: carnival at Nuremberg, 1450–1550. *Representations*, 13: 1–41.

Kipling, Gordon. 1977. Triumphal drama: form in English civic pageantry. In *Renaissance Drama: The Celebratory Mode*, ed. L. Barkan, pp. 37–56. Evanston, Northwestern University Press.

Kligman, Gail. 1981. *Căluş: Symbolic Transformation in Romanian Ritual*. Chicago and London, University of Chicago Press.

Krakowski, Shmuel. 1984. *The War of the Doomed: Jewish Armed Resistance in Poland, 1942–1944*. New York, Holmes and Meier.

La Fontaine, Jean. 1982. Introduction. In *Chisungu: A Girl's Initiation Ceremony Among the Bemba of Zambia*, by Audrey Richards, pp. xvii–xxxvii. London, Tavistock.

Lakoff, George and Mark Johnson. 1980. *Metaphors We Live By*. Chicago and London, University of Chicago Press.

Lane, Christel. 1979. Ritual and ceremony in contemporary Soviet society. *Sociological Review* 27, 253–78.

Langer, Susanne K. 1953. *Feeling and Form*. London, Routledge & Kegan Paul.
 1965. The comic rhythm. In *comedy: Meaning and Form*, ed. R. W. Corrigan, pp. 119–40. San Francisco, Chandler.

Laski, Vera. 1959. *Seeking Life*. Philadelphia, American Folklore Society

Lavenda, Robert H. 1978. From festival of progress to masque of degradation: carnival in Caracas as a changing metaphor for social reality. In *Play and Culture*, ed. H. B. Schwartzman, pp. 19–30. West Point, N.Y., Leisure Press.
 1980. The festival of progress: the globalizing world-system and the transformation of the Caracas Carnival. *Journal of Popular Culture*, 14: 465–75.
 1983. Family and corporation: celebration in central Minnesota. In *The Celebration of Society: Perspectives on Contemporary Cultural Performance*, ed. F. E. Manning, pp. 51–64. Bowling Green, Ohio: Bowling Green University Popular Press.

Lavie, Smadar. 1984. The fool and the hippies: ritual/play and social inconsistencies among the Mzeina Bedouin of the Sinai. In *The Masks of Play*, ed. B. Sutton-Smith and D. Kelly-Byrne, pp. 63–70. West Point, N.Y., Leisure Press.
 1986. The poetics of politics: an allegory of Bedouin identity. In *The Frailty of Authority*, ed. M. J. Aronoff, pp. 131–46. New Brunswick, N.J., Transaction Books.

Lawrence, Denise. 1982. Parades, politics, and competing urban images: doo dah and roses. *Urban Anthropology*, 11: 155–76.

Leach, Edmund R. 1961. Two essays concerning the symbolic representation of time. In *Rethinking Anthropology*, pp. 124–36. London, Athlone Press.
 1966. Ritualization in man in relation to conceptual and social development. *Philosophical Transactions of the Royal Society of London*, Series B, no. 772, 251: 403–8.
 1968. Ritual. *Encyclopedia of the Social Sciences*, 13: 520–6.
 1976. *Culture and Communication*. Cambridge and New York, Cambridge University Press.
 1984. Conclusion: further thoughts on the realm of folly. In *Text, Play, and Story: The Construction and Reconstruction of Self and Society*, ed. E. M. Bruner, pp. 356–64. Washington, D.C., American Ethnological Society.

Lee, Dorothy. 1959. *Freedom and Culture*. Englewood Cliffs, N.J., Prentice-Hall.

Le Roy Ladurie, Emmanuel. 1980. *Carnival: A People's Uprising at Romans, 1579–1580*. London, Scolar Press.

Levinsky, Yom-Tov. 1957. *The Book of Times*. Tel-Aviv, Dvir (in Hebrew).

Lévi-Strauss, Claude. 1966. *The Savage Mind*. London, Weidenfeld and Nicolson.
 1981. *The Naked Man*. New York, Harper & Row.

Lewis, Arnold. 1985. Phantom ethnicity: 'Oriental Jews' in Israeli society. In *Studies in Israeli Ethnicity: After the Ingathering*, ed. A. Weingrod, pp. 133–57. New York, Gordon and Breach.

Liebman, Charles S. and Eliezer Don-Yehiya. 1983. *Civil Religion in Israel*. Berkeley and London, University of California Press.

Lincoln, Bruce. 1981. *Emerging From the Chrysalis: Studies in Rituals of Women's Initiation*. Cambridge and London, Harvard University Press.
 1985. Revolutionary exhumations in Spain, July 1936. *Comparative Studies in Society and History*, 27: 241–60.

Linenthal, Edward Tabor. 1983. Ritual drama at the Little Big Horn: the persistence and transformation of a national symbol. *Journal of the American Academy of Religion*, 51: 267–81.

Little, W. Kenneth. 1986. Pitu's doubt: entree clown self-fashioning in the circus tradition. *Drama Review*, 30, no. 4: 51–64.

Lofland, John and Michael Fink. 1982. *Symbolic Sit-ins: Protest Occupations at the California Capitol*. Washington, D.C., University Press of America.

Logan, Alice Pomponio. 1978. The Palio of Siena: performance and process. *Urban Anthropology*, 7: 45–65.

Longyear, Christopher R. 1979. The dutiful dreamer: representations in machines and mortals. In *Communication and Control in Society*, ed. K. Krippendorf, pp. 513–26. New York and London, Gordon and Breach.

Ludtke, Alf. 1985. Organizational order or Eigensinn? Workers' privacy and workers' politics in imperial Germany. In *Rites of Power: Symbolism, Ritual, and Politics Since the Middle Ages*, ed. S. Wilentz, pp. 303–33. Philadelphia, University of Pennsylvania Press.

Ludwig, Jack. 1976. *The Great American Spectaculars*. New York, Doubleday.

Lukes, Steven. 1975. Political ritual and social integration. *Sociology*, 9: 289–308.

Lundberg, Craig C. 1969. Person-focused joking: pattern and function. *Human Organization*, 28: 22–8.

Lupton, Tom. 1963. *On the Shop Floor: Two Studies of Work Organization and Output*. London, Pergamon.

Lyotard, Jean-Francois. 1984. *The Postmodern Condition: A Report on Knowledge*. Manchester, Manchester University Press.

MacAloon, John J. 1984a. Introduction: cultural performances, culture theory. In *Rite, Drama, Festival, Spectacle: Rehearsals Toward a Theory of Cultural Performance*, ed. J. J. MacAloon, pp. 1–15. Philadelphia, ISHI.

    1984b. Olympic Games and the theory of spectacle in modern societies. In *Rite, Drama, Festival, Spectacle: Rehearsals Toward a Theory of Cultural Performance*, ed. J. J. MacAloon, pp. 241–80. Philadelphia, ISHI.

Mahoney, Daniel and Brian Sutton-Smith. 1976. The player as a random generator. *TAASP Newsletter*, 3, no. 3: 9–11.

Maimonides, Moses. 1956. *The Guide for the Perplexed*. New York, Dover.

Makarius, Laura. 1970. Ritual clowns and symbolical behavior. *Diogenes*, 69: 44–73.

Manning, Frank E. 1977. Cup match and carnival: secular rites of revitalization in decolonizing, tourist-oriented societies. In *Secular Ritual*, ed. S. F. Moore and B. Myerhoff, pp. 265–81. Assen, Van Gorcum.

    1983. Cosmos and chaos: celebrations in the modern world. In *The Celebration of Society: Perspectives on Contemporary Cultural Performance*, ed. F. E. Manning, pp. 3–30. Bowling Green, Ohio, Bowling Green University Popular Press.

McCall, Grant. 1975. More thoughts on the Ik and anthropology. *Current Anthropology*, 16: 344–8.

McCracken, Grant. 1984. The pre-coronation passage of ElizabethI: political theatre or the rehearsal of politics? *Canadian Review of Sociology and Anthropology*, 21: 47–61.

McDowell, Jennifer. 1974. Soviet civil ceremonies. *Journal for the Scientific Study of Religion*, 13: 265–79.

Melograni, Piero. 1976. The cult of the Duce in Mussolini's Italy. *Journal of Contemporary History*, 11: 43–74.

Miller, Stephen. 1973. Ends, means, and galumphing: some leitmotifs of play. *American Anthropologist*, 75: 87–98.

Milner, G. B. 1972. Homo Ridens: towards a semiotic theory of humor and laughter. *Semiotica*, 5: 1–30.

Ministry of Education and Culture. 1967. *Ḥannuka, Festival of Lights*. Jerusalem, Ministry of Education and Culture [Israel] (in Hebrew).

Mitchell, J. Clyde. 1959. *The Kalela Dance: Aspects of Social Relationships Among Urban Africans in Northern Rhodesia* (Rhodes-Livingstone Papers no. 27), Manchester, Manchester University Press.

Montrose, Louis Adrian. 1977. Celebration and insinuation: Sir Philip Sidney and the motives of Elizabethan courtship. In *Renaissance Drama: the Celebratory Mode*, ed. L. Barkan, pp. 3–35. Evanston, Northwestern University Press.

Moore, Elenora Haegele. 1959. *Fives at School*. New York, Putnam's.

Moore, Sally Falk. 1975. Epilogue: Uncertainties in situations, indeterminacies in culture. In *Symbol and Politics in Communal Ideology*, ed. S. F. Moore and B. Myerhoff, pp. 210–39. Ithaca and London, Cornell University Press.

Mosse, George L. 1975. *The Nationalization of the Masses: Political Symbolism and Mass Movements in Germany From the Napoleonic Wars Through the Third Reich*. New York, Fertig.

1979. National cemeteries and national revival: the cult of the fallen soldiers in Germany. *Journal of Contemporary History*, 14: 1–20.

Muir, Edward. 1979. Images of power: art and pageantry in Renaissance Venice. *American Historical Review*, 84: 16–52.

1981. *Civic Ritual in Renaissance Venice*. Princeton, Princeton University Press.

Myerhoff, Barbara. 1982. Life history among the elderly: performance, visibility, and re-membering. In *A Crack in the Mirror: Reflexive Perspectives in Anthropology*, ed. J. Ruby, pp. 99–117. Philadelphia, University of Pennsylvania Press.

Naftali, N. and N. Nir-Yaniv, eds. 1974. *Subjects of Instruction: Day-Care Centres*. Jerusalem, Ministry of Education and Culture [Israel] (in Hebrew).

Nakamura, Hajime. 1981. Time in Indian and Japanese thought. In *The Voices of Time* (2nd ed.), ed. J. T. Fraser, pp. 77–91. Amherst, University of Massachusetts Press.

Nemec, Thomas F. 1972. I fish with my brother: the structure and behavior of agnatic-based fishing crews in a Newfoundland Irish outport. In *North Atlantic Fishermen*, ed. R. Anderson and C. Wadel, pp. 9–34. St. John's, Institute of Social and Economic Research, Memorial University of Newfoundland.

Newton-Smith, W. H. 1980. *The Structure of Time*. London and Boston, Routledge & Kegan Paul.

Norbeck, Edward. 1967. African rituals of conflict. In *Gods and Rituals*, ed. J. Middleton, pp. 197–226. New York, Natural History Press.

Obeyesekere, Gananath. 1981. *Medusa's Hair: An Essay on Personal Symbols and Religious Experience*. Chicago and London, University of Chicago Press.

Oguibenine, Boris. 1983. Identity and substitution in Vedic sacrificial ritual: essay on a case of figurative disguisement of the formal scheme. *Semiotica*, 47: 165–79.

Ohnuki-Tierney, Emiko. 1981a. Phases in human perception/cognition/symbolization processes: cognitive anthropology and symbolic classification. *American Ethnologist*, 8: 451–67.

1981b. *Illness and Healing Among the Sakhalin Ainu: A Symbolic Interpretation.* Cambridge and New York, Cambridge University Press.

Ong, Walter J. 1959. Latin language study as a Renaissance puberty rite. *Studies in Philology*, 56: 103–24.

Orgel, S. 1975. *The Illusion of Power: Political Theater in the English Renaissance.* Berkeley and Los Angeles, University of California Press.

Ortiz, Alfonso. 1969. *The Tewa World.* Chicago, University of Chicago Press.

1972. Ritual drama and the pueblo world view. In *New Perspectives on the Pueblos*, ed. A. Ortiz, pp. 133–61. Albuquerque, University of New Mexico Press.

Ortner, Sherry. 1978. *Sherpas Through Their Rituals.* Cambridge and New York, Cambridge University Press.

Ostor, Akos. 1980. *The Play of the Gods: Locality, Ideology, Structure, and Time in the Festivals of a Bengali Town.* Chicago and London, University of Chicago Press.

Ozouf, Mona. 1975. Space and time in the festivals of the French Revolution. *Comparative Studies in Society and History*, 17: 372–84.

Paine, Robert. 1983. Israel and totemic time? *RAIN*, 59: 19–22.

Parsons, Elsie Clews. 1916. The Zuni Mo'lawia. *American Anthropologist*, 29: 392–9.

1917. *Notes on Zuni*, Parts I and II. Menasha, Wis., Memoir of the American Anthropological Association.

1929. *Organization of the Tewa of New Mexico.* Menasha, Wis., Memoir of the American Anthropological Association.

Parsons, Elsie Clews and Ralph L. Beals. 1934. The sacred clowns of the Pueblo and Mayo-Yaqui Indians. *American Anthropologist*, 36: 491–514.

Peacock, James L. 1967. Javanese clown and transvestite songs: some relations between 'primitive classification' and communicative events. In *Essays on the Verbal and Visual Arts* (Proceedings of the 1966 Annual Meeting of the American Ethnological Society), pp. 64–75. Seattle, University of Washington Press.

1978. Symbolic reversal and social history: transvestites and clowns of Java. In *The Reversible World: Symbolic Inversion in Art and Society*, ed. B. A. Babcock, pp. 209–24. Ithaca and London, Cornell University Press.

Phythian-Adams, Charles. 1972. Ceremony and the citizen: the communal year at Coventry, 1450–1550. In *Crisis and Order in English Towns*, ed. P. Clark and P. Slack, pp. 57–85. London, Routledge & Kegan Paul.

Pierssens, Michel. 1972. Market, fair and festival. *Diogenes*, 78: 1–17.

Pina-Cabral, Joao de. 1986. *Sons of Adam, Daughters of Eve: The Peasant Worldview of the Alto Minho.* Oxford, Clarendon Press.

Pocius, Gerald. 1979. Hooked rugs in Newfoundland: the representation of social structure in design. *Journal of American Folklore*, 92: 273–84.

Pocock, David F. 1964. The anthropology of time-reckoning. *Contributions to Indian Sociology* (N.S.), 7: 18–29.

Pratt, Jeff. 1980. A sense of place. In *'Nation' and 'State' in Europe: Anthropological Perspectives*, ed. R. D. Grillo, pp. 31–43. New York and London, Academic Press.

Price, S. R. F. 1986. *Rituals and Power: The Roman Imperial Cult in Asia Minor.* Cambridge and New York, Cambridge University Press.

Rabinbach, Anson G. 1976. The aesthetics of production in the Third Reich. *Journal of Contemporary History*, 11: 43–74.

Rabinowitz, Esther, ed. 1958. *Holidays and Times in Education*. Tel-Aviv, Urim (in Hebrew).

Radcliffe-Brown, A. R. 1952. *Structure and Function in Primitive Society*. London, Cohen & West.

Rapoport, Anatol. 1978. Reality simulation: a feedback loop. In *Sociocybernetics: An Actor-Oriented Social Systems Approach*, vol. II, ed. R. F. Geyer and J. van der Zouwen, pp. 123–41. Leiden and London, Martinus Nijhoff.

Rappaport, Roy A. 1979. *Ecology, Meaning, and Religion*. Richmond, Cal., North Atlantic Books.

Rearick, Charles. 1977. Festivals in modern France: the experience of the Third Republic. *Journal of Contemporary History*, 12: 435–60.

Reuther, Rosemary Radford. 1977. *Mary – The Feminine Face of the Church*. Philadelphia, Westminster Press.

Richards, Audrey. 1982. *Chisungu: A Girl's Initiation Ceremony Among the Bemba of Zambia*. London, Tavistock.

Ricketts, Mac Linscott. 1966. The North American Indian trickster. *History of Religions*, 5: 327–50.

Roberts, John M. 1964. The self-management of cultures. In *Explorations in Cultural Anthropology*, ed. W. Goodenough, pp. 433–54. New York, McGraw-Hill.

Robertson, Margaret. 1982. The symbolism of Christmas mummering in New-foundland. *Folklore*, 93: 176–80.

Rossiter, A. P. 1950. *English Drama From Early Times to the Elizabethans*. London, Hutchinson.

Roy, Donald F. 1959–60. 'Banana time': job satisfaction and informal interaction. *Human Organization*, 18: 158–68.

Ryle, Gilbert. 1975. *The Concept of Mind* (13th ed.). London, Hutchinson.

Sanches, Mary. 1975. Introduction: metacommunicative acts and events. In *Socio-cultural Dimensions of Language Use*, ed. M. Sanches and B. Blount, pp. 163–76. London and New York, Academic Press.

Schechner, Richard. 1981. Restoration of behavior. *Studies in Visual Communication*, 7, no. 3: 2–45.

1985. *Between Theater and Anthropology*. Philadelphia, University of Pennsylvania Press.

Schieffelin, Edward L. 1976. *The Sorrow of the Lonely and the Burning of the Dancers*. New York, St. Martin's.

Schipper, Kristofer and Wang Hsui-huei. 1986. Progressive and regressive time cycles in Taoist ritual. In *Time, Science, and Society in China and the West*, ed. J. T. Fraser, N. Lawrence, and F. C. Haber, pp. 185–205. Amherst, University of Massachusetts Press.

Bibliography

Scholem, Gershom. 1971. The Star of David: history of a symbol. In *The Messianic Idea in Judaism*, pp. 257–81. New York, Schocken.

Schmitt, Jean-Claude. 1983. *The Holy Greyhound: Guinefort, Healer of Children Since the Thirteenth Century*. Cambridge and New York, Cambridge University Press.

Schwartz, Barry, Yael Zerubavel, and Bernice M. Barnett. 1986. The recovery of Masada: a study of collective memory. *Sociological Quarterly*, 27: 147–64.

Schwartzman, Helen B. 1981. Hidden agendas and formal organizations or how to dance at a meeting. *Social Analysis*, 9: 77–88.

    1984. Stories at work: play in an organizational context. In *Text, Play, and Story: The Construction and Reconstruction of Self and Society*, ed. E. M. Bruner, pp. 80–93. Washington, D.C., American Ethnological Society.

Schutz, Alfred and Thomas Luckmann. 1973. *Structures of the Life World*. Evanston, Northwestern University Press.

Scribner, Bob. 1978. Reformation, carnival and the world turned upside-down. *Social History*, 3: 303–29.

Sennett, Richard. 1977. *The Fall of Public Man*. Cambridge, Cambridge University Press.

Shamgar-Handelman, Lea. 1981. Administering to war widows in Israel: the birth of a social category. *Social Analysis*, 9: 24–47.

    1986. *Israeli War Widows: Beyond the Glory of Heroism*. South Hadley, Mass., Bergin and Garvey.

Shanin, Teodor. 1972. Models and thought. In *The Rules of the Game: Cross Disciplinary Essays on Models in Scholarly Thought*, ed. T. Shanin, pp. 1–22. London, Tavistock.

Sharon, Douglas, 1978. *Wizard of the Four Winds: A Shaman's Story*. New York, The Free Press.

Shemer, A., ed. 1966. *Ways of Work in Kindergartens*. Tel-Aviv, Tarbut v'. Hu. Kin Hebrew).

Shils, Edward and Michael Young. 1956. The meaning of the Coronation. *Sociological Review*, 1: 63–82.

Shulman, David Dean. 1980. *Tamil Temple Myths: Sacrifice and Divine Marriage in the South Indian Śaiva Tradition*. Princeton, Princeton University Press.

    1985. *The King and the Clown in South Indian Myth and Poetry*. Princeton, Princeton University Press.

Shulz, Jeffrey and Susan Florio. 1979. Stop and freeze: social and physical space in a kindergarten/first grade classroom. *Anthropology and Education Quarterly*, 10: 166–81.

Shure, M. 1963. Psychological ecology of a nursery school. *Child Development*, 34: 979–92.

Sider, Gerald M. 1976. Christmas mumming and the New Year in outport Newfoundland. *Past and Present*, 71: 102–25.

    1980. The ties that bind: culture and agriculture, property and propriety in the Newfoundland village fishery. *Social History*, 5: 1–39.

    1984. Family fun in Starve Harbour: custom, history, and confrontation in village Newfoundland. In *Interest and Emotion: Essays in the Study of Family and*

317

Kinship, ed. H. Medick and D. Sabean, pp. 340–70. Cambridge and New York, Cambridge University Press.

1986. *Culture and Class in Anthropology and History*. Cambridge and New York, Cambridge University Press.

Silverman, Sydel. 1979. On the uses of history in anthropology: the Palio of Siena. *American Ethnologist*, 6: 413–36.

1981. Rituals of inequality: stratification and symbol in Central Italy. In *Social Inequality: Comparative and Developmental Approaches*, ed. G. D. Berreman, pp. 163–81. New York and London, Academic Press.

1985. Towards a political economy of Italian competitive festivals. *Ethnologica Europaea*, 15: 95–103.

Simmons, Leo W., ed. 1942. *Sun Chief*. New Haven, Yale University Press.

Singer, Milton. 1972. *When a Great Tradition Modernizes: An Anthropological Approach to Indian Civilization*. New York and London, Praeger.

Skorupski, John. 1973. Science and traditional religious thought, Pts. I-IV. *Philosophy of the Social Sciences*, 3: 97–116, 209–31.

1976. *Symbol and Theory: A Philosophical Study of Theories of Religion in Social Anthropology*. Cambridge and New York, Cambridge University Press.

Smith, Brian K. 1986. Ritual, knowledge, and being: initiation and Veda study in ancient India. *Numen*, 33: 65–89.

Smith, Jonathan. 1970. Birth upside down or right side up? *History of Religions*, 9: 281–303.

Smith, Pierre. 1982. Aspects of the organization of rites. In *Between Belief and Transgression: Structuralist Essays in Religion, History, and Myth*, ed. M. Izard and P. Smith, pp. 103–28. Chicago and London, University of Chicago Press.

Speck, Frank G. and Leonard Broom, with the assistance of Will West Long. 1951. *Cherokee Dance and Drama*. Berkeley, University of California Press.

Staal, Frits. 1979. The meaninglessness of ritual. *Numen*, 26: 2–22.

1986. The sound of religion. *Numen*, 33: 33–64.

State of Israel. 1983. *Statistical Abstract of Israel*, no. 34. Jerusalem, Central Bureau of Statistics.

Stephen, Alexander M. 1936. Hopi Journal of Alexander M. Stephen (ed. Elsie Clews Parsons). New York. *Columbia University Contributions to Anthropology*, vol. 23, no. 1.

Stevenson, Matilda Coxe. 1904. The Zuni Indians. *Annual Report of the Bureau of American Ethnology*, 23: 1–608.

Steward, Julian H. 1930. The ceremonial buffoon of the American Indian. *Michigan Academy of Science, Arts, and Letters*, 14: 187–207.

Stewart, Susan. 1979. *Nonsense: Aspects of Intertextuality in Folklore and Literature*. Baltimore and London, Johns Hopkins University Press.

Story, George M. 1969. Mummers in Newfoundland history: a survey of the printed record. In *Christmas Mumming in Newfoundland*, ed. H. Halpert and G. Story, pp. 167–85. Toronto, University of Toronto Press.

Straus, Erwin W. 1966. *Phenomenological Psychology*. London, Tavistock.

Street, Lloyd. 1958. Game forms in the factory group. *Berkeley Publications in Society and Institutions*, 4: 44–55.

Sullivan, Lawrence E. 1986. Sound and senses: toward a hermeneutics of performance. *History of Religions*, 26: 1–33.

Sumberg, Samuel L. 1966. *The Nuremberg Schembart Carnival*. New York, AMS Press.

Swain, Barbara. 1932. *Fools and Folly During the Middle Ages and the Renaissance*. New York, Columbia University Press.

Swiderski, Richard M. 1986. *Voices: An Anthropologist's Dialogue with an Italian–American Festival*. Bowling Green, Ohio, Bowling Green University Popular Press.

Sykes, A. J. M. 1966. Joking relationships in an industrial setting. *American Anthropologist*, 68: 188–93.

Sztompka, Piotr. 1974. *System and Function: Toward a Theory of Society*. London and New York, Academic Press.

Szwed, John F. 1966. *Private Cultures and Public Imageries: Interpersonal Relations in a Newfoundland Peasant Society*. St. Johns, Institute of Social and Economic Research, Memorial University of Newfoundland.

   1969. The mask of friendship: mumming as a ritual of social relations. In *Christmas Mumming in Newfoundland*, ed. H. Halpert and G. Story. Toronto, University of Toronto Press.

Tambiah, S. J. 1979. A performative approach to ritual. *Proceedings of the British Academy*, 65: 113–69.

Tarn, Nathaniel. 1976. The heraldic vision: a cognitive model for comparative aesthetics. *Alcheringa: Ethnopoetics* (N.S.), 2, no. 2: 23–41.

Taylor, Jerome and Alan H. Nelson, eds. 1972. *Medieval English Drama: Essays Critical and Contextual*. Chicago and London, University of Chicago Press.

Thomas, Keith. 1976. *Rule and Misrule in the Schools of Early Modern England*. Reading, University of Reading.

Thompson, E. P. 1971. The moral economy of the English crowd in the eighteenth century. *Past and Present*, 50: 76–136.

Titiev, Mischa. 1944. Old Oraibi: A Study of the Hopi Indians of Third Mesa. Cambridge, *Papers of the Peabody Museum of American Archaeology and Ethnology*, vol. 22, Harvard University.

   1971. Some aspects of clowning among the Hopi Indians. In *Themes in Culture*, ed. M. D. Zamora, J. M. Mahar, and H. Orenstein. Quezon City, The Philippines, Kayamanggi.

   1972. *The Hopi Indians of Old Oraibi*. Ann Arbor, University of Michigan Press.

Toulmin, Stephen. 1983. The construal of reality: criticism in modern and postmodern science. In *The Politics of Interpretation*, ed. W. J. T. Mitchell, pp. 99–117. Chicago and London, University of Chicago Press.

Trexler, Richard C. 1980. *Public Life in Renaissance Florence*. London and New York, Academic Press.

Turnbull, Colin M. 1973a. *The Mountain People*. London, Jonathan Cape
   1973b. Human nature and primal man. *Social Research*, 40: 511–30.

Turner, Edith. 1987. *The Spirit and the Drum: A Memoir of Africa*. Tucson, University of Arizona Press.

Turner, Terence S. 1977. Transformation, hierarchy and transcendence: a reformulation of Van Gennep's model of the structure of rites de passage. In *Secular Ritual*, ed. S. F. Moore and B. Myerhoff, pp. 53–70. Assen, Van Gorcum.

Turner, Victor W. 1964. Betwixt and between: the liminal period in rites de passage. In *New Approaches to the Study of Religion* (Proceedings of the American Ethnological Society, 1964), pp. 4–20. Seattle, University of Washington Press.

1967. *The Forest of Symbols: Aspects of Ndembu Ritual*. Ithaca, Cornell University Press.

1969. *The Ritual Process: Structure and Antistructure*. Chicago, Aldine.

1974. *Dramas, Fields, and Metaphors*. Ithaca, Cornell University Press.

1977. Process, system and symbol: a new anthropological synthesis. *Daedalus*, 106, no. 3: 61–79.

1978. Comments and conclusions. In *The Reversible World: Symbolic Inversion in Art and Society*, ed. B. A. Babcock, pp. 276–96. Ithaca and London, Cornell University Press.

1985. The anthropology of performance. In *On the Edge of the Bush: Anthropology as Experience*, ed. E. Turner, pp. 177–204. Tucson, University of Arizona Press.

Turner, Victor W. and Edith Turner. 1978. *Image and Pilgrimage in Christian Culture*. New York, Columbia University Press.

Ulich, Robert. 1955. Symbolism and the education of man. In *Symbols and Society*, ed. L. Bryson *et al.*, pp. 205–25. New York and London, Harper & Brothers.

Vainstein, Yaacov. 1953. *The Cycle of the Jewish Year*. Jerusalem, World Zionist Organization.

Van Gennep, Arnold. 1960. *The Rites of Passage*. London, Routledge & Kegan Paul.

van Gunsteren, Herman. 1976. *The Quest For Control*. New York, John Wiley.

Versnal, H. S. 1970. *Triumphus: An Inquiry into the Origin, Development and Meaning of the Roman Triumph*. Leiden, Brill.

von Wright, Georg Henrik. 1971. *Explanation and Understanding*. London, Routledge & Kegan Paul.

Vogt, Evon Z. and Suzanne Abel. 1977. On political rituals in contemporary Mexico. In *Secular Ritual*, ed. S. F. Moore and B. Myerhoff, pp. 173–88. Assen, Van Gorcum.

Waddell, Helen. 1946. *The Desert Fathers*. London, Constable.

Walens, Stanley. 1981. *Feasting With Cannibals: an Essay on Kwakiutl Cosmology*. Princeton, Princeton University Press.

1983. Analogic causality and the power of masks. In *The Power of Symbols: Masks and Masquerade in the Americas*, ed. N. R. Crumrine and M. Halpin, pp. 70–8. Vancouver, University of British Columbia Press.

Wallace, Anthony F. C. 1966. *Religion: An Anthropological View*. New York, Random House.

Waller, Willard. 1932. *The Sociology of Teaching*. New York, Wiley.

Walzer, Michael. 1985. *Exodus and Revolution*. New York, Basic Books.

Warner, Marina. 1978. *Alone of All Her Sex: The Myth and Cult of the Virgin Mary*. London, Quartet Books.

Warner, W. Lloyd. 1961. *The Family of God: A Symbolic Study of Christian Life in America*. New Haven, Yale University Press.

Webber, Jonathan. 1981. Resacralization of the holy city. *RAIN*, 47: 6–10.

Weil, Shalva. 1986. The language and ritual of socialisation: birthday parties in a kindergarten context. *Man* (N.S.), 21: 329–41.

Weiss, M. S. and P. H. Weiss. 1976. A public school ritual ceremony. *Journal of Research and Development in Education*, 9: 22–8.

Welsford, Enid. 1935. *The Fool: His Social and Literary History*. London, Faber and Faber.

1961. *The Fool: His Social and Literary History*. New York, Doubleday Anchor.

Werbner, Pnina. 1986. The virgin and the clown: ritual elaboration in Pakistani migrants' weddings. *Man* (N.S.), 21: 227–50.

Werbner, Richard. 1989. *Ritual Passage, Sacred Journey: The Form, Process and Organization of Religious Movement*. Washington, D.C., Smithsonian Institution Press.

Westwood, Sallie. 1984. *All Day, Every Day: Factory and Family in the Making of Women's Lives*. London and Sydney, Pluto Press.

Weyl, Hermann. 1952. *Symmetry*. Princeton, Princeton University Press.

Widdowson, John. 1977. '*If You Don't Be Good': Verbal Social Control in Newfoundland*. St. John's, Institute of Social and Economic Research, Memorial University of Newfoundland.

Wilden, Anthony. 1977. *System and Structure: Essays in Communication and Exchange*. London, Tavistock.

Willeford, William. 1969. *The Fool and His Sceptre*. London, Edward Arnold.

Williams, Clyde. 1969. Janneying in 'Coughlin Cove'. In *Christmas Mumming in Newfoundland*, ed. H. Halpert and G. Story, pp. 209–15. Toronto, University of Toronto Press.

Williams, Raymond. 1975. *Drama in a Dramatised Society*. Cambridge, Cambridge University Press.

1977. *Marxism and Literature*. Oxford, Oxford University Press.

Willner, Dorothy. 1976. Ritual, myth, and the murdered president. In *The Realm of the Extra-Human: Agents and Audiences*, ed. A. Bharati, pp. 401–20. The Hague, Mouton.

Wind, Edgar. 1958. *Pagan Mysteries of the Renaissance*. London, Faber and Faber.

Wolin, Sheldon. 1985. Postmodern politics and the absence of myth. *Social Research*, 52: 217–39.

Wright, Patrick. 1985. *On Living in an Old Country: The National Past in Contemporary Britain*. London, Verso.

Wyschogrod, Edith. 1985. *Spirit in Ashes: Hegel, Heidegger, and Man-Made Mass Death*. New Haven, Yale University Press.

Yates, Frances A. 1969. *Theatre of the World*. Chicago and London, University of Chicago Press.

Yamamoto, Yoshiko. 1978. *The Namahage: A Festival in the Northeast of Japan*. Philadelphia, ISHI.

Yerushalmi, Yosef Hayim. 1982. *Zakhor: Jewish History and Jewish Memory*. Seattle, University of Washington Press.

Zanbank-Wilf, A. 1958. The kindergarten as a component in creating a holiday atmosphere at home. In *Holidays and Times in Education*, ed. E. Rabinowitz, pp. 57–9. Tel-Aviv, Urim (in Hebrew).

Zerubavel, Eviatar. 1982. Easter and Passover: on calendars and group identity. *American Sociological Review*, 47: 284–9.

  1985. *The Seven Day Circle: The History and Meaning of the Week*. New York, The Free Press.

Zerubavel, Yael. 1986. The holiday cycle and the commemoration of the past: history, folklore, and education. Mimeo.

Zijderveld, Anton. 1982. *Reality in a Looking Glass: Rationality Through an Analysis of Traditional Folly*. Boston and London: Routledge and Kegan Paul.

Zucker, Wolfgang M. 1969. The clown as the lord of disorder. In *Holy Laughter*, ed. M. C. Hyers, pp. 75–88. New York, Seabury.

Index